MW00749554

MEETINGS
WITH
MARITIME
POETS

MEETINGS
WITH
MARITIME
POETS

INTERVIEWS

Anne Compton

Fitzhenry & Whiteside

Meetings With Maritime Poets
Copyright © 2006 Anne Compton

First Published in the United States in 2007

All rights reserved. No part of this book may be reproduced in any manner without the express written consent of the publisher, except in the case of brief excerpts in critical reviews and articles. All inquiries should be addressed to:

Fitzhenry and Whiteside Limited, 195 Allstate Parkway, Markham, Ontario L3R 4T8

In the United States:
311 Washington Street, Brighton, Massachusetts 02135

www.fitzhenry.ca • godwit@fitzhenry.ca

Fitzhenry & Whiteside acknowledges with thanks the Canada Council for the Arts, and the Ontario Arts Council for their support of our publishing program. We acknowledge the financial support of the Government of Canada through the Book Publishing Industry Development Program (BPIDP) for our publishing activities.

Library and Archives Canada Cataloguing in Publication
Compton, Anne
Meetings with Maritime poets : interviews / Anne Compton.
Includes bibliographical references.
ISBN-13: 978-1-55041-996-2
ISBN-10: 1-55041-996-X
1. Poets, Canadian (English)—Maritime Provinces—Interviews.
2. Poets, Canadian (English) 21st century—Interviews. 3. Poetry,
Canadian (English)—Maritime Provinces—Criticism and interpretation.
I. Title.
PS8081.1.C64 2006   C811'.6099715   C2006-904451-1

United States Cataloguing-in-Publication Data
Compton, Anne.
Meetings with Maritime poets : interviews / Anne Compton.
[400] p. : col. photos. ; cm.
Includes bibliographical references.
Summary: Sixteen Maritime poets explore the relationship between poetry
and place with Anne Compton.
ISBN-10: 1-55041-966-X
ISBN-13: 978-155041-966-2
1. Poets, Canadian (English) — Maritime Provinces — Interviews.
2. Poets, Canadian (English) — 21st century — Interviews. I. Title.
811.5409   dc22   PR9190.5.C66 2006

Cover art: Dan Steeves, *Familiar Voices*, crayon etching 1993. www.dansteeves.com
Frontispiece: Detail from untitled etching, Gerard Collins (1957–), Canadian
Cover and interior design by Karen Petherick Thomas, Intuitive Design International Ltd.

Printed and bound in Canada
1 3 5 7 9 10 8 6 4 2

For John Thompson and Alden Nowlan,
with thanks for the poems

CONTENTS

Perfection of tables: crooked grains;
and all this talk: this folly of tongues.

Too many stories: yes, and
high talk: the exact curve of the thing.

~ John Thompson

A pleasant walk, a pleasant talk,
Along the briny beach.

~ Lewis Carroll

⚔ PREFACE

CONVERSATIONS WITH POETS IN NOVA SCOTIA, PRINCE EDWARD ISLAND, AND NEW BRUNSWICK

Poetry in the Maritimes is undergoing a resurgence similar in energy and excitement to that of the 1950s – the formative decade in the careers of Alden Nowlan and Milton Acorn – but different in kind. In the past 10 years, close to a dozen significant new poets have emerged. Their writing, like that of their more-established colleagues – poets with two or more books – ranges widely in manner. Some are formalists; others test the pliability of free verse and the vernacular. There are poets whose material is the personal life; others are observers, investigators, of the world around. The high metaphorical manner of one poet contrasts with the plain-speaking of another. The present surge of poetic speech, unlike that in the earlier decade, is characterized by proliferation rather than the pre-eminence of a pair.

Scholarship, however, has not kept up with the burgeoning poetic output. In teaching courses in Maritime poetry, I witness students' frustration at the scarcity of critical materials. Their questions, unsatisfied by outdated critical materials, prompted me to begin a peripatetic project – interviews with Maritime poets who continue to live in the area and with those making return trips from the places where they now live. My conversations with Maritime poets were intended to document, through journal publication, the poets' accounts of the writing life, their attachment to place, and the relationship, if any, between place and poetics. As the interviews – which I thought of as essays in the colloquial with two speakers – began to accumulate, I realized that bringing these documents together in a book might create something like a dialogue between and among my subjects. That is, a fuller story could be realized by setting one interview side by side with another in a collection.

In and around my other projects, I kept the conversation going for seven years and many miles. Interviews took place on the Fundy flats, on ferry boats and airplanes, in homes and cafés, in gardens and winter blizzards. In this inquiry, I was the representative reader, an emissary for my students, and a fellow enthusiast asking questions about the poetic process that preoccupy both readers and writers. The 16 interviews appear roughly in the order in which they were done, spanning a period from 1998 to 2005.

Inevitably, the questions posed in these interviews reflect my own biases – an interest, for example, in poetry's kinship to science and to metaphysical matters, and, above all, the suspicion that nearness to the ocean – or in the case of the Islanders, the sea that surrounds them – shapes consciousness. These proclivities led me to certain persons and their poetry. I wanted to talk to poets with a strong sense of place, but given the ocean frontage in the word *Maritime*, I had a pronounced interest in their interest in the contraries of boundedness and boundlessness in terms of both time and space – a preoccupation that's exacerbated when the ocean's around you, before you. Identifying a dozen or so accomplished poems in a collection was reason enough for my setting out. Technical excellence in that dozen suggested a poet thoughtful about the practice of poetry, someone in possession of a poetic, someone able to answer the question: *How does a poet's quotidian experience of where he or she lives get transformed into an art that offers its audience an aesthetic and affective experience of place?* These are poets in their maturity, men and women past the proverbial 39, who have thought about such things. There were, of course, many other accomplished poets with whom I had hoped to talk – Lynn Davies, Robert Gibbs, David Helwig, M. Travis Lane, Harry Thurston, to name a few – but, frankly, I'm of an age, and the process was arduous. As for Newfoundland poets, that would be another book. Their poetry differs from Maritime poetry in voice, syntactical structures, idiom, and accent. Moreover, theirs is a different topography even though they share with Maritime poets an Atlantic lookout.

Preparing for an interview, I read everything the poet published – prose and poetry – and everything I could find written about her or him. If the poet had new work with a publisher, I read the manuscript. From that reading, I shaped questions. In most cases, I travelled to the poet and spent a minimum of three hours, sometimes a full day, taping the conversation, after which I transcribed it, returning the document to the poet. Further edits were my responsibility. One interview, verbatim from the tape, ran to 79 pages. In every conversation, our point of departure was the poems themselves – images and ideas, lines and phrases, forms and patterns. I wanted to travel back with the poet the path of the metaphor. I wanted to know the mind in the poetry and how that mind lived the world, how the particularities of time, place, and culture manifest in the poetry, *and* in fiction too if the author happened also to work in that genre. Often, I interrupted the poet's productivity:

I wanted that sense of his being in the midst of things – the pages of a proof, inked with revisions, on the table between us.

When I set out on an interview, I avoided rereading earlier interviews. I didn't want to repeat questions, and I had no mantra – some wise man's words about poetry – to which I asked everyone to respond. Inevitably, though, every conversation came around to issues of common concern to any poet: Creation, not to mention publication, it would seem, is infused with joy, beset with anxiety. The governing metaphor for the interviews was travel – through a body of work. Indeed, in some cases, we were literally travelling together. I came with a map of questions, but we weren't bound by the route I'd sketched in advance. In each case, I chose one or two books by the author, not always the most recent, as the area of exploration, but I allowed for, expected, side trips into the poet's other work at any time.

The poets did not see the questions in advance, which means theirs was an off-the-cuff speaking. I did not want long-considered, tailored responses such as you might get in an interview by correspondence. In the latter circumstance, the respondent tends to fall back on what he or she has said in other interviews or in articles. I hoped for nomadic thoughts. I wanted the poet full of surprise and accident. In editing, I have tried to retain something of the hesitation, self-contradiction, and backtracking that happens in thinking aloud. As well, I've tried to preserve the poets' speech habits: George Elliott Clarke's explosive "Absolutely," "Definitely"; Sue Goyette's illustrative metaphors; Brian Bartlett's penchant for lists; John Smith's polite, but qualified, words of assent, "Probably so," when a question of mine sounded summative. I wanted to know if a poet's everyday speech habits matched the voice or voices I heard in the poems. I have preserved, as well, the barely concealed hostility I sometimes encountered when I asked a stupid or an invasive question.

You have to be something of a chameleon to do interviews. I entered the poets' territory, geographically, and before that, I entered their poetic territory in immersing myself in their way of perceiving the world. I needed to talk their talk. There was no point inquiring about personal background if I had recognized reticence in the poetry; no point in my coming to him or her with theory if the poet wasn't a theorist. To some extent, I had to suppress my own talk. The interview is a balancing act: I wanted an exchange, but I didn't want my own views getting in the way. Somewhat like a psychoanalyst, I needed to get the talk flowing, allow anything to be said, so that productive shocks could happen. To some degree, I wanted the respondent to feel as though she were talking to herself. I wanted to overhear.

Partly, too, I was looking for a third way. I've published my share of articles – I know that politic – and I've harvested from publishers' spring and fall lists, feverishly reviewing the new books, getting my say in. But what would happen, I wondered, if you took time, really took time, to explore, in the company of the poet, the work he or she had created? Done with neither the deadline of the reviewer, nor with the control of the critic – interviewed people talk back – an interview of this sort is both impersonal and intimate: The critical analysis, done in preparation, is subject to the revisionary warmth of conversation.

Poets are sometimes dumbfounded when it comes to talking about their own poetry – its origins, the process of writing, even the poems themselves. I wanted to push against that dumbfoundedness. I have little patience with the claim – and I heard it more than once – that the poem says it for me. If a poet says, "I really don't know a lot about my own work" (Bowling 12), then who does know? The creative process may be mysterious – "tied up with not-knowing, with willing ignorance" (Hoagland 42) – but surely a poet must stand behind the published work and be prepared to talk about it. Otherwise, why enter the public domain? As Thomas O'Grady says here, "Creativity comes from inside and is given expression, but as soon as it is on the page, it is performative ...." Performance is public. The audience is entitled to ask questions. If my poets were occasionally resistant or, as one poet said, worried that our talk would "demystify" a poem, they soon moved beyond resistance and talked for hours. Repeatedly, what impressed me was the seriousness with which they spoke of the writing enterprise even if they remained puzzled by the "how" and "why" of it. Many of them had thought long and deeply about the making of poetry, and were prepared to share it. As the project proceeded, and I moved from the occasional interview to a book-length collection, reactions began to seep back. At an after-a-reading dinner one night, a friend reported an interviewee's description of my visit, "Exhausting," and down the table the poet I was to interview next heard, "Accosted."

WORKS CITED
— • —

Bowling, Tim, ed. *Where the Words Come From: Canadian Poets in Conversation*. Roberts Creek, BC: Nightwood Editions, 2002.

Hoagland, Tony. "Three Tenors: Glück, Hass, Pinsky." *American Review of Poetry* 32.4 (July/August 2003): 37-42.

INTRODUCTION

In East Coast poetry of recent decades, productivity divides fairly evenly between the genders, and between the Maritime-by-choice poets and the native-born. One of the interesting features of recent publication is the number of first-book poets of mature age. While there are younger beginners as well, the idea of a career-building move is not part of their thinking. Gone are the days of a Milton Acorn type of move to Montreal, or somewhere else, for the sake of poetry. Gone too the motive. Goose Lane Editions and Gaspereau Press – to name just two local publishers – include Maritime poets on their lists, and on any corner you can have a conversation about poetry. Sadly, for Maritimers, as for other Canadians, *poet* is not a career choice. Whatever else he did, in terms of jobs, Acorn was pre-eminently a poet, a bard. Alden Nowlan, too, in the last 15 years of his life was a full-time poet, a sage in all matters poetic. In these interviews, you'll meet bar-tenders and teachers, statisticians and novelists, editors and librarians and actors.

Unquestionably grounded in Atlantic Canadian landscape, some of these poets are transatlantic. Participating in a European writing community as well as a North American one (Liliane Welch, Thomas O'Grady, for example), publishing here and overseas, and referring frequently to European models of excellence, these poets are redefining what it means to be an East Coast poet. Similarly, in their conversations, you'll hear about a Boston-PEI axis of poetic activity, a New York-Nova Scotia axis. In more than one sense, these poets are seaboard. It is not surprising then that the migrant Ulysses occasionally turns up in their conversation and their poems. If climate, culture, and topography constitute the "bedrock" of Maritime poetry, the sea – and the poets' sea gaze, poetically speaking – preclude insularity. As Brent MacLaine says, "the meditative impulse is there in [the] positioning" of a speaker on the shore. He might be speaking for all the native-born Maritime poets when he explains how "connecting landscape and family over time" – in his case, five generations – leads quite naturally "to much more metaphysical or cosmological speculations about time simply through the geology of the place." The record of familial habitation – fossilized in Maritime earth – is centuries, not millennia, old. You look back, according to MacLaine, through the generations and then "it's wide open." A move from inland to shore, from landscape to seascape, is one of the differences between his first collection, *Wind & Root*, and his second, *These Fields Were Rivers*. An increased formalism is also noticeable. Following a first collection – which tends to be the poet's own story, or the familial one, in a familiar landscape – subsequent collections, broadening in subject matter, rely to a greater extent on received forms. This was the pattern I saw in reading in preparation for the interviews and it was confirmed in the conversations.

A greater interest in, and use of, forms obtains in second books by Anne Simpson and John MacKenzie, collections that move into the "wide open." MacKenzie's second collection, *Shaken By Physics*, is more "mind-oriented," more conceptual than his first. Physics and time are the preoccupations of Simpson's *Loop*, her second collection. As she says here, "[W]hat's to stop us from considering these things in poetry? ....You can't afford to be afraid: You have to be fearless." This notion that poetry can be, or can contain, "all things" is linked perhaps to the preponderance of sea symbolism in her work. The sea, according to Simpson, "contains an infinitude of meanings .... [I]t can be all things." You have to wonder if fearlessness as to subject matter, like the sea symbolism in her work, is attributable to the fact she "live[s] near the ocean," on the Nova Scotia coast, a place she now thinks of as her "home landscape." Speaking of the same coast, Sue Goyette says, "It's very important to me to go to something I can't see the edge of." Peter Sanger describes a trip he made "out to Cape John, which juts out into Northumberland Strait. Like a Hopkins' poem, it's a place that's full of wind and waves, really utterly unencompassable."

For Simpson, MacLaine, and John Smith, range happens to take the form of a speculative inquiry about the nature of time. For other Maritime poets, the distant gaze takes the form of poems about an ancestral background that is pre-Maritime (Clarke, O'Grady); poems of travel and exploration (Bartlett); an involvement with European topography and culture (Welch); a preoccupation with the sublime (Leckie); the romance of constellations (Wilson); or the conscious effort by a poet to carry on a dialogue with poetic predecessors (Sanger). However Ulyssean their interests and their imaginative wanderings, Maritime poets – whether they are immigrants, exiles, or residents – are unapologetic in their local attachments. Some, if they happen to be recent arrivals, aspire to such an attachment. By contrast, "the geography of Eastern Canada is noticeably absent" from the most recent Atlantic short fiction collection, *Victory Meat* (Bigge D17). Novelist and poet Elisabeth Harvor – more than 20 years absent from her native New Brunswick landscape – explains the difference in terms of genre: "[T]he ability of landscape to offer up images is so much more useful to a poem, and can even be the life of the poem, whereas imagery and scenery can sometimes get in the way of the narrative in a story." Harvor's poetry, rather than her fiction, returns frequently to the Kingston Peninsula area of New Brunswick where she grew up: "No landscape, in the present or future, will affect me in the same way."

For Maritime poets in exile, the landscape's "great hold," as Harvor describes it, can mean either a refusal to return – in order to preserve memories – or, as in Thomas O'Grady's case, a frequency of return "to re-root myself." For the Island-born, Boston author of *What Really Matters*, "What is so important for me when I write is the authenticating of the place." In O'Grady's Island poems, selectivity and scrupulosity of detail preclude sentimentality. The exile may, in fact, be more watchful than the resident: "[R]eturning home to the familiar lends one a heightened awareness of place specificity – of what makes that place distinctive," according to O'Grady. The "place specificity" in the poetry of George Elliott Clarke, Alan R. Wilson, Harvor, and O'Grady – the poets in exile – is generational as well as topographical. If "People are made of places," as Elizabeth Brewster says in one of her poems (31), the reverse, according to these poets, is equally true: Place is generationally inscribed, knowable really only through the lives spent in "Making Land," as MacLaine calls it (*These Fields* 36-38). And what is true for Seamus Heaney is true for these poets: "[R]etrospect is not relapse" (Miller 49). The present must fetch the past, but that doesn't mean that anyone has to get stuck there.

For the Maritime-by-choice poets – the immigrants – rootedness can be synonymous with an epiphanic sense of arrival. Liliane Welch, like Simpson, connects finding "a home here" with her beginnings as a poet: The region around Fundy is, Welch says, "the primordial, originary, landscape of my life." In an essay in *Seismographs*, the Luxembourg-born poet writes, "When I saw it [Fundy] first in a wild February storm, a desire arose to pierce the secret still withheld from me. A language had to be invented to make this ground sing" (53). For Welch, "Intensity comes from facing the elements," an experience as available to her in Fundy as in the mountains of Europe. The Nova Scotia poet Carole Langille, arriving from New York, similarly describes a first encounter: "I remember going to a lake here, very clear. You could see right to the bottom. It was warm, early September, and there was no one on the beach. And I thought, *I have arrived*." Maritime landscapes enter their poetry if not as direct subject then as templates of human desire and aspiration. As Langille says, "The great beauty in the natural world makes it possible to use it as a medium to talk about the erotic or the religious." For Welch, "When the sun is on the mudflats, after the water has withdrawn, it is, perhaps, the most erotic landscape in the world, a landscape of bare flanks."

Not all immigrant poets experience an epiphany upon arrival or the need, so immediately, to invent a language commensurate with this ground. For some, the process of settling in is longer, but no less crucial to their poetry. The British-born Nova Scotia poet Peter Sanger describes his decision to dig in "in the physical sense, the topographical sense ... but also imaginatively .... [F]or the kind of poet that I wish to be, that is what I had to do. You have to understand the weather, the animals, the trees, the way things grow, the procession of the seasons. You have to listen to sounds. To me, that's very important. The sounds of the leaves, the sounds of the birds. They all have to enter into the work in one way or another. You can only do that over time." After eight years of living beside the St. John River, Ross Leckie published *Gravity's Plumb Line* (2005), devoting a sequence of poems to the river. The experience of eight freshets can do that – re-route the imagination.

Topography and climate "enter into the work" of these poets, but among the poets themselves, there is a bemused-to-fierce resistance to the locution *Maritimes*. It is, rather, the Fundy or the St. John River Valley or the Annapolis that matters to them. And the ocean. As Brian Bartlett says, "Facing the power of the sea, even a few days of the year, can get under your skin ...." *Power* is the significant word here. Of late, storms on the Atlantic coast have been erasing the dunes, leaving a wreckage of wharves and boats. The poets' interest in the sea is not merely the result of proximity. And it isn't some relic emotion left over from the days of a predominantly fishing-based economy. Theirs is an interest in a great energy, in an amoral, inhuman force that draws them to the edge and provokes questions of a metaphysical nature. The ocean, Elizabeth Bishop says in one of her poems, "is like what we imagine knowledge to be: / dark, salt, clear, moving, utterly free, / drawn from the cold hard mouth / of the world ...." (74).

Several of these poets – interviewed between a first and second book – spoke of their deepening interest in forms. Others, including Smith and Sanger – veterans of metred and stanzaic verse – or Clarke and O'Grady – both of whom write sonnets, both of whom name "beauty" as a motive for their art – spoke eloquently, and at length, about the historical implications in their use of form. Free-verse modernism, it would seem, never really took root in the Maritimes. "[S]onnets, quatrains, and rhyming poems of one sort or another," according to Clarke, "are the forms that we have literally inherited because our parents, grandparents, great-grandparents loved and adored and used these forms .... This is the common perception of what poetry should be here in the Maritimes. I can't see that not affecting poets." For

Sanger, the ballad quatrain, in particular, is "a central form" carrying "what was most important in Maritime poetry of European origin during the 19th century. It gives us still an entry into the economical narrative method and profound psychological world of the Anglo-Scottish ballads." The quatrain is Sanger's preferred form. In a parallel way, O'Grady takes his bearing "from the Irish poetic tradition, which tends still to be traditional and formalist. It draws from the 19th-century English tradition that it emerged from and from the older Irish tradition, which is very rigorous in form and has a special sensitivity to language ...." Most of these poets, though, work in a combination of free verse and form, moving between the two, as Simpson does in going from what she refers to as the stone-breaking work of the sonnet series "Seven Paintings by Brueghel" (*Loop* 19-25) to the improvisational manner of "Gesture Drawings" (*Loop* 26-36). Overall, couplets, it would seem, dominate in the work of these poets whether they are the unrhymed, long-lined, margin-challenging couplets of Sue Goyette or the "prosy" couplets of Robert Moore, who, like Goyette, likes them for their tension, a "very particular kind of tectonic, a tension not available in an arrangement of three- or-four line stanzas." There are, of course, Maritime poets, such as Elisabeth Harvor, who revel in the un-"confined" freedoms of free verse, poets for whom formalism is not "liberation," and to whom the revisionary formalist mood is alien.

If modernism settled lightly here, perhaps postmodernism is more consonant with what was already present by mid- to late-20th century: The wryly ironic habit of Maritime speakers – such as you hear in poems by Nowlan – or the tendency, in regards to received forms, to reinvent as Acorn did in *Jackpine Sonnets* (1977). Among the poets included here, MacKenzie makes "Dissonnets" of the sonnet (*Shaken by Physics* 27-42). John Smith, in *Maps of Invariance*, using the freest of free-verse forms – the prose poem – creates paragraphs whose movement mimics the sonnet. Forms are as liable to erosion and reformulation as the sandstone cliffs that define so much of the Atlantic coastline. Nature, especially as it exists at the seashore, teaches that design persists even as forms change. If postmodernism has contributed an elasticity of form, a skepticism about language, and a comedic-ironic turn to poetry – as Moore suggests – such contributions are, in light of a half century of Maritime poetic practice, complementary rather than earth-shattering.

Certain things become obvious in reading a poet's body of work in preparation for an interview: Each poet has one or more favourite tropes, favourite poetic devices – Simpson's frequent use of onomatopoeia, Leckie's orchestration of assonantal sounds, Bartlett's preference for synaesthesia over the single-sense image, Sanger's fondness for out-of-the-way words, Moore's affair with irony. Part of the fun in interviewing a poet is bringing him or her news of recurrence – Goyette's fondness for copula metaphor, MacKenzie's and O'Grady's habitual use of the noun-phrase metaphor, something they share, incidentally, with Acorn, the use of which reflects the noun-dense phrasing of Island speech. In our conversations, we queried these habits, thought about how such habits affect and direct the poetic process, which, along with place, was the subject of most importance in these conversations. Because these interviews focus on manuscript work as well as published books, the poets – finding themselves in this in-between position – were in a mood for rigorous self-appraisal. In re-evaluating the published work, they identified practices that they'd like to change. With impartial professionalism, they considered, among other things, their past habits in figurative language. Moore is "less enamoured" of the metonymic in his second (and forthcoming) collection, more interested in "metaphor and the magic thinking it allows." Between collections, MacLaine moves from the "reluctant comparison" of the simile to the "greater confidence" of the metaphor. This was the move that Sanger, similarly, made between *The America Reel* and *Earth Moth*.

Given the opportunity, the poets offered definitions of poetry, speculated on the poet's role, and named – in the course of talking about such things – those poets whose practices were, for them, models of excellence. John Thompson and Elizabeth Bishop were frequently named in this regard; Alden Nowlan and Milton Acorn less often, although the interviewer does go on about the latter. Contemporaries such as Czeslaw Milosz, Seamus Heaney, Derek Walcott, or predecessors such as Wallace Stevens, and further back, William Wordsworth, all affectionately named, recur from interview to interview. Here and there, a poet finds another to admire, to love. *Here,* it would seem, means in this area; *there* means overseas or the Atlantic seaboard to the south of us. My line of inquiry did not regularly include questions about influences, but if a respondent went in that direction, I followed. It wasn't often our talk on that subject took us west.

A poem starts, Carole Langille says, "with a beautiful word." *Maritime,* I say, is a beautiful word, and reason enough to begin a book even though politicians and journalists use the word in the plural, and with derogatory intent, as an equivalent for the "have-not provinces." I made a road trip through the "have-provinces" in literature. These poets will tell you what they've had here, gained here. A view, yes, but a view enlarged by the always variable, vanishing horizon of the sea.

WORKS CITED

ANNE COMPTON

— • —

Bigge, Ryan. "They roar, but don't rant." Rev. of *VictoryMeat: New Fiction from Atlantic Canada*. Ed. Lynn Coady. *Globe and Mail* 7 June 2003: D17.

Bishop, Elizabeth. "At the Fishhouses." *The Complete Poems*. London: Chatto & Windus, 1969. 72-74.

Brewster, Elizabeth. "Where I Come From." *Coastlines: The Poetry of Atlantic Canada*. Eds. Anne Compton et al. Fredericton: Goose Lane Editions, 2002. 31.

MacKenzie, John. *Shaken By Physics*. Vancouver: Polestar, 2002.

MacLaine, Brent. *These Field Were Rivers*. Fredericton: Goose Lane Editions, 2004.

Miller, Karl, ed. *Seamus Heaney in Conversation with Karl Miller*. London: Between the Lines, 2000.

Welch, Liliane. *Seismographs: Selected Essays and Reviews*. Ed. Richard Lemm. Charlottetown: Ragweed P, 1998.

✠ ACKNOWLEDGMENTS

Several of these interviews – sometimes in a longer version, sometimes shorter and, occasionally, under a different title – were published in journals. My thanks to the editors.

"Standing Your Ground: George Elliott Clarke in Conversation" – *Studies in Canadian Literature*

"Ascension: Liliane Welch Talks About Poetry" – *Canadian Literature*

"Physics and Poetry: The Complex World of Alan Wilson" – *Canadian Literature*

"Doubly-Crossing Syllables: Thomas O'Grady on Poetry, Exile, and Ireland" – *Studies in Canadian Literature*

"A Many-Veined Leaf: Minutiae and Multiplicity in Brian Bartlett's Poetry" – *Studies in Canadian Literature*

"The Theatre of the Body: Extreme States in Elisabeth Harvor's Poetry" – *Canadian Literature*

"Writing Paintings and Thinking Physics: Anne Simpson's Poetry" – *Canadian Literature*

The New Brunswick Arts Board provided a documentation grant to cover travel and other costs. My thanks to John Ball, editor of *SCL*, for writing on my behalf.

By adjusting my teaching schedule, the Department of Humanities & Languages at UNB Saint John enabled me to complete the project.

Jena Schmitt, reader of the manuscript, made many helpful suggestions.

David Collins and Heather Craig, graduates of UNB Saint John, helped with the transcription of the tapes.

With his usual grace and good humour, Evan Jones edited the manuscript. Richard Dionne generously accepted the manuscript for publication and supervised its publication.

Above all, I want to thank the poets for their participation, the pleasure of their company, their conversation.

STANDING YOUR GROUND:
GEORGE ELLIOTT CLARKE IN CONVERSATION

Born in Windsor, Nova Scotia, George Elliott Clarke is a seventh-generation African Canadian. Clarke has published three books of poetry – *Saltwater Spirituals and Deeper Blues* (1983), *Whylah Falls* (1990), which received the 1991 Archibald Lampman Prize for poetry, and *Lush Dreams, Blue Exile Fugitive Poems: 1978-1993* (1994). Radio and stage versions of *Whylah Falls* were performed in Canada in 1996 and 1997. *One Heart Broken into Song*, a made-for-television movie, is set in the fictional rural Black community of Whylah Falls. Committed to research interests in nationalism, postcolonialism, and New World African literature, Clarke has edited *Fire on the Water: an Anthology of Black Nova Scotian Writing* (1991-92), *Eyeing the North Star: Directions in African-Canadian Literature* (1997), and he co-edited *Border Lines: Contemporary Poems in English* (1995). A playwright, as well as a poet, anthologist, and essayist, Clarke's verse-drama *Beatrice Chancy* will be published by Polestar in 1999. A "transplantation" of Shelley's tragedy *The Cenci* to the Annapolis Valley, *Beatrice Chancy*, the opera – libretto by Clarke, music by James Rolfe – premiered in Toronto in June 1998. The same year, the Nova Scotia Arts Council awarded Clarke the Portia White Prize for Artistic Achievement.

At the time of this interview – August 1998 – Clarke was teaching English and Canadian Studies at Duke University, Durham, North Carolina. Since then, he has joined the faculty of English at the University of Toronto, where he holds the E.J. Pratt Chair in poetry, but wherever he goes, Nova Scotia holds first place in Clarke's work: "this is where the world as we know it begins, / all blue and beguiling ..." (*Lush Dreams* 39). In the intervening years, Clarke has published *Beatrice Chancy* (1999); *Execution Poems* (2001), winner of the Governor-General's Award for Poetry; *Blue* (2001); and two chapbooks, *Gold Indigoes* (2000) and *Blue (II)* (2001). His acclaimed debut novel, *George & Rue*, appeared in 2004. Clarke's essays – some of which are discussed in this interview – appear in *Odysseys Home: Mapping African-Canadian Literature* (2002). In 2005, the Pierre Elliott Trudeau Foundation, which awards an annual prize in the social sciences and humanities, named Clarke a Fellow. Clarke published two collections in 2006 – *Black*, and *Illuminated Verses*.

For three hours on *The Princess of Acadia* – the ferry that crosses the Bay of Fundy – Clarke and I talked about Maritime poetics, politics, and his poetry. The commotion of late-summer travellers spilled around us in the lounge, and from time to time Clarke's fans and friends interrupted the interview to greet him. At one point, we were called upon to help out on a crossword puzzle. Our conversation looked forward to Clarke's forthcoming work as much as it looked back at his poems, essays, and anthologies in print.

AC   • *Whylah Falls* seems to be the centre of your work. It has blossomed into a play and a movie, *One Heart Broken into Song*. The forthcoming *Beatrice Chancy* shares more than setting – Nisan and Nova Scotia – with *Whylah Falls*. Is this an accurate account?

GEC • It's a scary statement. I think, like most writers, I don't want to be known as the author of one work. On days when I feel dispirited about my progress as a writer, I go back to it. "If I could do that," I say, "couldn't I do something as good or better?" What's also scary about it for me is that it showed a way forward for me that I may not, as yet, have actually taken. For some reason, I stumbled into a way of writing in *Whylah Falls* that I have not always replicated in my present work or in the work that immediately followed it. One of my present aims is to try to get back to the way of writing that I was pursuing when I was putting together *Whylah Falls*. The poems in that book flowed out of life. Even though it is a work of fiction, it is based very much on real people, real events.

AC   • *Whylah Falls* mythologizes a specific place, Weymouth Falls, and an event – the killing of Graham Cromwell – but it does even more than that. Under the pressure of events, including the razing of Africville, it reconceptualizes a people and a 200-year-old history in mythic terms. Is there some sense in which you, as author, felt incidental to this articulation, an amanuensis of a myth book?

GEC • Oh, absolutely, definitely. I took that role on. I guess it was really conscious because I was literally sitting in people's living rooms, writing down what they had to say – stories, jokes, sayings, proverbs – and

ANNE COMPTON

trying to weave it into longer poems or keeping it as a short snippet in longer pieces of prose. I did see the work as an attempt to embody the oral literature, the oral folkways, of a people I was living with and working among, particularly in 1985-86, although there are some childhood stories and some family stories in the book as well. If I can sum this up, *Whylah Falls* was for me a kind of falling into consciousness, not merely a racial consciousness, which was always there, but a poetic consciousness, an understanding finally that while there was a great world of Anglo-American poetry out there, there was this Black Nova Scotian, Africadian poetry that was rooted in the voice and in these shared jokes, stories, proverbs. If I really wanted to be a strong poet, I felt that's the material I had to work with. I think I went through a period, particularly when I went off to university, when I put all of that behind me and focused on how I could write the next *Paradise Lost* or follow the Cavaliers, and, of course, Shakespeare and all the greats.

AC • I'd like to understand the aesthetic and political ramifications of geography's collision with canon, and by geography I mean cultural as well as physical geography. Were you self-consciously ranging across the forms, raiding canonical forms?

GEC • I think I was. What happened was I spent two years writing these dreadful pieces of blank verse, just as exercises, and then something happened when I was about to leave Waterloo, where I had attended university, to come back home to Nova Scotia. One night, the week before I left, I stayed up all night, and I started remembering this community [Weymouth Falls] I had spent time in as a youth, and all of a sudden a poem, "How Exile Melts to One Hundred Roses" (22-23), came out of it. And in a sense, this was the first *Whylah Falls* poem. I wrote it in blank verse. It was an attempt to capture a miniature story of my visits to that community that I had suddenly begun to remember as I prepared to return to Nova Scotia. There was complete innocence in terms of writing. I had no idea that there was going to be a book or that I was going to develop this further.

AC • So you didn't know what you were starting at that point?

GEC • I was excited by the fact that I was taking this great Miltonic instrument and writing something that was, finally, out of my own experience, instead of trying to write poems for William Lyon Mackenzie King or something like that.

AC • Not only is *Whylah Falls* comprehensive in terms of canonical forms, but also it is a botany book of flowers and a lexicon of food and drink. What is this drive toward inclusiveness in your work? I see it, as well, in the forthcoming *Beatrice Chancy*.

GEC • Well, that's there because Black Nova Scotians have been left out of so much. And in a sense, we are very much still outside the canon and whatever else. This inclusiveness is also a response to all those travelogues about Nova Scotia from Will R. Bird's *This is Nova Scotia* to Margaret Morley's *Down North and Up Along*, particularly those about the Annapolis Valley, my favourite part of the province. Most of them did not mention Black people, or they mentioned them condescendingly. This jarred with my recollections and my knowledge of Black communities in the Annapolis Valley because they were, to my mind, not exotic but simply part of the valley, part of Nova Scotian life. Therefore, they had imbibed all of the culture that creates Nova Scotia from English literature to various foods. Just in terms of being true to what I knew of these places and people, it was natural to include catalogues of foods as well as to range across the canon. Another point to make about the canon is that it is our canon too. Even though it was imposed on us, it still belongs to us. I am told that I have to accept these writers as great writers, and that, in terms of English poetry, these are the models I have to use, but perhaps we can take these models and blacken them. We can make them speak Black English. We can adapt the forms. In everyday life, I see people adapting the English language all of the time to suit their own needs.

AC • Xavier Zachary, the character in *Whylah Falls* who is known as X, is, by times, a pastoral swain, a sonneteer, a cavalier. In his courtship of Shelley, and of Selah also, X churns out Petrarchan similes, but the vocabulary of praise in the conceits is transformed to ebony, indigo, apple blossoms, honey, pine, and so forth. The conceit undergoes a "double transplantation" – cultural and geographic. Is this "double transplantation" a characteristic of Africadian writing?

GEC • That's really intriguing, and I think that you're right, and this "double transplantation" is also a reflection of a double resistance. If we've been taught to think certain things about dear old England, or for that matter about the United States, vis-à-vis our own culture, which is understood to be inferior to England's and America's, then in order to come to terms with these "superior cultures," we need to reconfigure

ANNE COMPTON

them in our own terms. I think that is what I was trying to do in terms of *Whylah Falls*, especially there. We've been given these devices, these forms, genres, techniques, tendencies in English literature. What do they have to do with being a Black Nova Scotian? How can I use them to articulate who we are and create an English literature with a Black Nova Scotian accent? It's the only way to come to terms with it.

AC • You take it over, but you reconfigure it at the same time?

GEC • It's a kind of robbery.

AC • In the poem "April in Paris," you say, "I wander among the graves of poets, / Stalk inspiration with a loaded pen" (*Lush Dreams* 42). This is more than "anxiety of influence." Is the metaphor of the "loaded pen" the kind of thing that you are talking about at the moment?

GEC • James Baldwin, the African-American novelist, said it best. He said that the Negro is a kind of bastard of the west. There is a lot in that. Because of slavery, and the machinery of slavery and colonialism, we were displaced, centuries ago, generations ago, into this different set-ting, this strange setting – into a transplanted European culture in North America. Since the majority culture insists on proclaiming this as the epitome of human achievement – in terms of literature, in terms of everything cultural – the question is, where is our voice? How do we fit in? What do we do with it? We are forced into a kind of negotiation with the master tropes, master genres, master language. In order to sur-vive, in order to maintain some specificity for ourselves, we have no choice but to try to claim it for ourselves, to pretend that Shakespeare comes from Weymouth Falls or that Virginia Woolf comes from North End Halifax. I mean, why not?

AC • You appropriate the forms and redo the tropes, but at an even more particular level, you take up and reissue lines. For example, a line of Michael Ondaatje's becomes: "There's a trick with a verb that I'm learning / To do ..." (*Lush Dreams* 17). Is it parodic *homage* or a taking over?

GEC • It's a bit of both and also a response. One of the strange conditions of being Black Nova Scotian is that one is colonized in three different ways – by British culture, by American, and also by Canadian. We have to tussle with the Canadian as well. From the standpoint of Toronto, my little community that numbers 30,000 people, which counts for about 10 per cent of the Black Canadian total population, has little to contribute to the history and discussion of an African-Canadian presence. We literally do not count. So part of my strategy as a writer, in responding to my status as the scribe of a marginal and colonized community, is to sack and plunder all those larger literatures – British, American, Canadian, French, African-American, Caribbean – and to domesticate their authors and their most famous or noted lines. In other words, my acts of homage are acts of damage.

AC • You have described the Maritimes as the Canadian Orient and its poetry as East Coast pastoral ("Orienting and Disorienting" 52). Readers of Alden Nowlan and David Adams Richards might have difficulty recognizing the pastoral in their depictions of the Maritimes. What is it that you are trying to recover or to reclaim in your assertions of Maritime pastoralism and in your own practice of the pastoral, as in *Whylah Falls*?

GEC • What I was really trying to do was oppose the survival thesis, [Margaret] Atwood's survival thesis and that of other commentators, particularly those in the '60s and '70s. Thematic critics of Canadian literature kept finding all this emphasis on survival, and on how harsh and bitter life is for Canadians. That may be true but, at the same time, there is, at least in the Maritimes, specifically in parts of Nova Scotia – the Annapolis Valley – but also in Prince Edward Island and New Brunswick, the possibility for gardens, as opposed to wilderness, where one is, more or less, at peace and where one can find beauty. I find in the Annapolis Valley a very pastoral landscape. The vegetation is lush in the spring, summer, and fall. It's luxurious. You can luxuriate.

AC • The oft-told story of Maritime experience is the bleak, born-into-failure state of entrapment. Are you giving the backhand to the mentality of defeat?

GEC • I don't know if it's that because I believe we should be defeatists. I am not entirely opposed to that. And in *Whylah Falls* there is defeat because the killer of Othello Clemence is never brought to justice. But, at the same time, what I find most interesting is how people who do not have a lot of money can access a sense of beauty, or can create a beauty. And that is what I saw in the Black communities where I was working in the Annapolis Valley. Times are tough. People are on welfare; people are unemployed. There's racism. The police are unjust. The justice system is a joke. At the same time, while all of that is true, people insisted on creativity, on art, on cuisine, music, beauty for themselves.

ANNE COMPTON

This wasn't a question of going to museums or buying records. It was a question of making things, making your own music, singing your own songs. This ability to find one's own beauty, and to define beauty for one's self, is also politic. It is an act of resistance against all people who declare your community a slum, or who define you personally as ugly or ignorant, or on the margin.

AC • Which is what you say in a poem in *Lush Dreams*: "Hinterland is that country / you cannot even begin / to imagine" (77). Who is the "you" being addressed here?

GEC • That came out of when I was living in Toronto in 1981-83. It was written in Toronto, looking back on here. Basically, I felt that the Toronto intellectual elite despised folks from Atlantic Canada. I felt that they tended to view us as model mongrels, as *Deliverance*-style dog faces. "Hinterland" is a reaction to that brain-numbing prejudice.

AC • At the end of *Whylah Falls*, Shelley says, "we are responsible / for Beauty" (151). Yet, at the centre of that book, there's a crucible of pain. Is that the burden of words then, to find beauty in pain?

GEC • I think it is the means to find the strength to continue. Being able to see beauty, to create beauty, to know beauty, is an antidote, a means of balancing the pain, especially for the oppressed. We see that oppressed communities everywhere tend to be creative, a communal kind of creativity. I'm thinking of music especially. Music comes out of that and sometimes even art, such as wall murals, and these are created to express a communal consciousness. People may not even think of it as being *beautiful*. It exists as a necessity, something they have to do to manifest their existence. It says we have a right to be here even if we are oppressed; even if we are forced to suffer, we will continue to be here. We have an existence, and we have a means of defining our own existence for ourselves. Identity doesn't depend upon a ruling class or an over-group or a majority group. We have ideas and ideals. And I think, therefore, the artist, the poet, the writer, the musician has an opportunity – I don't want to say "a responsibility" – to articulate a communal consciousness. Depending on one's own philosophical orientation, one may find materials that strengthen one's own work in terms of the interest of the collective. A poet can reflect a community's art back to the community.

AC • Isn't this what *Whylah Falls* does: Gives back the beauty that can be claimed from terrible experience?

GEC • I'd like to think so. Another intention I had in writing that book was that I wanted to write something that I could read to my community. One of the problems I ran into with *Saltwater Spirituals*, even though many of the poems in that work talk about Black Nova Scotia, was that many of the poems are at an abstract, intellectual level. The difference between the two books is that the poems and stories in *Whylah Falls* were deliberately written to be read aloud and to be read in front of my own community. I had this horrifying experience, which I think every writer should go through at one time or another. In the spring of 1986, I was invited to take part in a fundraising event put on by the Black Cultural Centre of Nova Scotia. I was the only poet on the programme. Everyone else was a performer. I was there as *the poet*. I read in the way I had been taught to read in the university, which is very formal and very Atwood-like in terms of being plain, no emotion, just straightforward recitation. But this was in front of an audience of my peers, of my own community. So people started yelling at me, "Get off the stage." It was very direct: "You're boring. Go home." The people didn't want to hear some dry shit.

AC • That's interesting because *Saltwater Spirituals* seems to come directly out of your community. It begins, after all, with the dozen church poems, and it's the story of Richard Preston [Black refugee, 1812; founder of the African United Baptist Association]. So the difference must have to do with the way you present your material in the two books. *Saltwater Spirituals* has a different line from *Whylah Falls*, a very short, free-verse line as compared to the blank verse of *Whylah Falls*.

GEC • That's very true, but there is also a difference in terms of substance and tone and direction. *Saltwater Spirituals*, even though it was a reflection of, and a reaction to, my Nova Scotian history, was at the same time very much informed by what I had been studying in a way that hadn't yet been filtered out. The material hadn't yet been transmuted into my own voice. I was writing the poetry I thought I should be writing as opposed to stuff I had to write. And that was, I think, the difference. When I heard this audience reaction – there were 200 people there that night – I was, of course, shocked but luckily I had just written a piece, "Love Letter to an African Woman," which is in *Whylah Falls* (58-59), and I read that, and they loved it. The people got quiet and

ANNE COMPTON

they started to say, "Preach it! Testify! That's it, brother!" And the applause at the end was rich. It was intense. And I said to myself, *I will never write again anything I cannot read before my own community.*

AC • So is poetry performance for you now?

GEC • I think it always should be. For me, poetry is not only a printed form, a printed art. It is also an oral art, and it should always be. The two should never be separated. One should have a poem that reads silently as well as it does vocally.

AC • Yet *Saltwater Spirituals* has an oratorical quality, especially in the latter half where you are presenting Richard Preston's life story and where he is speaking.

GEC • That's very true. I think there has always been a drive towards rhetoricity for me. I am interested in that, having grown up in the Baptist Church where I listened to someone orate or preach. I wanted to do a couple of pieces of that sort in *Whylah Falls*. And, of course, the Reverend Langford character was my way of doing that. I find that kind of speaking spellbinding. Last weekend, I attended a Black church service in Durham, North Carolina, and the way the minister performed reminded me so much of the Cornwallis Street Baptist Church in Halifax. He didn't even use a text. He just performed. It was a 20-minute address that had people standing and shouting and laughing. At the same time, it was very spiritual. And I think that quality is there in some of my poetry where I am attempting oratory.

AC • Were you, at one point, headed toward the ministry?

GEC • Oh, God. That's a telling statement. Yes and no. What I mean is that at different times in my life, I've been pulled towards Christianity. I've read the Bible three times completely through and mean to do so again. At one point in my life, I considered myself to be "born again," but it didn't last very long. I still have a respect and interest in all that. From time to time, late at night, I'll tune into the Christian TV channel just to see what's going on. There's this one guy, a Black minister, evangelical, no notes, an extemporaneous, revival-fashion preacher, who said, "You've got tons of dirt on your Bible." I thought, *That's a great line.* So I stole it and put it in *Beatrice Chancy*.

AC • Alliteration seems to be the preferred rhythmic device – accenting stresses – in *Saltwater Spirituals*. Between *Saltwater Spirituals* and

Whylah Falls, do you make a shift from the psalmic alliterative line to Renaissance blank verse, and is that because of the epic inclination in *Whylah Falls*?

GEC • Absolutely. Also, my analysis at the time was that the blank-verse line is the basic line in English poetry, and it's the line we are stuck with no matter where we are from and no matter who we are. I think in Canada, because of the fact that we fall between Britain and the US – where the poets have felt freer to move away from the standard line – a lot of poets are closer to blank verse. I've never felt comfortable with completely unfettered free verse even though I was writing it in *Saltwater Spirituals*. I always felt that there was something else that I needed. I found that with blank verse, although with deviation from it. In my work, the iambic line is really messed up, complicated, abruptly stopped at points by my heavy use of spondees, trochees especially, and, of course, pyrrhics. This is the way we speak.

AC • Among Maritime poets, there's a tendency toward disciplined forms as in the work of Milton Acorn, Fred Cogswell, John Thompson. Is this regard for form among Maritime poets an aspect of what you refer to as "anti-modernity modernism" ("Birth and Rebirth" 72)?

GEC • These are the forms that we have literally inherited because our parents, grandparents, great-grandparents loved and adored and used these forms, which are still around. The Nova Scotia Poetry Society publishes, every few years, a collection of poems by its members, and they are almost always sonnets, quatrains, and rhyming poems of one sort or another. This is the common perception of what poetry should be here in the Maritimes. I can't see that not affecting poets. So even though we may be well aware of free verse and all the other forms and techniques that may be available to us, our poetic consciousnesses have been formed in this environment where people still expect you to be able to produce a sonnet.

AC • There are at least eight sonnets in *Whylah Falls*, and *Beatrice Chancy* has a number of them. Do you see your work in the sonnet as existing in a continuum with the work of Acorn and Archibald Lampman, who used the sonnet for social-political purposes?

GEC • I am knowledgeable about their uses of the sonnet, particularly Acorn's, and to a certain extent Lampman's as well; my only deviation from it is that my lines tend not to rhyme, but it was the same for Acorn.

AC • Acorn was writing 17-line sonnets, nine-line sonnets, and yet, for him, they were still sonnets because they had the structure, the dialectical structure – as formerly in the octave and sestet – of the sonnet. He wanted to free the sonnet from the 14-line form.

GEC • I think this also is postcolonial. We have inherited this thing. Now, what can we do with it? How does it work here on this side of the Atlantic? This is one of the interesting things about East Coast poetry in general. On the one hand, our landscape is somewhat reminiscent of the British Isles. And the seasons are somewhat similar, although our seasons are far more intense. That makes us feel on the East Coast that we can access British poetry. It's not completely alien to us, or even to our way of speaking. But at the same time, we are different; we are in America so there is a tendency toward a little more freedom, a little less formality, a little more abruptness in speech. All of that gets translated into the poetry. Although there is still this tenuous connection with British poetry, it is specifically with British poetry no later than Dylan Thomas. I don't think anyone follows more recent British poets unless it's the work of Seamus Heaney or Derek Walcott, who also counts as a British poet, I think. But for the most part, when we think about British poetry, it ends for us with Thomas.

AC • Yeats certainly enters your own work.

GEC • Definitely, but, then, so does Pound, a poet I have a lot of trouble with, and for good reasons. Nevertheless, his drive for a powerful simplicity – a simplicity still encoded within form – is very attractive.

AC • Is it the musicality of Yeats that is so consonant with the Maritime voice?

GEC • There's a poem by Harry Thurston, in a collection called *Clouds Flying Before the Eye*, which is written in the voice of a next-door neighbour. Its rhythm, its muscularity, its at-homeness, and the plainness of the speech is very Yeatsian. It's what Yeats was doing in his later poems.

AC • A few moments ago you were talking about poetry in terms of geography, and in one poem you talk about our "beach-broken speech" (*Saltwater Spirituals* 49). You seem to be saying that geography has gotten into poetry in the Maritimes.

GEC • That's so even in terms of the way people speak. There is a very distinctive way of speaking in Newfoundland – but not just in Newfoundland – also in Nova Scotia, New Brunswick, and PEI. There's an accent difference – different from the kinds of English spoken in Ontario, and for that matter, different from Quebec, or anywhere else in the country – and there's a different word stock. It's an elemental diction, which is, at the same time, quite picturesque. Look at some of those South Shore phrase books ....

AC • ... which you raided for *Beatrice Chancy*.

GEC • Oh, I certainly have, and also for *Whylah Falls*. They were like Bibles. I picked up Lewis Poteet's phrase books and that got me listening very closely to what people have to say. There's a line in *Beatrice Chancy* that I got from my uncle [Rex Mendes]. He was talking about crooked politicians, and he said about this one guy in Halifax: "He's so greedy, he'd even steal the leaves off the trees." I love that.

AC • I like the *Beatrice Chancy* line where Deal says, "Dice ain't got the sense God gave a dog in a fit."

GEC • That came from Kishi. She's right over there [George's friend Kishi, Darlene Djomgué, née Lawrence, happened to be on the same ferry crossing].

AC • You're fairly obsessive about light. There's "J.M.W. Turner's Nova Scotia" (*Lush Dreams* 80), where light "raptures" what it touches; the as-yet-unpublished "Paris Annapolis," where light, as the title indicates, collapses the geographically remote. And, of course, there is the poem that begins, "drunk with light / i think of maritime country" (*Saltwater Spirituals* 24). Is it light that nails us to Maritime space?

GEC • That's a really interesting idea. I know that there is a particular kind of sky that one sees in Nova Scotia in April, which I really like. There's a certain quality of light that is very moody and changeable and full of various colours, kind of stormy. A turmoil of colour in the sky and in the light. And it is well known throughout the Maritimes that we can have a cloudy day, and a rainy day, and a sunny day, often within a few minutes of one and other. I've always found that variety very enticing.

AC • You say that the persistent concerns of Africadian literature from its inception in 1785 – with the work of John Marrant, the African-American Methodist missionary – to the present are liberty, justice, and faith. Is it accurate to say that *Saltwater Spirituals* is the book of faith; *Whylah Falls,* the book of justice; and *Lush Dreams,* the book of liberty?

GEC • That's a nice way of putting it. I would never have thought of that myself. There's another formulation I've come up with. I'm struck by the revolutionary slogans that are usually tripartite: "land, bread, justice," the Soviet Revolution and, of course, "liberty, fraternity, equality," the French Revolution. Africadia also seemed to have a tripartite slogan, or a statement of what it is we are questing for. I thought "liberty, justice, faith" summed it up pretty well. But then in *Whylah Falls,* it's "beauty, liberty, and justice." So I would prefer to think of *Whylah Falls* as the book of beauty if one is going to trilogize my work.

AC • So, then, where is *Beatrice Chancy* going to fit in?

GEC • Realism is the word that comes to mind.

AC • I wouldn't think of *Beatrice Chancy* as a realistic work.

GEC • Not realism in that sense. Perhaps pessimism is a better word.

AC • I began by saying that I found *Beatrice Chancy* to be a lot like *Whylah Falls,* but it's also very different from *Whylah Falls.* There's metaphysical grief in *Beatrice Chancy* in spite of its intense physicality. In *Whylah Falls,* faith is abiding – at the end, faith is still in place – but in *Beatrice Chancy,* they're beyond faith. Is that so?

GEC • I think so. This is going to sound really grandiose, but I was reading a lot of Dante, so I look at *Whylah Falls* as the "Paradiso" and *Beatrice Chancy* as the "Inferno." It wasn't really intentional; it was just the direction *Beatrice Chancy* was going in. I knew I wanted to write a tragedy and not one where there was going to be any easy sort of resolution at the end. She does take action; it's good action, positive action. At the same time, it results in her own destruction. But sometimes that is necessary if you're going to strike that blow for liberty, independence, and freedom. Sometimes you suffer and lose. She's in a situation where she doesn't have any other choice but to act.

AC • She goes through an amazing transformation from the girl we meet in the beginning, who is carrying apple blossoms and a Bible. She is so very innocent and abounding in faith in the beginning, and then she becomes the instigator of revenge. Beatrice epitomizes the libretto's metaphysical, and political, concerns when she describes the Bible as "wasps' paper that wants burning" and denounces prayer as futile. *Beatrice Chancy* is far bleaker than what has preceded it, but nothing as compared to that manuscript of poems that I've gotten from you recently.

GEC • Oh, yes, those nasty things.

AC • They're Vesuvian, volcanic – venomous and vituperative. But they are, also, misogynist.

GEC • You think so? That's dangerous. Problematic.

AC • In one poem, there is "slut" and "whore" and "bitch," and in another, "Seraphic virgins … gush bilge and crap" ("*Res lascivas seu obscenas*"). Are you surprised I found them misogynist?

GEC • I know I'm going to be critiqued on that basis for some of them. What I was trying to do, and this may not be much of something to try to accomplish, and maybe it's just dangerous and stupid, and, as you say, misogynistic, but these are poems that I'm planning to publish as part of a manuscript that I'm calling "Out." What I'm interested in doing in these poems is exploring the modes of unacceptable thought and just letting the poems be there as ugly, awful, nasty, and as difficult, as they are. There's something in it to offend everybody; so I'll never be able to publish another book in my life![1]

AC • But there is, also, tremendous word energy in those poems. They are like the work of the young John Donne – bluntly unromantic, spoken with force, hurled. You seem to be reacting against your own earlier romantic work.

GEC • "Out" is divided in terms of the seven deadly sins, and so some of those poems, which will most likely be seen as misogynist, will appear in the section called "Lust"; some will appear in "Wrath"; some in "Greed," and so forth. "Depression" is another category, a modern sin, as is "Fear."

AC • A different kind of canon this time!

GEC • I have Blake in mind – *The Proverbs of Hell* and *The Songs of Experience*, as opposed to *Innocence*. Sade is also an influence.

AC • In the "Out" poems, are you giving voice to Francis Chancy, the villain in *Beatrice Chancy*?

---

1 "Out" was not published. The tone and attitude, and indeed some of the individual poems, appeared in *Blue*, 2001, and will appear in the forthcoming *Black*, 2006.

ANNE COMPTON

GEC • Maybe. Yes, definitely, because there are sentiments like these given to him in *Beatrice Chancy*. This is a weasel answer, but "Out" is all of the above. Some of it is stuff left over from *Beatrice*. Some of it is there just because I thought the lines were strong even if they are nasty and awful. All of this is stuff you shouldn't think, and certainly shouldn't say, but my desire here is to say it anyway and see what happens. Not that I expect anything positive to happen, or even that I'll get the book published. I've just sent the manuscript out to a potential publisher. Not everything in it is going to be offensive though. "Paris Annapolis" is in it, and other pieces of that sort, and some reflective pieces. What I really have in mind for "Out" is that these poems will enter the world and cause ripples, but I am not writing just for the purpose of provoking people or to cause a disturbance. For my own mental health, I want to get the stuff out there. Then I can just put it away and say, "OK, there's my nasty Inferno, Part 2," and then I can move on to other things.

AC • The question is, how far can anyone go with bold language? That issue arises in *Beatrice Chancy* as well, where there are some extraordinarily bold lines. There is, for example, what Lead says when he comes into Lustra's room after killing Francis Chancy: "Encunted, the dagger fucked his left eye." The line begins with an invented word, a neologism, doesn't it?

GEC • No, it's not. It's a translation from Sade. I can't claim it as an original. How can I put it? This new material is violent, and violation. It's stuff I haven't really explored before. I think *Whylah Falls* is a very "nice" work because it has that tapestry, the music, the flowers, and the food, and it has a good moral in all of that. I see these recent poems as acts of war.

AC • Who's the enemy?

GEC • It's not very well defined, but there are some people whose names are in that long poem ["*Contre la nouvelle trahison des grimauds*"], a long bitter satire, 150 lines, using a six-line stanza, about various writers and critics. If the order I have in mind for "Out" works, it will be the first poem in the section called "Wrath." I feel that there are a lot of issues that we never really talk about in Canadian poetry. I was thinking specifically of the folks in Toronto and how there is a certain kind of official political line that one has to toe, and an official poetic that one has to respect. And I just wondered, so what happens if we don't follow that? You probably really get throttled. Let's kick down the door a little bit and see what happens. I don't expect it to be very well received. I see it as something I just have to do. But I am also very interested now in the collision of words. In this manuscript, I am interested in colliding words together and seeing what happens. I am struck by all the potential inner rhymes and the playful hidden rhymes you can make with English words. I'm interested in the sound combinations that can happen.

AC   • It happens with vulgar words as well as with beautiful: Language breeds maggots as well as beauty.

GEC • You could say that I'm on a quest for boisterous language. But you know in that poem you were just talking about ["*Res lascivas seu obscenas*"], I was really paying homage to the "Seraphic virgins" who celebrate [Leonard] Cohen and [Irving] Layton and [John] Glassco. I was writing it in the spirit of Layton, who I read as a kind of Sadean voice, a poet and thinker full of piss and vinegar, and fire, sheer nastiness. There's no one doing that right now in English poetry in Canada. "Out" is a work in homage to Layton.

AC   • Is "Out" the abrogation of the anonymity of X in *Whylah Falls*?

GEC • Yes, I suppose that "Out" is a kind of reversal of X's anonymity, especially if you consider X to be a persona for myself. I guess that I felt safer projecting my own attitudes through X and letting him take the heat, so to speak, even though he is close to me. "Out" is, of course, a naked statement of my horrid personal failings, my own addictions to lust, wrath, greed, envy, pride, depression, fear, and accidie. Still, I think a semi-persona is at play in "Out." Then again, I'd like to think that I'm not the only one who feels, from time to time, immoral, sinful, and politically unrighteous impulses and thoughts. An example of what I'm getting at here is my poem "The Abortion," which describes the process in monstrous terms. It reveals, perhaps, my ambivalence for the procedure, even though I logically, conscientiously, correctly affirm a woman's right to decide the fate of a pregnancy. Similarly, in that long howl of satirical hatred, "*Contre la nouvelle trahison des grimauds*," I denounce hypocrite and sycophant writers because I, too, have been too much a hypocrite and sycophant. The presiding spirit in "Out" is Layton – his penchant for speaking raw war.

AC   • You have moved some distance then from the earlier position where desire is the generative force in your poetry. Is that so?

GEC • Maybe it's a different kind of desire. I think it is still there as a kind of yearning, but there is more voice now for anger, which I have never expressed much before. It's been there on the margins, but most of the poems said, "This is terrible, what has happened, but we're resigned to it."

AC • You describe *Whylah Falls* as a "dictionary of innocence and experience" ("Discovering Whylah Falls" 51). Does *Lush Dreams* extend that dictionary since its second section, "Gehenna" – poems about assassinations and crises – depicts the murder of innocence by experience on a worldwide scale in the 20th century?

GEC • For me, *Lush Dreams* is a kind of accident. A lot of the poems had been around for a long time. Some of the poems in the "Gehenna" section were written in the early '80s. I was planning, at one point, to publish this one book called "The Book of Liberty." I was going to include all the poems on assassinations and political events, but then *Whylah Falls* came along and knocked that project out of the water. Then when interest in my work picked up, because of *Whylah Falls*, there were some people who were interested in getting hold of *Saltwater Spirituals* and wanted to see it reprinted. But Lesley Choyce, at Pottersfield Press, wanted to do another book and to select for it some of the poems from *Saltwater Spirituals*. I knew this would be a place where I could get rid of, so to speak, these poems which had been sitting around for so long, poems that had been published but had not appeared in book form. I decided to set up the collection in terms of states of mind. The "Gehenna" section was the most coherent. I always knew I was going to have poems dealing with the assassinations in the '60s because I had grown up with them. They were part of my universe. I almost feel like turning against *Lush Dreams*. I don't see it as being the kind of book that I would have done if I hadn't been asked to do it. I don't feel as close to these poems.

AC • "Gehenna" isn't the strongest part of that book, but there are some wonderful poems in it such as "Watercolour for Negro Expatriates in France." It works well at the beginning of that section. The speaker asks the expatriates: "What are calendars to you? / And, indeed, what are atlases?" (14) Are the expatriates of no atlas, no calendar, rebuked by the 20th-century calendar of political saints and martyrs that follows in "Gehenna"?

GEC • I think there is an even more immediate rebuking that is going on. In fact, I didn't understand it at the time that I wrote the poem, but I now know that I was reacting as a Black Canadian to Black American experience. I was doing a kind of Canadian critique of Americans except they happened to be Black Americans and I am a Black Canadian. What I was doing in that poem, at the age of 18, was responding to African-American experience, which has been the defining experience for Black Nova Scotians even though it is not our experience. People complain about this sometimes: "Black Nova Scotians celebrate Martin Luther King Day and do all this other stuff that is oriented around the United States. What does that have to do with them really? Why aren't they celebrating Nova Scotian notables? Why does it always have to be some African-American hero?" I think I was reacting to that by picking on this little group of expatriate artists for fleeing a country where they couldn't pursue their art. It was tongue-in-cheek, partially ironic. But, at the same time, I wrote that poem in Windsor Plains! For crying out loud! Nobody left Windsor Plains and went to France! It was another postcolonial thing, except the people I was reacting against were African-Americans. While really appreciating what they had created, what they had done, I was also seeing in their flight a kind of evasion of responsibility. It was, of course, really easy for me to make that statement from my standpoint.

AC • Not only there, but in other places you reprimand "Ulyssean" roaming – the urge to be a traveller or a wanderer, a permanent migrant. In your work, there is a tension between home and "Ulyssean" roaming. Is that a tension that you yourself feel now that you are living in the States?

GEC • I think that I've been feeling it for a while, ever since I left Nova Scotia for the first time when I was 19. I was back home in 1985-87, which is an instructive period for me because that's when I started to write *Whylah Falls* – without really knowing it. That's when those poems began to generate but then I finished it in Ottawa. Basically, I've been away ever since. I haven't had an address in Nova Scotia since 1987. How can I write about this place anymore when my connection to it is so tenuous? I really feel this dilemma between being away and wanting to get back. In fact, one of the projects I had in mind for this particular visit was to look for a cottage so I can come back here in the summers and write and be around people and steal their lines! And have more material to work with.

AC • That sounds like nostalgia, but there are also conflicting feelings about home, aren't there?

GEC • Definitely. It's possible to write pastoral poetry about Nova Scotia, but there is also prejudice, narrow-mindedness, a degree of provincialism, which is actually the same everywhere, so this is not an anti-Nova Scotia or anti-Maritimes statement. Although we are always being accused of being provincials and doing provincial things, the whole country of Canada is provincial from an American point of view. What is this game I see some critics from Toronto playing – if it comes from the Maritimes, it's automatically provincial?

AC • Maritimers live degrees of marginality. We are the Maritime margin relative to Toronto, but we are the Canadian margin in regards to the States. You yourself talk about your culture being marginal within the Maritimes ....

GEC • Absolutely. So why should the world pay any attention? Why should anyone who reads English in Australia care about anything we have to say in Nova Scotia? On the other hand, we have no choice but to try to articulate some degree of our reality and of our consciousness as Maritimers, our way of looking at the world, whether that is one way or several ways. But that has to go into the writing if the work is going to have any kind of resonance. This is why I so admire Yeats and Walcott, whose work I've just reread again. I see in both of these poets a real insistence upon the geography, upon place, and a willingness, an insistence on speaking to the whole world from their location. Writing about the Caribbean, Walcott says, "Yeh, it's true. We don't have any history. Everything is all broken down. Nothing ever works. We're poor. But here we have stories, here we have our own history."

AC • I want to pursue a slightly different angle on the subject of community and ask about the conservative revolution that you talk about in "The Birth and Rebirth of Africadian Literature." In "Letters to Young Poets," you say, "Every poem must be a living insurrection ... striking revelation or revolution," but in "Birth and Rebirth," there is, as well, the burden of conservativism, the call to preserve the past. What about this paradox of the conservative revolution?

GEC • I'm attracted to Red Toryism. I'm attracted to the idea of revolution as a means of creating a more equitable society but, at the same time, I'm also interested in the idea of tradition and the sanctity of tradition.

Tradition is something that needs to be maintained and upheld, as long as it's not oppressive, because it's a way of defining one's existence, as a group, as a people. So there is this Janus-faced approach one has to have, or one should have, as a poet. On the one hand, you're looking forward to the future, but, also, you're not afraid to look back and say, "This is important," and carry it forward into the future. There is a tyranny of newness that can sometimes happen: "Sonnet. That's finished. We don't need to do that anymore. That ended in 1916 in the trenches in France. Nobody does sonnets anymore. Forget about Wilfred Owen too."

AC • This is the battle against liberalizing, homogenizing modernity that you talk about in "The Birth and Rebirth of Africadian Literature"?

GEC • One should be able to say that this form, this technique, is still interesting, still useful, and we can still do things with it. I like the fact that some of the poems in *Whylah Falls* are in the form that John Milton takes to a particular limit in *Paradise Lost*. All these forms are there to be renewed. I appreciate the L=A=N=G=U=A=G=E poets and the more self-consciously avant-garde poets, but I also insist that there is a way to be avant-garde that looks at the past and recovers what is still useful. That, also, can be radical. Revolutionary writing is not simply writing that is disembodied or very abstract or particularly vulgar as a means of claiming some kind of newness. And what about the audience? Can people read it? I still think we have a job to tell a story. Everybody can play games. We can all do that. We can write word games, and other people who write word games will enjoy them. But what if you desire to be read by your next-door neighbour, the person down the street, your relatives? Shouldn't the writing be accessible to them?

AC • The narrative line is important to you?

GEC • My horror is to be a writer who is not read by his own community. I like to think that I am giving back too. I am saying to the world this received line, or this image, deserves to be enshrined in print and given to everyone because, at this moment, it is poetic. It is poetry, and it should be given the permanency of print. I like reading folklore and phrase books. I just finished reading the *Encyclopedia of Black Folklore*. Writing *Beatrice Chancy* I read all sorts of slave narratives to find the odd suggestion of a line.

AC • You've written frequently about George Grant. ["Oh, God," the interviewee groans.] He is quoted in "Discovering Whylah Falls," referred to in "The Birth and Rebirth of Africadian Literature," and you wrote a long review article on *George Grant and the Subversion of Modernity*. So you and George Grant? Is it fair to say that you are in sympathy with his thinking?

GEC • For a long time, I think I wrote rather uncritically about George Grant, up until I read that Céline essay [Grant's essay, included in *Subversion*]. I read more or less without the kind of criticism that I now know I must bring to his work. What I originally liked about Grant was that he was able to provide a model for viewing social issues that allowed for a progressive agenda while at the same time bringing forth a kind of classical morality. I still do like that. I still think that *Lament for a Nation* is a very powerful piece. At the same time, I now know I have to part company with him at certain points. In the Céline article, for example, particularly in the version that was published in the *Queen's Quarterly*, he veers into anti-Semitism. It seems to be very clear that that's what it is. I'm surprised that *Queen's Quarterly* published the article. The end of that essay, "Céline: Art and Politics" [QQ 1983], is vicious, not simply ill-advised. Basically, it is a ridiculous piece of writing that calls into question everything that he puts forward in *Lament*, which is a kind of humanitarian conservatism, if I can call it that. It allows for a critique of capitalism, a critique of the United States particularly, which is always heartening for a Canadian. The problem with conservativism, like any "ism," is that it can be taken too far. And I think Grant does that. I will say in his partial defence that Céline has been recovered by a whole lot of people of very progressive political stripes. I think Grant is a richly significant and important philosopher and thinker, particularly in terms of the English Canadian – if not in terms of the entire Canadian – context and he had a progressive impact on people like Dennis Lee. Grant single-handedly created English Canadian nationalism in the 1960s. There is something to be said for that. He took principled stands on Vietnam and on corporate control. A lot of his pronouncements in terms of the drive of the whole world towards a bland homogenizing globalism seem to be taking shape. In fact, in 1965, he predicted the collapse of the Soviet Union. He foresaw the rise of the global capitalist state. And if that's what we're going to have, it's back to Marx! Even though communism as a means of organizing a society, as a government, has been a complete fiasco, the theory is still showing life because its critique of capitalism remains valid. We need to have some global means of controlling capitalism.

AC • If a strong Canadian nationalist position, such as Grant advocates, is one of the things that would be a bulwark against globalization, doesn't that very nationalism, at the same time, make it difficult for the Maritimes to have, and to express, its uniqueness? You can't have it both ways.

GEC • I think you can have it both ways. There's a difference between nationalism and patriotism, love of one's own place. I think you have to manifest that love of place. There is no way you can simply be a bland poet. I was looking at an anthology of love poems, and John Clare was there. It gladdened me that he was there. Clare's work is very local. I love the fact that he is willing to celebrate the woman who lives across the field. The language reflects that; it's an everyday, work-a-day language of the rural people of England in his time [1793-1864]. His language is homely, even frumpy, bumpy, and lumpy. It is so much out of where he is. I think a Maritime poetic idiom should reflect place in that way. And it's not opposing anybody else; it's simply being true to your own roots. That's a struggle because there are a lot of people out there who will tell you that your roots don't mean anything. If I can't speak in the rhythms and nuances, use the diction and vocabulary, of the people I grew up with, then what am I saying – they are not worth anything, that the way they speak is a nullity in the world? It can't be for me. I come from that. If they're a nullity, I'm a nullity. If I don't want to be a nullity, I have to do as much as I can to give voice to their voices, their experiences. There's a certain beauty in that. For instance, I've just written a poem, which I'm never going to publish, called "Queries for Kipling." I take his story "Gunga Din," and try to imagine how that would play out in the north end of Halifax. This is how I have to address Kipling. Not in terms of the British Empire, or what Kipling did in India, but rather, what did the British Empire mean for me as a Black kid growing up in Nova Scotia, a Black kid who sang "God Save the Queen" and meant it; who had a Union Jack in his classroom and loved it; read *The Jungle Book* stories and loved them. So how do I react to that? I can't talk about that by writing about the Caribbean or writing about Africa. My relationship to history and literature has to come through where I come from. That's what I respond to in other people's writing. Another British writer I like is Hardy because he has such a strong sense of place.

AC • Northrop Frye, whom I gather you are not very fond of, said that identity is regional and local and rooted in the imagination. It's how the imagination engages with where it is that makes for potent speech. From your localness, you engage in an argument with someone like Kipling. From your own ground. Perhaps that's what "standing your ground" – an interesting phrase, isn't it? – really means.

GEC • That's a beautiful metaphor. This is the ground upon which I received these figures, this culture, these impositions. I didn't receive them anywhere else. They came to me here. I have to respond to them from the same context. In a poem I've just published, "Antiphony," I am responding as a Black Nova Scotian to various literary figures and talking about the fact that they meant nothing to men and women who were probably illiterate, who worked as labourers and gypsum miners, or who worked in "service" as domestics. What did Shakespeare mean to them? Nothing. Why should he have meant anything to them? What kind of relationship, then, should I have to that literature, a literature of colonization? How do I work through that? By realizing that, while our language derives from this enclosed language, it is, at the same time, a de facto reaction against it. I see myself as being in a combative dialogue with English poetry, with American poetry, especially with African-American poetry, and with Canadian poetry.

AC • If you have all of these dialogical relationships, are you also, as a Black poet, in a feisty dialogue with Maritime literature?

GEC • I don't feel that I am, or certainly not as much. I see myself as being in alliance with Acorn and Alden Nowlan and other poets from here. I don't see myself as having any kind of tussle with them.

AC • But if we move to the next geographic sphere, then the dialogue is combative?

GEC • Definitely. For instance, as much as I may admire Atwood's poetry, I think it comes out of a very different growing-up experience – the bush in Northern Ontario. That's valid for her, but to say that *that* is the voice for Canadian poetry sticks in my craw. It's an important voice, a distinctive voice, a rich voice, but it's not my voice, or the voice of my experience. But of course it is not her job to give voice to my experience.

Meetings With Maritime Poets

AC • In talking about Maritime poets, you haven't named one woman poet!

GEC • I knew you were going to mention that. When I think of Maritime women poets who mean something to me, I think of Kay Smith, who hasn't published a lot, but whose work I admire very much, and of Elizabeth Bishop, although she's a long-distance Maritime poet. When I was a younger poet, Bishop was the poet I was reading.

AC • You talked about how your dialogue with other Maritime poets is cooperative rather than combative. Is there, then, another community in the Maritimes, the community of contemporary women poets?

GEC • I think such a community exists, and I think that I have a cooperative relationship with it – with Maxine Tynes, Sylvia Hamilton, Janet Pope. But at the time I came to poetic voice, so to speak, the poets I was reading are the ones that I have mentioned. Nowlan was born where I was born – Windsor, Nova Scotia. Then again, I think the strongest women's voices for me are those of my aunt [Joan Mendes, née Johnson] and my mother [Geraldine Elizabeth Clarke, née Johnson] and Kishi, and many, many other women I have known in my community.

AC • But what about those women's voices that have not been mediated through a male voice?

GEC • I am not sure I've been that much of a mediator. I've done some shaping, some nipping and tucking, here and there, but often I'll simply write it down as I hear it. Not as appropriation, but as homage. For instance, the movie *One Heart Broken into Song* grows, in part, from a conversation I had with a woman who hauled me into her house and sat me down and said, "I'm going to tell you the story of my life," a story about a poisoning. What I am doing is not so much giving Black women voice, but creating community.

AC • I don't know how long we've been talking, but that's the Nova Scotia coast up ahead. What you've just said about voice and community goes back to our earlier conversation. Since we've circled back as well as crossed the bay, this is a good place to stop.

ANNE COMPTON

WORKS CITED

— • —

Clarke, George Elliott. *Beatrice Chancy*. Vancouver: Polestar, Forthcoming 1999.

— — — . "The Birth and Rebirth of Africadian Literature." *Down East: Critical Essays on Contemporary Maritime Canadian Literature*. Ed. Wolfgang Hochbruck and James O. Taylor. Trier: WVT Wissenschaftlicher Verlag Trier, 1996. 55-80.

— — — . "Discovering Whylah Falls." *Quarry Magazine* 40.4 (Fall 1991): 80-89.

— — — . Introduction. *Eyeing the North Star: Directions in African-Canadian Literature*. Ed. George Elliott Clarke. Toronto: McClelland & Stewart, 1997. xii-xxviii.

— — — . "George Grant, Subversive." Rev. of *George Grant & the Subversion of Modernity: Art, Philosophy, Politics, Religion, & Education*, ed. Arthur Davis. *Books in Canada* 26.7 (October 1997): 14-17.

— — — . "Letters to Young Poets." *Germination* 11.2 (Spring 1988): 14-15.

— — —. *Lush Dreams, Blue Exile: Fugitive Poems: 1978-1993*. Lawrencetown Beach, NS: Pottersfield, 1994.

— — — . "Orienting and Disorienting." *Books in Canada* 31.2 (March 1992): 52-53.

— — — . "A Primer of African-Canadian Literature: George Elliott Clarke's short but filled-to-bursting history." *Books in Canada* 25.2 (March 1996): 7-9.

— — — . *Saltwater Spirituals and Deeper Blues*. Porters Lake, NS: Pottersfield P, 1983.

— — — . *Whylah Falls*. Vancouver: Polestar, 1990.

ASCENSION:
LILIANE WELCH TALKS ABOUT POETRY

Born in Luxembourg, Liliane Welch has lived for 31 years in Sackville, New Brunswick. A professor of French Studies at Mount Allison University, Welch is an avid explorer of the Fundy Marsh, a territory that is often the subject of her poems and essays. She is the author of 15 books of poetry, the most recent *Fidelities* (1997), and two collections of essays, *Seismographs* (1988) and *Frescoes* (1998). With her husband, the philosopher Cyril Welch, she co-authored *Emergence: Baudelaire, Mallarmé, Rimbaud* (1973) and *Address: Rimbaud Mallarmé Butor* (1979). *Fidelities*, like her earlier work, is full of movement and travel, and whether the speaker is touring paintings that hang in European museums, climbing mountains, or driving beneath Maritime skies, there is a sense of urgency in the travel. In the autumn of 1998, Luxembourg saluted Liliane Welch's literary achievements by electing her to the Institut Grand-Ducal.

Since this interview – Sackville, NB, 1998 – Welch has published five new collections of poetry.

AC   • Recognizing that *Word-House of a Grandchild* (1987) initiated the return to the past, is it fair to say that *Fidelities* is the most autobio-graphical of your collections as its first section, "Where are the images," returns to your Luxembourg childhood?

LW   • That question is discomforting to me because I do not believe that there is an autobiographical writing that is strictly autobiographical. All writing that is worth anything is fiction. Everything that a poet does with reality transforms it. Otherwise, it is not art; it might as well be journalism. I don't really think that you can take the "I" who speaks in these poems as my empirical "I." I believe what Rimbaud said: "'I' is an another." We receive from our experiences certain calls, and certain impressions, and they are the trampoline from which we leap into something else. *Word-House of a Grandchild* is above all a "word-house." I never met my grandfather. Everything in that book about my grandfather is fictitious. I have very beautiful images of my grandmother, but again those are *images*. Our past and all of reality around us is very dynamic and elusive. We can never really hold it or grasp it, or understand it once and for all.

AC • When the imagination goes to work on what was – the actual past – it is, of course, transformed. It becomes framed, but you *do say* in *Word-House*: "When I explore the paths of my background, I write poems" (9).

LW • Yes, but "paths" has to be understood in the widest way. When I explore the paths around Fundy Bay or the paths in the mountains, I also get pushed to write poems. I think that in those concrete places, it has something to do with our relatedness to the earth or to reality. I believe – and I don't want to push this too much because it might sound romantic or elated – our mission as poets is to bear witness to where we are and what we are doing. And, of course, bearing witness is, in the end, to praise, to give an affirmative response. A poet can do that. When you praise, when you affirm, you bring out the best in whatever you face. I have a long teaching career – 30 years here and, before that, at several other universities – and in that long career, you can imagine, one sees the spectrum of humanity in one's colleagues. I could never understand how some colleagues could go into the classroom with hatred or negativity in their hearts, rather than with an affirmative stance toward their subject and students. They end up denigrating the teaching situation. Similarly, poetry or writing can be that way. There are some writers with negative, evil agendas. Theirs is a work the opposite of praising and testifying. You have to be able to love whatever you write or do.

AC • Not only paths and roads, but also passageways, mining shafts, and waterways tunnel through *Fidelities*. Is the job of poetry connected in some way to this underground?

LW • Notice in "Winter Fires" (29) that the gladiators are running through the dark passageways towards the sun. In that case, they run towards their deaths, but, in general, the point is to get out from the underground into the sun. You just have to think about Plato's cave.

ANNE COMPTON

AC • Are these images of the underground a master trope for the writing of poetry?

LW • I think certainly in our Western tradition that theme comes up over and over again. Also, in the natural context, the underground of water wells to the surface. Undergrounds are very mysterious places. Look at those Icelandic pictures with their beautiful underground caves. [These photographs appear in *Mosaics: Music, Images, Words*, a book and CD (1999). Text by Welch.] Perhaps the underground is that which conceals itself so that we will be put onto the search, be forced to make a clearing, find something. That, too, is a trope in Western literature – *dévoiler* – this wanting to unveil, not just women, but reality, the need to take away covers.

AC • So searching the underground is really plumbing mystery ....

LW • ... which always withdraws itself. It might appear as a facile difference between science and poetry to presume that scientists might have an explanation of this mystery. All great scientists maintain that they, too, come up to the unknown, the *other*, which points to human limitation.

AC • Does that image cluster – tunnels, caves, mines – appear to a greater extent in the work of women than in the work of men?

LW • I wouldn't think so. I don't look at literature in terms of genitalia. For me, it is literature. Whether the author is a man or a woman does not make that much difference to me. I think it is, rather, something that goes through our culture. Maybe those images go through other cultures too, but the one I know best is our Western culture.

AC • "[B]ooks and mountains / Convene my days" (*Fidelities* 11), one speaker says. Are these the guides, the things by which this speaker finds his or her way?

LW • Yes, and they are forms of transcendence also. In the mountain, there is, of course, ascension, and that means transcendence of a lower region. Books, I think, are similar. Great books take us out of the everyday and light up that other domain. I always read with my students Baudelaire's "Elevation." To me, it is one of the most beautiful poems because you can take it as a guide. The narrator of the poem does what the Christian mystics might have done. He goes over nine different realms of our reality – oceans, mountains, plains, and so forth – until he comes to an emporium of peace and fantastic light. He breathes in this divine liqueur, the air, but, strangely, right there occurs, also, the most sensuous image of the poem. The narrator feels that he is a very powerful swimmer, going through that air as though he were rolling through waves. The poem, in a Baudelairean way, shows that he is far away from the morbid valley miasmas. The students all cheer. Wasn't this the point – getting away from all those trappings that we have to put up with down here? But then comes the last line, where the narrator addresses his spirit, says that lucky or happy is the one who can, like the morning lark, take an ascension and can understand the language of flowers and mute things. So you ascend to that region because you want to look down and get a real understanding of the things that you missed when you were down below. When you were caught up in the traumas and the miasmas, as Baudelaire calls them, you never look at what is close, what addresses you, beckons to you, which, in all the machinations, you never bothered to be a witness for.

AC • So the ascension enables us to see the inconsequential things in their consequences? There is a line in Rilke where he asks us to address the inconsequential things.

LW • The French poet Francis Ponge, in his book of prose poems, *Taking the Side of Things*, writes of all the *seemingly* inconsequential things that we use and use up, misuse and maltreat, by not paying attention and respect to them. This also is a theme in the work of [Martin] Heidegger – the need to care for what is closest to us, rather than ignoring it. Often, in climbing, when we reached the peak of a mountain, I have thought about Sackville and those aspects of Sackville that I neglect because I am caught up in my professional life. Similarly, when you read a good book, it gives a different light to your everyday experience, validates it in some sense.

AC • We go back, not away, by going up?

LW • Yes, the ascension grounds us more authentically on the earth.

AC • Things in their sensuality, persons in their sensuality, get noticed in your work. Do we owe our loyalties, our fidelities, finally, to our desires and passions? The second section of *Fidelities* begins with people such as the cyclist and the fisherman, "Still Life" (19) and "Marriage" (20) respectively, who are divided from their desires.

LW • For the fisherman, his desire was his labour, his work. It is a question of whether you can keep the fidelity. Infidelity means not completely giving yourself to this labour or to whatever, veering off into other directions before the "marriage" has been consummated.

AC • The poem "Marriage" suggests that the "mind's speed" (20) has to do with body's speed.

LW • Intensity comes from facing the elements. For me, mountain climbing, or hiking at Fundy Bay, is an exposure to the elements. That has always been a source of inspiration to me. My source of inspiration would be exposure to the winds and the sun in rough circumstances.

AC • Would you say that your poetry is against austerities and for the passions?

LW • I like the word "openness." Any kind of repression I abhor. Repression comes under many forms, many mantles – words and smiles – different guises. To remain open in one's passions, to remain alert and curious, to get beyond the masks and the self-imposed chains, that is important.

AC • *Fidelities* moves between Europe and North America. Is this the traversal of most importance in your poetry?

LW • It certainly seems to come back as a constant theme in my poetry.

AC • Perhaps the best expression of the Europe-Canada traversal occurs in the "Diptych" that introduces *Dream Museum*. In the second sonnet, winter is "A cathedral navigating angels / and miracles home through the dark" (13). Is this what the Maritime winter is for you?

LW • Yes, the Maritime winter is well elicited in that image. The plentitude I experience here in winter, I've never felt in the "splenetic" European winter months.

AC • Your last book, the collection of essays, *Frescoes*, is a very European book.

LW • *Frescoes* is not without America too. There is the essay on [Edmond] Dune and the essay on "Minescapes." Both relocate European poetry, that of Dune and that of Anne Blanchot-Philippi, into the Maritime context of my poetry classes. Places, like other images, shift and travel.

AC • Do you think of yourself as a migrant, an immigrant, or a Canadian?

LW • I am a Canadian. I feel at home here. I like the word "pilgrim," and I like the idea of journeying for adventure. Although I must say that when I compare my travels now with that period when we used to do extreme climbing, it is the earlier travelling that would qualify – at least in the public's mind – as adventure. Mind you, the mountains have been for me so heightened, so filled with plentitude, as a result of seeing them in the works of artists like [Alberto] Giacometti and [Giovanni] Segantini and Giacometti's father [Giovanni]. I love to go into the Bregaglia Valley where Giacometti hails from. When I look at those mountains now, after having looked at them in paintings, they are so much richer than when I only climbed them.

AC • So painting helps you to see and to experience the landscape?

LW • In Holland, on the coast, we were surprised all the time by the showers, and we metaphorically flew into the museums. We thought then that we were right in the paintings. It was quite a wonderful experience. You can't walk very long on the dykes without being showered.

AC • Every summer you return to Europe for the mountains and what might be called an immersion in culture. What would happen if you stayed all year round in Sackville?

LW • There are many things to be had, and still to be discovered, here. Eventually, when I am too old to fly, I'll stay here, buy myself two dogs, and with them, Cyril and I will run around the countryside all year long. Many of the *Frescoes* travel pieces speak of the return home to Sackville. The travellers long for the Maritimes.

AC • The point of the compass in the *Fidelities* poem "Winter Fires" is *north*. And in another poem, from where the speaker stands, the woods extend a thousand miles beyond "journey[ing] / to grounds unknown" (44). Is *north*, like the mountains of Europe, access to the unknown?

LW • Yes, I have that feeling particularly here in Canada. I don't have it in the European forests because they are so different, so well-cared for. You have to have a permit to fell trees there. They have a different relationship to their by-now-cultivated woods.

AC • "Six Personae" are all women, all house-bound. The woman in "Dream Land" (53) wants to trade "this stained north" for Florida. Other women, in these poems, are able to transform where they are through books or work. The transformation is imaged as "parachute" or as the "awakening" of the angel "lost in [the] body" (*Fidelities* 52, 51). Is this another version of the elevation pursued by climbers?

LW • Many angels appear in my work. As an artist, I am interested in angels as messengers. That woman, in "Mornings at Home," with the angel lost in her body, is someone who might still answer to the call of that messenger. We have the choice in life to answer, in different ways, to those calls.

AC • Your earlier word was "mission." Is the angel, or the messenger, the one who offers the mission?

LW • He brings a message. In Greek literature it was Hermes, the messenger of the gods, the patron saint of interpreters. In my literary criticism class, I tell my students that I want them to become hermeneutes, to deliver the text, to open its message. The angel's work would be in the framework of those images.

AC • Rilke, you say, "called ordinary existence life unlived" (*Fidelities* 68), but in your Vermeer poem, it is the radiant ordinariness of Vermeer's figures – the way they handle "household tools" – that seems to make "everything possible" (67). What are the avenues to this exaltation in the midst of the mundane?

LW • It is a certain bearing on the part of the individual. If you look at Vermeer's milkmaid, her way of pouring that milk becomes a creative act. It all depends on whether you can make out of an ordinary experience, or a simple thing, something creative. Each Vermeer painting contains a very ordinary act. His work is a praise of those acts that normally escape us. Whereas Rilke, especially when you get to the *Duino Elegies*, conceives of the "mission" as something much more dramatic.

AC • Rilke does say in Elegy Eight, after all his struggle with the angels, "Perhaps we are here in order to say house, bridge, fountain ...." He says that naming the ordinary is what we are here for.

LW • Yes. And it is why he finished his literary life by writing very humble and simple French poems. The epitaph on his gravestone – "Rose, oh pure contradiction, delight / Of being no-one's sleep beneath / So many lids" (*Frescoes* 66) – can be read to mean the human word does not violate the natural thing.

AC • The work of many painters – Giovanni Giacometti, Alex Colville, Hans Memling – as well as Vermeer, is honoured in *Fidelities*, and in your other collections as well. In the poem "Holland," you say, "We sailed to those urgencies / Only paintings can hold" (66), and in another poem, the painting is a "portal" (*Dream Museum* 36). What does this door open onto?

LW • A painting always invites you to go over a threshold. A transformation occurs. When you go into a dwelling – a painting, in this case – you have to purify yourself in some sense. It is almost a religious experience.

AC • In *Frescoes*, you talk about entering a painting – it's a Memling, I think – and that entrance requires a shift: "you must break to a different language, purify your words" (26). In one poem, the painting is an altar (*Dream Museum* 39). Has painting – and the other arts – replaced religious ritual as an approach to the divine?

LW • For some people it has. However, the arts have always been competitors of religions, have been a kind of religion for those who practice them and for those who take them seriously. Still, that does not necessarily mean that they replace the traditional religions. Some churches today are filled with people who avoid museums, where you step over that portal and experience some sort of enlightenment. Although today when I contemplate the spreading of popular culture – its power on the minds and the bodies of the young – I often wonder about the chance of the arts in this new configuration. I believe that the arts will always be for the esoteric. That doesn't mean that there won't be herds of people racing through the museums. The deeply felt and procreated experience of art is never going to be that of the wide masses of people, or of the advocates of the herd-mentality.

AC • Is there any way in which it could be made to do so?

LW • Not any that I can see today. You can take a van Gogh, or other painting, and you can blow it up huge and have it flashing from billboards and from screens, but look what you have done. You have turned it into popular culture. It is no longer a religious experience of conversion or change. It has become trivialized. Being ripped out of habitual patterns, seeing with different eyes – that is what art does.

AC • So is that liability for change open only to those capable of "esoteric" experience?

LW • I think anybody can have that experience, but you are never going to get it in a group.

AC • "The herd" is what you said earlier. Is art, then, in its many forms elitist?

LW • I would say that it is condemned to be that way. This is not an easy burden to bear. Many poets yearn to be popular poets, and would do anything to be popular poets. Even great poets fall into that trap when they go on endless reading tours. Even great poets feel the need to be confirmed. I like [Albert] Camus' story "The Exile and the Kingdom" about the artist who doesn't know that he exists and, therefore, seeks confirmation. The truly great works of art are never going to be heroic flags for mass and popular culture. Sad thought.

AC • Was it otherwise once? What about the groundlings at the Globe the-atre watching Shakespeare? Or, to put it in the Maritime context, poets like Bliss Carman and Sir Charles G.D. Roberts had a wide public fol-lowing. Is this a 20th-century phenomenon: Popular culture split off from the allegedly elitist culture? Were they once one?

LW • We are today living in a different world. The mass media have done so much and so little at the same time. When there was no television, when all that we take for granted was absent, people had the time and interest then for even more elitist literature.

AC • In "Chateau," you speak of "those airy cathedrals, / erected for a God already withdrawn" (*Fidelities* 70). If God and the angels are not in the cathedrals, have they gone from the world?

LW • Speaking now as a critic – the poems have to stand on their own – I would say religion in its traditional form, the godhead as it was con-ceived, is dead, as Nietzsche says. And remember, he said too, that human beings have killed him. That doesn't mean that the sacred is gone. The sacred undergirds our existence here on the earth. The sacred is far removed from all of the myths or stories that say if you do this or that, you are going to get your bonbon after you die, and you will be singing in the choirs of the angels. And if you don't do that, you will go down into the frying pan. That type of reckoning, merchan-dising, mechanical explication of God, I have always found repulsive. Already as a child, I combatted the priests on that notion of the god-head. Hölderlin talked about the gods having fled and the poets and the artists being the wine god's disciples. They are going through the night searching for the new gods who have not yet come. I think that the sacred is there, but we are on the brink of losing it if we give ourselves over to the labyrinths of the Internet, for example.

At this point, the interview moves to the area made famous by Sir Charles G.D. Roberts, the Westcock Marsh, where the dykes, built by the Acadians, rise above the reddish-brown flats. We are walking along the coast and looking for a spot that is sheltered from the wind so that we can carry on with the interview.

LW • At first when I saw the Bay of Fundy, I was stunned – I'd never seen water like that – but now I really love it. When the sun is on the mud-flats, after the water has withdrawn, it is, perhaps, the most erotic landscape in the world, a landscape of bare flanks.

AC • Europe was your birthplace, but coming to New Brunswick was your birth as a poet. Why did that move provoke poetry?

LW • I wrote [my] first poem on our first sabbatical leave away from New Brunswick. We went from Europe, where we were on leave, to Los Angeles for three weeks. To go from Europe to the farthest extremes of Western culture brought on quite a culture shock. It must have been around 1976. When I went back to Europe for the rest of the sabbatical leave, I suddenly started writing poems. I was also in the process of co-writing a book of literary criticism, *Address: Rimbaud Mallarmé Butor* (1979). The parts on [Stéphane] Mallarmé and [Michel] Butor were being written at the same time as the first poems. It was living here in New Brunswick that sparked my poetry. I don't think I would ever have written poetry if I had stayed in the United States. All the years previously spent down there never elicited poems from me. So it was very important that I came to New Brunswick and found a home here.

AC • Your Maritimes are "primordial" (*Seismographs* 58), not pastoral. You speak of the "defiance and savagery" of the Tantramar Marshes and the looming forests. After 30 years of living here, do the Maritimes remain, for you, "primordial"?

LW • Yes. That has never changed; it's truly amazing. When we come back from Europe, we go out to Wood Point [on the Fundy coast] and beyond to the last possible point. I always have exactly the same feeling – this is the primordial, originary landscape of my life.

AC • So you wouldn't use the word "pastoral" to describe this landscape?

LW • You have only to come here in the winter – the whiteouts, the fierceness of blizzards – and you couldn't possibly say it was pastoral. Also,

ANNE COMPTON

in the winter it becomes a landscape of gigantic constructions done by some enormous force. The tide, as it comes and goes, deposits huge blocks of ice right up to the dykes. It might look pastoral now because it is green, but there is a long, long period of the year when it is not like this. Someone from Toronto might see us here now – two women sitting on the dyke – and think that we came right out of a pastoral painting, but that is just one side of this landscape.

AC　• In an essay on Sackville in *Seismographs*, you say, "When I saw it first in a wild February storm, a desire arose to pierce the secret still withheld from me. A language had to be invented to make this ground sing" (53).

LW　• Yes. That is true. The Romans used to talk about the genius of the place. I believe that every place has a different genius. In Europe, too, there are different voices in the ground.

AC　• What, I want to know, are the features of the language that speak this ground? Is there a Maritime poetic?

LW　• I think that my poetry answers that best.

AC　• In the essay "What Are Poets For" (*Frescoes* 78-84), you raise the question: Is poetry private or public?

LW　• In that essay, I try to give you the experience that I had when I went to one of the most important poetry gatherings currently held in Europe. I went there as an invited Canadian poet, but I was also thinking about the meaning of the whole enterprise. There were poetry readings and also big debates about whether poetry could still stand as a force in today's culture. The answer is there in the last sentence of the essay: "Poetry does not just tie us to the invisible, but also to the visible world, and to our fellows." Actually the question "What Are Poets For?" is the one that Hölderlin asked. He was a man who took his position as a poet very seriously. His question goes on: "What are poets for in needy times?" I tried to loosely attach the essay to that question.

AC　• Silence is the word and the condition often associated with Canada in your work, but silence is also associated with the mountains of Europe. Is the achievement of silence – and the achievements in silence – what connects these two experiences: Winter in Canada and the mountains of Europe?

LW • I have friends in Europe who go to the cafés because they must have noise around them to write. I must have something of the monk in me because I value the silence most. I like music very much too, but it has to come out of the silence.

AC • It seems to me that there are three Europes in your work. There is the Europe characterized by the church and domestic rigidities and social formalities – guardians of morality. Present-day Europe, which has replaced that earlier order, is characterized by bankers, finance, and cities thick with truck traffic. Then there is the Europe of your mountains and museums. Do these distinctions explain why the final section of *Fidelities* is called "The Past Released and Held," which seems to encode a gesture whereby the speaker would let some things go and yet hold onto others?

LW • There is another Europe: The Europe of my friends. To go even further – beyond the three Europes that you discern – Europe is now something very dynamic and changing, especially if I compare what Europe used to be – during the war, after the war – with what it has become, not just financially but also culturally. There are so many cultural opportunities pulsing. It is really booming culturally. Even a small country like Luxembourg, which at one time was considered a provincial place, is now cosmopolitan. The leading musicians on tour in Europe think that Luxembourg is the place, better than Paris, to perform. In Luxembourg there is a very demanding public. Of course, they have a conservatory there. This renewal and vibrancy is connected with a united Europe. They are aware that they are, together, a very important political, economic, and cultural world power. They have great hopes for their future. Europe is a place that has a lot going for it right now. If Europe had not become an economic power, it would not have the cultural vibrancy that one finds there today.

AC • In *Frescoes* there is a fear of the commercialization of the very art that has been enabled by that economic growth.

LW • Commerce and art are always rivals. Baudelaire expounded a fierce hatred of commerce in his vilification of the merchant. Commerce for us is a necessary evil.

AC • In *Fidelities*, Europe is an old lady who "believes in ruins" (57). Yet the New England nuns who visit can expect to find "deceit under marble floors." What is that deceit?

LW • Those nuns go to Rome; they do not visit the rest of Europe. In Rome, they examine the Vatican's and the church's power. That poem talks about what can be expected today of the Roman Church. The deceit is linked to whatever has been constructed in that seat of power. Actually, now I find the church to be a very interesting historical phenomenon. As a young child, memorizing the catechism, the church didn't appear interesting to me at all.

AC • In your essay on Rilke in *Frescoes*, you say, "Rilke's line 'Beauty is nothing but the beginning of terror' ... forced me to look at myself and at poetry with straighter eyes, with a sword in my hands" (66). Does this forecast a new direction in your poetry?

LW • There are always changes occurring. I'm still in the process of change.

AC • The Blakean image of the sword in the hand suggests something revolutionary, but you mean there will be no more change in your poetry than there has always been – a gradual change?

LW • I would have to look into my diaries to see what I did the day after I visited Raron, where Rilke is buried. I must say I was extraordinarily moved. I go there regularly, and I am moved every time I go there to pay my respects.

AC • Earlier you were talking about art and the spectator's willingness to be converted by art. Was that moment at Rilke's grave such a moment for you?

LW • I think we all have moments of enlightenment when we see with completely different eyes, with "straighter eyes." My first visit to Raron was very much that way. We also drove to Muzot, the house where Rilke lived. I was very affected there. Sometimes when you go to places where other great spirits have been, they seem to have left something there that speaks to you.

AC • The poets whom you admire – such as Rimbaud and Rilke – were wanderers. Is there a link between travel and the transgression of boundaries, of limits?

LW • Yes. All travelling is a transgression of boundaries. That is particularly true in mountain climbing, but it happens in reading too.

AC • Critics have focused a lot of attention on the cosmopolitan qualities of your poetry – its learning and culture – but actually you are, as well, an excavator of the domestic life, as in the "Accounts" series in *Dream Museum*. Husbands and wives have different accounts of their lives, and in the parent-child poems, parents thwart and deform their children's lives, unaware they are doing so. Are we all living different stories even when we live intimately together?

LW • A lot of people – not everybody – but a lot do lead different stories. You will find a lot more on that theme in my very early books, *Syntax of Ferment*, *Assailing Beats*, and *October Winds*. On that cover [*October Winds*] you see, by the way, a picture of this dyke. I was preoccupied then by that topic, not so much anymore. The writing of poetry provides wonderful occasions to vicariously live other lives. I feel that often when I write poems about people. It's a chance of living another existence.

AC • In *Life in Another Language*, the polarities are "well-plotted days" or "sedition" (16). Must the poet, in your opinion, live "Outside Approval," which is the title of the piece containing that pair?

LW • I would say that poetry, as all art, lives "Outside Approval," and is fundamentally revolutionary. Sadly, our educational institutions have been the instruments, over the centuries, for eroding that which is powerful in poetry, taking the revolutionary punch out of it. They reduce poetry to traditional frameworks and categories, and overlay it with obfuscations.

AC • You have published a book of prose poems, *Life in Another Language*, an epic family narrative, *Word-House*, and you have just published *Frescoes*, narrative wall paintings of places visited. What effect do these excursions into prose have on your poetry?

LW • I have written prose and poetry together for many years. I don't think that there is any particular effect. They go side by side. All the essays in *Frescoes* were written at the same time that I was writing poems. I write all of the time. Writing prose or poetry is a good way of living well.

AC • In *Frescoes*, you give us not only a map of Europe by way of your travels, but also a calendar of engagements, and the artists with whom you are engaged in that book are strong male artists. The book does end with an Emily Dickinson quotation, but otherwise the artists are male ones.

ANNE COMPTON

LW   • Male and female artists came up naturally, without gender differen-
tiation in the landscapes I visited for *Frescoes*. I don't like to see male
and female pitted against each other for purposes of "agendas." When
we did the extreme mountain climbing, in conditions of extreme
danger, the only thing that mattered was getting to the top alive in a
common effort. It is a terrible shame that today in universities young
women are taught to hate males or to see themselves, which is even
more criminal, as the victims of men. Writing poetry is also an extreme
situation. Questions of gender are beside the point.

AC   • You make the people and places of *Frescoes* feel familiar to the reader.
And you make those artists and their work familiar, but the woman of
note that I remember meeting in that art world is "Annetta," the model
(41-45).

LW   • Annetta Giacometti, as far as I am concerned, is one of the most
interesting women in the history of art. For more than 50 years she was
the model not just for her husband [Giovanni Giacometti] but also for
her son [Alberto]. There is no other woman in the history of art that
has been depicted as many times in paintings and sculptures. She is one
of the strongest women that ever lived in the Bregaglia. Even today, a
long time after her death, you meet people who either had relatives who
knew her or have heard of her, and they still speak of her.

AC   • Your poetry has an East-West axis, but perhaps your permanent res-
idency is in a house of books and pictures. I'm sorting through your
library – reading the poems that you have written on poems. Are you
– to use your phrase – "in conversation" with these earlier pieces of lit-
erature?

LW   • All reading and writing is a conversing with artworks, present and
past, with other artists – poets, musicians, painters, and so forth. My
work is part of the house of art. That house is grounded on the earth.
And changing the wording of Heidegger's phrase, I would add, "Art is
the house of being."

Welch, Liliane. *Dream Museums*. Victoria, BC: Sono Nis P, 1995.

– – –. *Fidelities*. Nepean, ON: Borealis P, 1997.

– – –. *Fire to the Looms Below*. Charlottetown: Ragweed P, 1990.

– – –. *Frescoes: Travel Pieces*. Nepean, ON: Borealis P, 1998.

– – –. *Life in Another Language*. Dunvegan, ON.: Cormorant Books, 1992.

– – –. *Seismographs: Selected Essays and Reviews*. Ed. Richard Lemm. Charlottetown: Ragweed P, 1988.

– – –. *Word-House of a Grandchild*. Charlottetown: Ragweed P, 1987.

Welch, Liliane and Cyril. *Address: Rimbaud Mallarmé Butor*. Victoria, BC: Sono Nis P, 1979

Published since the interview:

– – – . *The Rock's Stillness*. Ottawa: Borealis P, 1999.

– – – . *Unlearning Ice*. Ottawa: Borealis P, 2001.

– – – . *Untethered in Paradise*. Ottawa: Borealis P, 2002.

– – – . *The Numinous Bond*. Ottawa: Borealis P, 2003.

– – –. *Dispensing Grace*. Ottawa: Borealis P, 2005.

ANNE COMPTON

SEVERAL WINDOWS OF SEPARATION:
CAROLE LANGILLE'S POETRY AND BACKGROUND

Carole Glasser Langille, a writer and designer living in Lunenburg, Nova Scotia, has published two children's books and two books of poetry. *In Cannon Cave*, her second book of poetry, was nominated for a Governor General's Award in 1997 and for the Atlantic Poetry Prize in 1998. Both *All That Glitters in Water* (1990), her first collection of poetry, and *In Cannon Cave* (1997) manifest a high order of craftsmanship. *Where the Wind Sleeps*, her second children's book, was the Canadian Children's Book Centre Choice for 1996. She holds an MFA from Brooklyn College, New York, and has received a MacDowell Fellowship and a Canada Council grant for poetry. Her artwork – plate designs and Zen tiles – features the architecture of Lunenburg, where she lives with her two sons. The wind, the sea, and the Nova Scotia landscape are everywhere present in her poetry. When she writes about the distances and depths of the interior life, she draws her analogies from landscape and from the tidal movements of Maritime seas. Like the cave that shelters darkness, but whose walls glow with a rich phosphorescent light, Langille's poetry has the ability to go to the dark places of the soul and make them incandescent.

Since this interview – Lunenburg, 1998 – Langille has published a third collection, *Late in a Slow Time* (2003), and *Interview with a Stick Collector* (2004), a children's book.

AC   • *In Cannon Cave* was shortlisted for a Governor General's Award. Do you see this book as a step forward from the first, *All That Glitters in Water?*

CL   • Some of the poems in the first book were quite old even when the book was published, and that was seven years ago. Some of them John Ashbery had seen in poetry workshops. He was the Head of the Creative Writing Program at Brooklyn. Just being around him was an interesting experience. He was very smart, very generous. I remember after I had published that book, I wondered if I'd ever be able to publish another book. I wouldn't have John Ashbery to look over the poems anymore. But, of course, that changed, and experience has helped a lot – leaving the country I was born in, having children. I feel that I was in a fog for many, many years and that fog has lifted.

AC • How long have you lived in Nova Scotia, and do you think of it as home?

CL • Oh, yes. I'm a Canadian citizen. I've lived here 10 years. My husband and I are divorced, and one of the unsettling aspects at the time of the divorce was my fear that I would have to leave the country. I didn't know during that tumultuous time, but that was probably what I was most fearful of. But that didn't happen. I'm glad of that. The marriage didn't work, but the country worked for me. Actually, he said to me, "You ought to live in Nova Scotia," and he was right.

AC • Your poetry is involved with the topography of the Maritimes, but less so with its culture. Do you lead a solitary life?

CL • I wish it were more solitary. I feel it's very busy. The mornings, when the kids are at school, I try to work. When people knock on the door, I don't answer it. I hide. I need that time. I take solitary walks. Occasionally, a friend will say, "Do you want to take a walk together?" But I don't want that. I have a lot of friends here but, you know, most of them are from away.

AC • And did you have jobs before children?

CL • I did. None very satisfactory. I taught remedial English and English 101 at Brooklyn College and at LaGuardia Community College, and at a few other community colleges. It's very hard to make a living that way. I worked as an administrative assistant to the Dean of Engineering at Pratt University. A horrible job. He was one of the worst human beings I have ever met. It was not the job for me. The last job I had was working at the ad agency, Young & Rubicam, on Madison Avenue. This was not the job for me. But it was only part-time so I could write in the afternoon. People would dress very elegantly there, and I would have to take the subway every day. I was proofreading and toying around with the idea of doing some copywriting, but I was saved from that. It would not have been good for me to have been a copywriter. To spend your life selling vodka does something to you.

AC • Now, however, you have children and, indeed, you have poems about your sons. Do women who have young children tend to write poetry, rather than prose, and is this a time issue?

CL • I have never written prose. It's a process I'm not really familiar with. I admire anyone who has the discipline to do it. And I've thought about this quite a bit because I thought it would be a good discipline for me. And yet, in reading many novels, I think, I would not have liked to have put my energy into pages and pages of rendering, of description, moving a plot along. It doesn't interest me. When I read a brilliant poem by a poet I admire, I think that is what I want. A novel creates a certain period of time, and a poem freezes time. I'm more interested in that. Good days are when I have a new idea [for a poem], but then the next day I'll rework it, and that's part of writing too. Reworking old poems, that's a very important process and a very enjoyable process, but it's much more exciting when something new is happening.

AC • When you're writing the poem – which, as you say, is the exciting part – do you feel that something is claiming you, soliciting you? Is there a certain wildness in it? I'm thinking of that line of yours: "And in that quiet – / wildness" (*CC* 18).

CL • Sometimes late at night I'll have an idea for a poem and I'm too tired, but in the morning I know I'll write it. Thomas Hardy, as an old man, wrote to Virginia Woolf, saying something like, "What you need to write poems is lots of energy," and I think that's true.

AC • So that wildness or excitement when the poem is first occurring, is that a language excitement?

CL • Usually it starts with a word, a beautiful word. And that explains something, opens something up. And I think, *Oh, I can go there*. It often starts with a word, and then I see where the word can take me. It's language led.

AC • Before the poem is language, before the poem is verbal, is it a state of mind?

CL • It's definitely a chemical process, an excitement that takes over.

AC • But which comes first: The state of mind that changes the way you use language or the fluke in language that opens up the state of mind?

CL • You stumble upon the word, but that's not always the time when you can write the poem, so I write down the word. And I think, "What is it about this word, this phrasing, odd and peculiar, that opens my heart up?" But if you have this strange fluke of language, and you have the time, and you have the energy, you can put those three things together. Odd things I hear open a door, and I know they will take me someplace.

AC • In the poem "Prayer," the speaker talks about "being translated, painstakingly ... / into everything that breathes" (CC 11). Do you think of poetry as a translation of what's occurring in the mind?

CL • It's a translation not so much of experience as of something evanescent, something there are no words for. Charles Simic, the American poet, said poetry tries to do the impossible. Well, I say yes to the impossible. There are no words for it so I just try to approach it. Translate what there are no words for. Poetry veers towards it, approaches it. That's the most poetry can do.

AC • And after you have tried to translate the untranslatable, after the poem, do you feel you have not quite made it?

CL • The poet must wrestle with what is not accessible or comfortable. A poet must be willing to live with uncertainty and confusion in the work until he or she finds out what needs to be told. That's why the poet keeps on writing. The desire to write the poem that says what can't be said. That's alright. It's a life process. The truly evolved, the enlightened, don't need to write at all, having reached a certain stage, but thank heavens I'm not there!

AC • So what's on the page then? Is it a remnant of that experience, of that state of mind?

CL • I would like the same intensity that I feel to be on the page. That's the hope. What maddens me is when I read poems and they feel lifeless. I'm enraged by that because to me it's the antithesis of what a poem should be. There's a certain vogue for the very intellectual, dead, sophisticated poem. I don't want that. I want raw, a certain raw quality.

AC • Is there a certain quality of attention, as Don McKay would say (24), that precedes or accompanies the writing of the poem? And how does that quality of attention differ from the everyday?

ANNE COMPTON

CL • It's almost as if I try to tune out a lot of things. I try to conserve my attention and not to notice too much. There's so much mail, piles of mail. I'm a member of The League of Canadian Poets. It's very oppressive because you get reams and reams of paper. This poetry and that poetry. It's disheartening. It's so competitive. Up-to-date poetry biz. Such clutter. The kids also bring home reams and reams of paper, this and that activity. There are mothers who are on top of all of that, but I have to make a decision not to get caught up in it so much. There's so much I want to read and think about.

AC • Fred Cogswell has a poem called "Black Swan" in which he says that "all thought is developed out of words" (*Folds* 46). Is non-linguistic thought possible? Is it possible to think without words?

CL • I don't think so. For me it's not, as far as I'm aware. Visual artists may be able to.

AC • Is poetry, as a kind of thinking, different from other kinds of thinking? Is it a different order of thinking?

CL • It's more concentrated and alert.

AC • If there is another order of thinking – and if it occurs when you are writing a poem, or painting a picture, or in any of the creative processes – why don't we live that way more of the time?

CL • When I finish my writing time, I'm tired. I don't think I could sustain that energy all the time. For me, I can't truly relax until I've finished the poem. I'm pulled through to the end of the poem. Unless I regularly go to that place where poems come from, I don't really want to be doing other things. That seems to me the important work. You know, when I put my attention to other things like that paper I wrote for Poets Talking [a series of talks by poets at UNB Saint John], I could have spent another few weeks making it much finer, but after a certain point I want to write poems. That was not enough of a pull for me. I'm thinking of writing a review, but I know there will be only a certain amount of time I'll put into it. I'm constantly doing that. I don't feel that way about a poem. I feel like I can put in all the time that is needed. It's the only thing in my life that I don't stint on. I'll spend hours and hours, and then the poem won't work, but that's OK. It's so ironic because what are poems for?

intrinsic value
more fulfilling in
the end.

AC • How does that process of being "pulled through to the end of the poem" work?

CL • I was in a writing workshop led by Carolyn Forché, and she talked about the hinge of a poem, that line, or lines, that takes the poem to another place and the reader to another level. The hinge can be anywhere in the poem, but it signifies a shift.

AC • Do good poems by other poets have a physiological effect on you?

CL • Absolutely. I was reading *Best American Poets of 1996*, and there was this poem – "The Case," by Karen Volkman – very unusual and original, and I was inspired by it. There was a certain boldness in the poem. And I thought, *I want this: fearlessness.*

AC • Did you grow up in a literary or artistic household?

CL • My parents were communists, and this was their religion. I think they used it to buffer themselves against the world. Poetry, too, was considered the opiate of the masses. My father was very wary of poetry. Nonetheless, he was an emotional man. When Martin Luther King died, he sobbed. And I feel that there was poetry in him, although he wouldn't acknowledge it. My mother is a wonderful artist, and Aunt Estelle is a painter. I remember being given a children's book of poetry and loving it and reading Stephen Crane's poems, including "A Man Saw a Ball of Gold in the Sky," like a Buddhist koan. I was thrilled by those poems. I remember reading one to my father, and he didn't approve very much.

AC • Did your father prohibit reading poetry?

CL • He didn't prohibit it, but he didn't approve because it wasn't talking about workers or bread. I read poetry as a child, though, and I wrote it when I was very young.

AC • Was there a lot of political talk around the dinner table?

CL • My father was a pretty volatile man so that he would do a lot of the talking. There was a lot of political talk. I remember asking as a very young kid, "Is he a good or bad man, Dad?" That's what I wanted to know: "Is this politician good or bad?" I figured as long as I had him to tell me ....

AC • Did you go to rallies with your parents? Did you march with your parents?

CL   • I remember going with my sisters to Washington, marches against Vietnam and that sort of thing. I was very political in school. As a kid, I pretty much mouthed what my parents felt. It seemed to make sense to me. It's interesting because I remember my mother mentioning that her grandfather was a rabbi. And I have asked her questions recently, but she didn't want to talk about it: "There are more important things to talk about." She couldn't be bothered. I have a strong spiritual leaning, and so do both of my sisters. Yet we come from a strictly atheist background. We couldn't mention God.

AC   • I wondered if your parents were first-generation immigrants because many of your references tend to be to European writers – the epigraph, from Antonio Machado, in your second book, for example.

CL   • Well, that's interesting because my parents don't talk about their past at all, and I don't know what I would like to know, although I have questions. My mother was born in Toronto, and my father was born in the Bronx, but his first language was Yiddish, and he taught his parents to speak English.

AC   • Was Yiddish spoken in your household?

CL   • It was, but it was spoken so the kids wouldn't understand. My mother's parents came from Poland, and my father's parents from Russia. From Georgia, I think. My father's family were serfs, and they were glaziers. That's why my last name is Glasser.

AC   • That might explain why there are so many windows in your poetry. Windows and doors.

CL   • The story, apocryphal or not, is that when my grandfather left Russia, he first went to Edinburgh. And then decided he didn't want to live there and went to the States. Now I'm going to Edinburgh to give a reading.

AC   • So you did not have an Orthodox upbringing?

CL   • I didn't, although I remember we had this book about Judaism in the house, and we would celebrate Passover with relatives. My parents said it was important to acknowledge that we were Jewish and to stop the threat to Jews, to stop any racist threat. At the same time, my parents were very pro-Palestinian. They were anti-Zionist. They felt this was reactionary. I was sent to communist camps where Pete Seeger would come and entertain us.

AC • Was there any persecution because of the communism?

CL • My uncle, who was a very fine actor – he was in the movie *The Hospital* – was blacklisted in the McCarthy period. Even talking about this, I have a little twinge. This was a secret. I certainly didn't talk about this when I was growing up. I think I always felt that I was leading a double life.

AC • There's a lot of doubleness in your poetry. There is disguise (*CC* 20) and invisibility: "It's the invisible me who won't forget" (*CC* 37) and "I became invisible" (*CC* 48). Is everyone, in some way, in disguise?

CL • I tend to think not, and I hope not. I don't think of myself as in disguise either, but I do think the inner world has to be protected. The inner world chooses when to show itself and to whom. For our own protection and safety in how we navigate in this world, we make choices. I don't think we are even aware of all the choices, or why we are making them, or that we are making them. The unconscious knows a lot more than the conscious, and is more astute.

AC • Coming into Maritime landscape, did you have a sense of arrival, as suggested by "In the Harbour" (*CC* 23-24)?

CL • We arrived here in September. We were driving from Yarmouth to this area around Lunenburg, and there were no cars on the road. I wondered what was going on. From Manhattan traffic to the 103! I couldn't believe it. I remember going to a lake here, very clear. You could see right to the bottom. It was warm, early September, and there was no one on the beach. And I thought, *I have arrived.*

AC • Did your arrival here somehow complement your interior life? Was it really the interior life that came into synch with Maritime landscape?

CL • It's so beautiful here, and so comforting and spacious. It's hard for me to believe that it wouldn't be liberating for anyone – as opposed to being packed into a subway. I know people get exhilarated from spending time in New York City, but it's an awfully difficult place to feel any expansiveness or beauty. It's so hard to see the sky. And birds were non existent where I was. Even the winter here is beautiful and a comfort, and I would think that would be enriching for everyone who lives here.

AC • The Nova Scotia landscape is everywhere in your poetry, but not as a direct subject. Landscape is the vocabulary of the interior life. Love is connected with bodies of water – oceans, lakes, and wells. Also, there are caves, chasms, dens. In an erotic poem, the speaker says, "It's all feeling in this chasm / where we find ourselves and there's – what – grace?" (*CC* 38). The word "grace," which is usually linked to the religious life, appears here in your most explicitly erotic poem. What is it that is common to the religious life and the erotic life so that both can be linked to landscape?

CL • It seems to me that Eros is god-linked. When we are in the moment – any experience, certainly in the erotic experience – we are nowhere else. That's what the religious experience is, too. Being very present so that the borders dissolve, the borders between one body and another, one thing and another in this world. That's what religion is, it seems to me, a dissolving of the borders – a real unity, a real rejoicing in our kinship, in how we are all related. So there is that parallel. The great beauty in the natural world makes it possible to use it as a medium to talk about the erotic or the religious. You know, I love houses too. I remember a Mark Strand poem – I probably read it in *The New Yorker* – where he is walking with his wife past a beautiful chalet and he says, "Ours the more for not being ours." And I feel that is true – there are houses that are truly mine, especially when I draw them, although they are not mine, and yet because they are manmade, they are not as holy or as exalted as a deserted beach or as rocks on the shore or as seaweed in winter.

AC • Is this the reason why your religious sensibility gets played out through landscape imagery?

CL • It seems to me that has always been the case for poets. All poets that are properly called poets are enraptured by the physical world.

AC • That religious sensibility is particularly obvious in Part 1 of *Cannon Cave*. Perhaps a better word for it is meditative. A speaker is frequently absorbed into landscape – "Every hour I am disappearing / where sun collides with icy leaves ..." (11) – and this seems like a happy achievement, a consummation, but is it also dangerous?

CL • It's not dangerous because of nature. It's just that there's danger in this world. For so long, fear was predominant for me, and now I feel it isn't. There is one poem where fear is a black moth that flew away ("Fear Ghazal," *CC* 64).

AC • It seems to me that there are several worlds in your poetry, the least important of which is the world of daily reality, which is only a point of departure. There is the world of the dead, and the dead look across at our world reassuring us: "'The body / has good will'" (*CC* 15). There's an interiority entered by way of certain states of consciousness or through sex: "We are going deeper into our own world" (*CC* 34). Your speakers are always crossing borders between one world and another. Is that why landscape is so important to you?

CL • I wouldn't have thought of it that way, or analyzed it that way, but I do think the grandeur of the natural world, with its depth and enormity, does lend itself to describing the inner worlds.

AC • In the epigrammatic "Five Doors," we are told, "The body, our great ally, / knows what it's here for" (*CC* 67), and that also is the message from the dead. Is the body, finally, the only thing that can be trusted?

CL • The dead tell us to "trust everything," don't they (*CC* 14)? I don't know if the body is the only thing – I don't think it is – but I do think you can trust it. Many dangers arise from not listening, not being aware. But anything that is listened to is a great ally. Anything that is ignored is a danger.

AC • Actual landscapes, as different from interior ones, are read like a text: "If there's something I need to know – / earth, foam, water – *let* me know" (*CC* 17). What is it that you think landscape can disclose?

CL • I know that there is something it can disclose and that's what I seek out whenever I go for a walk: "What is here for me?" The as-yet-undisclosed.

AC • What is erotic in "Through a Slit in the Tent"(*CC* 32-33) is not so much the drama of the man and the woman as it is the expression or repetition of this eroticism in everything: "night slide[s] / onto the sand" and "a glissando of water ... moistens a deep, splayed channel." The speaker says, "This is what brings / the sky to the ground."

CL • I am talking about everything being Eros – the wind that touches her shoulder, the water fingering the shells by the water – and all of this brings the sky to the ground, and the sky is down on the ground, giving up all of the rain inside it.

AC • Your poetry has a lot of water in it and a lot of winter, but it also contains much light. Some of your poems remind me of Vermeer paintings where the figures go about their mundane tasks enveloped in tremendous light. In your poem "Breaking," the speaker says, "Whatever we do or don't do, / we live, finally, by shining" (*CC* 62), and in "Looking at Houses," the dead see the living by the "light streaming around us" (*CC* 14). Is this light in your work painterly or spiritual?

CL • I thought that Vermeer, in his work, was using that light to talk about an inner light. These women, solitary on the canvas, were going inward, and the rich and beautiful light around them reflected that. And although I wasn't consciously thinking of that when I wrote the poems, I'd say that light is the metaphor for the great light.

AC • There are references in your poetry to Sylvia Plath and to Anne Sexton. Do you think of your poetry as confessional?

CL • You know, I don't think of it as confessional. I don't like Sylvia Plath's work. I'm not so much interested in biography as in poems that transcend that. The poets that I gravitate towards are really more reticent – like Elizabeth Bishop. You don't even know what she is referring to and yet there is a great passion beneath that reticence. I like Czeslaw Milosz also. The poets I appreciate the most are those who take care to observe the world rather than reveal their own private lives.

AC • Restraint issues in great feeling: Is this the paradox of poetry?

CL • In her poem "Filling Station," Bishop describes in exquisite detail the "oil-soaked, oil-permeated" place (149). It's a family filling station and the poet wonders if the family lives there. She notices the dog on the wicker sofa, the doily, the begonia. Bishop describes it so carefully, a picture can be drawn. Yet where does this description take us? The penultimate sentence in the poem says, "Somebody / arranges the rows of cans / so that they softly say: / ESSO – so – so – so ..." (150). This, to me, is the hinge of the poem, a zoom lens focused so we see someone's care in the almost talismanic act of arranging the cans. In the last line, the gate swings open, and we see where the poet has taken us. She writes, "Somebody loves us all." Certainly her attention to this filling station, and then to the poem itself, is an act of love. This poem, as restrained and ordered as it is, is passionate. For all its understatement, what comes through strongest is poignancy. Often the formal poem that demands restraint, by its very boundaries, becomes a structure allowing and containing great feeling.

AC • I've heard you say that it was Elizabeth Bishop's poetry that first got you interested in Nova Scotia.

CL • I read her poems about Lower Economy and the Tantramar Marshes. Even the word "Nova Scotia" sounded exotic and beautiful to me. When I arrived here, my husband and I visited Great Village, and met a relative of Bishop's. We happened to arrive when the town was showing a movie in which the poets James Merrill, John Ashbery, and others praised Bishop's work. When I lived in New York and heard that Bishop had died, I cried. I would no longer get the chance to study with her. But I did hear her read. That was at the Guggenheim Museum, one of the last readings she gave before she died, and I remember looking around the room and thinking, *Everyone here loves poetry*. I could hardly understand her garbled words. She wasn't a good reader, but it was enough to see her, watch her smile, notice the dress that she wore. And when I found myself living in Nova Scotia, coincidences kept occurring, which reinforced my feeling of connection with her.

AC • Your own poetry sometimes has the quality of a riddle. Actually, riddles appear in four poems. Some of those riddles are of the ancient or medieval kind: "Tell me what I am." What is the function of these riddles?

CL • Probably in the momentum of writing the poem, there's a corner I can't see past it. A certain momentum in the poem suggests that this is the course that the poem has to take. When you are trying to explore a certain area, and you're blind and you're groping, there's only so many things you can use. There are times when the question comes up in that riddle form. A certain pace in the poem brings me to the riddle.

AC • There are the long-lined, longish poems in the conversational manner – "What You Need You Continue To Need ..." (*CC* 38-39), "On This Ocean" (*CC* 34-35), and so forth – but there are also quatrains, triplets, and couplets, and in these last, particularly in the ghazal, there is the quality of riddle. David Milne, the Canadian painter, says, "The thing that 'makes' a picture is the thing that 'makes' dynamite – compression" (*Visions of Light and Air* 63). Do you think that is true of poetry as well?

CL • For me it is. If I read a poem and find extraneous words, I am so disappointed.

AC • Among the longer poems, there is "Through a Slit in the Tent" (*CC* 32-33), sectioned 1, 2, 3, where each section is like a film shot. Has film shaped your poetry?

CL • I don't think so. It was a hard poem for me to figure out how to record because this is a story that begins at the end. And it really isn't a story, yet I can see how it could be seen to have that cinematic quality. It's more visual than the other poems. I set out to write an erotic poem. It was an assignment for myself. There was a visual sequence that I wanted to record in that way.

AC • For all its attention to landscape, there is in your poetry, as you mentioned a moment ago, a preoccupation with houses. "Women at Forty," in their hopefulness, believe "houses will be cheaper" (*CC* 30), and there is "Looking at Houses" (*CC* 14-15), and other poems. Also, there are plenty of references to doors and windows. I am reminded of Gaston Bachelard's saying, "Great dreamers profess intimacy with the world. They learned this intimacy, however, meditating on the house" (66). *In Cannon Cave* opens with a poem about "being translated ... into everything that breathes" (11). That absorption of the self into landscape begins, however, from the house, doesn't it?

CL • I feel a great affinity for houses, but they are not the ecstatic of the natural world. A friend said to me that anything that is rendered intimately enough is universal. I think that is true. To know anything well and intimately is to know that which is beyond.

WORKS CITED

— • —

Bachelard, Gaston. *The Poetics of Space*. Trans. Maria Jolas. New York: Orion P, 1964.

Bishop, Elizabeth. "The Filling Station." *The Complete Poems*. London: Chatto & Windus, 1969. 149-50.

Cogswell, Fred. *Folds*. Nepean, ON: Borealis P, 1997.

Langille, Carole. *In Cannon Cave*. London, ON: Brick Books, 1997.

McKay, Don. "Baler Twine: thoughts on ravens, home, and nature poetry." *Poetry and Knowing: Speculative Essays and Interviews*. Ed. Tim Lilburn. Kingston, ON: Quarry P, 1995: 17-28.

Visions of Light and Air: Canadian Impressionism, 1885-1920. Exhibition catalogue for Americas Society Art Gallery, New York, 27 September - 17 December 1995. Curated by Carol Lowery. New York: Americas Society Art Gallery. 1995.

THE POETRY OF NUMBERS:
ALAN R. WILSON

Alan R. Wilson is the author of two books of poetry – *Animate Objects* (1995) and *Counting to 100* (1996). The New Brunswick-born author lives and works in Victoria, British Columbia, making frequent trips home. Trained in physics and astronomy, Wilson is an analyst and statistician at the University of Victoria. *Before the Flood* (1999), his first novel, is set in the 1960s, in Woodstock, at the juncture of the Meduxnekeag and St. John rivers. The novel spans the construction period of the massive Mactaquac Dam which, by the final chapter, has altered forever the free-flowing St. John River. In the first chapter of the novel, the young narrator, Sam MacFarlane, writes a school essay extolling the project, quoting the glib slogans prominent on town billboards. In the final chapter, Sam – with two of his friends – canoes the river, from Woodstock to Fredericton, the day before the *diversion sluiceway* is permanently sealed. Wilson's idea is that the past is not walled off from the present: The *sluiceway* remains open if we have the wit to find it. *Before the Flood* is the first novel in a projected series. Wilson is at work on the second novel, "The Burning Season," and he has a third collection of poetry, a book of sonnets, "The Sonneteer's Sky Atlas" – winner of the CBC Literary Competition – ready for publication. This interview took place in October 1999 in Rothesay, New Brunswick.

In 2000, Wilson was awarded the Chapters/*Books in Canada* First Novel Award.

AC • Alan Wilson, to use the jargon of the sociologist, you are a Maritime out-migrant. Living in Victoria, do you think of yourself as a Maritime writer?

AW • Yes, I do. I live in British Columbia because that's where my job is. I got my physics degree at UNB, and went to BC for graduate school. They gave me a job and I stayed. I don't like being poor. I tried being poor, and I wasn't very good at it.

AC • Do you think that if you were in the Maritimes, you would be poor?

AW • More likely. Statistically, yes.

AC • Your poem "Scene with a Shirt" (*AO* 23) is reminiscent of Alden Nowlan's "Red Wool Shirt," and your carpenter, in the poem of that title (*AO* 7), reminds me of Milton Acorn's several poems on that figure. Do you see your work as participating in a local tradition that features scenes and characters of Maritime life?

AW • For those two poems, yes. "Scene with a Shirt" and "Falling Landscape" (*AO* 3) come directly from Albert County [NB], where I have ancestors, but generally the poetry is less rooted in a particular place than the novel, *Before the Flood*.

AC • Economy, precision, and exactitude characterize your work. Do you think that these are bound to be the qualities of a poet who is trained in the sciences?

AW • I'm not sure which comes first – the nature and predisposition to the physical sciences or the precision that follows from that study. I don't think my studies in the physical sciences did that. I think that was already there. I've always had the idea that the literary image and the scientific image are manifestations of the same thing. I never quite managed to separate the two like I was supposed to. I don't see the two as separate [spheres] as others seem to.

AC • The above-named qualities are characteristic of the work of W.W.E. Ross, a Canadian Imagist poet who was trained as a scientist. Would you describe yourself as an Imagist poet?

AW • In these two books, *Animate Objects* and *Counting to 100*, I'd say the words have to do something or they are out of there. There are very few freeloading words. In that sense, I'd say I am [an Imagist].

AC • I am interested in the way in which the narrative drive of myth and the minimalism of Imagism combine in your work in a poem like "Carpenter"(*AO* 7). Do you think that the minimalist manner under-lines the way in which the mysterious inheres in the everyday?

AW • In physics and astronomy you are looking at reality at a very funda-mental and basic level. If you look at anything closely enough, it stops making sense. You start seeing the strangeness, the underlying reality.

Physics, supposedly, is a reductionist method, but it is not. It's just the opposite. You're pushing away all the foliage and you're looking into something very complex and very strange. You're pulling one layer away to find another layer even more complex. There's a pattern there that our minds can't get around. There's a limit to our understanding because there's a limit to our [mental] architecture. Nobody understands quantum physics. Einstein didn't understand it. Our minds are not structured to handle that depth of nature. Where the rational ends, I guess, is where mysticism starts.

AC • Characters in your novel *Before the Flood* are aligned through their names – Noah, Arthur, Vergil – with myth, and *Animate Objects* contains the poem "Song of the Magi" (*AO* 8-9), which uses an epigraph from *Gilgamesh*. Why are myths so important to you as a writer?

AW • I do keep going back to the myths. The hockey story in *Before the Flood* [chapter 4] is a variation, and development, on that particular poem. Both are the Sumerian underworld. I go back to the Sumerian pantheon, which I found interesting because it is the first one we know of, pre-Greek, pre-Indian.

AC • The magi bring gifts to a female immortal (*AO* 8-9). Who is that immortal?

AW • She is the destructive goddess born out of the nuclear holocaust. There is a science-fiction aspect to "Song of the Magi." After the holocaust, this mutated creature is born. That's who she is. It's a black treatment of the Ishtar figure [*Gilgamesh*].

AC • In *Animate Objects*, there are poems about things breaking down – "Equipment Failure," "Falling Landscape" (*AO* 2, 3). Buildings and equipment are at the mercy of the elements. The world of manmade things is remarkably unstable. Do you find yourself in sympathy with the forces of elemental nature?

AW • Common and everyday things are no longer working; our bodies are no longer working. I have a Luddite streak. Manmade things don't last. The elements keep coming back. So the answer is yes. I don't know if I would use the word "sympathy," but I do have a respect for, a fear of, those elements. The gale is going to get them anyway, so we might as well vicariously enjoy it.

AC • "Anguished Poet Seeks Self in Verse" (*AO* 12-14) is a witty comment on authorial presence, which seems to send up romantic verse.

AW • That poem is a parody of a certain Canadian poet. I read one of his books – a very prolific poet – and I thought, *This should never have been published*. It was sloppy and maudlin, and there was just not much in it. It made me kind of angry that it was published. So I decided to parody the style of the poet. His poetry was "I'm unhappy and you all should be interested in it." I found that egocentric and I get impatient with that.

AC • You're not the kind of poet who is going to write confessional poetry?

AW • Absolutely not. I'm basically a boring person. I don't consider the way I live to be interesting. I think that I do make connections with things that can be interesting, but there is too much "I" poetry. I wanted to make sure that I didn't slip into it.

AC • There is in your poetry an inclination to catalogue. It is there in "Elemental" (*AO* 4-6), "Newton's Laws" (*AO* 39), and in "Twenty-Four Poets' Haiku" (*AO* 15-18), a catalogue of poetic styles. What is this impetus to catalogue?

AW • That's a major part of what the sciences do – to categorize and catalogue to help people make sense of the world. "Elemental" does reflect reality. Those elements are there in the world. They are not inventions. That particular catalogue is the structure of nature. It was originally intended to be a whole book and then I pulled back. I thought enough is enough. "Newton's Laws" is another example. I thought, *I can write poems about these laws*. It's my way of defying the separation of poetry and science.

AC • How would you describe the kind of mind that finds poetry in the periodic table?

AW • Obsessive. For a moment I thought unimaginative, but of course that is totally wrong.

AC • In the poem "The Moon" (*AO* 21), philosophers are concerned with the moon as paradox – "lifeless sphere" casting a light "very brilliant, very white" – but the astronomers, interested in the nature of light, and the moonstruck lovers, interested in each other, could care less. What is the poet's attitude toward the moon?

AW • The astronomers and the lovers are the same. The poet is all the above.

ANNE COMPTON

AC • In your view, is the poet principally an observer, a recorder, of the world?

AW • That's what I have been. There's "I" poetry that's interesting. I can't do it. Others can. I have to step back.

AC • So observer or recorder would describe your position in the first two books?

AW • Yes, although, as in "Equipment Failure" (*AO* 2), I'm not exempt from the things that are going on, but they are not particular to me as an individual.

AC • You have poems such as "Poets Write Haiku on Office Stationary [sic] ..." that are about the writing process. How do you experience that process?

AW • The pleasure principle. There are times when things occur to me and to ignore them would be more difficult than to deal with them. Writing poetry is like the adult equivalent of building a tree fort. It is fun to build these things out of words even if it does look serious. And there is a natural urge or inclination to do it.

AC • If "I" is lost and "he" is on the run, is "it" the only stable entity?

AW • One of the underlying ideas of *Animate Objects* is that there is no such thing as "it." We think of this [the water glass] as an "it," a chunk of glass, but the book says that it's an animate object. What pronoun we use doesn't matter because "it" has a kind of strange life of its own. In the normal way we use "it," the word is demeaning because the word suggests the object has no life.

AC • If objects are "animate," what are humans?

AW • We are animate too. In my poetry, I bring objects closer to the living world, so does that mean that humans have to go higher up? In the book, it's very democratic. Humans are interacting with objects.

AC • So it's a community of animate entities?

AW • I don't know if I believe that, but that does seem to be what the book is saying.

AC • "Scene with a Shirt" (*AO* 23), an edgy, rather unnerving poem, suggests that there is another reality lurking around the edges of physical reality. Isn't that a blasphemous position for a scientist?

AW • No. Not at all. Lots of scientists believe in God. Science is another way of looking at the world.

AC • "Exercise," rather similar to "Shirt," presents the world from a ghost's perspective. Ghosts, in your work, seem to want to be rid of the clutter of human emotions to listen in on the universe – "radio / of wind and rain"; "background static of worms" (24). Is the poet, in some sense, a ghost presence in the world?

AW • I never thought of it that way, but I suppose you're right. The ghost is a kind of detached observer too.

AC • Yours is a precisely observed world with craziness in it. The dead, distant ancestors, and the proximity of another reality haunt these matter-of-fact poems. Is the universe a place of several kinds of realities?

AW • The universe is far more complex than we can imagine. J.B.S. Haldane, the geneticist, said, "My own suspicion is that the universe is not only queerer than we suppose, but queerer than we *can* suppose" (262-63). That's about capability and about the world. The two don't exist separately. We're in the world: The world is bigger than we are, and we can only see bits and pieces of it. So "are there separate realities?" No. There's only one reality that we can only glimpse at. We can view it, or treat it as separate realities, but it is probably all one reality.

AC • Your work has been described by reviewers as "classicist" (*Denham* 180), but there is also a gothic quality in it. The classicism could be tracked to your training in science, but where does the gothic come from?

AW • Phyllis Webb called me a formalist. To me, gothic means that you're drilling a little deeper than we normally go. You're getting into the dark world, the underworld that underpins it all. When we do that – go deeper – things start to look very strange, creepy, kind of scary.

AC • You write of a world of objects and these are neither silent nor dead. William Carlos Williams' "No ideas but in things" is rendered literally: Things, in these poems, have ideas, are communicative. Does your poetry recommend that we tune into a world that we have hitherto been deaf to?

AW • I'm not recommending anything, but the poetry does say that if you look at things a little steadier than we normally do, you'll start seeing them differently. That's how I see the world: It's infinitely strange.

ANNE COMPTON

AC • In your poems, the human is very small indeed, as compared to forces, regular ones like gravity, and irregular ones. Is this repositioning of the human a result of your training as a physicist?

AW • Science certainly emphasizes that we are part of the physical world. We're not left out of things, but the physical sciences don't care about people per se. They look at the world independent of human concerns. And the poems do that too. We're not the whole game; we're just part of it.

AC • A sense of menace is never far away in your poetry, as, for example, in the poems "Tale" (*AO* 19) and "Solitary Image" (*AO* 37). What is the source of this menace?

AW • We are not as important in it as we would like to think. We are not exempt from those forces. We have few choices. The story has been written for us. The world is scary and the world is uncontrollable. We can admire it, enjoy it, but in the end, we can't control it, except in an illusionary way. In the gothic world, the gothic sensibility, humans are demoted. It's an unreasoning world in the sense that we think of reason, so we are demoted. I think that is both truer and more interesting than the picture where we are the colossus, the focus of interest.

AC • "Solitary Image" (*AO* 37) seems to collapse the urban and a prehistoric fear of the beast. Is the urban as liable to incursions of the beast as the world of *Gilgamesh* (Humbaba) or *Ulysses* (Cyclops)?

AW • Of course. The gothic view of things is that the city is no protection. *It* is still out there even if the immediate things you see are the things that humans have built. It's there underground, in the air, just over the horizon.

AC • In "Fascist Haiku" (*AO* 41-42) an SS officer or some soldier of the Holocaust is reminded of a lover by the light of the distant fires. Does the Imagist cleanness of the haiku make it a particularly suitable vehicle for the tamping down of sympathy that enables this soldier to compartmentalize his feelings?

AW • I found the whole concept of a Nazi writing in haiku so incongruous. The reality is that there probably were Nazis who wrote in haiku. Here are two things that you'd think cannot possibly be related, and I found the idea of pulling these two unlikely things – the gentle, subtle haiku and the Nazi fist – together so interesting. If a Nazi wrote haiku, what would they look like? The incongruity, the fact that they did not belong together, appealed to me. I wanted to try putting them on the same plane.

AC • Is the fascist more likely to write in haiku than in another form?

AW • No. I would expect a dramatic monologue. A haiku is the last thing I'd expect.

AC • Your formal range is impressive, including cinquain, villanelle, haiku, limerick, and so forth. Does a poem's content lead to the choice of form?

AW • Mostly the form is first. Once you have the form, certain things are eliminated. The form is a spotlight.

AC • And now there's to be a book of sonnets?

AW • The series consists of 88 sonnets, one for each of the constellations. I think of the sonnet as the siren of poetic forms. It's both hard to understand and to resist its appeal, and in the end I didn't try. Like the relationship of love and the sonnet, the cosmos and the sonnet are made for each other. A match made in heaven, if you will. The majority of the poems in the sequence consist of seven couplets with a shift of mood or direction at line nine, where the sextet begins. I like that format because the six blank lines that cushion the couplets function as a kind of ventilation system for a sometimes intense or heated perspective. And visually I've never found the eight- and six-line clumps that form the traditional sonnet that appealing. I've also included a couple of variants that I've labelled, sort of seriously, prose sonnet and hypersonnet. I wrote some hardcore Petrarchan sonnets too that come fully armed with end rhyme, iambic pentameter, and capitals at the beginning of all 14 lines. The trick with those was to end up with a poem that was organic, that didn't look like an exercise.

AC • Was writing sonnets a radically different experience from the earlier poems?

AW • In many ways it was, in that it required a change from a style where tightness and economy of language were paramount to a kind of sensuality and controlled flamboyance. It required a willingness to experiment, which put me where astronomers, I think, have always stood, namely at the limit of their own vision.

AC • What are the relative satisfactions of the two kinds – the intricate sonnet form and the Imagist-like poem?

AW • I have to say that I found writing under the self-imposed strictures of the sonnet more satisfying. There seems to be something in the contours of the sonnet that can shape the imagination without limiting it. For me, it helped free my mind by providing a structure on which to ascend. As the writing proceeded, I got so pulled in that I didn't want to write anything else but sonnets. Sounds like an addiction!

AC • Windows are everywhere in *Animate Objects* – "Weather" (45), "Windows" (50), "Solitary Image" (37). Why are these so important to you?

AW • If our abilities are limited to simply looking at the world through portholes, where we can only get bits and pieces of the world, then looking through a window is what we do our whole lives. We look through different windows and try to make sense of the world.

AC • Is the window a metaphor for poetry writing?

AW • It would be a good metaphor for a lot of things, poetry among them. It would be a good metaphor for what scientists do. We're locked in the house. We can't get out of the house. There are different ways of looking out. Writing is one of them and so is science. God is one of them.

AC • Your second book, *Counting to 100*, is more abstract than your first. Numbers have replaced objects in the title and as a point of focus in the poems. What was your thinking in this move?

AW • The idea was to do something that is not supposed to work because numbers and poetry don't go together. I did the first two or three just as toss-offs. They were discussed in workshop, and Derek Wynand [workshop leader] really liked them and the class didn't. There were complaints – This is not poetry. And of course when they said that I was determined that I was going to continue with them because I disagreed so strongly and wanted to prove them wrong. Originally, I was just going to write 1 to 10, and then it got out of control.

AC • How easily did these number poems come to you, and in what order? Did you write 88 before you wrote 8, for example?

AW • There was no sequence at all. When the idea would come, I would sit down and write.

AC • Certain numbers, such as 6 and 8, are body types; others are anorexic (21) or dyslexic (62). For you, do numbers have physical presence and personality?

AW • In that book, the numbers are at varying distances from human beings. Some of the numbers are beings in themselves. They speak and have their properties. They are in their world, but then there are other ones, like the number 5, that are not about the number at all. That one is about the five fingers. It's a step closer to us. For some of the number poems, it's the references that I tie in with the number. They are not animate at all. And some of them are their own beings.

AC • Would you consider 6 and 8, the ones with physical bodies, animate?

AW • Absolutely. The poem in each case is about this being, this creature. Thirty is not animate. That's our world. It only exists in relation to our world.

AC • Some of these poems (7, 9, 13) refer to the mythic or folk associations of numbers. Are you saying something about how human-storied numbers are, how often numbers are part of the stories humans tell?

AW • Sure. The book says that. I went on a search mission. I tried to find a reference wherever I could. Eighty-six, for instance, is the one where the mathematician is in the strip club, and I got that from *M*A*S*H*. Eighty-six means "to eject." The mathematician is impressed with the numerics of the woman's body and he ends up getting thrown out on his nose.

AC • Thinking of the 35-millimetre camera, the .38 pistol, and the 45 record, are numbers, in some sense, as significant as artifacts in being the museum of culture?

AW • Of course. Some of those numbers would not work in a different culture, at a different time, in a different part of the world. Heinz 57 is not going to work in Greek culture.

AC • So this book is a museum of culture?

AW • Yes, pop culture. Though some go deeper. The 33 is Christ's age.

AC • Many of these poems are literally riddles. Are you drawing attention to poetry as riddle?

AW • They are telling a little set of jokes or riddles and some of them you get quickly and some of them you can't, which makes you want to go back. It's game-playing. It's seduction. I like books that do that. That's what I enjoy doing. A couple of reviewers didn't like that. They thought it was beneath poetry to be doing that sort of thing.

AC • Some poems are created around a number's quality – its indivisibility (17) or its perfection (25) or the multiples it contains (24).

AW • Look at this one [34]. It adds up every way. I can't take credit for that one. It's called a magic square. To me, that was the riddle. It scared people. That is quite gothic, quite weird. That's what is scary about the world.

AC • In doing public readings from this book, which numbers do you choose to read?

AW • I tend to pick ones that are quickly accessible. I read 1 and 2 to get started and 13 because of Wallace Stevens' poem. I read 20, which is about perfect vision. And then there's 73, which also has good vision, but realizes that infinity – all those digits – is stretched out across the horizon. That's kind of a critical poem because of the eerie buzz of infinity. In a way, that is about us: Our realization that this world is very small, and that there is more out there. That one, 73, is what the book is about.

AC • Has the number book been as successful with readers and reviewers as *Animate Objects*?

AW • To some reviewers it wasn't real poetry because it falls out of their range of experience. But Stephen Scobie gave it probably the best review I'll ever get. He said it was a kind of numeric epic. But some thought a grown man shouldn't be doing this. The book was partly me breaking windows, a natural cussedness.

AC • There are occasions when you don't choose the obvious thing. The alphabet poem is 27, not 26.

AW • Noah's ark is the obvious thing for 40, so it's nice not to do it.

AC • Speaking of Noah, there's an early scene in *Before the Flood* that I particularly like. Vergil and Sam, the protagonist, are in the Baptist church, and three levels of language – Vergil's note to Rachel, the reverend's sermon, and phrases from Sam's essay – get interwoven. Is this interweaving across language levels your notion of how language works?

AW • Not only language, but also life moves across different levels. There are many things occurring at once, and language is a reflection of that. You have these three worlds going on at the same time. There are not three solitudes here. We bounce things off one another.

AC • There's an inner darkness in Reverend Hart that emerges as madness from time to time. Has religion in the Maritimes had a particularly distorting effect?

AW • Woodstock and Carleton County [New Brunswick] are part of the traditional Bible belt. When I grew up there, went to high school there, the Baptists were still in the Old Testament. They still are to a certain extent. So there was a destructive element to the religion in that area. There was a very positive element as well, because there was a focus on things that are not materialistic. So there were these two aspects to it that I find interesting and appealing. There is the side that can destroy weaker people, but there is the side that can make people greater than they are because they don't focus upon the latest sale at the KMart. What they see may be distorted, but they are nonetheless looking up. Hart is a tortured man, but he is also a good man. In the last chapter, he's trying to console Miss Jonah because her cats are about to die. That's the other part of his religion: The part that makes him better than he might be otherwise. The kind of ranting sermon that he gives can be distorting, poisonous, especially for young people, although these boys are ignoring him.

AC • Yet, if we can go by Hart's sermon, his is a gorgeous, metaphorical, adjective-rich language. Does religion's bequest include both gorgeous language and guilt?

AW • The sheer richness of Christianity and its length of time, its two thousand years, have left behind quite a rich tradition. It's also given people a lot of time to get all twisted around. This religious base is a form of living history. Biblical language is one of the areas of conflict between the liberal and the conservative branches of Christianity. The liberal branch wants to translate it right into modern vernacular English, and the conservatives want to hold onto the older stuff. I think I am probably on the conservative side.

AC • Noah Perley is always in sight on the river, but never present in anyone's company, and unlike his namesake, he drowns when the river, because of the dam, drowns. Does this say that the dam is not an ark, and that we're lost for sure this time?

AW • The dam – as far as semi-mythical time goes – is the end of the world. The world is over. On the other side of the dam, there is something else, but it is not this world anymore. I am not even saying the next is a worse world, but that's why the book I'm writing now is not a sequel. It comes before the world of *Before the Flood* because that world is finished. The building of the dam is the border, and the boys live through that border-building period.

AC • Arthur Netherwood, Sam's friend, barely distinguishes the local landscape – the island at the juncture of the rivers – from a similar Mesopotamian geography that he has read about in *Gilgamesh*.

AW • Arthur is a very imaginative fellow, and he looks at this town, because he is so young, as new to him. And he connects it with Mesopotamia. He goes back and forth. He switches them very easily. You don't have to go to Paris to write exotic books. You just have to look at where you are.

AC • This novel says that time is not what we think it is. It is not linear. Tell me about your conception of time.

AW • In the novel, the past and present are beginning to coexist, and people get confused. The past keeps sticking up in the present, which is just a slight embellishment of what happens anyway. These ghostly figures are real people who are lingering. The past and the present are jumbled up.

AC • "The wonder of physics lay in its power to equate things that on the surface appeared unrelated" (104). Are you talking about physicists or poets?

AW • Both.

AC • Sam finds the book on astronomy, *The Heavens*, in the religions section of the library. What's your point here?

AW • It wasn't misfiled. It is exactly where it is supposed to be.

AC • In the very accurate descriptions in your poetry, you often suggest that there is more present than what is available to sight. Peripheral vision, night vision, and seeing into shadows are attributes of some characters in *Before the Flood*. What's the difference between sight and vision?

AW • Sight is what we see with our optic nerves, and vision is all the rest of it. In the novel, vision is the sight of what others have seen [of] the past, or what Reverend Hart sees. All of that goes into the experience of what these characters, Sam included, go through. There are bits of the past that become visible. Those things are crossing the border into sight. The demarcation [between sight and vision] appears to be more abrupt when we are older, for whatever reason. Although there are situations in times of stress when adults may see things.

AC • *Before the Flood* is a novel of beautifully conceived parallels: Tennyson's poem "Crossing the Bar" and the sandy bar of the Intervale; the pattern of fire hydrants on the ground and the pattern of stars in the sky. Is this parallelism a device of narrative structure or is the world for you full of uncanny parallels?

AW • The latter. In the hydrant story, Sam soon forgets about the telescope that he wants because the universe has come down to earth. There he is on the hill looking down. The effect is as if he were looking up. He is looking at this town and that's one of the things a small town is – a complete universe. He's looking at the town, and it is the sky. So what has happened, especially in that chapter, is that he has taken a big step in his appreciation of his immediate world. Seeing the earthbound constellations brings that about.

WORKS CITED

— • —

Denham, Paul. "Various Alphabets." Rev. of *Counting to 100*, by Alan R. Wilson. *Canadian Literature* 155 (Winter 1997): 180-81.

Haldane, J.B.S. "Possible Worlds." *Possible Worlds*. London: Evergreen, 1940. 262-263.

Scobie, Stephen. "Poetic Pre-texts." Rev. of *Counting to 100*, by Alan R. Wilson. *Monday Magazine* 23.6 (30 January - 6 February 1997): 16.

Wilson, Alan R. *Animate Objects*. Winnipeg: Turnstone P, 1995.

– – – . *Before the Flood*. Dunvegan, ON: Cormorant Books, 1999.

– – – . *Counting to 100*. Toronto: Wolsak & Wynn, 1996.

DOUBLY CROSSING SYLLABLES:
THOMAS O'GRADY'S POETRY

Prince Edward Islander Thomas O'Grady, Director of Irish Studies at the University of Massachusetts-Boston, published a remarkable first collection of poetry, *What Really Matters* (2000), a book that went into a second printing within a year. In his poems, and in this interview, O'Grady is an advocate for poetry's return to formalism. His poetry unites depth of feeling and formal mastery, local lore and wide reading, the Irish diaspora and Maritime out-migration. A scholar and a poet, O'Grady has published extensively on Irish writers and on poetics. He is currently writing a book on the Irish writers William Carleton, Patrick Kavanagh, and Benedict Kiely.

In July 2000, following the Island launch of *What Really Matters*, we met for a conversation about the Island and Irish writers, exile and poetry. Every summer, O'Grady and his family travel back to the Island from their home just outside of Boston. Our conversation took place in Southport, east of Charlottetown, overlooking the Hillsborough River, a scene of some importance in O'Grady's work. Cormorants stood sentinel on the river bank.

AC • *What Really Matters* is a poetry that takes place in Ireland, Boston, and on the Island. Where's home?

TOG • Home is PEI. Absolutely. It's where my heart is. It's where my identity really does reside. In the Boston area where I live, I certainly can't play myself off as an Irishman. Despite my career, my title as Director of Irish Studies, I don't make any pretence to being Irish because I couldn't get away with it. I'm not inclined to, anyway. My natural impulse is to look to where I came from. The Island is definitely home.

AC • Is the Island a subject in which literary journals have been interested?

TOG • The first two poems that I got published were actually Irish-related poems, and both were published in Irish journals, the first one in

Poetry Ireland Review, in 1990, and the second in an academic journal *Studies: An Irish Quarterly Review*, a year or two later. Writing those poems, I was responding to what was close to what I was working on in Irish Studies. I was provoked into writing in that way. But my commitment to writing began with the Island poems. The first time that I realized that there might be an audience for Island poems was when the *Kansas Quarterly/Arkansas Review* published "Transmigration," "Auguries," and "Valediction" (*WRM* 37-38, 39-40, 45-47). It stunned me when they accepted those three poems. That made me aware that poetry could transcend the negative notions of regionalism that some editors and some journals might have.

AC · You began with transatlantic and American publication. So Canadian publication was the third layer of publication for you?

TOG · I had poems accepted by *The Fiddlehead* and *Dalhousie Review* quite early on. I was appreciative of both those editors because there is not a PEI poetic tradition that my poems could be seen to be coming out of, or a school of poetry, or even a cohort of poets.

AC · You didn't belong.

TOG · There's nothing to belong to.

AC · Would you say that except for Lucy Maud Montgomery and Milton Acorn, there's been little, or no, literary rendering of the Island's cultural past?

TOG · I wouldn't go so far as to say there's not been any. Frank Ledwell's *North Shore of Home*, a very moving collection – which I reviewed when it came out, appropriately praising it – validated the Island subject in a lot of ways. At the same time, it wasn't my Island that Frank was recording because it's a generation removed, and his background is much more rural than mine. When I come to the rural, I come to it as a city boy, immersing myself in the rural partly by standing on the South Shore, where we went each summer. Also, my identification with my mother's rural family was intrinsic all along, but when I began to write, I became aware of how important it was for me to know that my family had been rooted on the Island since the 1830s.

AC · The speaker in *What Really Matters* refers to that family as "sea-crossed souls" (15) and as a family "choosing transportation overseas" (11). Why does that exile, generations in the past, remain so fresh?

TOG • I would have to make a distinction between the paternal and the maternal lines of my family. One of the dimensions of my father's side of the family that strikes me with great poignancy – it's registered in the poem "East Side Story" (72-74) – is that his parents came from Ireland to New York City, and my father came from New York City to PEI, and then I went from PEI to Boston. There is a diaspora effect at each generational level. On the maternal side, my ancestors came from Ireland in the 1830s, in pre-famine time. They came willingly, and settled here, and made their homes here. I value the rootedness of the maternal link at the same time that I'm acknowledging the paternal pattern. I'm trying to work through the relationship of those two strains in terms of my own identity.

AC • That gives us the ancestral record, but it doesn't explain the fresh feel of exile in *What Really Matters*.

TOG • My first real awareness of the Island as home was the product of the first time I left the Island, which was when I went to Ireland, in 1977, to do my Master's degree at University College, Dublin. I was away for a year and a half. Ireland is very beautiful in all its richness, but upon my return, in the summer of 1979, I was absolutely stunned by how beautiful the Island is and what that beauty did to me. The point at which I became aware that I wouldn't be living on the Island was around the time that I got tenure at University of Massachusetts-Boston. I was fixed in a job, had a house, a family. Knowing that this was where I was going to grow old is what provoked me to write the poems. There's a little poem "Land and Sea" that's not in the book. It's a quasi-translation of a lyric by Theógnis of Mégara, a Greek poet. For a few years, before I actually reworked that poem, I would come back to Boston [from PEI] in late August and I'd read that poem. His longing for place consoled me, but then I had to make the poem my own. So I reworked, rewrote it as an Island poem, and then I really had a way of saying, "This is how I feel about having just left." The poem "Valediction" (45-47) is also true to my yearly experience of leaving the Island. Every year, the evening before we leave, there is a great grief that I have to come to terms with.

AC • Sight is inflected with loss?

TOG • There is always a looking back over my shoulder. One of the wonderful dimensions of the ferry was that you could stand on the ferry and look at the Island receding.

AC • When I first read your poetry two years ago, I said that it was located mid-strait. There's a whole bunch of exiles out there – stranded – because there is no ferry to take them home.

TOG • "Lament for My Family, Lost at Sea" (11-12), which is a sestina, is a parable about my family. Seven children. Six of us have left the Island. That poem actually started as a villanelle that didn't work, but I still had to locate myself lost at sea. I mined the villanelle for images that had to do with the tidal pull. Something obviously did take me off the Island, but there is something just as strong pulling me back. I'm neither here nor there in a lot of ways. The mid-strait perspective is, indeed, an interesting conceit for where I am, and where others are too.

AC • The speaker in *What Really Matters* fears that his heart will harden (10) or grow "sere in a foreign land" (13), but he also fears that "words [will] turn brittle" (13). Is exile as much a loss of language, as a loss of place?

TOG • I think so. I think there are elements in my poetry that I am self-conscious about in hindsight rather than in foresight because I didn't set out with an agenda when I started writing poems. I didn't know I was going to be a poet. Five years ago in the summer of 1995, I made the commitment: I said, "I'm going to see if I can be a poet." One of the tests is the Wordsworthian one – natural language, the language of the people, and its accessibility. When my editor at McGill-Queen's was editing the manuscript she came to "Cattle Crossing at Argyle Shore," and wondered about the phrase "our having gotten caught" (16). She said, "That doesn't sound right," but I thought that's how an Islander would say it. I didn't write it self-consciously. When she alerted me to the fact that it was non-standard in some way, I thought, W*ell, how else would you say it*? I don't make a conscious attempt to sound like an Islander or to use Island dialect unless they are words that I myself would use. Those two images – "sere" and "brittle" – reflect the times when I have blocked out my emotions concerning my exile. It's a self-defence mechanism.

AC • Memory itself is like a tide, according to "Exile" (10). It washes the encrustation off the exile to reveal a soft-bodied heart. So the defence mechanism breaks down, doesn't it?

TOG • The poem "On Unquity Road," containing the phrase "my words [grow] brittle" (13), was written out of the same anxiety as

ANNE COMPTON

"Transmigration" (37) that contains the image of the blue heron, which represents my displaced soul. It concerns my removal from civility, which I associate with the Island – romantically or otherwise. Seamus Heaney has a wonderful poem, "Making Strange," in which he talks about the need to be both adept and dialect (221-22). He can still go back to south County Derry and walk in the bogs with the farmers and talk with them. I feel that I can come home, bump into old friends, and there is no distance between us. I feel very at home when I am at home.

AC   • Jonathan Bate, in *Romantic Ecology*, says that place-naming is a way of finding identity by dwelling in the land, but how does place-naming, of which there is a lot here, function for the exile?

TOG • To borrow one of my own phrases, it's "a finger-hold (and no more) / on a solid sandstone shore" (43). One of the licences for that is the Irish poet Patrick Kavanagh, who is one of the subjects of the book that I am writing. He has a marvellous sonnet called "Epic" in which he names the Duffys and the McCabes fighting over a little strip of land. I can remember reading Kavanagh back in 1977, when I was a student in Dublin. My poem "The Field" has the line "*Naming ... is the love-act and its pledge*" (41) from Kavanagh's "The Hospital."

AC   • When you use place names, such as "Belvedere" ("Bloodlines" 7-8), hundreds of miles away from the place that you name, does that constitute a renewal of the "pledge"?

TOG • It does, and it validates the poetic place that I am writing about. In *Poetics*, Aristotle talks about the recognition that the audience experiences from the familiar. Acknowledging the familiar is important to me. The first poem to make an impression on me was Langston Hughes' "The Weary Blues," where he names Lennox Avenue. In 1984, I took the bus into New York City and going through Harlem, I saw Lennox Avenue. It was an incredibly emotional moment for me because suddenly this place that he had made so real for me in the poem was so real in this other way. The real place validated the poem, but the poem had also validated the real place. It was an epiphanic moment for me. Some of that has carried through for me in "A Poem Leaves No More Mark" where it was so crucial for me to name "the Point Prim // beacon" (43) right across from our cottage. It is not "a lighthouse": It's specifically "the Point Prim // beacon."

AC • In almost every poem you name a place. In "Cormorants," for example, you name the "Hillsborough Bridge" (9). It's as if you start from a specific geographical location when you think a poem.

TOG • In some cases, I start from a location; in others, I end up at there. "Cormorants" is an interesting example. The first time I saw cormorants was 20 years ago at Pictou Landing. I saw them sitting on posts by the dock. Cormorants weren't common on the Island when I was growing up; or they weren't ubiquitous the way that they are now. In the interval, while I have been away from the Island, more and more cormorants have come to be on the old pilings of the Hillsborough Bridge and out at St. Catherine's. Their presence became a symbol of change for me: My departure, and an influx of new Islanders. I could name envy not in a vicious way, but with longing: They are now enjoying that "wingspread ease" (9) of being Islanders. The cormorants have come in and made themselves at home while I have been removed. The blue heron is a much more important symbol for me as a kind of embodiment of my own soul, but the cormorants do function in a naturalistic way to mark time.

AC • Is the exile, especially the one who makes return visits, more watchful than the inhabitant of a place?

TOG • Recently, I came across a wonderful image in the poetry of the Swedish poet Tomas Tranströmer that comes close to describing how I feel when I return to the Island: "I don't know where I / turned my head– / with a double field of vision / like a horse" (93). I think that returning home to the familiar lends one a heightened awareness of place specificity – of what makes that place distinctive. As a corollary to this, I wonder whether we can ever know a place that is not home.

AC • There's a family history in this collection – a poem about a maternal grandfather (a railway agent, 19); a great uncle ("an idler," 25); and a paternal grandfather (a soldier, 27). Except for the mention of the railway agent's wife ("Bloodlines" 7), you remember back through male forbears. Is that right?

TOG • In the cases you cite, there are specific stories behind the poems that lend the poems their resonance. Also, I suppose that the world of male activity, outside the house, is more intrinsically compelling for me. That is not, of course, to invalidate the domestic world: It is simply not a world that I've plumbed the depths of ... at least not yet. In fact, somebody recently observed that my poem "Bloodlines" may take for granted – when it really should question – the contentment and patience that I attribute to "the railroad / agent's wife who set meals on the table / timed to the minute the station clock showed" (8).

AC • When you name yourself, what word – Islander, Maritimer, Canadian – most readily comes to mind?

TOG • If we're travelling someplace, usually for convenience's sake, I'll say I'm from Boston, but if I actually start talking to someone, they'll know I'm not from Boston. It immediately comes out that I'm from the Island. The first thing that would come to mind is Islander or Canadian, not Maritimer. I cannot think of anyone that I've met who would use "Maritimer" as a badge they would wear. For me, the Canadian part comes and goes, but growing up on the Island I didn't have a very extended or extensive sense of Canada. There were seven children, and we didn't travel much off-Island.

AC • In your academic life, you teach Irish Studies. Does your academic life complement, enrich, your poetry writing?

TOG • I think so. Much of my scholarship in the last eight years, while I've been writing the poems, has been related to place in Irish literature. I'm writing a book on three Irish writers – William Carleton, who is a 19th-century short story writer and novelist; Patrick Kavanagh, poet and novelist; and Benedict Kiely, novelist and short story writer, general man of letters, anecdotist, and memoirist. All three of the writers are from Southeast Ulster, from County Monaghan and Count Tyrone. This happens to be where the great majority of PEI Irish emigrated from in the 1830s. These are the writers I can identify with because their world is so familiar to me in a lot of ways. The codes and values are tribal, similar to the ones I have from Island culture. There are other dimensions of their writing that I'm interested in. How do they record place? What do they recognize as the factors that define place? Some of it is the topography and the topography as it affects the social structure. They are all writing in drumlin country with the rolling hills that define people's lives because they live in these little narrow valleys, where there are just a few families. E. Estyn Evans, the great Irish geographer, said that there is no sense of horizon in drumlin country. I'm very interested in how these writers create place through language, through the interaction of the people, and the social codes that get rooted in a place. Through the material culture of the place and through the popular culture of the place – the music, the stories, and poems, the oral culture. I am interested in the "how" of registering place. But what also intrigues me is "Exile and the Epic Imagination," which is the subtitle of my book. All three of these writers left Southeast Ulster and moved to Dublin, and wrote about their place from that distance. I am interested in the impulse to return constantly in the imagination. The recurring emphasis, perhaps in about 90 per cent of their writing, is going back even though they are not physically going back to reside there. Their attraction to place and their writing about it from the position of exile is part of the licence, or authority, for me to do it, but it also tells me that it has to be done with care.

AC • In your scholarship, you are excavating the very thing that is the underlay of *What Really Matters*?

TOG • Yes, though I would make a distinction. Heaney has written several wonderful essays on Kavanagh. In one of the later ones, he takes a phrase from one of Kavanagh's poems where Kavanagh refers to County Monaghan as "the placeless heaven." Eventually, Monaghan became more important to Kavanagh as an imagined place (Heaney, "Placeless Heaven" 4). For me, the Island has not become a "placeless heaven" yet. I still have family here and close friends. I hope that I won't move toward simply the idea of a place. That's why it is so crucial for me to get back every year, to re-root myself.

AC • The imagined place and the real place are not the same place, are they?

TOG • What is so important for me when I write is the authenticating of the place. Part of that has to do with the naming of the place, with the details that make their way into the poem. I have an Island "informant," and I have tested a few poems with him. He would not let me distort, corrupt, or romanticize. If I can pass his litmus test for authenticity, then I know that I've got a poem that speaks some form of the truth.

AC • The epigraph on the title page of the second section is from the Gospel of St. Thomas: *"If you bring forth what is within you, what you have will save you. If you do not have that within you, what you do not have within you [will] kill you."* Is poetry salvational?

TOG • It is for me as a writer of poems and as a reader of others' poems. That epigraph functions as a sort of gloss on where my poems come from. I don't write unless I have something to write about, some issue that I need to work through or explore. When I have found the proper words and appropriate form, then I do feel some sort of uplift, some sort of release. The epigraph thus implies that if I were not to find release through the poems, then I would be consumed from within.

AC • There are a number of religious references in this book – poems entitled "Redemption" (58) and "The Miracle" (59), images of ark and grail, and a creed is voiced: "Belief / is still what saves us in the end," but is this any longer religious belief?

TOG • Most of the religious images are probably cultural references: I grew up a Catholic. The occasional "religious" dimension to the poems involves the need that I think we all have, whether we know it or not, to believe, or the desire to believe, in *something*: God, music, art, poetry .... Conventional religious belief is difficult to maintain in this materialistic and cynical age. While I have evolved into what some priests refer to as a "cafeteria-style Catholic"– one who picks and chooses from the rules and the beliefs and practices – I am nonetheless a "cultural Catholic," and that makes its way into the poems.

AC • How do you keep a poetry that is so unashamedly attached to family and place from becoming sentimental?

TOG • I'm not a sentimental person. I'm not a dreamer. I'm very practical in a lot of ways. One of the things that I'm aware of from these Irish writers is that in one way or another you have to achieve distance from your subject. The physical distance I have is just right for what I need. I'm not so removed that I can't come back in a day. I don't have to have a "placeless heaven." I can have a real heaven. I do idealize the Island in a lot of ways, I suppose, although I'm selective about what I write about. Because it's lyric poetry, it's very much filtered through my own emotional grid of experience. Authors who write about places that they know intimately use comedy or irony to distance themselves. James Joyce, writing about Dublin in *Dubliners*, says he's going to use his "style of scrupulous meanness" to remove anything that would be sentimental (*Letters* 109-10). Every writer who engages with place in a sweeping way throughout his writing has to find some device. I don't know how I would label my device. It isn't comedy or irony. There's a scrupulosity, although it's not "scrupulous meanness." It's a selectivity. There may be more that I'm not writing about. Maybe I'm not even aware of what I'm not writing about. The fact is I had a happy childhood. I grew up in a completely innocent way on the Island. I don't have childhood darkness that I need to explore. My relationship with the Island is one that has always been very healthy.

AC • Physical distance affords a kind of objectivity, you say. There is also, however, the naturalness of language in *What Really Matters*, and it coexists with strict forms. Perhaps the strict forms play a role in the disciplining of feeling?

TOG • What you are saying is interesting in light of the distinction that Kavanagh makes between craft and technique, and that Heaney picks up on in his own writing ("Feeling into Words" 47). Craft for both Kavanagh and Heaney is the ability to know the rules – iambic pentameter and the rhyme scheme of the sonnet, for example – but technique is what the individual infuses the poem with that distinguishes it as *that* poet's sonnet. It's a vision that is distinctive and unique to the poet. Perhaps for me craft and technique merge. Form is part of my vision.

AC • Neither of the section titles of the book, "Transmigration" or "Between Two Worlds," suggests arrival, yet the book testifies to a deep attachment to place. Is there a paradox here?

TOG • Over the years, as the poems were accumulating, I began thinking in terms of a book. My working title as I wrote poems and inserted them into the manuscript was "Between Two Worlds." There was a completely different order from the present order of *What Really Matters*. The Island poems were all at the back of the book. I was frontloading it with my sense of not being on the Island. The phrase "Between Two Worlds" appears in the poem "East Side Story" (72-74), which is about my father's experience with his father and the phonograph they had in their New York City apartment. It's about the transporting power of music to take someone back. You are in one world physically, but you are in another metaphysically so that you end up "Between Two Worlds." It's actually a wonderful phrase in Irish: "*idir dhá shaolta*." You look the words up in an Irish dictionary and it means not just between two worlds, but between two times, two states of mind. It resonates with multiple meanings. That phrase worked very well for what I wanted to capture on a literal level, but it also resonated for me with my grandfather's experience, my father's experience, and with my own. "Between Two Worlds" is exactly what I have felt.

ANNE COMPTON

AC • I had thought the title of the second section, "Between Two Worlds," came from Matthew Arnold – "between two worlds, one dead, / The other powerless to be born" (187), which is quite glum.

TOG • The poems in the second part of the book – its title has no connection to Arnold – tend not to be Island related unless it's incidental. They are not working through my relationship with the Island. There's a more cosmopolitan sense of self. Ireland is there; America is there. The fiddlers of the first part of the book become Stéphane Grappelli and Niccolò Paganini in the second half. David Blackwood's painting appears there. There's a different engagement: The Islander not being dialect but being adept, if I can borrow from Heaney again.

AC • If I say Thomas O'Grady is a formalist and a Romantic, would you have a quarrel with that?

TOG • Not with the formalist part and not with the Romantic if it refers to the poetic tradition. No one has ever accused me of being a "romantic" in real life. I think the valuing of experience processed through the imagination is vital to my poems. There's a real effort, on my part, trying to locate myself relative to natural process. In "Valediction" (45-47), I see the heron homing to St. Peter's Island, and we are going to Boston the next day, wanting to believe that is the right place for us to be going. There is a desire to see my experience, and the tugs and pulls, as being part of a larger cycle of being.

AC • You read the natural landscape for portents and auguries. That's a Romantic gesture. There's individualism: The self is sought in various ways. Also, this is a poetry that seems to come from the inspired moment. Central aspects of the Romantic aesthetic – the natural world, individualism, and inspiration – are present in your poetry. At the same time, in terms of craft and technique, you are a formalist even when you are not dealing with fixed forms.

TOG • One of the touchstones for me formally – and, as you know, sonnets are my great weakness – is Wordsworth's "Nuns Fret Not," where he explains why people write sonnets. Sometimes we like the rules and constrictions, and like to work against them. Wordsworth is someone who licences me. The other influence, a very specific influence on the first published poem that I ever wrote – "The Test of the Bow" (75), a sonnet variant – was Keats' poem "On the Sonnet," where he advocates the loosening of the sandal straps. So the first published poem I wrote was influenced by Keats and also by Wordsworth. It would be romanticizing to say that I was destined to write sonnets by way of that first poem.

AC • This is a poetry that is highly allusive in its many classical and literary references, yet it is extraordinarily tactile. Is that a balance you strive for?

TOG • The first word of the sestina, "How a Poem Begins" (81-82), is "Coincidence." Many of my poems come from stories, and it's usually not just one story, but two elements coming together and clicking. This is galvanizing for the emotional life behind the poems. Two agents come together and something comes out of that. A specific example of what you describe is "The Craft of Poetry" (33), which has the story of Jason and the Argonauts trying to return with the golden fleece through the Symplegades – a wonderful story – and the other agent was a woodworker's vice that was on my grandfather's workbench in Cardigan [PEI]. I had to find a way to bring the transcendent story of Jason and the Argonauts back down to my known experience, and not just have it as a metaphor for the vulnerability of the poet that I constantly feel. I had to make it the real vulnerability of getting my fingers pinched over and over again as a child at my grandfather's. Writing the poem, I was remembering something that I didn't even know that I was remembering.

AC • Both of the levels in that poem – the classical and the actual – become ways of talking about poetry itself.

TOG • Constant risk inhabits the making of poetry, or any art, for that matter. And art without risk is no art at all. Those aren't just good stories. They are a way of illuminating real experience, bringing them into my realm.

AC • But even when you are being allusive, you domesticate the allusion through tactile imagery. You bring these allusions, these stories, not only into your realm, but into the physical realm.

TOG • Another poem that does that is "Metamorphoses" (54-55), which starts off with Pegasus, and you have the Centaur and Ixion, the sire of the Centaur. Its origins include the one and only time I ever saw my father ride a bicycle. I saw how that transformed him. It includes, as well, the first time my daughters saw me on a bicycle. My pleasure in all of those poems – such as "A Prayer for My Daughters," which alludes to Yeats' famous poem – not just the ones that have classical references, is the ambitious, but I hope appropriately modest, attempt to have a dialogue with the poetic tradition.

AC • Do you think that a poem speaks to past poems, past literature?

TOG • In my poetic, they certainly do. I'm very aware of T.S. Eliot's talking about this, and W. Jackson Bate's speaking of the fact that there are always the precursors. I don't suffer from an anxiety of influence. I can acknowledge that the Irish poets have had a determining influence on my becoming a poet. My attraction to form is through the Irish tradition, but because I don't write as an Irish poet, I don't have an anxiety of influence. It's much more the pleasure of confluence, entering into the same stream that they are part of. I can explain it through some of my fiddler and violinist poems, especially the Paganini poem. Paganini actually is for me a kind of Yeatsian anti-self. He is a projection of who I am not. The fiddler or the violinist standing up with his music is the poet standing up with his words. Paganini and Grappelli are such wonderful musicians. I like to sidle up next to them.

AC • This is the opposite of the vulnerable poet that you talk about. This is the confident guy on stage with his fiddle.

TOG • I'm betwixt and between on this too, because there is also the cavalier dimension. That's very much a pose for me, the anti-self projecting a figure the opposite of who I am and trying to fulfill it. In one of the personal essays that I'm working on, I'm trying to sort out for myself the performative dimension in readings and the launches. But the writing of the poems is also performative. I've been able to trace the longing to be an artist back to a very particular moment in my life. I wanted to be a musician. I wanted to be the lead guitarist in a rock band. I wanted to go to Berklee College and study music, and that goes back to when I was 10 or 12 years old and my parents bought me a ticket to a Hank Snow and Wilf Carter concert at the Confederation Centre. Seeing them, something in me said, "That's what I want to do." I never imagined myself doing it as a poet, though. Creativity comes from inside and is given expression, but as soon as it is on the page, it is performative, and then on the stage, it is performative in a different sense.

AC • At a reading, you literally, as well as metaphorically, stand behind your words. There's the risk of seeming "to act big," isn't there?

TOG • I'm afflicted with that fear. That's the story of my life. Everything that I do in my life, I do quietly.

AC • Don't you think the fear of bringing on the accusation of "big feelin'" has been very damaging for Island artists and writers, for any ambitious Islander?

TOG • I've been trying to be (unscientifically) analytical about this. I think that on some level the "big feeling" creates the counterpart to the fear of failure, which is the fear of success. Is there a way on the Island to handle accomplishment or success gracefully when everybody is going to be squinting at you? In the States, there is an incredible sense of ego, of entitlement, that goes with political office, whereas here, the politicians are the guys you meet walking down the street and they are immediately accountable to their constituents. If they become egotistical here, they are voted out. As I put it in my Acorn essay, there is on the Island a "governor" that keeps your engine from running at full tilt.

AC • Do you think of yourself as an intellectual poet?

TOG • No. I'm very aware when I read a poet like Mark Strand, for example, that his poems start with ideas. The poetry of someone like Wallace Stevens has a different origin from mine. My poetry starts with an emotional impulse. When I finished *What Really Matters*, I was burnt out, but now I've started writing again and I'm trying to do something different, formally and thematically. Exile is not going to figure as much. I'm looking for, and finding, different formal strategies, which I think help complicate my emotional engagement with whatever my subject is. I'm finding it difficult to write sonnets. The four poems in the sequence "Land of Youth," which I've now finished, are all set on our shore, and it's a much different relationship with the shore. It involves the experience of coming home last summer – we hadn't been home the year before – and seeing that the cottage had fallen into disrepair. There was a lot more seaweed and sinking sand on the shore. The cliffs had crumbled. There was a sense of erosion. I was startled, shocked, and dismayed by the ravages of time. What is projected in the poems [of *WRM*] is this timeless, serene place. The name on our cottage is *Tír na nÓg*, the Irish for "land of youth." In a way, all of that damage was a measurement of the passing of time, the ravages of time, and created an awareness of mortality. The form that I've used for the four new poems is four rhymed quatrains. I take the comfort of

ANNE COMPTON

housing it in that form. It goes beyond the sonnet, which has a tendency to give you a gratifying sense of closure.

AC   • I notice in *What Really Matters* that you have a tendency to write sonnets in pairs – "Bloodlines" (7-8) and "Cattle Crossing" (16-17), for example. The dialectical relationship, formerly between octave and sestet, exists here between the sonnets in the pair. In these 28 lines, are you seeking the formalism of the sonnet yet the stretch of the pair?

TOG • That's an interesting way to look at it, but it's not the way I look at it. One of the appeals of the sonnet for me is what Paul Fussell, in his book *Poetic Meter and Poetic Form*, calls the principle of imbalance (115). The need to resolve in a smaller space what you have established in a larger space is very appealing to me. In my sonnets, and even in my free-verse writing that is arranged in couplets or tercets, I'm interested in the relationship between formal structure and rhetorical structure. The rhetorical structure is affirmed by the end rhymes, but, more importantly, the rhetorical structure *is* the structure. In those double sonnets, each sonnet works on that level. There are pairs because I'm indulging my narrative impulse. I have a storytelling impulse and that contributes to those sonnets.

AC   • Even as you pay regard to the formal requirements of the sonnet, you are trying to elbow your way out of the form.

TOG • From what I've been writing in the last six months, I have a feeling that I'm going to write a lot more sequences. I am aware of the strength and power of the stand-alone lyric, but also its limitations in acknowledging the complexity of human experience. In the sequence I've just finished, "Land of Youth," each poem stands alone, but when they come together, the whole is greater than the sum of the parts. Sequences allow me to extend beyond the nicely turned vase that the sonnet is.

AC   • A yearning for the epic and the narrative is present in this book in the related lyrics. Perhaps lyric sequences are the present-day epic.

TOG • In *What Really Matters*, there are probably a half-dozen, maybe even eight or ten, poems that make reference to my grandfather, my mother's father. It's a kind of connect-the-dots history of that line of our family. That's how I would describe the epic ambitions of my poetry, very modest ambitions, but the cumulative effect of a body of lyric poems is somewhat narrative. The trajectory of the poems tells the story not just of a poetic career, but also of a life.

AC • In this case, a cultural past is also expressed. In *What Really Matters*, the familial history *is* the Island cultural past. Although we have Acorn's mythic history of the Island in *The Island Means Minago*, nobody has started telling, in literary terms, the cultural past through familial stories. However, in spite of your narrative tendency, you use the word "song" for poetry (26). There are not a lot of people today who refer to poetry as "song." Does your use of this word declare a position?

TOG • One of the descriptions of poetry that I came upon this past winter was Emerson's. He says that in a poem every line should be a poem (253). That was wonderfully affirmative for me because that is not only what I aim for, but what I feel instinctively when I write. There's a musicality in my poetry. Not coming from an artistic culture or a culture where beauty was something that mattered, I had this fear of writing something beautiful – not only thematically beautiful, but beautiful in itself, having a texture to it. But I got over that. I said, *That's what I want to do: create something beautiful for myself*. In the beginning, I had no audience. I was writing poems because I wanted to create beauty.

AC • When you use the word "song" for poetry, you are referring, then, to the beauty that you want to create in poetry?

TOG • I can't imagine my poems ever being set to music, perhaps because of the musicality within them. Perhaps it's my frustrated musician coming through that wants to be melodic. I played a dozen instruments and can still do so if called upon. As I acknowledge in my recent essay, "Weights and Measures," Heaney licenced me to create beautiful poems. He has a remarkable musical capacity. In his essay "Feeling into Words," he talks about the way language as it is spoken in South Derry – the consonantal quality of it, in particular – became the sound system that he was working with when he started to write poems (44-45). When I started to write, what came naturally to me was a play that was at times verbal, at times sonic, that I didn't want to suppress. I wanted to acknowledge that this was the medium that I was working with. When I'm writing, I'm not worrying about whether this poem is going to work. I'm taking pleasure in where the poem is going and how it is going there.

AC • You go around modernist poetics. Your poetry isn't much affected by it?

TOG • I haven't read – to the extent of being engaged with – much 20th-century American poetry.

AC • You take your bearing from a 19th-century tradition?

TOG • Or from the Irish poetic tradition, which tends still to be traditional and formalist. It draws from the 19th-century English tradition that it emerged from and from the older Irish tradition, which is very rigorous in form and has a special sensitivity to language and a resonance with, what Heaney calls, "the verbal philandering of the Irish language" ("Poems of the Dispossessed" 34). I see myself as taking that same kind of pleasure in the use of language. I can't say that I came from an oral culture, but I came from a very literate culture, growing up in a house surrounded by books.

AC • Many of your poems are about poetry-making and the role of the poet. The identification of the poet as "idler" ("A Fiddler's Share" 25-26) is reminiscent of William Morris' phrase "the idle singer of an empty day" in *The Earthly Paradise*. Does the term "idler-poet" (26) convey the social perception, perhaps judgment, of the poet?

TOG • I can translate that back to my growing-up experience when Acorn was the only visible Island poet. As an example of the social public poet, there was an element of caricature in Acorn. As far as I can glean from the [Richard] Lemm biography and from [Chris] Gudgeon's, it seems that was partly a function of Acorn's personality. He was a little bit different, and he played that up and became a kind of persona. That for me was not a useful model for the poet. The poet, like anyone else, has to be a functioning part of some other structure. "A Fiddler's Share" does acknowledge the social perception of the poet, but what has stunned me and uplifted me about the reception of *What Really Matters*, especially where I live in Milton [near Boston], is the celebration of me as poet, and that is connected to the other dimensions of my life there.

AC • Acorn referred to himself as a "bard," as do you. Do you think of your work as at all similar to his?

TOG • When I read Acorn, I am constantly distracted by the politics – by the stridency of his expression of his politics. When I read certain poems in isolation, however, I find his lyric spirit altogether engaging. I admire his poem "The Island," and I recently took pleasurable notice of "The Stormbirds" for the first time. But I am also distracted at times by

Acorn's inattentiveness to craft: I think that he has written many poems that are just a word or a phrase or an image short of being objects of true beauty. There are other poems in which remarkable phrases or images get lost in an otherwise undistilled poetic concoction. It's the difference, once again, between "craft" and "technique," though perhaps he wanted that rough-around-the-edges effect to his poetry. I suspect that Milton would register mirror-image complaints against my poems: Not enough politics, too much polish.

AC • Like Acorn, you use clusters of hyphenated words that function as adjectives – "Brine-blackened sticks" (9); "wind-plagued place" (11); "salt-tattered sail"(12); "cattle-stalking flock" (17); "Sunday-collared countrymen" (72). Within these adjective clusters there are nouns. Why do you think you share with Acorn this linguistic habit?

TOG • I would certainly say that it is coincidental rather than influential. For me, what is going on in those phrases that you have named is the sonic texture. It is the assonance in "stalking flock" that matters and the consonance in "cattle-stalking." I use a lot of internal rhyme and consonantal play so that my poems, my most formal poems, my sonnets, are defined not only by their form, but also by their texture. To the extent that I can analyze it, I'd have to say that my biggest influence in these clusters of sounds is my closeted career as a blues guitarist in my younger days. I played obsessively from 10th grade through college with a blues pianist. The inflections of blues guitar – the repetition of notes, the bending of notes, the difference between the down stroke and the up stroke with the pick – all of that has made its way into the sounds in my poetry. I've just begun a six-poem sequence that is going to be about six jazz guitarists. It's my acknowledgment of the importance of guitar players not only as stand-ins for violinists, but also for the importance of the guitar in my system of hearing and of making sounds.

AC • I wondered if there was some common ground having to do with Island speech that might explain why two Island poets of different generations had this common linguistic tendency. You say this is a sonic feature, related to your background in jazz; nonetheless, in these adjective clusters, there are nouns which give the phrasing its tactility. Adjective clusters that contain nouns harden the adjectives.

TOG • I should acknowledge another dimension to this: [Gerard Manley] Hopkins and sprung rhythm. My poems are heavily iambic. Robert

Frost says that there are two metres that we can use – loose iambic and strict iambic (51). In using those clusters, I am able to strain against the strict iambic. Paul Fussell talks about the three degrees of "metrical competence," which are the absolute absence of it, where you are all over the place; strict adherence with no variation; and the third is the one where the metre is expressive. Adjective clusters make the line expressive. The adjectives are part of the texture of the line, but they are also part of the recuperation of the experience. That feature has a complex quality. I have never actually consciously written anything in Hopkinsesque sprung rhythm, but in the poem "Fox Tongs" (32), I was very aware of the strong stresses that were getting into the poem. That's a poem about forging something. Sprung rhythm provides a way to make the iambic expressive, and natural as well, so that you are not just aiming for that end rhyme. You've got other things going on that prevent the end rhyme from defining what the sonnet is.

AC   • Flexibility in the iambic line makes the line more expressive, but you also say, "rhyme keeps my grip / on what really matters" (53). Is there a place for recklessness in your poetry?

TOG • It goes against my ear.

AC   • You speak of Osip Mandelstam's "high faith in unfettered words" (67).

TOG • A poem like "Valediction" (45-47), which is a free verse poem with irregular line lengths, is a very dangerous poem for me because it could end up being sentimental. It also uses that lethal "O" twice. That's a poem that is a little bit "unfettered." I am able, however, to contain it through its structure. It's got two parts, and within each part there are sections. There is a relationship between the formal free-verse strophe and the rhetorical content. When I was citing Mandelstam, I was acknowledging what that poem departs from, but also I am recognizing Mandelstam's own life and career as a prisoner in the Gulag. When I say that "rhyme keeps my grip / on what really matters," rhyme is a stand-in for poetry in general. At the same time, the evidence suggests that rhyme itself is crucial to what I do. If you do the math on the free-verse poem "What Really Matters" (51-53), you see that it is masked heroic couplets all the way through to the end. This structural principle is as much as anything a textural principle. It gives the poem its music. These undercurrents of sound measure out wonderfully for me personally. The poem's structure of slanting lines creates a mimetic effect for the slope that the cyclist is going down. There is a lot of play that is visual. I don't do a lot of that. As the title poem in the book, it also carries a lot of thematic weight.

AC • Finding the poem in the empty field, the "stone-strewn field" (31), is compared to laying a hand upon Excalibur. In another poem, poetry is aligned with the sea-engaging Argonauts (33). This is a very high notion about poetry, isn't it?

TOG • Stompin' Tom Connors is poetry; Gene MacLellan [Island singer/songwriter] is poetry. They're working with words. They're making words do something. That for me defines poetry. My own poetry is what it is by virtue of who I am and my own particular take on the world. I try to read widely. I try to have a very catholic sense of poetic possibilities. I had my eyes opened a few years ago when I did a hitch as poetry editor for *College English* and read thousands of poems and accepted poems that I never would have imagined writing myself. I became aware of the range of valid poetic expression. I tried to accommodate that range within the few pages that I had each issue. I tried to get in variety and different poetic strategies.

AC • It is clear from *What Really Matters* that the craft of the wily peasant is present, but there is also the high as well. Poetry is compared with a "gilt-hilted sword" (31) and, contrarily, with fox tongs (32). Do these two analogies represent the poles of poetry for you: Heroic and aristocratic, on the one hand, and the wily peasant's craft, on the other?

TOG • As high as poetry may be, it should not be foreign to the "low audience" or to the audience accustomed to low culture.

AC • In "Whoso Pulleth Out This Sword" (31), the poem is found in the "stone-strewn field," and the question is: Who is able to pull the sword of the poem out of that field? There's a notion there of what poetry is.

TOG • Many people would know that story of the sword in the stone and would be able to respond to it. If that poem were seen as a stand-alone lyric, it could be seen as an egotistical, vain expression as if I were the Arthur who is going to come and do that, but the poem stops short of saying that I'm going to do that. Actually, when I was writing that poem, I was thinking of the absence of poetic culture on the Island. I end my Acorn essay, "Advice from Milton Acorn," with a glance at Yeats' "Under Ben Bulben," where Irish poets learn their trade by singing whatever is well made. This poem is saying to Island poets – but also to myself – There's something in the air, but we have to grasp it. We all have to be Arthurs, in a sense. We have to be bold enough and innocent enough to do that.

AC • But can we all be Arthurs? In the story, only one person can pull the sword from the stone. It resists everyone else. I'm not suggesting there is only one poet – God forbid that there is only one poet – but surely there is not an endless number of poets?

TOG • But maybe everybody needs to try it within their own narrative. Not everybody, but anyone who has the impulse, as I did myself, five years ago, when I said to myself, *I want to see if I can become a poet.* The writing I had done up until that point did not allow me to say it, but I can say it now. I wanted to know if this desire to create something that was beautiful, and beautiful in a performative way, would work. Would people read the poems and be enriched by them? I had to see if I could pull out that sword.

AC • Earlier you referred to your delight in sound linkages. In the Grappelli poem, the jazz artist's improvisations become "rapelling" (60). Is it sound linkages, rather than narrative or theme, that carries a poem forward in terms of its development?

TOG • Yes. One word leads to another. I don't know if I've ever had a sense of exactly what I was going to do in a poem. Poems are very much acts of discovery for me. I can predict the area that I'm going to land in, but not the spot that I'm going to land on. It's really a matter of following the impulse established in the first line of a poem. For me, the first line of a poem is really crucial. The last line of the Grappelli poem is from an interview that Grappelli did with *The New Yorker* in the 1970s. I actually read it back then, in the UPEI library, and although I didn't retain that line, I retained something else that is so crucial for my poetry. The interviewer asks Grappelli about improvising on the violin, and Grappelli cites the advice given him by a French cabaret singer: *You must start well and you must end well* (Bailliet 214). Nobody is listening in between. Starting well and ending well are important for me. I have a pronounced attraction to the closure of poems.

AC • "[D]oubly crossing // syllables" (80) seems to me a crucial concept in *What Really Matters*. Would you say something about that concept?

TOG • That phrase works in "As in Wild Earth a Grecian Vase" (78-80) on the literal level with the word *streelish*. The phrase actually went from

Ireland to PEI and then my mother wrote it in a letter to me when I was in Ireland. But "doubly crossing // syllables" can also describe a linguistic and a poetic heritage. There's a poem that I didn't include in the book that is a translation, or version of, a poem by a poet named Dáibhí Ó Bruadair, which is my mother's name, anglicized as "Brother." Working with dictionaries, with other translations, I have done a few translations of Ó Bruadair. I've tested them against Irish poets and they have worked. In the first of those, which *The Fiddlehead* published, the phrase was "*cairt chluana*," and the translation as it existed at the beginning of the 20th century was "beguiling verses," but when I translated it, I used "verses tickling her fancy." That was "doubly // crossing syllables" for me. Whenever I'm at a dry spell, I'll try to do a little bit of translation, and work with the Irish language. When I detach myself from my own use of words and look at someone else's, trying to recover them, it opens up a "wordhoard," to cite Heaney's *Beowulf*. "[D]oubly crossing // syllables" acknowledges for me the linguistic subtlety that, on some level, I grew up with. If you look at Terry Pratt's *Dictionary of Island English*, you'll find *streelish* there.

AC • But in Pratt's dictionary *streelish* means "sluttish," a sluttish woman.

TOG • *Straoille* means a "hag" or a "slattern." That was the original meaning, but my mother was using it to mean "unkempt." That's how it was handed down in my family.

AC • Words come from Ireland, land on the Island, pick up something Island, and go back to Ireland. "[D]oubly crossing // syllables" – that's the poetry that you write.

WORKS CITED

— • —

Aristotle. "Poetics." *Critical Theory Since Plato*. Ed. Hazard Adams. New York: Harcourt Brace Jovanovich, 1971. 48-66.

Arnold, Matthew. "Stanzas from the Grande Chartreuse." *Poetry and Criticism of Matthew Arnold*. Ed. A. Dwight Culler. Boston: Houghton Mifflin, 1962. 185-90.

Balliet, Whitney. "You Must Start Well and You Must End Well." Interview with Stéphane Grappelli. *American Musicians: 56 Portraits in Jazz*. New York: Oxford UP, 1986. 209-16.

Carleton, William. "The Fair of Emyvale." *Illustrated London Magazine* I (1853): 17-21, 57-66, 101-07.

– – – . *Traits and Stories of the Irish Peasantry*. 1830, 1833. Ed. D.J. O'Donoghue. 2 vols. London: J.M. Dent, 1896.

Emerson, Ralph Waldo. *Journals of Ralph Waldo Emerson*. 10 vols. Boston & New York: Houghton Mifflin, 1912. Vol. 7.

Fussell, Paul. *Poetic Meter and Poetic Form*. New York: Random House, 1967.

Frost, Robert. "The Constant Symbol." *Atlantic Monthly* 178 (October 1946): 51.

Heaney, Seamus. "Feeling into Words." *Preoccupations: Selected Prose 1968-1978*. New York: Farrar, Straus and Giroux, 1980. 41-60.

– – –. "Making Strange." *Opened Ground, Poems 1966-1996*. London: Faber and Faber, 1998.

– – –. "The Placeless Heaven: Another Look at Kavanagh"; "The Poems of the Dispossessed Repossessed." *The Government of the Tongue: The 1986 T.S. Eliot Memorial Lectures and Other Critical Writings*. London: Faber and Faber, 1988. 3-14; 30-35.

Hopkins, Gerard Manley. *Poems and Prose*. Ed. W.H. Gardner. Harmondsworth, Eng.: Penguin, 1963.

Hughes, Langston. "The Weary Blues." *Norton Anthology of Poetry*. 3rd. ed. Ed. Alexander W. Allison et al. New York: W.W. Norton, 1983. 1067.

Joyce, James. *Selected Letters*. Ed. Richard Ellmann. New York: Viking P, 1975.

Kavanagh, Patrick. "The Hospital." *The Complete Poems*. Newbridge: Goldsmith P, 1984. 279-80.

Ó Bruadair, Dáibhí. *Duanaire Dháibhidh Uí Bhruadair/The Poems of David Ó Bruadair*. Ed. and trans. John C. MacErlean, S.J. 3 vols. London: Irish Texts Society, 1910, 1913, 1917.

O'Grady, Thomas. "Advice from Milton Acorn." *Canadian Literature* 155 (Winter 1997): 139-153.

– – –. "Land and Sea." *Poem* 73 (May 1995): 22.

– – –. "Weights and Measures." *New Quarterly* 19.4 (Winter 2000): 11-20.

– – –. *What Really Matters*. Montreal & Kingston: McGill-Queen's UP, 2000.

– – –. "William Carleton's 'The Fair of Emyvale.'" *Abegweit Review* 5.1 (Winter 1985): 33-45.

Pratt, T.K. *Dictionary of Prince Edward Island English*. Toronto: U of Toronto P, 1988.

Tranströmer, Tomas. *New Collected Poems*. Trans. Robin Fulton. Newcastle upon Tyne: Bloodaxe P, 1997.

Yeats, W.B. *Collected Poems*. London: Macmillan, 1950.

"THE THEATRE OF THE BODY":
EXTREME STATES IN ELISABETH HARVOR'S POETRY

Elisabeth Harvor, who was honoured in 2000 with the Alden Nowlan Award for outstanding achievement in literature, grew up on the Kingston Peninsula in the Kennebecasis Valley of southwest New Brunswick. Her parents, Erica and Kjeld Deichmann, operated a pottery studio on the peninsula. After attending high school in Saint John, she studied nursing for two years. She now lives in Ottawa. Her first collection of short stories, *Women and Children* (1973), was later revised as *Our Lady of All the Distances*. Two more collections – *If Only We Could Drive Like This Forever* (1988) and *Let Me Be the One* (1996) – followed. *Let Me Be the One* was a finalist for the Governor General's Award for fiction. Harvor published her first novel, the critically acclaimed *Excessive Joy Injures the Heart*, in 2000. Her first collection of poetry, *Fortress of Chairs* (1992), won the Gerald Lampert Award, and her second, *The Long Cold Green Evenings of Spring* (1997), was shortlisted for the Pat Lowther Award. *All times have been modern,* Harvor's second novel, appeared in 2004.

Returning to the Kennebecasis Valley for a writers' workshop in May 2001, Harvor talked with me about the poetry that has won her the Confederation Poets' Prize, First Prize in The League of Canadian Poets' National Poetry Competition, the *Malahat* Long Poem Prize, and a National Magazine Award for poetry. The interview took place on the south shore of the Kennebecasis River, three miles, as the crow flies, from Harvor's childhood home.

AC • Both books of poetry use free verse in variable-length paragraphs. What does this form enable you to do?

EH • It wouldn't occur to me to write in any other way. I don't care to be confined. Although, in my experience as a teacher, I've found that if I give students restrictions, they will often respond with free writing that explodes into forgotten memories, emotions, and images that will surprise even them with its vitality or hilarity. Or terror. I have memories of writing certain poems. I certainly have a memory of writing "Afterbirth," the first poem in *Fortress of Chairs* (9-21). I had been reading a poem by Sharon Thesen in which she talks about tall blue glasses and music. It reminded me of the tall blue glasses from Mexico that my parents had. I started with that. And then it just became a series of freewheeling memories from childhood. At the same time, I was finding earlier notes and plundering other earlier things, poetry or fiction, that hadn't worked. I was writing with a deliberate deadline in mind because, at the last minute, I had decided that I was going to send the poem to the *Malahat* long poem contest. I stayed up all one night working on it and sent off what I knew was a flawed version by Express Post, but I kept on working on it. I rushed down to Britnell's bookshop and got Sharon Olds' *The Gold Cell*. Her poetry triggers me because she is so unambiguous. She is so much of a force. I thought, "I have to read Sharon Olds." I have to move close to that clinical fire to make sure that I pull everything that I can out of me for this poem. I wrote all that next night in a very strange fugue state. Then I sent a second version off to *Malahat*, thinking that if I had made the deadline with the first version, they would accept the second, which they did.

AC • You are describing the way in which other people's writing, in this case Olds', can be a stimulus for your own.

EH • As a writer, I am drawn to that kind of staccato authority. I had a feeling that I could get something from this. I could inhale something, and it wouldn't be *like* hers, but it would be triggered by her. Having said that, though, I should also say that she is a writer I'm not entirely drawn to. She doesn't have enough ambiguity for me. Her work doesn't have enough of an afterlife. She's all there on the first take. You don't need to go back. She's too grandstanding, boastful, harsh, and has too microscopic an eye. At the same time, I'm very grateful to her, and find her powerful and stunningly refreshing. She affects me very differently from [Sylvia] Plath, say, a poet I can go back to time and again. Plath is an absolutely primal force too, of course, but there's more invention in her work. There's greater metaphorical dazzle. There are greater leaps but, at the same time, there's somehow more room in the poem for the reader to do some of the work with her.

AC • Your flexible free verse allows for unpredictable developments, for surprise, and for lyrical associations between discrete moments. Do you think of yourself as a lyric poet or a narrative poet?

EH • Somewhere in between, I would say. Sometimes people say, "Your work is prosy," but I can think of any number of poets who are much more prosy than I am, whose language is not lyrical.

AC • There is a strong formalist tradition in the Maritimes. You are unique in that your poetry is such a pure form of free verse. I've never seen a sestina or sonnet by you. Or a villanelle.

EH • I've never tried to write one, although I know it could be intriguing – to see how I would fight my way around that limitation. But for me, form – being hemmed in that way – is not a liberation. Poets whose work I admire greatly have all done these things. I've never done any of that. I've never counted syllables. I have no idea about beats and so on, and when I read about other poets who work in iambic pentameter, I think, "No, I don't want to know." I just want the poem to be however it is, and I'll just take a look at it and sound it out.

AC • This is a poetry that takes its time. In one poem, the speaker says, "You need time for that, that kind of linkage / memory begetting memory / as water begat water" (28). Do these lines describe how a poem unfolds for you?

EH • Those lines would certainly describe the leisurely but eerie "Afterbirth" (9-21), but there are many shorter poems that feel condensed, at least to me – poems in *Long Cold Green Evenings* like "Snow and the End of Childhood" (29), "Her Children or God" (34-35), and "Snazzy Night" (43-44). Or even "Letter to a Younger Man in Another Country" in *Fortress* (69). Or a compact little poem like "This Is Our Life," which hasn't been collected in either of my books, and which is so short that I can actually recite it for you:

> This is our life,
> carnival on quicksand,
> house of balconies, wild flowers,
> trap doors, windmill and potter's
> wheel, kiln pit, lightning rods,
> staggered views of the river,

little steps up and down, crazy
quilts on the beds, upstairs
part of the house airy, unfinished,
life-sized hands our father carved
screwed into the ceilings to hold
lanterns, lantern light seasick
in storms or when someone
(in a rage) slams the door.

That ends more with a bang than a whimper. And also supplies at least some evidence that my aim, or one of my aims, is to write poems that are shorter and swifter. But it's also toppled in on itself because it refers to the surreal within the real. There was really so much daily dark and bright magic in that house.

AC • You mean in your childhood home?

EH • When my father was "throwing" a pot on the potter's wheel, for instance, I'd stand and watch him, mesmerized. The metamorphosis of each individual ball didn't even seem repetitive to me; it was always the same but always thrilling: Whirling from a hive to a hive with a nipple on top of it; from a breast to a thick-walled well; from a thick-walled well to a fast-spinning hollow tower; from a slower spinning hollow tower to a jug whose spout was made by a quick pinch of the wet clay. Actually, the lines that I've just spoken are the lines of a poem called something like "Our Father, Throwing a Pot" that appeared in *The Fiddlehead* in the spring of 1995, I think, along with some other pottery poems gathered under the title "Glassy Archives of a River."

AC • You haven't lived in New Brunswick since you were 21, yet the Kingston Peninsula and the city of Saint John generate some of your most powerful poems. What hold does this landscape exert over you?

EH • The landscape of the Kingston Peninsula, in particular, has a great hold over me because we were so very isolated there in the winters. We were isolated both physically and psychically from our neighbours. In summer, when there was a lot of foliage, we couldn't even *see* any of our neighbours. We were the only immigrant family in a settlement of Scots and Irish descendents. There was all that immigrant pressure: Our mother was forever giving us the impression that we must do better than everyone, that we must out-Canadian the Canadians, be more amazing at school, more amazing at everything. And although I can't remember any of these things being specifically said, we felt them. The feminine quality of the landscape, though, its rolling hills, must have had some maternal reassurance for me. I was really in love with that landscape. I haven't been able to go back. I lived in Fredericton in 1994-95 and had many chances to go down to the peninsula, but I'd heard that it had changed a great deal, and I couldn't go back. I think I want not to go back. I think too, my feeling for the landscape is tied up with a certain feeling of abandonment. I can remember standing on the beach, as a very small child, and watching my parents go out in the canoe, going around Black Rock so that they disappeared. I must have believed that they would be gone forever. In the winters, they would sometimes walk to Saint John by crossing the frozen river. Once, when I was still small, my brother followed our parents across the ice and got lost. The farm girl who looked after us organized a search party to go out on the ice to look for him. His tracks went as far as the crack in the ice that widened where the Bay of Fundy sends its salty tides up the river. It was assumed at first that he had drowned. But he was found alive. I remember my mother telling me all of this years later, and I cried so violently that she had to keep telling me, "But you see, it's all right. We found him," but I couldn't be consoled by this. Any indication that we hadn't been properly looked after got me very upset.

AC • If you felt that you weren't being properly taken care of and were worried for your safety, was the landscape the safe place?

EH • I think the safety of the landscape was maternal, but it also had to do with my father, who was a very kind person, a stable person. The landscape and my father were the couple. My mother was this volatile lizard or cyclone.

AC • In the poems, memory seems to blow a wintry chill on the present.

EH • When I was living in Fredericton and was driving around looking at the miles and miles of dark spruce trees, I just wanted to cry. Something about New Brunswick makes me want to cry.

AC • Is it the look of the place?

EH • It's the history of the place. There's a lot of open country on the Kingston Peninsula, and we owned a huge tract of land, but most of it was wooded. There was also a great bluff behind our house on the peninsula, with a small cedar forest leading into it, and I associate those cedar trees with a definite melancholy. The feelings also relate to the time of my being Writer-in-Residence at the University of New Brunswick, and so they have some emotional connection to the area around Fredericton, the sad tracts of trees, fir and spruce, the endless miles of dark trees. But I think it was the more public history of the place too, and this is especially true of Fredericton – the massacres on both the Indian and settler sides, the terrible winters, and the famines.

AC • Is it fair to say that this area – the Kingston Peninsula and the Kennebecasis River – is the psychological underground of your writing?

EH • Because I am no longer a child or an adolescent, no landscape, in the present or future, will affect me in the same way. A lot of the adolescent feelings about sexuality, or safety, might have been landscape connected. Romantic ideas about the future occurred while I was walking in the country. I remember coming home, so tired, as a student nurse, dragging a mattress out into the orchard, falling asleep there with apple blossoms falling all around me. I often dream now of living in the country and, yet I don't think I would like it day to day. I don't even think of the country as a safe place anymore. It's become a sinister place since Truman Capote's *In Cold Blood*. Movies like *Easy Rider,* and its descendents, have certainly helped to demystify the romance and safety of the country.

AC • The Maritime landscape is present to a greater degree in your poetry than in your fiction. Why is that?

EH • Partly because poetry – even my poetry – doesn't require characters, although there are many poems about women and landscape, or women *in* the landscape, come to think of it. And then the ability of landscape to offer up images is so much more useful to a poem, and can even be the life of the poem, whereas imagery and scenery can sometimes get in the way of the narrative in a story.

AC • "Memories ... might point the way / to this childhood, that childhood" (19). Does that mean that there are any number of versions of the past?

EH • Not really. I think I know about the past. I'm arrogant about what I remember, just as, I suppose, most people are, thinking that they remember everything exactly as it was. That line might be an instance where I am acknowledging the current thinking that there are many moods, many memories – that we might look at something one way

ANNE COMPTON

and then differently another day, or look at it through a politically conscious lens and see it differently. And yet I haven't revised my memories. You know how they say that when a parent dies, you revise your thinking about that parent. I haven't found that to be true. I didn't think differently about my father after he died. And if I survive my mother, I don't suppose I will think differently about her. She won't be established as a much finer or sweeter person. I have never doubted my memories or their veracity.

AC • Your writing comes out of a body of memories that you have about your personal past?

EH • Often. Although more often out of the marriage between the invented and the real. If I need to invent, I invent. Although, as most writers know, invention has a habit of becoming prescient in quite spooky ways. There's always a danger it can make you feel too much like God. But then life also has its habits, above all its notorious habit of upstaging art.

AC • Poems in *Fortress* include subjects such as periods (85-87), placenta (13), and giving birth. Are you insisting upon the connection between women's bodies and women's sensibility?

EH • Certainly not consciously, but I suppose I must always have been fascinated by the body, by illness, by theatrical life experiences that involve the body, like the woman giving birth out on the Kennebecasis River ("Afterbirth," *Fortress* 9-21). Living in the country, one was just more exposed to the theatre of the body.

AC • Not just the marvellous women of "Afterbirth," but many of the women – the women going down to the river to bathe in the poem "The Damp Hips of the Women" (*Long Cold Green Evenings* 14-16) – seem to have mythic stature. For you, is there in ordinary women a mythic quality?

EH • My mother was a great one for women friends. She made much of them, and they made much of her. My mother was the one who did things that were festive with her friends. While my father would be home working, or putting us to bed or cooking supper, my mother would be down on the beach with her friends or going off on little jaunts, or playing a trick with her friends on some other group of women. She was quite girlish with her friends. So in a way I saw them as girls together but, at the same time, as goddesses. They were the ones who called the shots, and my father was just there as background. That was not my view of him, of course. But it was their view.

AC • There is also a painterly quality to those images of women, those gorgeous, full-bodied creatures. "Down There" (*Fortress* 27-28) is reminiscent of Edgar Degas' paintings of women bathing. Do paintings lurk in the background of your poems? I know that Jack Humphrey, Miller Brittain, and all those Saint John painters were a part of your past.

EH • Of all those painters, I think the one that I admire most is Pegi MacLeod. And perhaps also Jack Humphrey. I can see that Miller Brittain was a great painter, but I wasn't drawn to his paintings so much. But I haven't visited galleries or done that sort of thing for years. Memories of paintings are very important to me. They are tied up with certain emotional times in my life.

AC • The poems of *Fortress* are full of decaying light (12), "decayed aroma" (25). The word "decay" recurs in *Long Cold Green Evenings* – "the air smelling of decay" (14) – and in your novel *Excessive Joy,* there's "decayed sexual heat" (20). In a *New Brunswick Reader* article, you speak of the "East Coast's fog and decay"(9). Did that attunement to decay begin back here?

EH • In a sense, that is my past and my childhood, though I hadn't realized that I was so fond of the word. I wonder if it has to do with the house that we lived in on the Kingston Peninsula before we moved down to the pottery. It was a very old farmhouse, very mouldy, very dark. There was a special smell in that basement. And as children we were always afraid to go down there. There was sand on the floor and a little stream bubbled up through it. It was like a landscape down there because of that stream. And there was an icehouse where a truck would come, every two weeks, with a huge block of ice wrapped in canvas. The iceblock on the sawdust floor smelled of decay. In the orchard, the apples would fall and decay, so there was a lovely smell of apple decay.

AC • You make poetry out of the intimate details of a life – the loves and hates between parents and children, the delight and terror of motherhood, the coming apart of marriage, and the terror of old age. Does the human heart in its entanglements accurately describe your material?

EH • I would say so.

AC • Few people write poems about children. The emotion so easily goes sentimental. The third section of *Fortress* contains poems on early motherhood and babies. Were these difficult to write?

EH • Slipping into sentimentality was a worry. When I sold "At the Horse Pavilion" to *The Malahat Review*, they wanted to cut the last line, "Until this moment I never knew what love is" (66). They wanted the poem to end earlier. I didn't agree with that, but I said, "Oh, all right," and then whenever I read the poem at readings, I would find myself putting the line back in. Their argument against the line was that it was already implied in the poem. When I was putting the book together, I put the line back in.

AC • Does that last line of "Horse Pavilion" put maternal love beyond every other kind?

EH • On some level, it's stronger, more primal. In the lover, there is always something of the father and something of the son, but women are so wired to protect their children when they are small, it makes that love very powerful. Any other love that you are fortunate enough, or unlucky enough, to experience is a frill. For people who have not had children, some of that primal love probably goes into the relationship with lovers.

AC • There is a lifetime in *Fortress* from the childhood of "Afterbirth" to the questions of "Bloom, Rain" – "How do we do it? / Learn how to be old?" (85). Did you set out to chronicle a lifetime in this first collection?

EH • No, I didn't. I wasn't thinking of that trajectory. When Michael Harris and I finally put the poems together, we did think, however, of that order. "Bloom, Rain" has a very intriguing history in relation to two other poems. I'd read Don Coles' poem "Self-Portrait of the Artist at 3 a.m." in his book about Edvard Munch. Munch is looking in a mirror and thinking about how old he is. The lines "How do we do it? / Learn to be old?" then came to me. That's what I began with. My poem then becomes very involved with rain. Barb Carey, another poet friend, wrote a poem called "Wire Kiss" about a teenage girl. There's something rain-saturated in her poem, which was affected by "Bloom, Rain." So through that cross-pollination of poems, we went from a very old man looking in the mirror, to a middle-aged woman thinking about getting old and being afraid of it, to a very young girl.

AC • There are four kinds of light in *Fortress*: The natural light of child-hood, the overly bright light of the hospital poems (Part 2), the watery light of the motherhood poems (Part 3), and the rainy darkness of age and the single life in the final section. Is light for you the register of emotional and mental states?

EH • Often. And some of the women-living-alone poems are filled with a kind of surreal or even cruel light. I'm thinking of poems like "In the Cold Sunlight" (66-68) and "Love After a Long Absence (of Love)" (108-10) in *Long Cold Green Evenings*.

AC • In *Long Cold Green Evenings*, in one poem alone, there is a "light-pricked / heaped twilight" and "light-flocked dimness" (92, 93).

EH • Light can symbolize so many emotions. Not only for poets and painters, but also for story-writers: Loss, hope, melancholy, regret, the understanding that we are going to die. But the tiny bits of light, the light-on-the-move in "light-pricked … twilight" and "light-flocked dimness" seem more philosophically energetic and buoyant, at least to me, and perhaps take a happier view of mortality.

AC • Your fiction favours the sensation of smell; light is favoured in the poetry. Is that so?

EH • I think smells do belong much more in prose. They don't seem as connected with clarity as light does. They seem more ordinary, more connected with the body.

AC • In your novel, *Excessive Joy*, Claire thinks, "there was some boundary of risk or tenderness you crossed if you were a lover ..." (207). As a writer, are you interested in extreme emotional states?

EH • Yes, I am. But also in the subtleties and complexities of ambivalent states. Ambivalence in all its forms, really.

AC • For me, your short stories are not as thematic – tyranny of mothers, internecine family warfare – as reviewers have suggested. Rather, they are glimpses into how the mind works: Registering the present, remembering the past, sifting information. Would you say that the mind and how it works is a subject?

EH • Yes. And the heart, too, and how it's connected to the mind. Or disconnected from the mind, as the case may be. A writer named Heidi Greco got this right when she reviewed *Let Me Be the One* for *Paragraph* and described the style of the book as "akin to synapses firing in the brain" and talked about the way the stories were "jolts of energy linking cliff to cliff, idea to idea" (35). As a writer who's a constant reader, I would have to say the mind is what I look for when I'm a reader, the mind and the heart, much more than I look for the architecture of plot. I read to meet the personality and soul of the writer. But as a fiction writer, I have to remember that plot is the bait, the device I have to use to get the reader, or at least some readers, to even want to encounter the heart and mind of the writer.

AC • You said in an interview, "An obsessive is an aristocrat of feelings" (Ross D20). I would have said "the drudge."

EH • It's only in her, or his, own delirious world view that the obsessive is an aristocrat of feelings. She sees the love object as unique, absolutely irreplaceable. She sees him not only as the only one, but also as the only one for all time. And so she inevitably sees herself as bathed in his shine. Whereas the much more objective outsider sees her as being *embalmed* in his shine, sees her as being dulled by it, sees her being made less than she is. Sees her as having such extreme tunnel vision that she's turned into, as you put it, a drudge.

AC • Although *Long Cold Green Evenings* continues the variable free-verse paragraph of *Fortress*, it favours a shorter, terser line. Would you say that the second collection is more cryptic?

EH • When the second book came out, one of my students asked, "Where are your long lines? I think of you as a long-lined poet," but I didn't want them. It was actually a technical decision. Some of those poems in *Long Cold Green Evenings* pre-date the *Fortress* poems.

AC • I could see that. In fact, I wanted to ask you if *Long Cold Green Evenings* was the underlay of *Fortress*?

EH • About half of this book coexisted with *Fortress*. *Long Cold Green Evenings* was about to be published by Coach House Press when Coach House collapsed. It was about a month away from being published. Then I took it to Signal Editions. This accounts for the very strange acknowledgment at the beginning of the book in which I thank Michael Harris "who (along with Simon Dardick) generously made room on the Signal Editions list for this book." Originally that sentence continued, "after the fall of Coach House Press," showing why it was generous of them to take the book at the last minute. Simon Dardick wanted me to take that phrase out because by that time Coach House had re-invented itself. Now it sounds very strange. It sounds as if I went pleadingly to them to make room. I regret that I allowed the wording to stay that way because it sounds like the poor little writer had no self-esteem and they generously made room. I'd love to get that misconception corrected.

AC   • "Snow and the End of Childhood" (29) is a poem that moves away from the usual narrative technique for enigmatic suggestiveness. Would you say that is a shift that characterizes this second collection as a whole?

EH   • That's an apt description for some of the poems in the second book. That particular poem ends with a metaphor. On the whole, I would say the poems in the second book are more suggestive and metaphorical. The second book might be a little higher and cleaner and colder than the first. Perhaps there are more ideas in it.

AC   • "Snow and Moon River" (30-33) opens with an image of snow falling on a glassed-in swimming pool; the pool and its swimmers are seen from nine storeys above. Is there increased attention in this second collection to bizarre perceptual experiences?

EH   • Yes. I have a fondness for bizarre perceptual experiences, for the dream-like or nightmare-like way that seeing something from a shocking or disrupting angle jolts you into thinking in new ways.

AC   • Dream is a "dressmaker ... cut[ting] and stitch[ing] our history" (67-68). Is poetry also a "dressmaker"?

EH   • What an intriguing idea. Yes, I think so.

AC   • In *Long Cold Green Evenings*, the river landscape seems ominous in a way that it wasn't in *Fortress*: "smaller [islands] / frightened groves / of trees // riding / the darkening water" (48-49). Is there more threat in *Long Cold Green Evenings*?

EH   • The landscape is standing in for time and life. I definitely think that *Fortress* is a younger book. It's probably a more hopeful, buoyant book. *Long Cold Green Evenings* is a more darkly realistic book.

AC   • Snow, which was benign or indifferent in *Fortress*, is quite sinister in *Long Cold Green Evenings*.

EH • I wouldn't say sinister: "Snow falls on snow, / snow falls on the swimmers ... / like a thoughtless promise from God / that can never be broken" (30-31). I think I see snow as very beautiful even though I don't like it. But I think you are right. In "Snow and the End of Childhood," its appeal weakens: "We sink up to our knees / in its cold fluff // and deeper // until we're / stopped short by it // and there's nothing to do / but fall face-down on it with a // sapped joy that feels sexual" (29). Snow has the power to slow you down, to stop you, to still you. It makes you feel tired. There's that brilliant line in Sylvia Plath's "Tulips": "Look how white everything is, how quiet, how snowed-in" (600). That part of the Plath poem makes me feel very tired. This is what I remember about growing up so isolated at the pottery in the winter. Just the five of us, these five unhappy people, with our mother reproaching our father about so many things. Not having any real friends in the community. Not having any grandparents or cousins. Not having anyone on this continent who would intercede for us. That feeling of being snowed-in is so claustrophobic for me.

AC • Snow creates an asylum, which can be either refuge or prison.

EH • Yes. And for us it was a prison.

AC • Would you say that the potential for violence is also present in the second book?

EH • I think the second book is less tender. I think there is no question: Violence could happen to the narrator in this book.

AC • *Fortress* has a time line – from childhood to the anticipation of old age. You said the collection turned out that way although it didn't start that way. What organizes *Long Cold Green Evenings*?

EH • *Long Cold Green Evenings* has more of a theme line.

AC • "The Damp Hips of the Women" (14-16) seems to me to be a love poem to the women of the 1940s. For all the gains that women have made, have certain womanly qualities been lost?

EH • To me, it doesn't really seem that way. It's *plus ça change* .... That scene could happen again another time in the future. After all, women in the 1930s – with their fedoras and their trousers, and their jobs, their smoking and their very free sex lives and so on – were quite mannish in a lot of ways. The war was very sexual, I think, in the way women felt about themselves with all those men around. And then after that, we came into a period of such prim abstinence. The 1960s was a blossoming out again in a rather pagan way. Certainly people now can talk about everything more freely, but in losing the innocence of sex, we've also lost some of the private excitement of sex. We lost so much of the privacy and mystery of it.

AC • "We Have Four Husbands" (17-22) is the poem in this collection most like a short story. When material presents itself, do you always know whether it will be a short story or a poem?

EH • I do, but I don't know how I know. I have a poem that I've written recently that begins: "Pure liquid and twist of birdsong at one a.m." I can't imagine these lines being the lines of a story. A poem begins for me with a line or a few lines, and they are not lines that I would use in a story.

AC • Is the key language?

EH • Language, not ideas. When I'm thinking about a story, I'm thinking of all sorts of character-based things, which you really couldn't do in a poem. Occasionally – for example, in the story "Through the Fields of Tall Grasses" (*Let Me Be the One* 142-76) – the ending is made from a plundered poem. The poem called "I Don't Ask For Real Happiness" was about a teenaged girl trying on the evening dresses of an older girl while she lives in a doctor's house. When my editor at HarperCollins wanted me to extend the ending of the story, I went back to the poem, which had been published in *Pottersfield Portfolio*, but had not been collected in a book.

AC • It is language, then, that determines the genre because the material could be either story or poem?

EH • Yes, almost always. And, in fact, the reason I could get away with an intensely poetic ending in that story is because the epiphany of that particular story allows for a more lyrical, staccato, forceful, dramatic use of language.

AC • Are you suggesting that a short story comes round to poetry in its ending?

EH • I think so. The final few lines or final few scenes can have that metaphorical intensity.

AC • Occasionally there is a honky-tonk feeling to this language, as in, for example, "You could fill a stadium / with the hearts you have broken ..." (69).

EH • I can see that it has a real twang to it now that you've pointed it out. And I am a country-and-western fan of the best country songs, partly because the best country songs – and also the worst country songs – are willing to go all the way into emotion. But I also like the more ironical and witty songs, the ones that are on the point of crossing over from country to folk. There's also a honky-tonk feel to "How Long Will It Last" (*Fortress* 78-80), a poem where the narrator is in love with a younger man. The narrator, after trying not to hear the "honky-tonk of the car horns" (79) at his imagined wedding, also tries not to hear him stamping the snow off his boots "outside the door / of someone younger" (79).

AC • *Fortress* undertakes the challenge of expressing maternal attachment. *Long Cold Green Evenings* explores the equally difficult material associated with aging – senility, abandonment, and loneliness – as figured, for example, in the old woman in "Snow and Moon River" (30-33). Is this the figure the persona fears becoming?

EH • Yes, but I imagine all women would fear becoming her. The old woman is like a spectre, but a sweet, addled spectre.

AC • There is a fear of lethargy and immobilization in "Snow and Moon River" (30-33). Is that something you personally fear?

EH • Being out of control and helpless, yes, I fear that.

AC • In "Cold Day in August," the speaker, while taking a drive with her sister, recalls how her mother used to sunbathe on the roof of the house. She says, "there were no / scraps of leftover light / for her two daughters" (37). This is redolent of folk or fairy tale with light substituted for food. Were you consciously working with fairy tale in this poem?

EH • On some level, I think that I was because there is something in that poem about the dark knitting: "all around us the bay's / broken bracelet of islands // their steep walls / of trees // knitted into / a sketched darkness / by someone who must have / kept whispering, You will / learn nothing here, there isn't / even the relief of a meadow..." (37).

AC • There's something else that's fairy tale or folk story in that poem. The woman is on the roof sunning while the men, with their horses and sleighs, are coming down over the snow-coated hills. The sleigh bells are jingling.

EH • And yet it is absolutely based on reality. It is interesting in terms of the seasons – the fact that it could be so hot on the roof while, at the same time, the men are travelling on snow. My father made my mother this little pen for sunning up on the roof. She was an exhibitionist about her body, but I still don't know if she was aware that those men coming down over the bluff could see her down there, totally naked, in that little pen.

AC • In "Cold Day in August," the "broken bracelet of islands" seems to say to the speaker who is crossing the Kennebecasis River, "You will learn nothing here ..." (37). Has the landscape become inarticulate to the returning Maritimer of this poem?

EH • I don't think there was anything as conscious as that. I think the poem refers more to questions about the mother and her superficial sexuality, which was not experienced as a deep womanly sexuality, but as a teasing – a jingling, high-jostling flirty kind of teasing. The two daughters, in the present, seem to be in a state of paralysed resentment. There is something dead in them relating back to the mother.

AC • They seem to find talking about the past erotic.

EH • It's an opening out. It's a release.

AC • Is there less effort in *Long Cold Green Evenings* to distance the speaker from the author?

EH • No. I don't think so. I mean, I don't think there was ever much of an effort to distance the speaker from the author.

AC • Do you expect your readers to identify the speaker with the author.

EH • I think that they probably will most of the time anyway. I think you could say about a poem like "My Mother, My Scalp" (*Fortress* 25-26), I don't give a damn if my mother, or my enemy, reads it.

AC • Was "Snazzy Night" (*Long Cold Green Evenings* 43-44) originally a part of the longer poem "Afterbirth" (*Fortress* 9-21)? Or is it just that the child's perception of adults in social interaction is a perspective of persistent interest to you?

EH • Yes, it is of persistent interest. "Snazzy Night" is also very much from the time of *Fortress,* although I don't think it was ever actually a part of "Afterbirth."

AC • But generated from the same memory?

EH • Yes, I would say so.

AC • "Snazzy Night" (43-44) returns to the party scene with which "Afterbirth" (*Fortress* 9-21) opens. Both of these poems are reminiscent of Virginia Woolf's *Mrs Dalloway.* Is Woolf a writer whom you admire?

EH • Yes, immensely. Not all of her books, but I very much admire *Mrs Dalloway* and *To the Lighthouse.* I've read *Moments of Being* and find it extraordinary.

AC • Why is the mother here so closely associated with light? Around her there are "no / scraps of leftover light" (37) and her laughter "scatters light" (44).

EH • When you're a child and even if you have a very bad relationship with a parent, you can't stand to see that parent humiliated. These children want to run to her and tell her the bad news – she's being mocked by the women at the party – to protect her, and they are stopped because they see her turn to laugh and the light scatters. It's a scattering of energy and they can't move toward her.

AC • Is there power in that scattering of the light?

EH • Yes, it backs them up into a corner.

AC • The mother is a taker of light?

EH • Yes, and the scattering of light means that she doesn't have to be warned. Adulthood isn't as dangerous as the children thought even though her friends are being catty about her.

AC • In "The Dark Clouds Between the Ribs" (54-60), the child-speaker says, "there isn't a word // in the world it isn't too late for" (54). Is the child's dilemma, thus expressed, also the poet's?

EH • God, I hope not.

AC • For the child-speaker returning home, after a stay in the doctor's house, home is "beloved, terrible" (59). Would that accurately describe your own adult return to your Maritime home?

EH • It accurately describes my adolescent returns to my home. We [my brother and I] were away for two years living with a doctor and his wife, though not all the time. In the fall and the spring, we were home because then we biked to the ferry and rode across the river, but in the winters we were in Saint John. And it applies to other times when I was away – at summer camp or when I was away living with the doctor's family when I was much smaller. Home always seemed both beloved and terrible to me. The "beloved" is my father. The "terrible" is my mother. The house itself, and the charming way it was arranged, and the landscape around it, were also beloved. At the same time, so many terrible things happened in the house – so many accusations, door slammings, temper tantrums, but at the same time these were set in a matrix of so many sing-songs and picnics and skinny-dips on starry nights.

AC • *Long Cold Green Evenings* follows the childhood physical illness poems with poems about being "lovesick." Is anything being suggested by this proximity?

EH • I don't think so. "One of the Lovesick Women of History" (69-72) is a fairly playful poem, followed by a more resentful poem, "In the Cold Sunlight" (66-69). "A Breast, Our Hearts" (69-72) is about mass infatuation. I wouldn't say that any of those poems are really anguished. "In the Dark" (88-91), which is in another section of the book, seems to me a much more anguished poem than those playful ones.

AC • For the "lovesick" speakers, being looked at is a great fear, but then not being looked at is equally scary.

EH • To paraphrase Oscar Wilde, the only thing worse than being looked at is not being looked at.

AC • One "lovesick" woman experiences the "fine old grand fear of falling," which is worth it, though, because that's "a small price to pay for being / given so much to hope for" (65). Hope and fear: Are these the aspects of love that interest you as a writer?

EH • They interest me as the trappings of love. Men who are charismatic and withholding become attractive to certain kinds of women because they provide both hope and fear. But the healthy thing is to hope to be close to someone. The woman in that poem is seduced by the trappings themselves, by the on-again, off-again, now-he-loves-me, now-he-doesn't, flirty feelings.

ANNE COMPTON

AC • Lovers and male doctors seem interchangeable in "A Breast, Our Hearts" (69-72). Your novel, *Excessive Joy,* is about a woman's obsession with her therapist. Why is the medical erotic?

EH • It's the power and mystery of it all. These men know something that could help you or save you and, therefore, they must be protective lovers. We meet them in a place that is supposed to be perfectly safe. So that if something is transgressed, there is the excitement of that. There are all those possibilities for transgression.

AC • Would you say that *Long Cold Green Evenings* is a more gothic book than *Fortress?* I'm thinking of "South of the Brain" (81-83) where a mother is studying a medical book with her sons and sees "my childhood making / a bow to your childhood / through the wet glass / and we all get afraid" (83).

EH • Not more gothic, exactly, but certainly spookier. Or, let's rephrase that. There's an increased awareness in *Long Cold Green Evenings* of how the darkest fairy tales still apply.

AC • Art gives "instruction through seduction" (17), you say in the introduction to *A Room at the Heart of Things.* What instruction does your poetry give?

EH • It might give instruction on how to cope with disappointment in love. If there is instruction, it is very deeply embedded in the poems. I would hate to think that I was writing poetry prescriptively. My poetry is not meant to be instruction to anyone, but if someone reads it and feels it emotionally and takes direction from it, I have no quarrel with that.

WORKS CITED

— • —

Greco, Heidi. Rev. of *Let Me Be the One,* by Elisabeth Harvor. Paragraph. (Summer 1997): 34-35.

Harvor, Elisabeth. *Excessive Joy Injures the Heart.* Toronto: McClelland & Stewart. 2000.

— — — . *Fortress of Chairs.* Montreal: Signal Editions, 1992.

— — — . "Hell, that's swell: A meditation on Saint John, art, war, emigration, and what makes us remember." *New Brunswick Reader* 23 May, 1998 6-13.

— — — . *If Only We Could Drive Like This Forever.* Toronto: Penguin, 1988.

— — — . *Let Me Be the One.* Toronto: HarperCollins, 1996.

— — — . *The Long Cold Green Evenings of Spring.* Montreal: Signal Editions, 1997.

– – – , ed. *A Room at the Heart of Things: The Work That Came To Me, An Anthology of New Writing*. Montreal: Véhicule P, 1998.

Plath, Sylvia. "Tulips." *The Norton Anthology of Modern and Contemporary Poetry*. Eds. Jahan Ramazani et al. 2 vols. 3rd. ed. New York: W.W. Norton, 2003. 600-01.

Ross, Cecily. "Interview: Recovering Obsessive." *Globe and Mail* 14 October, 2000. D20-D21.

ANNE COMPTON

UNDOING THE FIELD:
CONFLICT AND COMFORT IN BRENT MACLAINE'S ISLAND
POETRY

Brent MacLaine, the author of *Wind & Root* (2000), is a fifth-generation Islander. His great-great-grandfather, emigrating from Lochbuie, Isle of Mull, at the time of the clearances, settled at Rice Point, Prince Edward Island, where succeeding generations of the family have remained. The younger of two sons, MacLaine grew up on the family farm, a landscape of fields and hills, woods and marsh, and several miles of Northumberland Strait shoreline. Although visitors to the area like to suppose that Rice Point was named for a rice-laden cargo ship that went aground here, the fact is, Captain Samuel Holland, an 18th-century surveyor, named the point after an Englishman, one Colonel Rice.

On a hot June day, in 2002, I drove down the Rice Point Road to the MacLaine place, to MacLaine's new house, which is next door to the still-beautiful, but now vacant, homestead house. Just as the poems promised, it was all there: "red sandstone cliffs, a blinding bay /... waves welcoming the shore." In the cool of his kitchen – over tea and cookies and Rice Point pudding – we talked about the origin of his poetry in this place, his years of travel, his academic work, and the new manuscript, "Where the Branch Bends." A literary critic and an award-winning professor of English literature at UPEI, MacLaine is the co-editor of *Landmarks: An Anthology of New Atlantic Canadian Poetry of the Land*.

Two years after this interview "Where the Branch Bends," the manuscript discussed here, was published under the revised title *These Fields Were Rivers*.

AC • You grew up in the landscape where you now live. What does it mean to a writer to have a landscape?

BM • I have a very strong aesthetic response to landscape yet, in some ways, I'm conflicted in my response. I'm not a farmer, so I can't claim a farmer's rootedness, although as a child I did do farm work. I do have that background as a shadow, perhaps as a possibility, of a direction in which I could have gone. But I didn't enjoy farm work. Farming is awful work. I'm quite sure I would have been very ill-suited to it. My father was sensitive to the possibility that his sons would not be farmers, so when he had opportunities to buy land for his sons, he didn't. There was no particular push from him in that direction. So for me the response to landscape is visual and aesthetic. When I walk over these fields, go to the hilltop, I'm looking at proportions, the amount of sea to green land. I'm looking at colour. And what we have to realize is that this is a constructed landscape. It's not natural. This is a farmer's landscape. Environmentalists and biologists don't particularly like farmers because they denude the landscape. These beautiful green fields, these red fields and plowed fields, are unnatural but, at the same time, they create a beauty of visual contrasts.

AC • History has been written on the landscape.

BM • That's right, and all of that goes through my mind when I'm situated here, but this landscape is also associated with memory and childhood. When I look out of this window to my left, I know that is the wood where I used to go picking raspberries with my aunt, where I had my first bee sting. And a little further on, that's where the bait shed for the fishermen used to be. So all of those associations and memories are constantly available.

AC • A writer who lives in the landscape he experienced as a child is someone who lives in a memoried place.

BM • And yet I'm cautious about that. Perhaps I'm overly guarded about sentimentality and nostalgia, but who, in midlife, wants to exist in a haze of nostalgia for one's past? It's very easy to slip into that.

AC • Those memories can be wretched as well as wonderful. You go around a corner and meet the worst of your past as well as the best. That's a kind of insurance against nostalgia.

BM • That's something that hasn't been picked up on in *Wind & Root*. Tough moments are hinted at and suggested. This landscape is not all pastoral.

AC • In relation to that, I wanted to ask you about the E.M. Forester epigraph in *Wind & Root*: "Men yearn for poetry although they may not confess it ...." Does a Prince Edward Islander of rural background feel some awkwardness in being a poet?

BM • I would have felt some awkwardness if I had not removed myself from this landscape for 18 years. Coming back with academic credentials and so forth allows me a certain scope that belongs partly to the educated image. Actually, I have to qualify that some because if I look around my community, there is a kind of stubborn appreciation for a certain kind of poetry. Even in the one-room schools, during Christmas concerts, we did what were called recitations. They would have been ballad or narrative poems. We memorized them, and our parents would have been appreciative. At family events – weddings and anniversaries, homecomings and housewarmings – my aunt was noted for presenting addresses. The address would have been a poem, roughly scanned, rhymed, and witty. The idea there would have been to bring in as much personal and anecdotal material as possible to celebrate the occasion. You can write a certain kind of poetry here without awkwardness and embarrassment.

AC • Billy O'Shea, a character in the final "Timothy Harbour" section of the book, dies of an inappropriate "gentleness" (103). Is that quality in a man "unseemly" on the Island?

BM • Partly. I had in mind that rural PEI could be a rather rough place for a "cultured" sensibility. On the other hand, there is an admirable gentleness in that culture, but it can be harsh, unkind, and ignorant.

AC • The collection, as the title *Wind & Root* suggests, veers between rootedness and roving. Were your travels to Australia, England, China, and Singapore important in your development as a writer?

BM • My development as a writer must be quite strange. I remember as an adolescent having quite a little bundle of poems. These were chiefly descriptive of the landscape. I must have had a strong childhood response to landscape, and that response would have been unmediated: No interference. There was something quite spontaneous about that. I was desperately trying to catch in a poem the excitement of seeing a red-winged blackbird. Virginia Woolf jokes about young poets trying to get a particular shade of green. There seems to be a kind of ache to duplicate the world. So there was that. I did write some poems during my undergraduate degree here [UPEI], but when I decided to take the academic route, I must have unconsciously decided I was not going to be a poet. I was going to be an academic and a critic. During most of my 20s, I did virtually no writing. Travelling and family became preoccupying. Distance, physical distance from this place, seeing other cultures, and all of that was important. In 1991, when we returned here, even before I was settled in this house, when we were still living with my parents – with the computer set up in an awkward corner of an upstairs bedroom – I started writing the first poems of *Wind & Root*. And it strikes me now that it was very unlikely.

AC • After travelling, you returned to the landscape that had prompted childhood poems in the first place?

BM • There's probably something unconscious, something deeper than I understand, in that.

AC • In reviewing *Wind & Root*, I said that the collection was as much about time as it was about place (19). Was I right in that observation?

BM • Landscape and time may be related. As a child I was probably more interested in, and fascinated by, family history than most children. Family and landscape were my way into time. The farmhouse that you see next door was built by my great-great-grandfather. Nobody but my immediate ancestors have lived there. So there is a continuity from its construction till now. Donald MacLaine, who immigrated from Scotland, homesteaded the place. As a child, I could find my grandfather's photograph in a shoebox in the cupboard, and in the upstairs spare room I could find a large oval-framed portrait of my great-grandfather. And in the attic, I could find letters and deeds belonging to my great-great-grandfather. So you see the time line goes up as well as back. I remember in high school doing family histories. I don't think very many kids did that. So what was that fascination but connecting landscape and family over time?

AC • Do you think that behind the personal attraction to time, as delivered through a genealogical chart, there lies an interest in abstract time?

BM • I suspect that's right. In the current manuscript, in the sequence "The Story of My Land," for example, there is an interest in geological time. What was here before this was farmed? What was here before there were roads? Oh, there were woods. And you go back and back, and you think about Mi'kmaq history or the French sailing into this harbour.

They would have sailed in right there [*gestures east*] when they first landed at what became Fort Amherst or Port la Joie. I find it fascinating that nothing like the grand history of Europe can be found here. I could go into that field and dig for centuries, and I'd not find a single bone or a charred pit. You'd just find earth. It's not been trampled over by civilizations the way that China or Europe or India have been. Maybe it's a feature of living in a North American colonial society: The genealogical history and the economic history, the agrarian history, are really quite connected. What's beyond that must lead you to much more metaphysical or cosmological speculations about time simply through the geology of the place.

AC • So you look back through five generations and then ....

BM • ... it's wide open. And that's what is behind the poem "Where the Breeze Has Been" (73-74) in the new manuscript.

AC • What does the narrator of "A Wind Not a Root" mean when he says, "I need the distance of high air" (13)?

BM • That was a hedge against nostalgia because I am acutely aware that there are hazards in looking at family history. Rootedness can become a kind of trap. Margaret Laurence makes this point in *The Diviners*. Morag spends a lot of time thinking about her split family history, about the Scots part in particular. She makes a very sentimental journey to the Western Isles, from where my own ancestors came, to rediscover her ancestors. And when she gets there, she is very disappointed. She realizes that this has nothing to do with her. Her identity as a contemporary Canadian woman is quite separate and removed from the way that she had been thinking about that place. I do worry sometimes about getting mired in an oppressive family history. The "high air" is meant to suggest that what is needed at times is a more objective long view, the metaphysical view. What is this short human history in terms of the cosmological history? And, of course, I associate the wind with travel. On the one hand, families are wonderfully supportive and warm, gift-giving and picnic-planning. On the other hand, they can be terribly constraining and restraining. You want to get beyond them. I think that I had always felt that tension quite keenly, even as a child. I may have always felt slightly outside.

AC   • So however much you may have felt at home in the landscape as a child, the appetite for roving, metaphorically and literally, was already in you?

BM   • Very early. A poem yet to be written involves a travelling event narrated by my mother. It's one of those events where I am confused as to whether I'm remembering it or remembering its being told. It's July and I must have had a fondness for winter because I managed to get my snow sled down from a hook in the garage and dragged it over the red dirt road down to the beach and took it out on a sandbar. Of course, this is potentially dangerous – a child wandering by the water with a sled. A fisherman was keeping watch, amused more than anything, I suspect, until I was retrieved. I think I was always running off. I always liked to get away, see things beyond here.

AC   • I'm glad you mentioned the snow sled because that reminds me of the eerie transformations worked by snow in your poetry, a topic taken up in three poems in *Wind & Root*. I'd expect an Islander to take snow for granted, but you don't. In one poem "road and sky and snow / ... lose all category and referent" ("Who Would Have Guessed" 39).

BM   • That's certainly a very dark poem. It comes from the experience of driving in a PEI winter storm, an experience of erasure. The snow was erasing the dark lines, the shadows. The road I was on goes by a farm where there would have been Holsteins in summer, and you could just imagine the PEI summer clarity being erased. In that snow, all the lines in the landscape seemed to be converging in the distance. For me, that was an obvious metaphor for death. We usually think of death as entering a darkness, but there is also a long literary tradition of death being associated with whiteness.

AC   • Is the erasure of an identifiable landscape the erasure of identity?

BM   • Yes, if you lose that, you lose everything. Identity is tied up with landscape.

AC   • You like the word "smudge." It appears as a verb (14, 40); otherwise, as a noun (16, 29). Why does this word recur?

BM   • I think that you could fit it into what I was just talking about. It suggests a transformation from something clean to dirty, from something clear to something blurred. My mother was fairly clean-obsessed. One of the early poems talks about her cleaning windows, and the phrase I

ANNE COMPTON

use is "index fingering the rag into the very origin of corners." She was never content with the broad strokes of cleanliness but needed the finite details of deep cleaning. There was a preoccupation with tidiness and cleanliness – and you can insert as much Presbyterianism as you like into that. If you look at our farmhouse next door, you'll see its crisp black and whiteness, its orderliness.

AC • Is "smudge" a fear or a desire?

BM • It could be both, couldn't it? At times, I have a wonderful fondness for tidiness and precision. And, at other times, I want the opposite of that. I see that tension in my poetics. I love that tension. When you are starting off, the poem is free. It's messy. It's unshaped and unformed. It's clay. And you know that there is always the possibility that you can shape and shape, order and form it, make it symmetrical and patterned. But is that too much? You need to find that balance between the two. Maybe all poems are "smudges." I like a tension between the two. I don't like poetry that's too free. It isn't poetry to me. On the other hand, it can be hammered dead. In this culture, the culture I grew up in, there is a tremendous reverence for fine, patient, repetitive detail. Witness when PEI women at the local agricultural exhibition inspect the quilts. They inspect the stitching to see if the stitches are even. The spaces between the stitches, and the length of the stitches themselves, indicate fine work. The highest bit of praise for that would be: "Look at the work in that." What's important is the time that it took to do that. I think such craftsmanship is not to be ignored or underestimated. Craftsmanship is a lot of work over a long time and a lot of skill and care in details. I wonder if we haven't lost some of that in contemporary poetry. And yet to do too much of that is a risk.

AC • Upon rereading *Wind & Root*, I found it to be not only a darker book than I had thought, but also I thought in this book, there is a wild man trying to get out.

BM • Sure. I see that as human. One of the enduring human conditions is the tension between order and chaos. One of my poems in the new manuscript, "When Red Stone Falls," draws its inspiration from the red stone banks of the shore where you can see that tension. The sea is coming in and undoing the field, eating away at the bank. The soil goes first and then the sandstone rocks. You don't see it, but at some point there must be great crashes of rocks. They shatter, and over time they are undone. They become sand. The long view, the geological view, will tell you, though, that over time the sand will become compacted and redone, restored to order. That cycle is in nature, and I don't see how we can escape it.

AC • Besides "Halitherses" (16-17), there are several old-men poems in *Wind & Root* – the address to Dr. Johnson (26-27) and "the ragged-haired man / explaining his old life with both hands / to a dog in a ditch that isn't there" (30). Do these old men have something in common?

BM • Those are very different old men. I don't connect them.

AC • They are all tellers-of-tales.

BM • That's true. That would be the common thread. You're telling me something that I wasn't aware of. That's fine. I'm interested in these patterns. The conscious force behind those, at least the Dr. Johnson poem, is the violation of family history because he was visiting my ancestors ....

AC • ... literally?

BM • Yes. When he was in Mull, he visited a castle in Lochbuie that belonged to my ancestors, and he insulted them. He didn't speak flatteringly of them. He thought it was a kind of dull place, and he was unhappy with the food. He was cranky. Because of Dr. Johnson's arrogance in relation to the Scots, it was just too good of an opportunity not to get back at him and defend the family honour. You can make something, if you like, of my fear and distaste for arrogance. That's very much part of PEI culture. In this culture, "big feelin'" or "donning airs" is something to guard against. On the other hand, "Halitherses" is a sage, a wise old man. And there I was more interested in exploring the dramatic monologue as a way of getting beyond the personal voice. It's a dodge, but it's also very convenient because, in a way, that setting is just the family farm again, the fields and the landscape that I know. I have a different voice, but there is a connection across time. When I read *The Odyssey*, I feel the folk connection to natural forces, to the bird life, and to the sea and the sky. The elemental life that you can see in the background of the eventful narrative of *The Odyssey* struck a chord with my relationship to the landscape and folk here. The folk rhyme about "One crow, sorrow; two crow joy ..." that my mother would recite is similar to Halitherses' reading birdflight.

AC • So in going away from the personal, through the dramatic mono-
logue, you were coming back?

BM • No question about it.

AC • Is the emphasis, though, in those three old-men poems on the word
"old"? Let me put the question in a different way. In *Wind & Root*, there
is one poem to your daughter, but otherwise the poems nod to gener-
ations past and passing. Why is the collection turned in that direction?

BM • One possible reason would be the desire to recover the past. But I
don't think that's it. In addition to the rootedness and all the farm cul-
ture, there's also discomfort, conflict, and darkness in *Wind & Root*.
There are things in there that I don't want to re-experience, things that
were awful. Also, I am aware of a general search for a father figure.
Maybe it's because my own father was too fatherly, too much a strong
and powerful presence. On the one hand, while there is a great deal of
admiration and respect for him, and for his values and uprightness,
there is perhaps a desire for a more grandfatherly father. That may be
in the nature of fathers or of some fathers, at least. I don't know. Fathers
don't have the luxury of indulgence and storytelling. They're busy with
work. I think of my father as mostly associated with work. There is one
poem in the new manuscript ("Photograph of a Sartorial Father" 62)
that touches on my resentment towards my father. I recognized in him
a great capacity for fun, but there was never much time for fun with
the sons. There were always matters of responsibility and duty, jobs and
chores. The storytelling aspect of the old men in those poems belongs
to my grandfather, on my mother's side. He was very much a figure of
fun, teasing, and tales. Those old men are more like him. Also, I think
I have a fear of turning into a ragged old man telling a story in a ditch
to someone who isn't there. There's a fear of becoming a mad old man.

AC • The opening section of "Boat People" (22-24) is reminiscent of
Joseph Conrad's *Heart of Darkness:* "I think of all of those who go forth
/ down river channels, swirling on muddy tides ..." (22). Why do you
give that context to the story of your ancestors' migration?

BM • The Conrad connection may very well be there on an unconscious
level. That's a text I know well and I am very fond of, so I can't escape
it. But the more conscious connection there is to the explicit news sto-
ries about more recent boat people: Vietnamese boat people to Hong
Kong, the Cubans who tried to get to Florida, the Indian Sikh stow-

aways landing in Charlesville, Nova Scotia. To this day, it is still going on. The Conrad imagery sort of seeps in to connect those. That's a poem about insecurity – and isn't that a surprise? Probably another feature of roving is the fear of insecurity, of un-rooting yourself. Uprootedness may be a more natural fate, and prominent condition, of humankind than rootedness. Rootedness may be the exception. Throughout history, being pushed around and travelling and roaming and warring and moving may be a more prominent feature of human life than the comfortable white farmhouse.

AC • There's a fear of its happening again?

BM • Yes. And, by the way, the thinking in "Boat People" takes place in the context of some very personal insecurities. Here I was, in 1991, back in my family landscape, which has a tradition of successful farmers and carpenters and so on, people making a good living, and here I am job-less, with a family, and worried terribly about my fatherly responsibil-ities as provider. Worries about penury were very much on my mind.

AC • This was before you got your appointment at UPEI?

BM • Which came very late. It may be difficult for others to appreciate the near trauma of that fear, especially when it comes with responsibilities. What do those people do when they are suddenly cleared – and of course I make hay of the phrases "cleared off" and "the clearances" – you have to set sail and start all over again. And that's terrifying. The other interesting family thing there – and this comes back to nostalgia – I can't find a trace of Gaelic in my own family. My father couldn't remember his grandparents speaking Gaelic. Why was that? If you go to Cape Breton, you can still find the Gaelic, but where is it in my family? I think that there are possibly two avenues for migrants. We assume that they bring their culture with them and transplant it. They speak the Gaelic. They do the dances and cook the food and so on, but I think that there is another way to migrate and that's to say, "God, that was awful. God, we were hungry. Let's try it new in this country. Let's outdo the English. We'll speak the English, make the money, and be prosperous and get ahead here as fast as we can. And be done with the past and move on." It may be that my family were of that latter kind. Isn't it interesting that you have in Montreal, and in Canadian history in general, as someone said recently at a conference, "bagpipers at the head of the line."

AC   • There is a great comfort in the familiar in some of these poems – "farmhouses / nestle in the hills like fat white sucklings ..." (23) – but security is not taken for granted here. What is it that lurks?

BM   • "Are you a participant or an observer?" is always the question when you go to a party. Well, I'm always the observer. I think that if you're a writer, that is what you have to be. I would readily admit to a crippling self-consciousness that makes me uncomfortable and awkward in many social settings, family or community or church or whatever. While recognizing the attraction, the welcoming nature and comfort of those, I don't think I ever really felt that I could naturally insert myself. At the same time, I always felt that those weren't quite me. You have someone who hasn't found a single state or single identity, someone who can go to Singapore and say, "Ah, perhaps this is where I belong." Or go to China and say, "Perhaps that's me." Poet, farmer, teacher: Which is the best identity? Perhaps I'm afraid of inclusion because it may close down possibilities for other identities. It's a fear of not being included, yet it's a fear of inclusion.

AC   • I could make an inventory of children's pieces in this book – the rhyme "One crow, sorrow ..." (16); the story of the three little pigs (21); and an echo of Dr. Seuss (41). Why do these remembered lines enter your poetry?

BM   • I don't have a theory about it except that quoting them is one way of tapping into the musicality and the formal aspects of poetry. I also suspect that I am using them as a template or palimpsest or shadow reference. There I am, an adult in my bedroom listening to a storm outside: I should be perfectly secure, but no, I am wondering if this newly constructed house will blow down. That's childish, but to connect to the child is also to connect to the elemental. You're going back to something true. You can't censure it. I like Wordsworth on childhood. I think he's got it right: "The Child is father of the Man." The other thing that occurs to me is that in terms of the inclusion/exclusion dichotomy, maybe I experienced a more comfortable inclusion in childhood.

AC   • There's a Wordsworthian sensibility in *Wind & Root*?

BM   • I would say so. I like what Wordsworth does with childhood, with landscape. When I was in England, I went to the Lake District and tramped around in the landscape and visited Wordsworth's home in Cockermouth. There are parallels between the Lake District and PEI. I like his descriptive force and the way he moves from description to metaphorical imagery.

AC • The question mark is ubiquitous in this collection. Is the poet's role really an interrogation of what others take for granted?

BM • Certainly I am aware of the principle of making the familiar unfamiliar, and looking at it as strange. In my academic work, I have spent a fair amount of time with the Russian Formalists. For all that it gets tiresomely mechanical after a while, I do think that they were onto something. They had an admiration for the way that art inspects the everyday and looks for what is unfamiliar. You have to work at that. Habituation of perception is one of the great hazards for the poet. You have to kind of shake your head and get rid of habit. I am always trying to do that. It never ceases to surprise me that something is right under my nose, but I just haven't stepped back and looked at it from a different angle. Also, about questioning, I'm very slow to answers. I'm not comfortable with answers, and the minute I formulate a response to something, the very next response is, "Is that right? Is that true? Is that final?" I can't be comfortable with finality. That goes back to the Island cultural suspicion of know-it-alls. Who wants to be a know-it-all? They're offensive. Skepticism and suspicion are necessary.

AC • Are they part of the Presbyterian heritage?

BM • You'd think not. You'd have to work through theological history and dogma to answer that definitively, but on the face of it, Presbyterians are pretty sure about how the world was, how it's going to unfold, and how you should behave in it. My elemental experience of the world told me something different. I couldn't see myself being comfortable – to this day – in the Presbyterian-defined world, although I have a great deal of respect for it. The questioning could be a response to the certainty and over-determination of Presbyterianism.

AC • In the barn-painting poem, "The Gable End," the narrator says, "My brush slaps on good Presbyterian sense, / an even-tempered work ethic / and proper consideration for the wintering of real cows" (65). How does "good Presbyterian sense" sit with the writing of poetry?

BM • Not very well. "Presbyterian sense" can work at odds to poetry, even while exhorting the virtues of the psalms and the poetry of the hymnal. I have not seen much evidence that Presbyterianism is very interested in secular poetry.

ANNE COMPTON

AC • Parenthetical asides – such as "oh, what the hell," "no doubt," "I guess," "I suppose" – abound. Are you consciously striving for the conversational mode?

BM • Yes. I like that tension between the formal and the informal. Back to Wordsworth again. I've always been amazed at how many poets over the centuries have made the claim that they're bringing the conversational mode to poetry, making it speak the language of the common man. There's Milton Acorn, the People's Poet, and so on, who do that. They all fail, really. I guess the asides are my gesture in that vein, an attempt to keep the poetry from being stuffy, to show that poetry can be casual, that it need not be a stilted and artificial language and diction.

AC • In "Wintering," people "stog rags" against draughts (106). "Stog" appears in Terry Pratt's *Dictionary of Prince Edward Island English*. There are other examples of punchy one-syllable verbs in this volume. Did that just come in or were you reaching for that kind of richness through Island vocabulary?

BM • Trying to be conscious about it won't work. If you sit down and say I want PEI diction and strong Anglo-Saxon words in this poem, you'd have a recipe for disaster. I couldn't do it. But if I'm writing a poem about the country cold and I'm in the world of gathering stuff up for the winter and thinking about preparations for winter on the farm – my parents, especially in their early days, spoke in Island diction – it will just come. When it just comes, of course I recognize it. I would recognize "stog" for all its semantic and aural advantages, and I would say, "Yes, I'll take it. I'll use that one." I don't think that I could do a really long sustained colloquial piece. In some of the poems in the "Timothy Harbour" section of *Wind & Root*, I'm trying to hear in my memory what they would have said. I can hear a lot of it, and I can invent a lot of phrases to get at how they would have spoken. I can recapture some of that, but it only goes so far.

AC • But you certainly seem to use quite naturally phrases such as a "floaty Ford" (79), a "throaty car" (80).

BM • Yes, well, those are probably in me in ways that I'm not even aware of myself. The poems allow some of that to come out in a way that my terribly stuffy classroom academic self does not allow.

AC • The most striking example of that is the expression "a field of hand-some hay" (76). That's very Island.

BM • Yes, I'm hearing my father in that phrase. Similarly, I've heard neighbours refer to my father as "dear." They'd say, "Now, Donald, dear," which is very unusual.

AC • Am I wrong in thinking that you remain fairly skeptical about the worth of words or at least about their durability? You speak of "the long erasure of their [words'] naming" (42) and there is an equation that goes, making words is "making flesh for worms or tinder for a flame" (61). Are they not to be trusted?

BM • No, they are not. This notion of literature and posterity, this looking for permanence or security through one's writing, is not to be trusted. Over the long view, this is nothing. It's going to disappear. If you are satisfied with a few centuries, well then, do your best. I've always put more faith in the process than in the product. The hard thing to grab onto with something like poetry – which in some ways is so product-centred – is ....

AC • ... forgive me, but if you are so interested in process, why bother to publish?

BM • That's a fair question. I will acknowledge that the only way to communicate the process is through a product. And here we are hovering around "the dancer and the dance" idea. But there is also the cultural suspicion of words and the Presbyterian suspicion of words. Loquaciousness, volubility, are not desirable because the devil can quote scripture. Words can pull the wool over your eyes, be deceptive. They do not always contain the truth. Truth for me is always much more intentional: What were the intentions, not what is in the thing itself? The end product may be approximate. I suspect our poems are approximations. Words are imperfect. All communication between reader and writer is necessarily imperfect. I feel that you should respond to what people are intending, the truly felt impulse behind their attempt to communicate. That, to me, is always more affecting or endearing or more human than what is said itself.

AC • You would rather trust the best intention of the speaker than the words themselves?

BM • I might have to draw a distinction here between spontaneous human speech and constructed speech, like poetry. Certainly carefully constructed poetic speech ought to be closer to the intentional gesture of communication than the everyday is.

AC • The poem "Finely Fashioned Things" expresses the desire to be rid of "the residue of self that clings to things" (64). What is the relationship between the "self" and the poetry that is written?

BM • That poem begins with a suspicion of, and a desire to be beyond, the material. I have an admiration for Ghandi. I've always been struck by the fact that he died with only a simple white robe, a rice bowl and chopsticks, and his sandals. That's all he owned. There were very few "things" for him to stick to. His self was elsewhere. Now, how that relates to poetry has to do with process. You can be too much stuck to the product. The poem and the book – when they are finished – are gone. When we read poems, we are reading a record of what happened when the poet was writing the poem. Poems may be an avenue into the past rather than into the present.

AC • It seems to me there are two lines to your answer. One is the anti-material stance: You are putting poetry in the same category as the tray over there. You don't want to be too attached to your poems. They're just material things. The other part of your answer puts the emphasis on the self rather than on things. You're wondering if the self in poetry isn't already out of date.

BM • Yes, I like that. The self in a poem is a momentary self, not a permanent one. Also, I have, I would admit, a fear of the personal, or the too personal, in poetry. I'm not comfortable these days with the use of the "I" in poetry. I think the confessional in poetry is hazardous. At the same time, I recognize that a lot of my best poems come out of personal responses to events and people.

AC • And, as you said earlier, you like the conversational mode. It's hard to employ that mode without the presence of the "I" – "I guess," "I doubt," and so forth.

BM • I guess what we're left with here is that I'm full of contradictions. But the "I" of "I guess" or "I doubt," the casual conversational "I" is quite different – in degree and kind – from the "I" of a sustained confessional or introspective poem.

AC • "[T]he ever-active mind flitting over things" (61): Is that what poetry is for you?

BM • Not really, although that image captures one part of the poetic process, a kind of relentless observing and speculating and analyzing, a kind of head chatter to the self. The poem itself, however, has much more *gravitas*.

AC • I counted nine father poems in *Wind & Root*, the feelings of which collect poignantly in "The Moment of Your Going" (69). Is it accurate to say that *Wind & Root* is a homage to your father?

BM • Much of it, but I think you'd have to accommodate the historical context there. *Wind & Root* was written awfully close to my father's death, which was traumatic for me, almost to the extent that I'm embarrassed by how traumatic it was. Real men should be able to handle their father's death without so much fuss. Why should my father's death be so special?

AC • As Hamlet's stepfather points out to Hamlet: Lots of sons lose their fathers.

BM • Respect and resentment are doubled up in my relationship to my father. The respect, admiration, and appreciation came very late, as it often does in young people. In *Wind & Root*, there may be an enthusi astic compensation in discovering how fine a person my father was. I take some pride in being able to capture his character, or at least some parts of his character, in that volume.

AC • Not only in the homages to your father, but also in poems such as "Southward to Kissimmee" (78-79) and "The Reprieve ..." (80), age and death appear frequently. Was *Wind & Root* prompted by familial deaths?

BM • It may well have been. I was certainly aware in 1991, when we were still in Singapore, that I was facing a rather important career decision. We could have stayed there for another three years, which would have made it six, and if you stay six, then you have to start thinking about emigrating. I could have had a career there. Part of the reason for returning to PEI was familial. I was concerned that my children were growing up without an extended family and without a landscape they could call their own. There was a real sense that to bring the family back here was the right thing to do. Coming back here initiated a flood of poetry, but it may well have been that much of what I was remembering was already passing away. The elegiac mode is an accurate description of some of *Wind & Root* – and I guess it is – for a passing way of life. It's the speed that gets me. It seems to have happened so fast. I can remember my mother driving the hayfork. Recently, I was thinking of that wonderfully complex system of pulleys and ropes, and women and horses and men on the farm. It was just yesterday, and that's not just a trick of my memory. I think if you did some sociological study, you'd see how that was still happening in the late '50s. In under 30 years, by the 1980s, all of that had disappeared. There is something disproportionate in the way that that life has been erased from PEI so quickly. The poem series "The Story of My Land" (32-43), in the new manuscript, ends with that kind of uncomfortable speculation. From the top of that hill just over there, I can see the trace of the farms and the way they used to be. But now they are subdivided, and I'm guilty because I have subdivided a corner of this farm. You can see the past giving way to this, and I'm not sure what *this* is, but I'm sure that I'm not entirely comfortable with it. Rice Point is now a bedroom community of Charlottetown.

AC • Over and over again, *Wind & Root* names rural work, and the objects involved in it, most spectacularly in "What You Left Behind" (73-74). Are you an archivist of rural work?

BM • Knowing my avoidance of rural work, my father would laugh at that. An archivist? Yes. In "Sunday Drive by the Lewis Place" (97-98), I am cataloguing all the barnyard objects that I can think of, and am familiar with. That's a museum piece in some ways. Yes, there is an element of the archivist in me. I think that it is important to get that stuff written down. I haven't done a survey, but I suspect that there are large chunks of Prince Edward Island culture, life, and stories that have not been put into literature. L.M. Montgomery and Milton Acorn have not had the last word on what it was like to live here. That image of my mother, ropes and horse and all, has been spinning around in my mind for some time. And I know that there is something there. See, this is what I mean about my interest in process. For me, the pleasure and joy is going to be in working that out and discovering what is there. I don't know if Wordsworth thought of it this way, but I suspect he did. If I have a strong memory or a strong image, I have faith that independently there is something important there. It's a matter of my discovering what it is. That image can't be purely accidental or casual. There has to be something purposeful or meaningful that lodged the image there in my memory.

AC • In your academic work, you have written about two subgenres of the novel, one of which is the "family album novel." Do you think there is "family album" poetry too?

BM • Oh, I would think so, and that is where I was going, to a certain degree, although it may have been a failed experiment in the "Timothy Harbour" section. What critical responses there have been to *Wind & Root* have been to the other parts of the book and not to that section. You'll recall that there is a genealogy of the MacFadyen family in the "Timothy Harbour" section. That's partly fictional. But I had in mind putting together a family in a community rather like Edgar Lee Masters' *Spoon River Anthology*. I wanted to do a kind of update of that for a PEI community. Also, you'll notice that there is a little map, which I drew. Mapping has been a very prominent preoccupation of my mind, and I suspect that it is in my poetry. As a child, with my cousins and friends, I would make, after a snowfall, not snow angels but a map. We would say, "This is Rice Point Road; this is the MacFadyen house," and we would make a lane and a circle. We would duplicate the community in paths in the snow. Why would children do that? Why would you do that when your world was already so clearly bounded? There must have been a tremendous desire to represent it, to write it, to put it down in snow. [Jorge Luis] Borges has that wonderful story, "Of Exactitude and Science," where the cartographers set out to make a map of the country. They do a pretty good job of it, and they're pleased, but they decide it's not quite accurate and detailed enough so they double the size of the scale of the map, and they're able to get more detail into it. Then they start making the map bigger and bigger. If you take that principle to the extreme, the map becomes synonymous with what is mapped, and you can't distinguish the two. There may be something of that going on in *Wind & Root*.

AC • What, for you, is the central poem in *Wind & Root*?

BM • A central poem would umbrella the others. It would have to gather the others under it, and I don't see any single poem doing that. You might be able to find more of the themes and concerns of *Wind & Root* covered in "Making the Middle Be" (107-08) than in some of the other poems. It does catch the local and the colloquial. It catches my own preoccupation with the edge and the inclusion/exclusion dynamic. It

ANNE COMPTON

offers a more or less expansive ending to time and space through its landscape and history.

AC • Your principles of a collection do not accommodate the idea of a central poem?

BM • That's right. In fact, I would add that I find arranging and sequencing poems a rather painful process. I would really rather not do it.

AC • The comic in this collection occurs when a poem's subject is sex, or attraction, or lust. Is sex absurd? Is it a topic you don't want to deal with?

BM • Probably. It's not a topic I think of writing about. That being said, in the new collection there are several poems, including "Such Love Was Dangerous" (55-59), which discovers a love-making couple right down here at the edge of the beach. "Album from the Forties" (60-61) is a very sad poem. I think sex in that poem is sad because when I look at photographs of young people in their youth, particularly ones of my parents, you see their handsomeness and the way that they flirted. Even in these Kodak Brownie photographs, you see a lustiness that leaps off the image. When I compare that to the sometimes wretched and painfully grim present, I find it really sad. You could see in that photograph the possibility of fulfillment, sexual or otherwise, and yet I know how that story ended. The other poem I was referring to, "Such Love Is Dangerous," is celebratory. It's love-making in the context of the landscape and the seascape. There is a sense of overstatement and amusement, I guess, from the authorial perspective. No question: I find it a difficult poetic subject. That being said, I don't feel any particular obligation to write poems about sex.

AC • There's lots of familial love in *Wind & Root*, but there are no love poems.

BM • I wrote a love poem once and showed it to a respected friend who laughed and said we can't write poems like that anymore. And that made me aware – and so skittish – that a direct approach to a love poem may not be possible in the contemporary poetic idiom. Ours is the age of irony, so the romantic, which I see as the genuine approach to the love poem, can't be negotiated. Even in terms of familial love it's difficult. I have an elegy which was read at my father's funeral and that too was disparaged for its sincerity of feeling. Sincere and direct feeling will be ....

Meetings With Maritime Poets   157

AC • ... unaccommodated in the ironic world. Of course we are in a new century so perhaps we're beyond the ironic age.

BM • You go first.

AC • When I move to the new manuscript, "Where the Branch Bends," I notice a shift away from the leisurely conversational mode. Are you more of a formalist in this second book?

BM • No question.

AC • There are sonnets, a villanelle, and a ballad in this new manuscript. Is there paradoxically more freedom in these than in free verse?

BM • Forms may provide opportunities that I wasn't aware of in free verse. The naive writer of free verse assumes that free verse is free and that formal verse is restricting. But we know that writing to a form can also lead to invention and possibilities that never would have occurred to one while writing in free verse. It isn't a simple equation: Formal equals restraint, and free verse equals freedom.

AC • Is it possibility rather than freedom that exists in form?

BM • For me, yes. But restraint and freedom are not categories that I think about. It is a matter of taste, and I am growing increasingly skeptical of free verse the more I read of it. It does not make use of all of the possibilities that the English language has to offer. Why shouldn't we use all of the features of English that there are in shaped verse and metrically arranged verse, scanned verse, and accented verse? Why shouldn't we exploit them for poetic purposes? The assumption is that something in stanzas is old-fashioned, that it is tight or limited, and I think that assumption has to be questioned. I'm already beginning to regret some of my own free-verse poetry. It's beginning to seem naive. I've moved the tension between form and dis-form to the formal side. I spoke earlier of my liking for the tension between shaped clay and pure clay, as I put it. Free verse is much more clay. I'm putting more fingerwork and more symmetries and patterns into the clay. I don't think that I have the skill or the mastery to write in the accentual-syllabic, perfectly rhymed verse of the previous centuries. However, I can do other things. I have a great fondness for internal rhymes. I do think of my poems sculpturally, almost as three-dimensional objects. I look through my poems for sound effects. What rhyme or half-rhyme or

ANNE COMPTON

near-rhyme do I have going on here? I try to arrange the poem and move it forward by musical principles.

AC • Those sound linkages are in *Wind & Root*, not just in your new manuscript. So even in your pre-formalist days, sound linkages were at work in your poetry.

BM • For me, those define poetry. Otherwise, it's prose. I swear I could get into a lyrically elegiac mode and write out stuff in sentences, chop it up, and call it a poem. To me, it isn't a poem. It is arranged prose. Of course it is a continuum. At one end, there is something like the minutes of a meeting, which I see as pure prose, and at the other end, the epitome of formal lyricism, Shakespeare's sonnets. You could place Virginia Woolf's prose *The Waves* in the middle.

AC • "One could infer from the evidence / of these stones an occasion occurred" ("When Red Stone Falls" 12) is an order of speech different from that in the preceding book. What explains this shift?

BM • There are times when I want to use a speculative, philosophical, metaphysical language. I don't see why that should be excluded from poetic speech.

AC • "Where the Branch Bends" is leaning further in that direction just as it is leaning further into forms?

BM • That's perfectly true, although "Where the Branch Bends," the new manuscript, is not without the personal. The formal and the speculative are just where I am going these days. These days, I have regular Monday lunches with the poet John Smith, and among a whole range of literary and philosophical issues we discuss cosmology and science much of the time. And, of course, family-as-subject must have its poetic limits. Maybe I've written it out. If you have an ambition to be a poet, you have to struggle with this. You have to think about what is going to sustain you. I have such an admiration for Yeats because he was of the nature that he was moved by different subjects at different times in his life. I'm undecided as to whether or not I have that ambition. I'm not entirely comfortable yet thinking in terms of a poetic career or even in thinking of myself as "a poet."

AC • If the new manuscript is more formal in its prosody, more abstract in its thinking, does it also rely to a greater extent on metaphor? I'm thinking of lines such as "while uncomprehending cottages / close their plywood eyes" ("North Shore Park" 16).

BM   • When it is pointed out to you by a very shrewd critic that you over-rely on the simile, you take such advice to heart. If I had to give a quick answer, I'd say that the metaphor shows greater confidence. A simile is a reluctant comparison, but a metaphor is a clear and more confident comparative statement.

AC   • Do you see "Where the Branch Bends" as a more confident book than the first one? Is "a leap ahead" too grand a way of putting it?

BM   • It's a slide ahead, perhaps. I think I know that there are limitations to the childhood-memory subject matter. I'm never going to apologize for those or say that they are limited because that would be to excise three-quarters of the canon of English literature. That subject has its integrity, but logically it can only go so far. What I'm trying to do now is open up the avenue of the meditative for poetry because that ulti-mately should be more sustaining.

AC   • In "The Poem I Have in Mind" (53), you sketch your ideal poem – "notable but not extreme," the product of "easeful creation," and "unobtrusive."

BM   • I associate "The Poem I Have in Mind" with "Finely Fashioned Things" (*Wind & Root* 63-64). It expresses a tiredness and impatience with the rhetoric of greatness, the rhetoric of the exceptional. I think a lot about the idea of centre and margin, which is a similar manoeuvre. "Centre" reduces it to one: "This is the best" or "We are at the centre, and that's the only place to be." These are ultimately statements of power and control. Those who are not at the centre are marginalized. I would rather strive for some kind of excellence in the ordinary, among the many, to share the excellence.

AC   • In stating these modest aims you are taking exception to the idea of an excellence that is singular?

BM   • I think that there are all kinds of beauties and excellences in the world that remain totally undiscovered. That's partly what I am arguing for in the common experience of this landscape. There's an excellence here that will never be central in a marketing or media kind of way, but it is just as wonderful. This lands us right in the middle of the whole local and regional and globalization discourse. That whole debate, and the presumption of the centre, really raises my blood pressure.

AC • By identifying ourselves as marginal, we are already conceding a centre, aren't we?

BM • Not necessarily. To use the word "margin" is not necessarily to define a symmetrical geometry. You can have a messy geometry. And in a messy or chaotic geometry there will be many centres. It's not just one circle. That's a tidy geometry.

AC • In a traditional geometry, the compass point can have only one centre.

BM • That's true. But that's not what I mean by a margin. I mean "margin" in the sense of "coastal." A coastline is irregular. My experience of living in other cultures and other countries is that all people, in a manner, live their lives as though they are at the centre. But only those who are arrogant or power-conscious, or hierarchical in their thinking, order the world into one big centre with lots of concentric circles. People who have a false sense of centre use the term "margin," but I can live at "their margin" and still know that my experience, my life, my culture, and my landscape are central.

AC • Whereas *Wind & Root* is field and farm, the poems in the first section of "Where the Branch Bends," the new manuscript, are frequently set on the shore. They are more coastal. What explains this move to the edge?

BM • That's a pattern that makes sense given the other shifts in the new manuscript. Robert Frost has a poem in which the people at the beach can look "Neither Out Far Nor In Deep." When people go to the shore, their backs are to the land, and they're all looking out. The meditative impulse is there in that positioning.

AC • "[A] broken road to St. Peter's Island" (32) appears twice in the section called "The Story of My Land." Why does your imagination attach itself to a tide-made road, a road that disappears regularly?

BM • Let's begin with the facts. From our farmhouse – before the trees were as high as they are now – you could see St. Peter's Island. There was a little community over there and a schoolhouse. We knew the people who lived on St. Peter's. Twice a day, at low tide, the sandbars are bared. That was the only means of transport from the Island. Of course, they always picked the highest or the hardest sandbars to cross on. That sandbar road would be broken by gullies and ponds, and at high tide it was gone altogether. To have a pathway to home coming and going like that is very striking because roads are usually stable and secure things. That was a shifting one. To the child's imagination, that is striking, for sure. I'm thinking also of the road that we talked about earlier, the road in winter that is always disappearing because the lines and perspectives are vanishing in the storm. This is the paradox: A road is a clear direction, an invitation to get the hell out of here, and yet, at the same time, it represents the fear that it leads to nowhere. You will get lost or you'll die if you go down that road.

AC • What serendipity. We're ending almost where we began, with your preoccupation with erasure and the way snow erases referent and category. Once again, in this new manuscript, in the central section, "The Story of My Land," you have a disappearing road.

BM • Let's not miss the other reading – good old 20th-century skepticism and loss of faith. I grew up in a religious culture. You take out that centre, that direction, what are you left with? You're left with questions and a kind of erasure.

AC • So the disappearing road is about losing one's way?

BM • Loss of certainty, for sure, but it's also about losing a prescribed way.

WORKS CITED

— • —

Borges, Jorge Luis. "Of Exactitude and Science." *A Universal History of Infamy*. Trans. Norman Thomas diGiovanni. Harmondsworth, Eng.: Penguin, 1970.

Compton, Anne. "Torn between rootedness and roving." Rev. of *Wind & Root*, by Brent MacLaine. *New Brunswick Reader* 9 June 2001. 19.

MacLaine, Brent and Hugh MacDonald, eds. *Landmarks: An Anthology of New Atlantic Canadian Poetry of the Land*. Charlottetown: Acorn P, 2001.

MacLaine, Brent. "Sleuths in the Darkroom: Photographer-Detectives and Postmodern Narrative." *Journal of Popular Culture* 33.3 (Winter 1999): 79-94.

– – –. "Window Cleaning." *Fiddlehead* 131 (January 1982): 83.

– – –. "Where the Branch Bends." unpublished ms.

– – –. *Wind & Root*. Montreal: Signal Editions, 2000.

Pratt, T.K. *The Dictionary of Prince Edward Island English*. Toronto: U of Toronto P, 1998.

Wordsworth, William. "My heart leaps up ..." *William Wordsworth's The Prelude with a selection from the Shorter Poems, the Sonnets, The Recluse, and The Excursion*. Ed. Carlos Baker. New York: Holt, Rinehart and Winston, 1948, 1954: 82.

SON OF A PREACHER MAN:
JOHN MACKENZIE, POET

Polestar-published, Prince Edward Island poet John MacKenzie works as a
bartender at Baba's Lounge, Charlottetown. An avid reader, MacKenzie
dropped out of school in Grade 8 and has been reading around in English lit-
erature, physics, geology, and anything else that he can get his hands on ever
since. To find his parallel in poetry, you have to think back to poets such as
Milton Acorn and Al Purdy, autodidact worker-poets. *Sledgehammer and
other poems*, published in 2000, was shortlisted for the Atlantic Poetry Prize
and the Gerald Lampert Memorial Award. The poems of *Sledgehammer* are
concrete, convoluted, and densely metaphorical; its speaker is, by times, a
romantic lover, an angry ecologist, and a road warrior. The collection narrates
a cross-country excursion.

At the time of this interview – in Cedars Eatery, Charlottetown –
MacKenzie's second collection, *Shaken by Physics* (2002), was about to go to
press.

AC • Other than what I've read on the back of your book, I don't know
much about you so let's begin with background. Has your family been
on the Island a long time?

JM • I'm not sure exactly when we came. We go back to the 1800s. Both
sides of my family come from Scotland. From four years old till my
teens, I lived in the Victoria-Crapaud area of PEI.

AC • You're one of nine children. Does that mean a Catholic family?

JM • No. Fundamentalist Christian, the Gospel Hall. There's a bunch of
Gospel Halls right across the country. Actually, it's an international
church.

AC • You left school in Grade 8 so you're self-educated rather than tutored. Was there a method to your reading?

JM • No method. Just whatever I got to next, whatever interested me. In elementary school, I'd get up early and read the *World Book Encyclopedia*. That was something I really liked to read.

AC • Were there any restrictions on your reading because of the fundamentalism?

JM • The only thing I can recall – and it had nothing to do with me – was one time we were visiting my family on the west end of the Island and my grandfather saw one of my brothers reading a Louis L'Amour book and he turned to my mother and said, "What are you letting him read that kind of stuff for? Do you want him to turn out to be a Son of Sam?"

AC • Tell me about reform school.

JM • That was the summer before I turned 14, break-and-entry and joy-riding. That involved going into a construction company and getting the keys and taking a vehicle out. We did it a lot. We wrecked a vehicle, rolled it.

AC • When and how did you come into poetry?

JM • My grandfather used to recite *The Cremation of Sam McGee*. In Grade 7, we had to read aloud in class and one of the textbooks included *The Cremation of Sam McGee*. I really liked that.

AC • What was it you liked, the sound of the poetry or the narrative?

JM • The words in themselves. I've always been fascinated by words. We didn't have television in our household, and the radio was only on for the news and the obituaries so our entertainment was what we could make ourselves. Most of us read a lot. Wordplay was a big thing for us. I did crosswords and acrostics in my teens and early 20s, but at home it was mostly verbal wordplay.

AC • Your father was a "go-preacher" (*Sledgehammer* 85), so he would have had oratorical skills.

JM • Yes, and he enjoyed a pun and nonsense. If I remember him with any fondness at all, it is because of his liking for words.

AC • What do you value most in others' poetry?

JM • The specifics – words and images. First of all, I look for joy in words. Freshness. Strangeness.

AC • You like the concrete, but by the look of your poetry, not to the exclusion of the abstract?

JM • I've been thinking about that lately. As I get better at what I'm doing, I'm able to use the abstract more without it diffusing the whole poem, making it less of a poem.

AC • Would you say the second book, *Shaken by Physics*, is more abstract than the first?

JM • It's certainly more mind-oriented, although there's a lot of concrete stuff there.

AC • Do you see your work as emerging from or participating in an Island poetry community?

JM • No.

AC • Tell me about The Secret Swarm.

JM • That was something that I stumbled upon just about the time when I decided that I wanted to write, or could write, poetry. That'd be around 1988. That year I went to the Island literary awards. Andrew Griffin had just come back from the Yukon – I didn't know him – and he read some of his stuff. I liked it more than anything else I heard. I ran into him on the street a few days later and he told me about this workshop that he was getting underway. He invited me to come and that became The Secret Swarm. That was when I began to show my stuff to other people and began to accept criticism.

AC • How did *Sledgehammer* come about?

JM • I was a bit crazy. Nineteen-ninety-seven was a bad year for me and so was most of '98. Early in '99 I took off for Vancouver Island and stayed with Lynn Henry for the first couple of months I was there. She'd been a member of The Secret Swarm a long time ago. I showed her what I was working on, a manuscript called "Sledgehammer." She told me to work on it some more and show it to her again. If she thought it was any good, she would suggest I submit it to Polestar, which is where she was working as an editor. So that's what I did. I gave them some 150 pages of poetry.

AC • And Lynn Henry found a book in it?

JM • I think that was a painful process for Lynn because she knew me. In fact, I know it was. Late July or early August, I came back to PEI and sometime in October, I got an e-mail from Lynn saying they had passed it around and decided, in the end, they couldn't do it. About two weeks later, I got another e-mail, this time from Michelle Benjamin, the publisher at Polestar, saying they'd gone over it again and decided they couldn't *not* publish it. I guess what had happened was that Lynn had decided that she was too close to me to be objective about the manuscript. They sat her down and talked sense into her.

AC • Does the title of your first book, *Sledgehammer and other poems*, identify your poetic?

JM • The reason that I wanted it to be called *Sledgehammer* was because two friends of mine, both painters, said that reading a poem of mine was like being hit with a sledgehammer.

AC • Do you think of your poetry as revolutionary? The poem "Sledgehammer" (65) talks about knocking things apart, about destroying, in order to open up.

JM • Mentally, it might be revolutionary. I think people should take their thinking apart and put it back together again. All I know is that one of the reasons I write is that I don't find all that much that I want to read.

AC • In terms of poetry?

JM • Well, maybe that's not entirely true. I am beginning to find things that I want to read. But I'm also finding a whole lot of goddam shit that no one should ever have inflicted upon them.

AC • Why is it getting published then?

JM • It may have to do with a dropping level of discernment – people's inability to discern between good and bad, good and mediocre, in the written word. There's a kind of levelling out going on.

AC • Do you write all the time?

JM • In spurts. When I write, I write a lot. During dry periods, I write down phrases and ideas in my notebooks.

AC • Is everything initially handwritten?

JM   • The first four drafts are and then I move to the computer.

AC   • You like to extend and modulate a metaphor over the course of a poem – "Me as an Archaeologist" (11-12) and "hearthouse" (20-21), for example. Does the elasticity of a metaphor determine the evolution of a poem?

JM   • Metaphor is not something that I think consciously about. In a way, though, I guess I am governed by metaphor. Once I begin a poem – without thinking of it as metaphor – I try to search for plays upon what I've begun through shifts or sequences. I carry that as far as it will go.

AC   • Your metaphors are varied. There are noun-phrase metaphors – "shattered pottery of desire"(11); modifying verbals – "petrified, unleavened love" (11); simple adjectives – "fossil eyes" (11). Did you study other poets' use of metaphor?

JM   • I don't have an academic background so I don't analyse or dissect poems in terms of metaphor or anything else. Metaphor comes from the family, I suppose. It's an abstraction or another version of the word-play.

AC   • There are *Sledgehammer* poems that use simple diction and a plain style – "Box O'Glass" (18) – but there are also poems containing a difficult technical language and complicated syntax: "On a late jurassic plain the diplodocus died, / decayed, descended – long before the jaded jurassic" (48) and "chemists & molecular engineers building gore-tex / & dacron universes / searching for molecules to depend futures from" (22). Did the more complicated diction and syntax emerge in the course of your writing career?

JM   • "Box O'Glass" is one of the oldest poems in *Sledgehammer*. That one and "Me as an Archaeologist" (11-12) were both written in 1992. Then there followed a period when I wrote hardly anything. Around 1995, I started working on the long poem "Far from the Sea (Portage la Prairie, MB)" (47-51). In between, I was reading a fair amount of poetry, and although I wasn't thinking consciously about how it was put together, I was absorbing and thinking all around the mechanics of poetry.

AC   • "A List (By Colour) of Things Left Behind" presents an inventory of objects but, really, or additionally, it is an inventory of clichés: "down at the mouth"; boots "down [at] their heels," and "rundown clocks"

(15). Do you find that clichés, sayings, and commonplaces are a great language resource?

JM • When I find ways to refresh them and reinvigorate them, yes. That's what's going on in that poem. It was a painful poem to write. My marriage had broken up and I hadn't seen my son for forever and I was on the opposite side of the continent. I was balancing the emotional pain with the fun I could find in clichés.

AC • Does that mean that intellectual wordplay can be a kind of solace for emotional hurt?

JM • Works for me.

AC • Although *Sledgehammer* travels Canada from west to east, the geography of *Sledgehammer* isn't always Canadian. In the love poem that opens the book, the narrator is an archaeologist of another's dead desire, and that desire is conceptualized as an ancient city that seems Mediterranean, Uruk or Babylon perhaps. How does this geography enter the book?

JM • That's my ex-wife's heritage. Her father is an Italian-Newfoundlander. Also, around the time that I wrote "Me as an Archaeologist" (11-12), I was reading a lot of Greek mythology and doing some reading on geology. So the Mediterranean comes from those sources.

AC • "[R]ubble" (12), "fragments" (16), and "broken bits" (16) recur in this book. Is poetry a way of putting a life back together again?

JM • For me it was, but it didn't have to be poetry. It could have been anything that I focused on and was fanatical about. It's a matter of redirecting, refocusing your mind on something that is complex. It could have been painting or – if I had the math skills – it could have been engineering or chemistry. If I'd started playing pool earlier than 13, it could have been pool-playing.

AC • In the poem "on hands and darkness," a palm-reader finds "the child line ... [f]aint ... distant blue, like hills losing oxygen" (16). That's a great simile, but it's terrifically sad.

JM • The distance from my son was a very sad time in my life. Poetry is about finding similes and metaphors to match the feeling.

AC • "Lamentations at Gravity's Feet" (24-40) is a series of ghazals. What does this form enable you to do?

JM • To connect things that normally would not be connected. After I had done the first couple, I realized I was working on a sequence. I read John Thompson's *Stilt Jack* in '89 or '90 and that was probably why I started thinking about ghazals.

AC • Why is gravity such a powerful and pervasive metaphor in your poetry?

JM • There's no escaping it, is there, at least not down here?

AC • Is there gravity in the afterlife if there is an afterlife?

JM • Dante set Hell at the very centre of the earth's mass so that's where gravity would be most of a force. I'm reading the John Cicardi translation of Dante at the moment.

AC • In the first of the "Lamentations," the narrator is "Here at gravity's feet" (25) and in another, he is "fallen to earth ... / Broken in gravity's hand" (32). In physical terms, this is the course of human life, but something else is intended here, isn't it?

JM • Gravity is emotional. It's about as low as you can be in spirits and still be here, still be alive. Gravity's the opposite of levity. That's part of what I'm trying to do: Find levity through gravity, through wordplay. Earlier we were talking about what I look for in poetry – joy in words, but the poetry doesn't have to be full of joy.

AC • The gnomic nature of the couplets in "Lamentations" creates the effect of folk riddles: "At least, with snow, / Where you have been disappears" (26) and "The old man with white wild hair insists / The faster I go, the heavier I get" (34). Is poetry close to riddle?

JM • I think so. The same compression. Each word should have as many meanings as possible, or at least you want a word to have more than one meaning, which is how riddles work. The "white wild hair" one is easy. That's Einstein.

AC • "All is flux, and contingent upon observation" (35). Are you a relativist?

JM • In some contexts I would be, and in others I'd be an absolutist. In terms of poetry, for example, what I like, I like absolutely. But then, I might like something absolutely today, but tomorrow I might not.

AC • Doesn't the line that I just quoted suggest that what we're looking at today won't be the same tomorrow?

JM • It does, but it also says the person doing the looking won't be the same. It's wonderfully unsteady.

AC • "[T]ime smears as easily as fingerprints, or lipstick" (37). Do the "Lamentations" suggest that gravity is a dependable force and time is not?

JM • In the first place, gravity is a force and time isn't. In that sense, gravity's dependable. Time is an abstraction. My perception of time changes. It can go by really quickly or really slowly, but gravity you can count on. Time and space, though, are too closely connected to completely separate them. Islanders, and perhaps all Canadians, tend to talk about distances in terms of travel time: "It's a good three hours." We conflate them. In terms of physics, time and space are intertwined. They're one thing, and gravity shapes space, meaning it also shapes time. The curvature of space is most obvious around objects of the heaviest mass, which makes the strongest observable instance of gravity.

AC • Old Testament prophets and angels arc everywhere in the "Lamentations," as you'd expect from the title. Are they another version of gravity?

JM • The angels aren't. They may be the only thing in "Lamentations" that aren't affected by gravity. For them, it's not a force. But there is the line about "one more stone angel" (32). That's an angel that's leaving its angel state behind. If angels allow themselves to turn to stone, they're subject to gravity. The prophets are the voice of the past. They're the voice of the preacher.

AC • Are the prophets connected to a personal past or the historical past?

JM • Both really, but they're connected in particular to my personal past and the absorption of the Old Testament as a child.

AC • In the part of *Sledgehammer* set in the Rockies and on the Prairies, geology and palaeontology enter the story. Do these geographical areas seem older than the coastal areas?

JM • That's the feeling I was after in that section. The Prairies seem physically vast and unending, so there's a conflation of time and space.

AC • There are "harrows," "combines," and "diggers" in "Far from the Sea (Portage la Prairie, MB)" (47-51). Did you do farm work on the Prairies?

JM • I was working for a farmer at one point. I loved being on the land, but I hated working for that farmer. Also, growing up, in my pre-teens, we spent a lot of time at my uncle's farm at West Point [PEI]. We were always around farm machinery.

AC • "Far from the Sea ..." says that the earth resents and resists the "ritual rending into straight lines" (49) and the "regimental summer" that inscribes "precision" on old black earth (50). Is poetry, by parallel, a regimentation of thought and the past?

JM • It is, but it's also a freeing of thought. I think poetry involves a more free arranging of the past than prose does simply because there are so many springboards in poetry. Every word is a springboard. In a good poem, you can go in many directions from each word. There is the doubling effect – the combining of meanings in a word – in order to set thought free.

AC • The narrator reserves his deepest scorn for Ontario where "imagination has merged with the digestive track" (52). And that expresses what perception of Ontario?

JM • Well, they've got their heads up their asses mostly.

AC • There are two kinds of chaos in *Sledgehammer* – nature's "No particular order" (57) and the chaos of "convenience mistaken for progress" (56). Is one of these benign, the other malignant?

JM • Human-made chaos is malignant, but I wouldn't say there was a benign chaos. That would imply that something was thinking.

AC • On September 11th, were you eerily aware of the rant, "Note to my few friends ..." (56-57), that posits a "yellow moon ... / A screaming sawblade ... /... to topple the CN Tower the / World Trade Center, world trade ..."(56)?

JM • I have the excuse of the car bomb. In that poem, I was thinking back to the car bomb that was planted in the garage of the World Trade Center in 1993.

AC • So you weren't being prophetic or an instigator?

JM • Perhaps an original thinker.

AC • The poem "Sledgehammer" says that the work of the hammer is "to break everything apart / in search of the pure in flesh grown dry / in bones & dust" (65). This sounds like Ezekiel. Is poetry's task resurrection?

JM • In a sense, it is. Just as "A List (By Colour) of Things Left Behind" (15) is a resurrection of clichés. Poetry is both reinvigorating the old and trying to find the new. Poetry is about getting out of routines in language and in life, in general. We get comfortable and stale. Language grows stagnant and complacent. The task of poetry has always been to refresh us and to break us out of our becoming set. Whether poetry does that through terror or joy, it's the newness, the startlingness, the strangeness that we look for in a poem. For over a year now, I've been mulling over a wonderful essay by Harold Bloom on strangeness.

AC • "[T]his Island suffers from a gentility of / low hills" (66). Does this mean that imagination is earth-bound here, no soaring in the high air?

JM • Not necessarily. I was trying to say that we tend to limit ourselves through politeness. For instance, there was a play at the MacKenzie Theatre [Charlottetown] a couple of years ago and the theatre was running advertisements about the 50th standing ovation. Islanders tend to do that with theatre and other things. They give people standing ovations for breathing.

AC • And that niceness does what?

JM • It dulls our discernment. If we're applauding everything, then nothing stands out. No standards. One of the things that makes us human is the ability to discern patterns and to notice anomalies, and to make judgments. Judgment is closely connected to imagination. In order to recognize something as strange or useful or fresh, you have to be able to distinguish between things.

AC • The same poem, "landscape, from lowdown," suggests that the Island is itself a portion of a beast "ancient & gentle," which will on "a whim

... wing away" (67). In another poem, the Island landscape is the place of the goddess (68-70), and in yet another, "the soil drank god" (90). Are you constructing or retrieving myth in these poems? Are you myth-making?

JM • Yes, I do think not just poetry but daily life – the moving through every day – is a process of myth-making: The making of the myth of ourselves. I have been sliding that into my poetry. Myths may limit us if we stick to them too long, but they are very important to us.

AC • "Ancient" is perhaps the most frequent word in *Sledgehammer*. Is it a term of affection? It's there in the first *Sledgehammer* poem; in "landscape, from lowdown" (66-67); and in "My love is strung with the ancient" (83-84), the father poem, and in other places.

JM • It's not a term of affection in the father poem. That's for sure. Perhaps it's a term of inevitability or inescapability.

AC • Another version of gravity?

JM • I hadn't thought of that but, yes. It's in "Lamentations" (24-40) too, now that I think about it.

AC • *Sledgehammer* tours a vast landscape. Sometimes, as in "Because I speak too rarely" (58), the body is a landscape that can be similarly toured, and the mind is a "landscape ... ripped & torn" (96). This tendency to view other things as landscape suggests that the visual leads in your poetry. Would that be accurate?

JM • I'm very visual in my poetry. Creating images was the first thing that I worked on when I started to think seriously about writing.

AC • In "Drinking with the Neurosurgeon" (73-74), an incision into the brain reveals God and a patient playing pool. Einstein said that God does not play dice with the universe. Perhaps he plays pool – "'Double, or nothing'" (74). Does he?

JM • God is at play in the fields of the brain.

AC • An echo of Leonard Cohen's line "I asked my Father. I said Father change my name ... " from his song "Lover Lover Lover," opens your poem "The Surface [:] Viscosity of Want" (79), and a Blakean line – "And all the flowers threw down their petals" – closes the poem. Are these poets with whom you identify?

JM • As I said, imagery was the first thing I started to work on and that was after someone had introduced me to Leonard Cohen's music. From there, I found his poetry, specifically *The Energy of Slaves*. That's the first modern poetry I can remember reading. His images really struck me. I wanted to capture that. I don't know Blake very well. I'm not ready for Blake. I'm attempting to read Blake, but I always hit a wall. So that's not a Blakean line. It's actually a reference to Chinese poetry, through Pound, a translation of Li Po: "It's like the flowers falling at Spring's end / Confused, whirled in a tangle" (59), the inevitability of it, no matter what we do.

AC • "This Binary Perception" (80) laments imprisonment in the present, the way that we are stuck "between behind and before," and other variations of that binary. The poem says "we believe // we cannot rattle unborn bones at the dead" (80), which implies, doesn't it, that but for limiting belief, we could?

JM • In that poem I'm thinking, once again, about physics, and that time is not necessarily a one-way flow. Some part of us, apparently, goes both ways in time. "[B]etween behind and before" is not necessarily being stuck in the present so much as being some here and some there, not being able to decide between the past and the future, not being able to look just one way.

AC • Reviewing *Sledgehammer*, I said with great confidence that "He Kept to Himself, Mostly" (81-82) was about Milton Acorn. Are you going to tell me who the subject of this portrait poem is?

JM • It's a poem about a serial killer.

AC • You must have gulped when I said it was about Acorn.

JM • The difference between what you saw and what I wrote isn't that great. The poem is about compulsion. Acorn was obsessed and compulsive about certain things.

AC • "He Kept to Himself, Mostly" (81-82) employs the body-as-furnace metaphor, which turns up in other poems and, second, it says that the body is a factory of love. In an earlier poem, "hearthouse" (20-21), the heart is a furnace. Do you see this poem (81-82) as central to the book as it collects together some dominant metaphors and motifs?

JM • In terms of the structure of the book, in its placement in the book, "He Kept to Himself, Mostly" is an echo or reflection of the earlier poem, "hearthouse." They share a metaphorical connection, and whereas "He Kept to Himself, Mostly" is about the inability to perceive love, "hearthouse" is about trying to express love through pain. It was written in immense pain without devolving into saccharine sentimentality. In "He Kept to Himself," I was thinking of sociopaths not having any empathy for other people, not having the ability to feel others' pain. They're the ultimate solipsists.

AC • Although there is a love story in *Sledgehammer*, a son's relationship to his father is of equal importance. In my review of the book, I suggested there was both a poetic father, Acorn, and a biological father. Now, I'd say that the biological father is also the poetic father. Is that so?

JM • Much as I hate to admit that, it's true. One of the reasons I love sounds and words, and am aware of the power of words and the power of rhetoric, is seeing my father preach. So yes, "My love is strung with the ancient" (83-84) is about my poetic as well as my biological father.

AC • The three father poems – "My love is strung with the ancient" (83-84); "Where I First Saw the Light" (85-86); "In Lieu of Flowers" (87-89) – clustered towards the end of the book are powerful. The most volcanic language in the book is in those poems. They look to me like the birthplace crater of the book.

JM • In a metaphorical sense, maybe even in a literal sense, they are. As a child and a teenager when I needed to make things stop happening, when I needed to escape, books were the places where I went, which reinforced my love of words and my desire to use them myself.

AC • "My love is strung with the ancient" is remarkable for its spitting, sizzling rage, but it is equally surprising in what it reaches for to describe filial love – from the "coil-spring" action of a dinosaur to "the destruction of hydrogen bombs" (83-84). Is this a poem that loves as much as it hates?

JM • I was angry when I wrote it. I couldn't decide between the two – love and hate. When I was writing it, I was feeling a lot of rage, but I was also trying to get a grasp on the nature of love itself. It's a poem that questions: "Is this what love is? Is it destructive?"

AC • There's a good deal of destruction in the imagery of *Sledgehammer*. It does seem to suggest that it's not possible to love without bringing destruction along. Is love – whether you're talking about romantic love, sexual love, or filial love – ever innocent?

JM   • Love is a manifestation of the human mind, so can it ever be innocent? Going back again to the Bible, to Genesis, and the Tree of the Knowledge of Good and Evil, when we begin to reason, we lose our innocence. If we define humans as reasoning creatures, love cannot be innocent.

AC   • The dialect speech that you use in "Where I First Saw the Light" (85-86) comes from where?

JM   • Comes from my youth. Comes from my mother.

AC   • There's just two years between the first book and the second, *Shaken by Physics*. That's a lot of writing in two years.

JM   • *Shaken by Physics* began before *Sledgehammer* was published. As in "Lamentations at Gravity's Feet" (*Sledgehammer* 24-40), I'm once again playing with ideas from physics.

AC   • You're not out from under gravity?

JM   • The style in *Shaken by Physics* may be different but the themes aren't.

AC   • The first book is personal, the second less so. Does the beginning poet have to get the autobiographical stuff out of the way to move on?

JM   • The byword in writing is to write what you know so writers tend to begin with that. Whether or not such things should be published is another matter. The stuff that is being published that I can't stomach is too autobiographical and not well done.

AC   • The poems in *Shaken by Physics* are less narrative than those in *Sledgehammer*. What replaces narrative thread in these poems?

JM   • Perhaps I'm trying to extend metaphor right through a series instead of just through a single poem. That extended metaphor in *Shaken* has to do with changing perceptions of the world and how we construct history.

AC   • *Sledgehammer* is unified through its cross-country excursion. What unifies *Shaken by Physics*?

JM   • The attempt to play with ideas of quantum mechanics and modern physics, including relativity, and not necessarily just in the poems

                       ANNE COMPTON

grounded in terms from physics. As the book moves toward its end, the terms fall away, but the effect of flux on observation is still at work.

AC   • So this book is more conceptual than the last?

JM   • Yes.

AC   • For all its physics, aren't the creation and the fall really the subjects of this new book?

JM   • That's a good part of it. It's funny you say that because I may be working on another manuscript at the moment which is tentatively titled "The First Mistake: Learning to Read," which refers to Genesis and the Tree the Knowledge of Good and Evil. It's more about the process of reading and synthesizing. Whether it's poetry or prose – if it's well written – it's teaching us to think, and once we begin to do that, we become open to different perceptions of things we're very familiar with, so it could lead to a fall, the loss of a certain kind of bliss.

AC   • Does reading jeopardize the garden?

JM   • It leads you right out of the goddam garden. It's the path out. And, really, you want out.

AC   • Again, are the creation and the fall subjects in *Shaken by Physics?*

JM   • They are not *the* subjects, but one of the very first poems in the book is "Now We Sing Our Descent" (12-13).

AC   • A retelling of Genesis?

JM   • Yes, it is, and the sequence towards the end, "Black Feather Poems" (57-69), is about a very specific fall. The poems in that series are an exploration of my state of being a month or so after the World Trade Center events.

AC   • "Now We Sing Our Descent" (12-13) presents a physics of the fall: A descent into distance, dimension, direction that leads to "purpose," which in your retelling becomes the "fruit we ate." Why is "purpose" our undoing?

JM   • Once we begin to think, we believe that we have to do something with our thought. It's inevitable that you'll find purpose once you begin to think, although we never attain our purpose.

AC • Was the story of the fall drummed into you when you were growing up?

JM • It was: "We are not in a state of grace. We must be saved ...."

AC • Is *Shaken by Physics* excavating the roots of "progress," which is what you excoriated in the first book?

JM • Technological progress sprang from classical physics and the new physics. Technology is the manifestation in physical form of those ideas.

AC • I'm trying to find the link between the critique of progress in the first book and the idea, in the second book, that "purpose" is "the fruit we ate."

JM • With purpose, everything becomes calculation.

AC • In that poem, "the wind sends its gusts through us" (13), so have reason and logic made scarecrows of the human?

JM • No, they don't make scarecrows of us. Perhaps they prevent us from being scarecrows. With over-indulgence in reason and logic, we become too full of ourselves to let the wind gust through us. The wind is a positive image: It's about emptying out, about going back before purpose.

AC • Physics is the obvious source of metaphor in this new book, but aren't the psalms the source of its language?

JM • That's quite possible, although it's not necessarily conscious. The King James version of the Bible does echo in a lot of my writing, not just in *Shaken by Physics*.

AC • "Lobster Boats, PEI" (15-16) is written against all the pretty "post-cards." Tourism panders to the easiest emotion, sentimentality, but what else is at stake in the proliferation of "postcards"?

JM • The postcard is the equivalent of repeating a word over and over again until it's meaningless. "Lobster Boats, PEI" is an early poem, from the time when I started to think about landscape and its effect on people. We are what we are because of landscape. If we lose the ability to perceive landscape as it truly is, we are in danger of losing ourselves: "We have sold this Island so far into scenery / We have forgotten its landscape, / Have forgotten landscape contains us ..." (15).

ANNE COMPTON

AC • You have a preoccupation with gods (Thor, Yahweh, Icarus) and birds. Any connection between these two?

JM • Birds tend to gather around human habitations to scrounge because the pickings are easy. Other than that, we aren't any use to them. They are unchanged by us. Whatever messages we take from them, we are creating in our own minds. The messages are not being brought to us. The crows come a half an hour or so before dark. You look up in the sky and there are multitudes of them winging towards Victoria Park [Charlottetown]. They seem to keep passing overhead forever. It's impossible not to notice them. The crows in *Shaken by Physics* are a tipping of the hat to Ted Hughes. The other thing is that in North American native mythology, crow is trickster.

AC • In terms of the human body, the hand gets a lot of attention, particularly in the first section of *Shaken* – the cramped hand of "This Is ..." (11); hands buried "to the wrists in red furrows" (14); and the hand holding a hatchet in "Red Sky in the Morning (A Murder of Crows)" (23). Why is this part of the human body so significant?

JM • Our opposable thumbs enable us to manipulate objects. It's another thing that makes us human. The hand is also how we connect with one another.

AC • Well, yes, the hand is important in human evolution and in human relationship, but is the presence of hands in those poems more personal than that? Is it just that the hand is the second most important thing after language?

JM • The hand can be both our curse and our blessing.

AC • A stylistic feature of your work is the title in brackets or partly in brackets. What's that about?

JM • The parentheses are a qualification of the title. They strengthen any ambiguity or ambivalence that might be in the title, or if it's not there, they create it. I'm trying to recognize ambiguity. I *am* a relativist!

AC • As in *Sledgehammer,* so also in *Shaken by Physics*, there is strong figurative language: "Look how its waters are / Remote as protestants" (35) or "The high octaves of trees ..." (33). Would it be fair to say that you think figuratively?

JM • I do, and also visually.

AC • A poem often pivots on a pun, but the entire second section of *Shaken* is constructed around the dissonance/dissonnets pun. "Dissonnets" contains 14 poems.

JM • No, actually, it contains 13. The 14th poem in that section can be read as part of the sequence to make it a meta-sonnet or it can stand apart from the sequence. What I wanted in that sequence was to create these 13-line poems, a truncation of the sonnet.

AC • Are you reworking the traditional form of the sonnet, dismantling it?

JM • After writing a couple of the poems, I realized they were close to the sonnet and I decided to keep working at it. The restriction to a specific length, and the form, fluid as it is, drive the poems. I came up with the word "dissonnets" and played on dissonance at the same time.

AC • In *Shaken by Physics* you are moving away from free verse and into formalism?

JM • I wouldn't say that I was moving into formalism any more than I would claim that I wrote free verse. There are almost as many forms as there are poems. In *Sledgehammer* the poem and the form found each other. That's my story and I'm sticking to it.

WORKS CITED
— • —

Compton, Anne. "Of Sons and Fathers." *Fiddlehead* 209 (Autumn 2001): 118-21.
Mackenzie, John. *Shaken by Physics*. Vancouver: Polestar, 2002.
– – –. *Sledgehammer*. Vancouver: Polestar, 2000.
Pound, Ezra. "Exile's Letter." *Selected Poems*. New York: New Directions, 1957. 56-59.

"A MANY-VEINED LEAF":
MINUTIAE AND MULTIPLICITY IN BRIAN BARTLETT'S POETRY

With the publication of his selected poems imminent, Brian Bartlett and I sat down to talk about his four books of poetry – *The Afterlife of Trees* (2002), *Granite Erratics* (1997), *Underwater Carpentry* (1993), and *Planet Harbor* (1989). Although *The Afterlife of Trees* was our chief talking point, our conversation included the earlier books, the forthcoming selected, and his prose. In a career that has spanned three decades, Bartlett has published three chapbooks as well as four full-length collections, a body of work characterized by generosity of spirit, a tone of humility, precision in word and fact, wit and playfulness. He has been the winner twice of the *Malahat* Long Poem Prize and the recipient, in 1996, of a fellowship to the Hawthornden Castle International Retreat for Writers in Scotland. In 2000, his poem "Foot-doctor for the Homeless" won the Petra Kenney Competition. His critical work includes essays on poets such as Tim Lilburn and Elizabeth Bishop. *Don McKay: Essays on His Works*, edited by Bartlett, will appear in 2004.

A professor of English literature and Creative Writing at St. Mary's University, Bartlett was born in St. Stephen, New Brunswick, raised in Fredericton. He lived in Montreal for 15 years before moving to Halifax in 1990.

On a clear, cold day in January 2003 – in the book-lined Bartlett home and, later, at the Heartwood Bakery and Café – Brian Bartlett and I talked about his poems, poetics, and the process of choosing poems for *Wanting the Day: Selected Poems* (2003).

A year and some months after this interview, Bartlett's *Wanting the Day* won the Atlantic Poetry Prize. In 2004, he published "Travels of the Watch," a chapbook.

AC • Certain declarations are made in your most recent collection, *The Afterlife of Trees*, among them: "What I want is what / shakes up the known" (17). Is this a statement of your poetics?

BB • Certainly I like to see things in a new light, give them a spin they don't ordinarily have. But I don't want to over-rely on that or insist upon everything being transformed or every move being iconoclastic. There are also things – an infinite number of things – to be found within the familiar.

AC • So your poetic is not the pursuit of quirks?

BB • Curiosities and exceptions are often what draw our attention, but I wouldn't want my poetry to become just a catalogue of eccentricities and little-known facts. If there were a whole book of poems like "Sloth Surprises" (*AOT* 16-18), it would soon stop surprising. It would feel like *Ripley's Believe It Or Not*.

AC • In "Listening on the Back Steps," the first poem in *The Afterlife of Trees*, the metaphor for a poem, or for poem-making, is "a box for small births" (3). If the poet is lucky, the words will take flight from that bird-house, but that's not a sure thing. And in "Hawthornden Improvisations" (*AOT* 37-58), the narrator says, "anything can happen" in a poem (52). Is there a lot of surprise for you in the writing process?

BB • Yes, definitely. For a reader, if there's no surprise, there's no poetry. The surprise may be subtle, low-key, rather than in-your-face. Surprises that are explicit and heavy-handed and outrageous can quickly lose their appeal. The surprises I'm most interested in don't give the impression of shock-effect. I'm not much interested in that kind of frontal assault – though now and then it's good to feel jolted.

AC • But is there self-surprise in the writing process?

BB • Especially in going from a first draft to the 15th or 20th, I find it surprising how far the eventual draft can be from the original. My first drafts tend to be quite tentative and groping. There may not be a single line that survives until the final draft. To use a sculpting metaphor, finding the shape within the stone can be a slow process.

AC • Do you write to "see who you are" (3) as the first poem in *Afterlife* seems to suggest?

BB • It's not something I set out to do, but it's a product, a bonus, of the process. Writing can help you gain a self-knowledge that you might not otherwise have, but like I say, I don't think of that as one of the more significant values of writing poems.

AC • Doublings or overlappings appear to be of interest to you.

BB • It seems to me the word "overlappings" appears in more than one poem. It's a word I'm attracted to just like I'm intrigued by the ways things fade into each other or mimic each other– whether it's a mockingbird picking up on other voices or sand on a beach shaped by the wind to look like waves.

AC • You're a highly visual poet, but sometimes, through synaesthesia, a visual image slides over into the auditory: For example, the flowers at McCormack's Beach are "sopranos to our sight" (*AOT* 15). In another poem, "[Charlie's] voice got entangled in the garden" (*AOT* 30). Is that entanglement of sensory experience truer to the way we experience the world than the purely visual?

BB • Yes, definitely. Synaesthesia is a reflection of the way our minds and our eyes work. It's not just an ornamental literary device. It's a tool that we use when we explore the world. In poetry, synaesthesia gives an accuracy to observation that's not possible if we stick to just one sense. In the same way, metaphor can be more accurate than a simpler transcription of what's seen.

AC • So experience comes to us through an entanglement of the senses?

BB • Sense experiences are simultaneous, and it's hard to get that simultaneity in poetry. I like imagery that's evocative to the mind's eye, but I also like to have the words ringing off one another, echoing. The way words work with each other should be pleasurable in itself so that the reader experiences the sounds of the words along with the observational power of what's presented. One of the primary things for me in a poem is the experience of sounds, the way words work together, and how that differs from language in everyday speech. Still, a lot of poetry is an intensification of daily speech. Poetry would be the poorer if it didn't include both the vernacular and uncommon turns of language.

AC • Although you are aware of the poem in a sculptural sense while you're writing it, do you have in mind the delivery of the poem?

BB • I often mutter the poem under my breath or aloud as I'm working on it. I want it to have a resonance and intricacy of sound when it's read aloud so that it will be appealing to the ear in the same way that the shape of it is appealing to the eye.

AC • Is the voice you use in a poem affected by the fact that you may be reading the poem in public someday?

BB • I usually think in terms of fairly intimate voices, rather than voices projected publicly to a crowd. I remember what Alden Nowlan used to say about the paradox of public readings. If he thought of a listener, he said, he thought of a single human being, not 50 people gathered in a room. The relationship I sense with the listener is more one on one than performance. It's hard to say, though. Maybe there are some poems, storytelling poems, where you might think of a larger audience, but I still don't think of my poems as *declaimed*. I trust in something faithful to the conversational mode, as opposed to something that's oratorical or spoken from the heights. One of the most exciting things in Yeats' poetry is how he'll be rolling along in his oratorical, heightened mode, then something more conversational breaks in, adding pathos or humility or uncertainty. I also wouldn't want to suggest I don't find oratorical modes exciting in other poets – Robert Bringhurst and Al Moritz, for instance.

AC • I want to ask you about the recurrence of the door metaphor. A voice can "swing open whatever is shut" (*AOT* 4); the effect of wind, according to one poem, is "a door opening" (*AOT* 10); and love is "your fingers unlocking / door after door after door" (*AOT* 49). I notice that this is also a significant metaphor in *Granite Erratics* and *Underwater Carpentry.* What does this pattern – the recurrence of the door metaphor – speak to?

BB • I'm astonished! Nobody's pointed out this pattern to me before. I'll probably never use another door metaphor! A door is a rather archetypal image, though. I imagine it's the sort of image that Gaston Bachelard might investigate. In fact, maybe he does deal with it in *The Poetics of Space.* Opening and closing is one of the most basic contrasts the human psyche knows. Opening is an image that suggests freedom and liberality and multiplicity, whereas shutting or closing is ....

AC • ... elegiac.

BB • I could see an elegy working in terms of opening as well, opening oneself to what's beyond the grief, to the memories of the person or thing mourned. I wouldn't think of elegies strictly in terms of shutting down.

AC • Does the door have to do with entrance into poetic space?

BB • In the case of the first poem of *Afterlife,* "Listening on the Back Steps" (3-4), which ends with the great saxophonist whose sound bursts through the doorway and "swing[s] open whatever is shut" (4), opening is an image of originality. This is the trail-blazing artist moving into something fresh, something that's not been done before. I was thinking of Charlie Parker, and the poem uses the names of a few music clubs he knew in his youth.

AC • Is poetry, like music, capable of "swing[ing] open whatever is shut, whatever needs more air" (4)?

BB • Sure. Like other poets, I've often felt a parallel between what poetry might do and what certain kinds of music do. Listening to more wide-ranging kinds of jazz has encouraged me to attempt poems like "Underwater Carpentry" (*UC* 89-102), which is mood-changing, mosaic-like, or improvisational, like "Hawthornden Improvisations" (*AOT* 37-58). I'm attracted to the idea of improvisation, but there's an irony involved in all of that because I also want the poem polished. I tried to get that irony out front at the very beginning of "Hawthornden Improvisations" where I say, "'Improvisation is the name of the game,' I vowed to write / months ago, in winter, walking slippery streets of home // an ocean away" (39). The decision to improvise is itself an un-improvised thing since it was based on a vow made on another continent months earlier.

AC • The words "Essay" and "Footnote" in "Lost Footnote from an Essay on Rhythm" (*AOT* 6-7) suggest the pedantic, but the pun on "note," like the word "Rhythm," draws attention to music. For you does a poem exist somewhere between music and essay?

BB • Pun on "note": I hadn't thought of that. I think some poems ache to be close to music. Others that are more discursive and digressive and lack that kind of sustained intensity might overlap at times into the realm of essay. The lyric uses compactness to the maximum; every line rings. But I'm also drawn to trying poems like "Hawthornden Improvisations" (*AOT* 37-58) that are sometimes leisurely and relaxed, that aren't always insisting on heightened emotion and intense sense experiences. Another source of that more leisurely mode is the diary or journal.

AC • I understand that for most of your life, you've kept a journal. "Hawthornden Journal," which parallelled the writing of the "Improvisations," is a published example. So, is the journal a ghost form that haunts your poetry?

BB • Yes. And I realize that not everyone is comfortable with the ghost. The Hawthornden poem had some very enthusiastic responses, but it also had some lukewarm ones. One of my friends thought the poem was too close to a diary. He said it struck him as "notes toward a poem," rather than a poem itself. I do feel now that if I went back to it, I might still cut out some stanzas.

AC • Are essay and music the poles between which your poetry moves?

BB • You might say that, yes. Even in "Sloth Surprises" (*AOT* 16-18), though it's concentrated in three-line stanzas and moves quickly down the page, there are elements of discursiveness – references to the Internet and quotations from various naturalists. In terms of the lyric, there are impure things there such as dropping in quotations and making a hokey joke about the *William Tell* overture, and yet, by the end, the poem moves toward a lyrical celebration. We were talking earlier about declaimed intensification, and when I'm reading that poem aloud, I'm aware that its ending – "Sloths swim with the might of eagles flying" (18) – might be a declaimed line. It almost has the feeling of a punchline, but I hope that it grows organically out of the poem and isn't just a cheap capping-off. One reviewer of *Granite Erratics* took me to task for punchlines. He said that I suffered from an unexamined weakness for snappy endings. I was glad that he'd said that because it made me wary ....

AC • ... but that can be dangerous.

BB • It can, and it can make you timid. In any case, I only caught wind of the review two years after it was published, too late for it to have any effect on *The Afterlife of Trees*. Years ago, in Montreal, I read Barbara Hernstein Smith's book *Poetic Closure*. She points out that the open ending is as much a convention as any other ending. It's just one of the options. Still, I don't want an ending that makes it feel as if the poem is shutting down, all loose ends tied up. As a reader, I resist poems of

ANNE COMPTON

that sort. Just before that review of *Granite Erratics* came out, I'd reviewed a book by a fellow poet and said there was a tendency toward overly emphatic endings in a few of the poems. So it was amusing when a reviewer said a similar thing about my work. You can't see the mote in your own eye.

AC • The speakers in the first section of *Afterlife* are often walkers – in parks, by rivers, through woods. Would you describe yourself as a naturalist-observer-describer?

BB • That would be accurate but incomplete. I hesitate a bit over the word "describer," although I do feel great reverence for the way things are before we do much with them – even if we only know things *through* our consciousness. Paying prolonged, patient attention to how things appear is one thing I respond to in poets like Elizabeth Bishop and Eric Ormsby. It's almost as if the act of looking closely at the object is sometimes enough, which is what Ormsby himself suggests in an interview (200). It's not like the poet has to manipulate the object or show off his or her own consciousness.

AC • But you hesitate over the word "describer"?

BB • For some people, the word might imply a clinical, detached approach. I'm interested in offering some details about the object that suggest a response to it, a sympathy for it, some sort of attitude toward it so that readers are still aware of the perceiver, even if he's somewhat invisible or half-hidden. The perceiver isn't making any claims to being scientifically neutral or god-like.

AC • The presence of the perceiver is part of what is delivered in the poem?

BB • All you have in the poem comes to you through the language of the observer. Every line of a poem reveals or creates its character, even if it's intensely focused on a red pepper, like in one of Sue Sinclair's poems. Even in the work of the haiku masters, who mostly avoid metaphor and try to present the thing or event as cleanly and clearly as possible, there's a reflection of personality and character.

AC • "Shuffles" (8-9), a two-part poem, limits itself to two instances of 12 words. Are you interested in what can be accomplished in verbal limitation and confinement?

BB • Yes. And I'm interested in how confinement can help spark freedoms of association. I suppose such freedoms are more obvious in relatively spacious forms like the glosa (*AOT* 72-73), with its 40 lines, but I hope they're also there in what I've called "shuffles." While I enjoy using limitation – partly just as a kind of play – I'm just as drawn to what's expansive, digressive, many-faced. *Afterlife* has one poem that's a single line long, and another that's 20 pages long. Many years ago a friend of mine said something like, "Poetry is a matter of leaving out," and I remember getting a bit hot under the collar and protesting that poetry is also very much a matter of including, embracing, multiplying.

AC • "Shuffles" (*AOT* 8-9), with its reference to footwork, although the title word is a pun, leads me to wonder about your preoccupation with feet. Later in this volume, we have "Foot-doctor for the Homeless" (82-83). In *Underwater Carpentry*, there's a poem called "Première Pédicurie" (35-36). I'm going to suggest – partly facetiously – that the feet and the eyes are the essential equipment for the poet according to Brian Bartlett.

BB • Are you saying I have a foot fetish! Although I don't think that it's finally possible to really escape yourself, walking and exploring are attempts to lose consciousness of the self and concentrate on what's out there, beyond you.

AC • In "Underwater Carpentry" (*UC* 89-102), the narrator wants "a voice / freed of all travels but those / inside ..." (98-99). Has that ambition been fulfilled?

BB • No, and I wouldn't want it to be. At that point in the poem, I was expressing an itch to write more transcendentally, to get beyond the specifics of one time and place – I recall thinking, *More like Rilke.* That sounds pretentious, I know! But right after what you just quoted, the poem goes on: "but the four elements / hold me hard." So the poet confesses he's got feet of clay, that "pure spirituality" isn't for him. And I sort of intended as a joke the lines "one way out / [is] to sneak in many times and places." That is, you can get away from one time and place not by slipping into a more abstract realm, but by multiplying your involvements in *various* places and times.

AC • Each of your last three books contains an especially long poem: "Hawthornden Improvisations" (*AOT* 37-58); "The Woods on the Way to School" (*GE* 27-34); "Underwater Carpentry" (*UC* 89-102). Are you moving away from the brief stand-alone lyric, and what explains that move?

BB • I don't think I'm moving away from the lyric because I still feel a strong fondness for the stand-alone shorter poem, but reading A.R. Ammons, spending so much time with his work and writing over 400 pages on it as a doctoral dissertation, helped deepen my interest in longer poems. He's done many long poems that are extremely free and improvisational. His first one, *Tape for the Turn of the Year*, is, incidentally, a diary.

AC • The long poem, the travel poem, and a gravitating toward the essay are interrelated tendencies in your work?

BB • The first long poem, "Underwater Carpentry" (*UC* 89-102), felt like a breakthrough. I wrote it soon after I moved from Montreal to Halifax. It was, in some senses, my farewell to Montreal. I felt a new sort of freedom, throwing so many things into it. Different metaphors – the catalogue, the mosaic, film-splicing – could describe that kind of writing. It's over 10 years since I wrote that, and I still feel I haven't tapped into what I started in "Underwater Carpentry." I'd like to get back into that. Soon after, I wrote another long poem, "Trailing Juniper" (*UC* 103-15), which was an effort in a similar vein, but I'm not happy with it. There are passages that don't hold together. But then you might ask, "Is it the purpose of these wide-ranging, dishevelled poems to hold together?" Is that just the lyric self saying that this poem has to be somehow consistent and tightly structured?

AC • Even in the case of shorter poems, you favour a multi-sectioned structure, the sections numbered or marked by asterisks. What does that multi-part structure allow you to do?

BB • Back at UNB, I did a Creative Writing class with Fred Cogswell, who said my work was "kaleidoscopic," and then at Concordia, Clark Blaise used the same word for my fiction. There must be some significance to that. You often gain something from combining things rather than having them stand on their own. I like multi-perspective. The McGill-Queen's editor of *Afterlife* wanted some of the multi-part poems in *Afterlife* cut back to one section. He wanted only the first section of "Under the Old Roof" (12-14), which is in three sections. The first section could have stood on its own as an intense lyric, but I thought it was going to lose too much – including the comic bits in the second part – if sections were cut. I was interested in the variety – the kaleidoscope.

AC • You like to look at things from opposite sides and consider an argument from opposite positions. I see this in "Two for the Winds" (*AOT* 10-11) and in the paired poems, "The Afterlife of Trees" (19) and "A Toss of Cones" (*AOT* 20-21), for example. Am I right in thinking that there is a dialectical inclination in your work?

BB • The word "dialectical" suggests thesis, antithesis, and synthesis, and I'd resist the idea that those pairings move toward a synthesis. But there's duality, certainly.

AC • "Two for the Winds" (*AOT* 10-11) presents, on facing pages, winds that differ in degree or kind. The second kind "break the reins of everything tamed" (11). Are you on the side of these winds?

BB • Yes. To be on the side of those winds doesn't mean, though, that you sell your soul to chaos. "[E]verything tamed" should have the opportunity to be loosened. It's the metaphor of the door opening again.

AC • Is it the ferocity of natural force that keeps you coming back to nature as subject?

BB • That's one of many factors. Ferocity attracts, for sure. The sheer energy in those winds whipping around may be comparable to the musicianship, the feeling of freedom, in the jazz improvisations of "Listening on the Back Steps" (*AOT* 3 4). At the end of "Trailing Juniper" (*UC* 103-15), there's a passage that describes an ice storm. Enormous force, bringing human activities to a halt, is exhilarating, a reminder we're not masters of the universe. Though hurricanes and tornadoes can be destructive, we're attracted to them – as long as they keep their distance, of course.

AC • Is it the sublime in nature or the minutiae that attracts you?

BB • I don't see those as contrasts. The romantic sublime is often associated with mountains and seascapes, the grand in scale, but near the start of his essay "Nature," Emerson suggests almost anything, looked at in the right frame of mind, can create a sense of awe.

AC • In writing of nature, your strategy is sometimes to establish abundance through negation. In "The Colours at McCormack's Beach," except for a willet, "Nothing / else veers into sight. No fin surfaces, / no boat slides past" (*AOT* 15), but the list of absences is followed by a catalogue of flowers whose names suggest nature's variation on the colour yellow. Why do you set plenitude in negation?

ANNE COMPTON

BB • "McCormack's Beach" was the first time I had the idea of embodying in a poem the suggestion that however unyielding and bleak, neutral and grey a landscape might be – as happened on that day at McCormack's Beach – if you look closely enough, there's something that flips that impression and shows you in some little pocket of that space a fullness and vibrancy.

AC • Is this amplitude of detail a desire for total immersion in sensuous reality?

BB • Immersion, yes, but not total immersion, which I don't think is possible. It's very hard to give up the observer no matter how immersed one is. In *Pilgrim at Tinker Creek*, Annie Dillard has a beautiful passage about the fall into self-consciousness. She speaks of experiencing an absence of herself, feeling immersed in what she's observing. As soon as she makes that reflection, self-consciousness kicks in. I don't particularly lament the fact that we can't lose ourselves. I'm not that drawn to the mystical ideal of giving up the self utterly to plunge into the godhead. The most interesting differences in existence are those between distinct phenomena, and the interaction between them. That's more interesting than the absorption of one self into another, or the loss of self-consciousness for a passive state of mind, giving up your complex human mentality for something that's pure and unconscious.

AC • Some fairly eccentric bits of information – "a white elm drinks fifteen hundred gallons of water / from a hot dawn to a hot dusk ..." (*AOT* 21) – is deployed in your poetry. Is this connected to the catalogic tendency in your observations of nature?

BB • Yes. I love catalogues in poetry and other kinds of literature. They're one of the most exciting aspects of Whitman's work even if the relentlessness of the catalogues sometimes cancels out their effectiveness. Catalogues are a rapid, but closely observed, succession of images from a wide-ranging perspective. They are one of the best ways of conveying amplitude and getting lyric concentration away from a narrow focus that pinpoints one thing. And yes, I suppose the cataloguing tendency is connected to the accumulation of eccentric information. They reflect the same passion, the desire to hear and to see a multiplicity of things. Sometimes, though, I want to express how information can be oppressive and even blinding. "[T]o an osprey" talks of getting sick of those "shiny-paged bird books" (*AOT* 95). In that poem, there's almost relief that the osprey is distant, not close. Sometimes I want that distance.

Sometimes that perspective results in greater recognition, greater respect, for the thing as it is. That respect can be achieved by just letting it be out there, wherever it is, by not wanting to put the binoculars on it, not wanting to break it into its parts, but just to let it go on its way, without itching to paint it in fine detail. That poem is against always using the eagle-eye for minutiae.

AC • This is related to something the narrator says in "Hawthornden Improvisations" about being a pilferer: "[S]ome days you need to stand back // and let everything go on its way, unpilfered, / unexamined ..." (*AOT* 57). Does that "stand[ing] back" result in no poetry or a different kind of poetry?

BB • One of the kinds of poetry that can result from that reflects upon detachment itself. Some people would argue that using language, even naming, is a way of trying to pigeonhole a thing. I dealt with that anxiety in a long essay I wrote revolving around a P.K. Page poem. You have to remind yourself that your authority is very limited. It's a naive misunderstanding to suppose that somehow you know more than a fraction of what there potentially is to know about a thing – or a person, for that matter.

AC • In "The Afterlife of Trees" (19), an objective tone and an enumerative manner explore the ways in which living trees, and trees in their afterlives, contribute to our lives, but the poem is thereafter personalized and elegiac. Is beginning with the objective a way of restraining emotion, holding it back?

BB • I'd question whether that poem has an objective beginning. I'd hoped that in the rhythms and in the undertone of excitement, emotion comes through: "Neither sheep nor cows crisscross our lives as much" (19). I'd hope that there was a sense of awe in that opening line, and that the richness of sounds – the alliteration and rhyme echoing in "fuller" and "finer" and in "lost" and "last" – as the verse continues, would carry a sense of celebration. I guess I'm pushing back against the word "objective" the way I did with "descriptive."

AC • My question is related to something I observe in the poem "Three Windows" (*AOT* 65-67). What seems to be autobiographical is cast in the third person and contains the self-reflexive remark: "Three is a handy number / and all stories use scissors" (67). Do you as a poet want to hold the personal, anything autobiographical, at a distance?

BB • Between poets writing autobiographically and those trying to keep autobiography out of their work, I think of my work as being some-where in the middle. I'm certainly not at either end of the spectrum. Many of the poems I write don't use the first person, and many of those that do use it, fictionalize. And, as you pointed out, other poems written in the third person have an autobiographical basis. In the end, for the poetry it's the poem that matters and not my personal life. That's why I don't have qualms about modifying autobiographical facts. I also find that putting things in the third person loosens up my imagination.

AC • Are you leery then of sentimentality and nostalgia?

BB • Overall, I'd say that I'd be more leery of cynicism and coldness. When people speak about their worries about sentimentality, I say, "Well, cyn-icism seems more *au courant* at times." Sentimentality occurs when a poet is enamoured of his own emotion. Such a poet doesn't give credit to the reader to share in what the poet's feeling. Personally, I probably have more of an inclination towards the elegiac and the nostalgic, even the sentimental, than I have towards the ruthless and the distant. So I'm not that worried about the cynical in my own work because it's not a big part of my personality. I might, therefore, be more cautious about sentimentality. But I want poetry to move people. I don't want all my poems to be of primary appeal to the intellect – language as an endless set of indeterminates.

AC • Would you say that of the four books, *Afterlife* leans further away from the autobiographical and the personal?

BB • I don't think so. The third section of *Afterlife*, "The World of Counting," includes the family poems, the three or four poems that include my son. The glosa (72-73) is one of the most personal poems I've ever written. And "Hawthornden Improvisations" (37-58), although it's wide-ranging, has quite a bit of personal stuff.

AC • Is it liberating to adopt personae as you do in "Foot-doctor for the Homeless" (82-83) and "The Sonographer" (84-85)?

BB • Yes, and I'd like to try it more. By the way, when I first drafted "Foot-doctor," it was written in the voice of the middle-aged female doctor, but before workshopping it with friends, I chickened out and recast it in the third person. At the workshop, I mentioned the change, and after talking about it for a while as a third-person poem, my friends asked me to try it aloud in the first person. After hearing it that way, everyone – all women, by the way – told me it worked better in the woman's voice. That was rather pleasing – though in that poem I suppose gender is less crucial than profession and age and personal history.

AC • "Hawthornden Improvisations" (*AOT* 37-58) is catalogic, epistolary in part, and a poetics. How did it develop?

BB • "Improvisations" came out of the diary mode that I'd adopted while I was at the writers' retreat. Each morning I'd draft a few stanzas of it, and then I'd work on a prose piece in the afternoon – something more literally a journal. I decided before I went there that I didn't want to write a bunch of discrete poems and use the notebook where I'd accumulated lots of things. I wanted to go there a blank slate and see what came out of the experience. I did take my notebook along, though, so that long poem ends up being a mix of the notebook and unexpected things that emerged out of the experience of being at Hawthornden. I'd never know exactly what was going to be in the poem the next day because it might grow out of something I'd experienced the day before. But I was also picking up flotsam and jetsam from the notebook I'd brought overseas. I say at the beginning of the poem, "I've sent no list of what I want, / the old image-bank is closed" (39). In a sense, that's a joke because the "image-bank" wasn't closed. Things from the past rush in there. Like many long narrative poems, though, it ends up also being about the process of writing itself.

AC • You do give form to "Improvisations." There's a five-line stanza.

BB • When I started the poem, writing one section a day at Hawthornden, I had a draft structure more like that of "Underwater Carpentry" (*UC* 89-102), where there are no sections, no regular pattern on the page. But "Improvisations" started feeling too diffuse. Frankly, I felt a bit defeated when I settled on the five-line stanza. Part of me felt like I'd copped out or given in. But then I was tickled one day to think those five-line stanzas looked like bars of music.

AC • "However small, each thing fed from its own nature" (43), the Hawthornden narrator-traveller observes. This reminds me of Gerard Manley Hopkins and inscape. Is your loyalty first of all to the inward quality of an object?

BB • Yes. And to its outward qualities, which, I suppose, we're better equipped to know.

ANNE COMPTON

AC • Unlike Hopkins, the speaker in "Improvisations" discounts any "cloud-hidden Puppet Master" (43) responsible for the beauty of things. For you, are things in themselves sufficient?

BB • Yes. I'm a non-idealist in the sense that I don't feel the necessity for another realm to justify our daily realm. Thoreau ends one of the chapters of *Walden* by saying, "Talk of heaven! ye disgrace the earth" (200). That feeling comes out in the anti-Platonic section of "Improvisations": "the river in the glen isn't mimicking a crystal river / smoothly rushing in a perfect place" (*AOT* 53). Those lines resist the idea that things in nature are second-hand, inferior. That's an aspect of Platonic thought I've always found alien. It's a way of thinking that's caused some terrible problems in Western culture. It makes it less likely you're going to celebrate what's immediate, what you experience with your senses. It favours the visionary and heavenly. The harder thing for me, though, is imagining my stance from the perspective of someone who's in dire circumstances, suffering from malnutrition or living in a war zone. What sense would it make to them to talk about the immediate beauties of existence or the glories of nature? For them, the imagining of another realm, a heavenly destination, is a balm. That's a real roadblock in my own non-visionary approach to the world. For myself, though, I don't feel the need for some alternative reality. If you feel the earth is a secondary, tainted realm, and that there's this other glorious place, you're not as likely to look after the world you were born into.

AC • Observing a chapel's "over- // flowing Gothic stonework" (*AOT* 44), the speaker's plea is "give me such mania, to chisel words like roots and petals ..." (44). So how does "mania" combine with the active noticing requisite to poem-making?

BB • The frenzied, inspired, rhapsodic carver uses the forms of nature as a basis for his work. His carving of "roots and petals" is contrasted to an art that has no relation to natural forms. But even abstract art, a Jackson Pollock, can be impressionistically connected to forms of nature. Certain things under a microscope can look like a Jackson Pollock and vice versa.

AC • In your journal-essay "A Long Fall For Poetry," you say, "writing is first of all a matter of using our language with the most practiced skills and the most fervent agility we can muster" (79). Is that "first of all" what poetry is? That could describe debating, couldn't it?

BB   • I suppose it could – as long as you don't get into the details of what those "skills" and that "agility" involve. With debating, they'd be directed more at reason and logic, wouldn't they? Poetry appeals more to the whole person or, at least, to a wider range of our responses. In "Long Fall," if I remember right, that comment about "fervent agility" was meant as a contrast to emphasis on themes, politics, psychology, anything but the poem as a work of art. No art deep down is apolitical, and we shouldn't ignore the politics of poetry. But a poem is short-changed when its paraphrasable meaning gets more attention than its music and language and structure, when its integrity not only as a poem but also as *this particular poem* is overlooked. We owe it to the poem – like to each thing in nature – to see it for itself rather than instantly trying to *use* it for something. A few years after writing "Long Fall," I read Seamus Heaney's prose *The Redress of Poetry*, and there I found passages that say more powerfully than I ever could things I was trying to get at in the journal. Let me get it off my bookshelf .... Heaney values poetry that "consciously seeks to promote cultural and political change," but he also talks about the need to "redress poetry *as* poetry .... Poetry cannot afford to lose its fundamentally self-delighting inventiveness, its joy in being a process of language as well as a representation of things of the world" (5-6).

AC   • In a recent interview, George Steiner says that the night worker on a geriatric ward "stands much higher on the scale of need and human value" (Wachtel 115) than the writer or critic. Does your reference to "quaint needlework" (*AOT* 56) express some doubt about the worth of poetry?

BB   • I don't think that it's an absolute denial of the tremendous values and powers of poetry but, in the improvisational manner, I was trying to capture a moment of doubt. In the despair, emptiness, inertia, and suicidal temptations experienced by some people, what value does the contemplation of a landscape or the contentment of everyday activities give? What kind of comfort can that supply to one who is truly in a state of despair? Sometimes [Czeslaw] Milosz writes out of that kind of doubt. The other day, I was reading some back issues of *Harper's*, where I came across a passage from "The Poor Poet," an early poem, where he imagines a poem as a tree branching over a page, and he says, "like an insult / to suffering humanity is the scent of that tree" (60). In "Improvisations," I talk about the personal experience of finding comfort in an insect or in a many-veined leaf, and wonder if that comfort is a special kind of gift or mercy that helps some people find significance in small things. The dismissive phrase "quaint needlework" recognizes that such comfort isn't available to everyone.

AC • The river is a powerful presence, perhaps a comfort, in your poetry, isn't it? In a *Planet Harbor* poem, "River There, River Here" (31-32), the speaker who is a "time-zone farther / into the continent" says, "if I turned around quick enough // here it would be at my back: a river ..." (32). Have you been accompanied by the St. John River?

BB • In imagination, yes. I grew up close to it and took it for granted all through my childhood and adolescence. As "Three Windows" (*AOT* 65-67) tries to convey – though it doesn't specifically mention the St. John – it was only after I lived out of the province for a few years and travelled to other parts of the country that I began to see what a gorgeous river the St. John is – why it's been called the Rhine of North America.

AC • Of the principal places that you've lived – Fredericton, Montreal (15 years), Halifax (13 years) – which is the ground from which your poetry comes?

BB • That's a tough question because a lot of the early sources and inspirations are New Brunswick places – like the Fundy Coast or the ocean – rather than specifically Fredericton ones. In my early stuff, there are actually more references to the sea than to Fredericton. Facing the power of the sea, even a few days of the year, can get under your skin in a way that something that you see every day can't. There's not a strong sense of Fredericton in my poems. Maybe because I moved to Halifax 13 years ago, coasts go on being reflected in a fair number of the poems, like "Granite Erratics" (*GE* 14-15) or the North Sea section of "Brimming" (*GE* 63-72). As for the geographical "bedrock" of the poems, I'd say Atlantic geography, Atlantic topography. Coasts, forests, mountains – though with mountains, we're pushing further west to the Adirondacks. On the other hand, in large parts of "Underwater Carpentry" (*UC* 89-102), I wanted to reflect urban reality as well. I have no desire to be specifically "a nature poet" or a poet with no interest in human interactions.

AC • In "At the Fishhouses," Elizabeth Bishop says of the ocean, "It is like what we imagine knowledge to be: / dark, salt, clear, moving, utterly free, / drawn from the cold hard mouth / of the world ..." (74), and in your essay on Bishop you say, "Such knowledge seems ... more likely to arrive, if it ever does, via the senses rather than the mind" ("'The Land Tugging at the Sea'" 95). So you are an empiricist?

BB   • Well, I wouldn't be ashamed to be called an empiricist, if that means putting high priority on our five senses as avenues into appreciating the world – and if it means our thinking processes are grounded in our acquaintance with material reality. I think the material is *prior,* even though once the mind is active – but dependent on the brain, not divorced from nature – it drastically influences how we perceive anything.

AC   • You also say, however, that "If *if* [supposition] weren't with us, the brain might be little more / than a register ..." (*GE* 14).

BB   • Yeah, I guess there's a sense of the limits of empiricism there. The brain would be wasted if it became nothing but a recorder. *Ifs* and *what-ifs* are needed to keep us open to possibilities not apparent now, and to fantasies of what will never be. I'd never want to disparage imagination in its most everyday sense.

AC   • The adult first-person narrator in the long poem "The Woods on the Way to School" (*GE* 27-34) reminisces about "the year he first knew he was / spellbound, when he detoured from the street / into a land of blue beetles and moss" (34). "[B]esotted" (*GE* 65) and "spellbound": Are these the conditions that are necessary for the practice of poetry?

BB   • For some poetry, yes. But there are poets in whom things like skepticism and discrimination are more key than besottedness and enchantment. Maybe the largest poets go in both directions, sometimes on the same page. Shakespeare clearly does.

AC   • In "A Handful of Tales" (*GE* 35-59), of which there are 11, you allow yourself exaggeration. These tales are somewhere between the fantastic and the real. *Afterlife* says, "If I allowed extravagance, I'd say ..." (91), but it's not allowed in *Afterlife,* is it? Between these two books did you put away extravagance and exaggeration?

BB   • "Put away" is putting it too strongly, I think. For instance, I'd hope there's something extravagant in the act of addressing an eight-part poem to eight species of birds. The extravagance might not be that of the tale-spinning in *Granite Erratics*, but I think there's some comic exaggeration in "Lost Footnote" (*AOT* 6-7) and "whippersnipper rant"

(*AOT* 28) or in "Work at Twenty-One" (*AOT* 61-64) and "After the Age of Parties" (*AOT* 68-69). The latter two, both narratives, might've been cast in moulds like those of the earlier "tales." I guess they're more realistic – but I still think they've got touches of the extravagant and the gothic.

AC • Except that it's lowercase and unpunctuated throughout, "This Bridge Is No Bridge," in *Brother's Insomnia* (1972) – with its concern for reflectivity, doublings, and blurrings in the natural world, its minute observations giving way to breadth of statement – might be at home in *Afterlife*. The development of a poet is not exactly linear, is it?

BB • Not usually, no. I feel my development was – is – at a snail's pace, despite the early publications. Maybe I've had a few turning points: What's suggested by the phrase "play in the lyric" in "Bluegrass in Japan" (*PH* 9-11); the first attempt to write long poems; the discovery that poems could generate each other in specific ways, like the hiking poems and the tales. But overall the learning has been full of side trails – including a certain scattering of energy that results from also writing fiction, reviews and other pieces on writing, personal essays, and a journal that will soon be 40 years old.

AC • Is your life with books – as writer, teacher, editor – continuous with your childhood? Was reading an important part of your childhood?

BB • To both questions, yes. I was an avid reader in elementary school and still remember – here goes some shameless nostalgia – the excitement of trips to the old Fredericton Public Library down by the St. John River: The sense of shelter there on winter days; the Walter R. Brooks and Enid Blyton collections – the Blyton *Adventure* series, not Noddy – and the rituals of the checkout desk. I wrote to Blyton's and Brooks' publishers and got autographed photos of both, which I still have buried away. By the time I was 10 or 11, I wanted to be a writer as well as a reader. As for the teaching, that was much less expected. Even though my immediate and extended family has included heaps of teachers, for many years I didn't think I was headed in that direction. I just wanted to write, but by the end of my 20s, the life of penury had lost some of its glamour. After hitting my 30s, I got on the track that led to a full-time university job. On the introvert-to-extrovert scale, I'm quite far along the introvert end of things, so I didn't imagine teaching as my destination.

AC • In reading the manuscript of your selected, some of your early poems – "November Mare" and "In a House Where Chastity Was Taught for a Century" (*WTD* 12, 130) – remind me of the early Alden Nowlan, as does "A Bear-Hunt Tale" in *Granite Erratics* (44-45), but I see more of Elizabeth Bishop in *Afterlife*. Of Maritime poets, are these the two of greatest importance to you?

BB • Hard to say. Bishop has certainly become increasingly important to me over time, and I'd say that in the past decade the textures of her poems more than Nowlan's have been on my mind. Nowlan had such a powerful presence in Fredericton when I was young. His best poems were an inspiration and remain so, even if I feel that his *Bread, Wine and Salt* set a standard for consistency that the later collections didn't rise to again. But one thing about Fredericton is that there wasn't just Alden. There was also Alfie Bailey, Bob Gibbs, Bill Bauer, Travis Lane – all very different from Alden. I suspect Bob's collections *A Kind of Wakefulness* and *All This Night Long* – which I think are overdue for republication in a single volume – taught me as much as Alden's poetry did. Looking further afield, I think it's great that we've had such contrasting models as Al Purdy and P.K. Page, or – going farther back, and abroad – Yeats and Williams. Some poets seem to feel the need to side with one poet or the other, but I'm convinced it's most rewarding to soak up influences from all over the place.

AC • Alden Nowlan was not a "mentor," you say, in the sense of "dispensing advice," but there were "lessons that Nowlan's poetry gave some of us" ("Nights in Windsor Castle" 54). What were those lessons?

BB • Faithfulness to concrete life. A mixing of immediate personal experience with history and fantasy. A range from deep emotion and compassion to irony and whimsy. And Alden's life was an example of stick-to-it-ness.

AC • These days the catchwords of praise for poetry are innovative, experimental, edgy. What kind of poetry do you write?

BB • It's something of a cliché to say that all memorable writing has a dimension of the "innovative" and the "experimental" to it, but I do believe that, however much the poetry may seem out of step with ideas of what the avant-garde is. The kind of poetry I *do* write is surely best for readers to describe. I can only talk about the kind of poetry I'd *like and hope* to write: Poetry that's musical in its sounds, sensuous in its

ANNE COMPTON

images, strongly rhythmical, closely observant, emotionally moving, welcoming but challenging, open to humour, surprising. Anyway, that's a beginning.

WORKS CITED
— • —

Bartlett, Brian. *The Afterlife of Trees*. Montreal: McGill-Queen's UP, 2002.

– – –. "For Sure the Kittiwake: Naming, Nature, and P.K. Page." *Canadian Literature* 155 (Winter 1997): 91-111.

– – –. *Granite Erratics*. Victoria: Ekstasis Editions, 1997.

– – –. "Hawthornden Journal: Notes from a Writer's Retreat." *Antigonish Review* 112 (Winter 1998): 147-64.

– – –. "'The Land Tugging at the Sea': Elizabeth Bishop's Coasts and Shores." *Divisions of the Heart: Elizabeth Bishop and the Art of Memory and Place*. Eds. Sandra Barry, et al. Wolfville, NS: Gaspereau P, 2001. 91-102.

– – –. "A Long Fall For Poetry: Reflections On Poetry In The Public Eye And The Private Realm Through The Last Months Of 1994, Including Greatly Exaggerated Reports Of Its Death and Resurrection." *Antigonish Review* 102-03 (Summer/Fall 1995): 63-81.

– – –. "Nights in Windsor Castle: Remembering Alden Nowlan." *Pottersfield Portfolio* 18.1 (Fall 1997): 48-55.

– – –. *Planet Harbor*. Fredericton: Goose Lane Editions, 1989.

– – –. *Underwater Carpentry*. Fredericton: Goose Lane Editions, 1993.

– – –. *Wanting the Day: Selected Poems*. Fredericton: Goose Lane Editions; Cornwall, Eng.: Peterloo Poets. Forthcoming.

Bishop, Elizabeth. *The Complete Poems*. London: Chatto & Windus, 1969.

Heaney, Seamus. *The Redress of Poetry: Oxford Lectures*. London: Faber and Faber, 1995.

Milosz, Czeslaw. *The Collected Poems*. Hopewell, NJ: Ecco, 1988.

Ormsby, Eric. "Going Down to Where the Roots Begin." Interview with Carmine Starnino. *Where the Words Come From: Canadian Poets in Conversation*. Ed. Tim Bowling. Roberts Creek, BC: Nightwood Editions, 2002. 196-212.

Thoreau, Henry David. *Walden*. Princeton: Princeton UP, 1971.

Wachtel, Eleanor. *Original Minds*. Toronto: HarperCollins. 2003.

WRITING PAINTINGS AND THINKING PHYSICS:
ANNE SIMPSON'S POETRY

Anne Simpson's first collection of poetry, *Light Falls Through You* (2000), won the Atlantic Poetry Prize and the Gerald Lampert Prize. The Lampert jury found the collection to be "strongly original – in its supple music and lucid imagery, its range of reference (to archaeology, painting, the mythological and natural worlds) and in the scope of its moral concerns." *Light Falls Through You* was also shortlisted for the Pat Lowther Award. In 1999, Simpson earned the Bliss Carman Poetry Award for her poem "Little Stories." *Canterbury Beach* (2001), Simpson's debut novel, set in Nova Scotia and Maine, was shortlisted for the Thomas Raddall Atlantic Fiction Award and the inaugural Chapters/Robertson Davies Prize. Simpson's short stories appear in various literary magazines and anthologies, including the *Journey Prize Anthology*.

Born in Toronto, raised in Burlington, Ontario, Simpson has lived in Nova Scotia for 15 years. In 2002-03, she was Writer-in-Residence at UNB. We met at Molly's Café, Fredericton, for this interview. Just a few weeks earlier, in March, Simpson's second collection of poetry, *Loop*, was released.

Six months after our conversation, Simpson's *Loop* was shortlisted for the Governor General's Award for poetry, and in June 2004, Simpson won the Griffin Poetry Prize.

AC • I've talked to a lot of poets, but I've not yet asked the question: "Why do you do it, write poetry?" It's gut-wrenching, time-consuming, and often one doesn't get to where one's going.

AS • I do it because there is no other way to express what I need to say. I painted for a long time, but I'm not painting now. Painting is one form of expression, but it's as if I want several forms. In practical terms, though, I knew I couldn't paint and write *and* raise children at the same time. I had to make a choice, and I thought writing was more portable.

But to answer the question – "Why write poetry?" – I guess there's something in me that exceeds everything else. Perhaps I come closest to it in poetry. It's as though there is a surplus. Poetry is a working out of ideas, but it's also play. Even if the ideas are serious, the play can be inventive. That's one part of it, and the other part is that in writing poetry I can bear witness to the world. It's not just a case of me writing about me. I'm more interested in the world and what can be said about being in the world.

AC • Do you wait for a poem to occur? Or do you write for a certain period every day whether or not you feel inspired?

AS • I write fiction every day. Fiction takes longer: You need the timber to build the house, to do the floors, the walls, and so forth. All that takes longer. I don't do poetry every day, but I don't wait for the inspiration to come and seize me. I do it regularly, but not as regularly as fiction. I don't want to be disparaging about inspiration, but there's a lot more to it. There's the hard work of putting poems together. There's also the convergence of ideas, and for me that takes a lot of reading and looking and thinking. Usually three or four ideas will come together at the same time. Once that happens, I can start playing around with them.

AC • You published three books in four years. Is this a sudden emergence or a long-nurtured development?

AS • For a long time, I didn't know that I was a writer. In fact, I still question it. It was a matter of gaining confidence over a long period of time. Also, I didn't have a whole lot to say when I was younger, or I didn't have it in me to say what I needed to say.

AC • Since we are not in your home landscape, would you briefly describe it for me?

AS • Nova Scotia is that place right now, but I'm also realizing that it is the place where I grew up, Burlington, Ontario, the landscape of suburbia, coupled with the steel factories of Hamilton. I'm beginning to see now what that childhood landscape was. But Nova Scotia is very strong in my thinking, and I use it a lot in my writing.

AC • You seem to be suggesting that you are only now digging down to the first layer.

AS • Yes, I guess I am. It was so exciting to write "Altarpiece" (*Light* 59-76) and to use a landscape that is part of me. The American poet Jack

Gilbert has Pittsburgh in his soul, and after reading his poetry I realized some of the places that are in mine.

AC • The observed and the imagined: Do you gravitate to one or other of those poles?

AS • Both, I think. In my long poems, the observed and the imagined work together. The observed landscape, for instance, is often peopled by characters who are frequently imagined. And these two things, the observed and the imagined, come together. I need to observe and think about most things and then discover how they are a way into the poem.

AC • In a paper that you presented at Banff – "Bowing Before the Light" – you say, "The movement from seeing, listening and wondering, to that of imagining, is the beginning of the writer's work."

AS • I often begin to imagine the characters as I am working out the ideas. It may not always be *A* followed by *B*, followed by *C*. I think there are centripetal forces in a given poem, particularly in long poems, but there are also centrifugal forces: The thing can fly apart. The initial ideas are a bringing together, a gathering of various things, a collage, which I try to make something of. It is a matter of "How will these things cohere?" and "Will it fly apart, and how can I hold it together?"

AC • Is it a bad thing if it flies apart?

AS • At the end of "The Trailer Park" (*Loop* 80-91), I came to a point where I could do no more. The poem had expanded to a point where I couldn't bring it back from the stars and the cosmos – into the world again. I had to let it go out.

AC • In *Light Falls Through You*, except for narrative-based poems such as "Deer on a Beach" (2-3), "Light Falls Through You" (4-5), and "Sea of Death" (17-18), you appear to favour a very short line, a line one phrase in length, so that a poem steps carefully from phrase to phrase. Do you determine line, and line length, through sound rather than by grammatical sense?

AS • I often go by what must be some innate sense of rhythm. I have been told by people that there is rhythm in my poetry, but I am not always aware of that as I lay down a line. I am very aware of how the poem looks on a page, so that may have something to do with why the lines break where they do. I worry about the long line. Can I impose control on a line when it gets to that length?

AC • These short lines enforce a quality of quiet in the reading process. As a result, the reader is acutely aware of your word choices. I am struck by certain-sounding words – "undulating" (*Light* 1), "undulate" (*Light* 14), "elongated" (*Light* 24), "indolence" (*Loop* 73), "embellished" (*Loop* 74) – that occur in your poetry. Do you gravitate toward certain sounds?

AS • I was reading "Altarpiece" (*Light* 59-76) out loud yesterday to a friend, and I realized that the words where I wanted a kind of laziness of tone – you mentioned the word "indolence" – seemed to be appropriate to the sense, the atmosphere, that I wanted. So it must be something done unconsciously.

AC • I know of no poet who uses onomatopoeia as extensively as you do. In "Altarpiece," alone, the reader finds "green acorns fall to the pavement – *snuk*, / *snak*" (63); "the golfer birdies / on the ninth (*tock, tock*)" (69); "barks of the crow / invade the room. *Ja, ja*" (71); "the century spins slower, slower, until the wheel / – *click, click, click,* – seems to stop ..." (72). Is there a mysteriousness that you are trying to get into poetry, one that is not available to the eye?

AS • I am striving for the same thing that I strive for in visual terms. That is, can I get at all the brushwork of the world? Can I get at the world as closely as possible, and how do I do that? For me, that involves getting at the sight and the sound of the world, and even trying to go so far as to get at taste and touch. For me, perception is the way we know the world; I mean *knowing* in the sense of deeply knowing. Sensation is our entry point, and from there we can move on to ideas.

AC • Section titles in *Light Falls Through You* – "Souvenirs," "Reliquary," "Altarpiece" – suggest a ceremonious memorialization of events or lives. Is poetry itself like one, or all, of these things?

AS • Yes, poetry is a way of remembering. I didn't realise that it was so ritualistic, but I suppose it is. Bearing witness has to be ceremonial to some extent. This act must be done with reverence, and I guess this is my attempt at reverence.

AC • If we live in a ritual-deprived world, perhaps poetry moves into that place.

AS • That's true. I think poetry is an attempt to remember as thoughtfully as possible. So if this means that it somehow becomes ceremonious and

ANNE COMPTON

ritualized, so be it. It is true that it's memory – and how we keep the things we keep and how we lose what we lose – in which I am most interested. When I was painting in Antigonish, during the years when my children were young, I spent a lot of time on very large paintings. At that time, I would often look at art magazines, and I remember picking up an art magazine in which Tony Urquhart's *Reliquaries* were pictured. I do think it must have had an impact on me to see those things. I must have been thinking of that when I titled one of the poems "Reliquary" (*Light* 53-57).

AC • The meditation on *fin-de-siècle* culture, "Altarpiece" (*Light* 59-76), says, "We should have seen it coming, that / shift from lament to indifference" (66). So if we live in a culture of indifference, does that mean that the poet has some responsibility to lament?

AS • That's exactly it. We have a responsibility. If the world can't grieve for itself, we have the responsibility to do the grieving for it. People often ask me, "Why are so many of your poems about grief?" But I think that is not seeing clearly enough. As much as there is a great intensity in grief, there is also intensity in celebration, and I think that's there in my poetry too. Poetry is about giving voice to intensity – whether it's lament or ecstasy.

AC • One of the registers of intensity in your poetry is grief, but there's also a lot of violence, especially in "Souvenirs," the first section of *Light*. Sometimes, as in "Chopping Wood" (7-8), the violence issues from accident, but more frequently, as in "Deer on a Beach" (2-3); "Grammar Exercise" (6); and "Octopus" (12), the violence is intentional, directed, gratuitous. Do you feel an obligation to face and to write about this kind of violence?

AS • Yes. We live in a beautiful but terrifying world. I think that it is something that comes up in "Altarpiece" (*Light* 59-76): Dread is facing something squarely. I am drawn to poets who do this: They look at things and do not look away.

AC • For all the violence, a couple of poems early on in *Light Falls Through You* come down to the words "marvelling" (1) and "miraculous" (11). Looking squarely at violence does not appear to breed cynicism. Is the world still a place of miracle for you?

AS • Yes, it's a place of wonder, surprise, grace. After all the terror and horror, and the unbearable things that happen, there is yet wonder and beauty.

AC • There's probably a thesaurus of symbols somewhere in which the sea takes up the greatest number of pages. "Sea of Death" (17-18) is a poem title in the first section of *Light*, but the very first poem in the book also presents a sea of death. Is this what the sea chiefly symbolizes for you?

AS • No, I think it is many things. There is a sea of death in the story of *Gilgamesh*. The pole that he is using "rotted in the poisonous / water" ("Sea of Death" 17). In that case, it is a sort of mythical sea. The poem "Descent" (1) refers to an actual ocean, the Atlantic, a harsh sea. But the sea, for me, is many, many things: It contains an infinitude of meanings. It is like the sky in the sense that it has no ending, no beginning, so it can be all things.

AC • In your poem "Shoulder of Water, Skin of Air" (*Light* 14), the sea is associated with birth: "Now I lie floating on the sea's hammock ....We lie newly born / tipping from one side to the other, / between water and air."

AS • I'm working on a long poem right now that has to do with the sea as a place of birth and death. I'm focussing on a woman in the 21st century – the short view – and trying to suggest the long view. I'm thinking of the sea as a place of transformation. It's clear to me that I wouldn't be examining the ocean in symbolic terms if it weren't for the fact I live near the ocean.

AC • Would you say that the place of poetry for you is not so much a geographical place, but rather – given the number of poems that focus on birth and death – a threshold?

AS • I think I come to the threshold again and again. Maybe poetry is an instance of coming to the entry place of another world, and looking on that world. There are so many worlds within us. This is a way to at least glance into those worlds.

AC • Asking that question, I am reminded of the work of playwright and poet Wole Soyinka in whose country, Nigeria, you spent two years. Soyinka writes of thresholds. What kind of impact did that stay in Nigeria have upon you as a writer?

AS • Soyinka did have an influence on me. Perhaps more so when I came back and I was doing a course on Commonwealth literature. Soyinka is very interested in myth, the myths that concern his world, and they are so different from the myths that I was used to, the Greek myths. So I was rediscovering Nigeria upon returning to Canada. While I was there, though, the impact was profound, but I found I couldn't write about Africa, and can still hardly write about it, perhaps because it was such a vivid experience.

AC • Did being in Nigeria determine your becoming a writer?

AS • There were a couple of things that happened there that had to do with writing. One occurred when I first got there – a Canadian teacher working there had just published a story in *The Fiddlehead*. I was so impressed. I remember thinking, "I have two years here. I could easily write a novel. There is enough time and no distractions." But I couldn't. Of course I was reading a lot because I was teaching. The first year it was a boys' school, fairly predictable teaching. The second year, though, it was more interesting, an advanced teachers' college, and I remember trying to teach T.S. Eliot's *The Waste Land*. It made such sense there because it was the dry season, and the poem resonated for me in a way that it never would have in Canada. Eliot's notion of thirst and dryness, and needing to locate the mystery of things, the water of life, became very significant in that place. So although I wasn't doing much writing, there was a lot of absorbing of experience there.

AC • I wanted to ask you about metaphors in your work that suggest a spatialization of the mind: In "A Head Like Hers," the mind is one of two "luminous places" (*Light* 13); in another poem, there are "rooms in the mind" (*Light* 17); and a third poem asks, "Where do any of us wander / but in the mind ..." (*Light* 22). Do you think of the mind as a many-roomed house?

AS • When I was young – a lot of kids must do this – I remember thinking that there's a world that I go to in my head. I could roam around in that world. I thought that it was pretty great to be able to go there. Later, I realized that imagination does have many houses, and we can visit each one, depending on the project. It was hard for me to come and live in Nova Scotia. I did feel very much that I had to pull something out of a hat, and it was to the imagination that I turned.

AC • Was Nova Scotia, like Nigeria, a turning point in your becoming a writer?

AS • At first I didn't know what I'd do with myself there. My husband had work; I didn't. I felt like I had to cobble things together. But it was the first time that I gave myself permission to be creative, truly creative. I was painting a lot and then I was writing a lot.

AC • If the mind is figured architecturally in your work, the body is often a landscape: "I see everything planted in you unfurling new leaves / and flourishing" (*Light* 4) and in another poem, "your // heart flowers on the tip of my / finger, while I respond with several // smaller buds, nested / up and down your spine ..." (*Light* 10). In both cases, the land-scape season is spring, so is the body a site of hope?

AS • Oh, I think it must be. I'm doing a series of poems about anatomy. It's a kind of long celebratory poem, though it's not that there's praise in every line or anything like that. But the body is so beautiful, and I don't mean that in terms of young women who are beautiful or that sort of thing. In art school, we had to draw figures carefully, and these could be old guys off the street. There was one I remember in partic-ular, George. I remember thinking how beautiful the body is, despite its ugliness. It is so remarkable a thing.

AC • Is the body, as you suggest in one poem, both "cities of pain ... gar-dens of delight" *(Light* 32)? You have a poem in which a woman listens to the sound of an octopus beaten on concrete and is reminded of "one body slapping against another // in the tedium of desire" (*Light* 12). In another poem, "the piercing of desire ... drives // a needle in the flesh and threads it through" (*Light* 17). The "cit[y] of pain" is often associ-ated with desire, isn't it?

AS • I think Jack Gilbert puts it really well in *The Great Fires*: We have to go "through the wildness of her sweet body already / in our bed to reach the body within that body" (9). We have to go through body to get beyond the body. It's the same thing with desire. We have to go through desire to find what's beyond desire. Is it love or is it pain? Is it a good thing or a bad thing that we get from desiring something? Is it going to give us suffering? Metaphorically, the body is always going to be both garden of delight and city of pain for me.

AC • Entire books are devoted to the question: *Where does poetry come from?* There's an odd reticence, however, around the question: *What is the connection between sexual desire and poetry*? Do you have any thoughts about that?

AS • There's a very strong connection. Poetry is often about longing as much as anything else; no, not as much as anything else. It's *often* about longing and desire and, yes, a lot of it has to do with sexual desire. I am very interested in all the aspects that make us human, but that in particular. We are desiring creatures. Why not talk about that? Because I'm a visceral, physical sort of writer, I'm interested – I think so many writers are – in what we make of sexual desire. Can we talk about it in ways that do justice to it instead of making it sentimental slop? Can we also be reverent about it? It's one of the deepest human things, so how are we going to deal with that in a way that is both implicit and explicit, hiding it to some extent and showing it as well?

AC • "I have closed thousands / of little doors in my skin" (4), the narrator says in the title poem, "Light Falls Through You," and in "Sea of Death" the lesson that the snake teaches is "to shed our skins a thousand times // in any given day" (*Light* 18). Does this recurring idea – the change-ability of skin – pertain to the slipperiness of identity?

AS • It seems to me that we are always in the midst of change, and this is one of those ways that we shuck off what we were and begin again. We are always beginning again. Skin is such an interesting thing, and this goes back to my fascination with the body and drawing the body.

AC • Not surprisingly, given the title of your first book, light is everywhere: "rectangles of light" (*Light* 7) represent the safety of domesticity. For the artists "In Italy" (*Light* 9), "what dresses us in light" is the landscape spread before them. But there's a third kind, which is neither natural nor manmade: "Light is an axe through the top of our heads. It splits us open, and for one moment we see" (*Light 57*). What is the third kind?

AS • Oh, I think it's a light that we're all after. It has to do with – as much as anything – our being sort of half asleep in the world. Can we ever wake to this moment of light? Can we stay with it? No, not very long.

AC • From their perspective on a hill, the artists "see / everything ... going back / hundreds of years" (*Light* 9). Similarly, in "The New Year," time has spatial dimensions: "for a moment ... century on century – frozen into place" (*Loop* 18). Why are you so drawn to the idea that time is visible?

AS • I think it happens in so many of the poems, even if it's not overt. I'm fascinated by the mystery of time, and how we look at time. Is it just a linear thing? Or can we see things happening that happened before? Can we still see them happening, and if so, then how do we give voice to those things that happened as though they were still with us in the present? Bearing all of the past into the present, to me, is the work of the poet.

AC • So does the poet, somehow, have to get around linear time?

AS • I've read that there's not just our universe, but multiple universes. I think they're called multiverses. This has implications for space, of course, but also for time. And what Max Tegmark tells us is that "All possible states exist at every instant, so the passage of time may be in the eye of the beholder ..." (48). Time may not be the way we tend to think of it at all. Something that I explore in poetry is the notion of things happening at once.

AC • Although the long piece "Usual Devices" (*Light* 35-52) is entirely immersed in Greek mythology, other poems use ancient myths in other ways. Our need for reassurance against loneliness is woven into Gilgamesh's futile search for immortality (*Light* 17-18). And in another poem, a revised version of Ulysses' story is juxtaposed with the narrator's bus travel (20-21). What does this invocation of myth allow you to do?

AS • It allows me to go back to stories and rewrite them in the way I want. For instance, in *The Iliad*, a lot of women do not get a chance to talk or be revealed. By revisiting myth, we're trying to retell it, to give voice to those who didn't have a voice. But there is more to it than that. It's that kind of timeless story that tries to describe what we are as human beings. Myth gives us something to hang onto. It tells us so much about who we are in war, in love, in this or that – although the gods are there and they are determining the game.

AC • The series title "Usual Devices" (*Light* 35-52) refers to editorial devices and these devices appear as titles on the individual poems. The title phrase is a pun, isn't it, referring as well to devices of torture?

AS • Oh, that hadn't occurred to me. I was thinking of divine devices such as the apple in the Greek myths or in the Christian story. As well as divine devices, I was thinking of the common devices we use in language to denote stops, pauses, or gaps. There are also mathematical devices: The addition and equal signs. I was thinking of devices that move language along, or change it, or help us to shape language – the little traffic signs, as Don McKay puts it – in language. It is a kind of self-reflexive move to call it "Usual Devices" because it says, "Look at the signs that I am using in this poem to title each section."

AC • The comma "deep in that flesh" is Menelaus' experience of Helen's absence (*Light* 39); the exclamation points are hacks in the flesh of Hekuba's children (*Light* 40); "Lust // ... a snake bite: Twin holes / in a wrist" is the colon (*Light* 45). Aren't you playing with the similarity between puncture and punctuation?

AS • Yes, you are right. These devices change or arrest the words. There's a way in which you could see them as devices of torture.

AC • Based on *The Iliad*, "Usual Devices" is, of course, filled with blood and guts, but it's also very sexy as in the simple, erotic line, "a man's hand, dark against white cloth, on her hip" (38). In this retelling, did you want to skew the original in a particular direction? Are you telling a more erotic version?

AS • These women and men, in the fullness of their lives, are of course driven by desire. Yet the women in *The Iliad* – not the men – were condemned if they explored who they were in any but acceptable terms: Helen's infidelity, for instance, is set against Penelope's fidelity.

AC • You studied visual arts for three years. What effect has that training had on your poetry?

AS • An enormous effect. I'm not painting right now, so everything's being poured into poetry. For me, the painting is a threshold – we were talking about thresholds earlier – you move into the painting and then almost past it. Every visual object that I become obsessed with is a door into something else.

AC • Two poems strike me as especially paintable – "White, Mauve, Yellow" (*Light* 26-27) and the cherries in the foreground of "Little Stories" (*Loop* 1-5). Do you think in terms of painting when you are writing?

AS • I paint when I write. I write paintings.

AC • Then I'd describe your palette as predominantly blue, sliding over to mauve, purple, indigo. Would I be right?

AS • You would be dead on – with little hints of red. The man who wrote *The Art of Colour*, Johannes Itten, asked his students to give [him] the palettes that describe their particular personalities (*Light* 77). There was one student who came up with four palettes, all different, and I thought that if there was one student I would identify with, it would be that student. It is not enough to say, "These are the colours that interest me." That's not enough. There are more. White, black, red, for instance, would be another palette. Colours, for me, are almost like ideas. They lend the poem its atmosphere as much as its idea. So much of the intellectual working out of the poem has to do with the kind of palette I'm using.

AC • In both books, the most ambitious of the poems – "Altarpiece" (*Light* 59-76) and "Seven Paintings by Brueghel" (*Loop* 19-25) – link 16th-century artworks and 20th-century civilization. What are the features in the work of the German Grünewald and the Flemish Brueghel that enable you to look at our time through their time?

AS • Here's the weird thing about choosing Matthias Grünewald: I had in mind the book I'd been reading, *The Age of Extremes: The Short Twentieth Century 1941-1991*, by Eric Hobsbawn. In it, Hobsbawn mentions that the 20th century was like a triptych. I immediately thought of the Grünewald masterpiece – *The Isenheim Altarpiece* – which has side pieces as well as a perdella, and opens up to present four painted surfaces. The three main paintings, though, are the Nativity, the Crucifixion, and the Resurrection. The paintings are bold and brightly coloured. They show us a strange and distorted world. Yet, this altarpiece resonates with the 20th century. Pieter Brueghel, one of the Flemish painters of the northern Renaissance, died about the time that Grünewald was born. But the interest in storytelling is consistent in both, and neither of them shrank from what they wanted to portray. They had a vision that took in the whole world. As Geoffrey Chaucer does, Brueghel revealed so much about human nature – all the greed, indifference, cruelty, capriciousness, kindness, nobility. He observed without flinching.

AC • In "Altarpiece" (*Light* 59-76), three historical moments – Grünewald's painting of the crucifixion; the installation in 1933 of Hitler as Chancellor; and end-of-the-century suburban culture – are folded together. So the poem itself re-enacts Grünewald's triptych, a folding altarpiece.

AS • The turning points in the 20th century I was most concerned with had to do with World War II: The advent of Hitler, the war itself, and the dropping of the atom bomb. There are smaller moments in the poem that echo that violence such as the near-fatal beating of one boy by another. All of that is set against the banal landscape of the golf course, those monster homes – affluent homes that you find in Burlington down by the lake – the steel factories in the background. So I was setting up a cluster of moments, one juxtaposed with another.

AC • Are these eras so situated in order to illustrate the idea that "Whatever happened will happen again" (63)?

AS • Certainly, I think we forget history; we allow things to happen again.

AC • When the Grünewald altarpiece is folded up, it is, as far as I know, one of the most horrific crucifixion paintings there is, and yet when it is opened up, we see inside three panels of great beauty. Are you suggesting in that poem that there is beauty within the violence of the suburban world.

AS • I set beauty against violence to see how these things come together.

AC • "Altarpiece" (*Light* 59-76), in its attention to the 20th-century suburb, depicts a tidy, tidy world, where orderly lawns, sprinklers, and sunshine camouflage lassitude and violence. Are these the perils of our era?

AS • I think we are blind to what is going on around us. All of those things going on in, say, the 16th century, are still going on today, but we have covered them up with such nice façades. We like to think they're not there.

AC • In this, and other poems – the paste and plastic of the Disney theme park noted in "Now What" (*Loop* 7-8), for example – you are a critic of present-day culture. Although your work, it seems to me, has been very well received, this aspect of your work has received the least attention. Do you think of yourself as a political poet?

AS • I didn't before, but I do now. It's not just a case of bearing witness, but it is also a case of – and I don't want to sound like a moralist – standing apart. There is a way in which you have to stand outside of your culture and look at it, and keep on looking.

AC • You refer to the linked sonnets based on the seven paintings by Brueghel as a "corona written for Staten Island, New York" (*Loop* 92). Could you say something about how these two things, Staten Island and Brueghel, came together in the making of these seven sonnets.

AS • I always need a place to write about – or I often do, particularly with a long poem. I was looking at photographs of the Staten Island landfill site. Staten Island was reopened, and all the debris from the Twin Towers was taken there. I had a 10-day period to work on that poem, so I was working hard. It was a little bit like breaking stones trying to write that corona because sonnets are awfully hard to do. I was trying to make these two things – Brueghel's paintings and the landfill site – connect, come together, and it was a bigger project than that one tragedy. It was a lament not just for the debris that was taken from the Twin Towers to Staten Island; I was also thinking of these paintings, each one a kind of door, as an entryway into what we have made. And what have we made here, but this, a tower of garbage? The life that we have made here has become a memorial. Each one of those Brueghel paintings helped me to structure the thing as a whole. But I don't mean to talk about just this one thing that happened, the tragedy of 9/11. I don't mean to talk just about that atrocity, but many atrocities.

AC • In spite of the forward momentum achieved through linking the last and first lines of succeeding sonnets, the sonnets themselves are comprised of fragments of sentences: "Shut in rooms. / Gone. *Tick*. The towers. *Tock*. Of fire. A fold / in air" (19). Is this syntactical feature – sentence fragments – meant to instil a feeling of the end of things?

AS • I could not write in iambic pentameter. I could only write in this disjointed, fragmentary language. No other language would do, though I was still trying to make the lines fit the sonnet form. There are 10 syllables in each line, and the end rhymes are there, but the flow of the sonnet is not Shakespearean. None of these seven sonnets sound like a sonnet. It's a way of getting language to show the breakdown of the world. It is getting language itself to bear witness.

AC • The syntax is meant to restate the condition?

AS • It is a way of constantly arresting the reader. It's hard to go forward. It does not move smoothly. It does not move like music. It does not move like a lyric ought to move, or the way you are used to lyrics moving. I realized as I was going along that the very fabric of this was different.

AC • A broken crown?

AS • Yes.

AC • These poems originate not with Brueghel's paintings of stolid, contented peasants, as in *Peasant Wedding*, but, rather, in his grimmer work. I was interested in the paintings you chose, but was equally interested in the ones you did not choose.

AS • Yes, I know. There is that very famous one, *The Fall of Icarus*. I did not choose that one partly because everyone chooses it. I wanted to choose ones that, yes, were known, but also ones like *Christ and the Adulteress* that are not known well. It is a panel in which the figures look quite austere. Brueghel is known for his paintings of crowds, with lots going on and with many stories being told, but in this case the painting is stripped down to the bare essentials. I was interested in that.

AC • In *Peasant Wedding*, the peasants are happy and there is a sense of, if not contentment, at least satisfaction, a physical kind of satisfaction. They are well-fed and jolly-looking, but you didn't choose that Brueghel.

AS • No, but that's a very interesting one because if you look closely there's a lot of drunken cavorting. It's a wedding at which people are getting out of hand. There's more than just the surface. Brueghel looks at all aspects of things: Happiness can tip over into unhappiness so easily.

AC • There's a little sliver of something wrong?

AS • Just as there's a wrongness in the world. In the corona, I realized that I was going to have to connect the last line up with the first line, and the first line – "These watches. Ticking, still. Each hour is cold" (19) – is very devastating. What that image draws on are photographs of watches that were found in the debris of the World Trade Center. What does a watch do besides tell the time? A watch itself is like a little room, but it cannot do any more than what it is designed to do – it *ticks*, it *tocks*. That's the end of it. So for me to come from the beginning to the end – "Love's breath. Things we can't hold: / these watches. Ticking. Still. Each hour is cold" (25) – was the most unbearable thing. There was a sadness in it: That it just comes to this. It's only these watches. We don't have the people. We've lost them. There is no light at the end of the tunnel for me in this corona. There might be little moments of uplift, but there's not a lot. That's the way I thought about that atrocity, but also about atrocity in general.

AC • Of the Brueghel paintings invoked in this series, the most placid is the scene *Hunters in the Snow*, one of his most lit paintings, although it is a dusk scene. Your poem of that title seems, however, to suggest that the return to domestic comfort is a deception: "Each thing / deceives. The counters, cutlery ... Some children skate; they laugh. / And history has no place" (24). Is the domestic, then, just another refusal of history?

AS • In this case, yes. In the context of this particular poem – this sonnet – history has no place because people want to forget. As for whether we think of ourselves as being part of something larger going on in the world, well, it's difficult for us to do that. It means we have to stand outside of the comfortable houses of our lives. But history has a way of invading and disrupting the domestic.

AC • Clocks (*Loop* 9), watches (*Loop* 19), and time would appear to be of great interest to you. I understand that *Loop* at one time bore the title "Time-Piece." Why is *Loop* the more suitable title for this material?

AS • I am very interested in form now, and in inventing form, in fact. The title *Loop* seemed to say more about the forms, how they circle back on themselves. That was one thing. Then, there's the theme about things recurring in time. So there are all kinds of loops. I've been trying for months to formulate why it is I'm fascinated with form. I think that the content is the saying of the poem and the form is thinking it out in terms of shape.

AC • "Little Stories" (*Loop* 1-5) is a 13-part poem with a radical sense of division. The 13th section contains three words, "we can't say" (5). What is gained through this enjambment not of line or stanza, but of section? You create divisions and then you compromise them.

AS • I think it was a matter of setting sections up in order to dismantle them, that is, in terms of the poem's form and structure. It's a kind of undermining of imposed structure. Here's the structure, well, let's play around with structure. Maybe it has something to do with marriage, which is what the poem is about. Here's the structure of marriage, so let's play around with that. What does it mean to go on in a relationship with someone?

AC • The poem contains the riddle-like line "a trick inside the trick" (2), which could refer to the form or to the subject, marriage.

AS • The form is riddle-like because the poem is trying to sort out what marriage is like. It is this thing which is so mysterious. That poem rests on Chaucer's story "The Franklin's Tale," which is really about fidelity. It's not just that the woman is learning about her faith in this marriage, it's also that her husband, the knight, has to learn it as well. I was playing with that story, which I leave behind at a certain point in the poem.

AC • Brueghel and Chaucer bode large in your poetry.

AS • I'm interested in how both of them want to portray not just a few characters, but the whole of humanity. They don't look away when they encounter something repulsive in human nature. They keep looking. It allows me to look at myself and others and be able to see all of these things and not to look away or be disgusted by human beings.

AC • It's very interesting to me that you are drawn to the work of these two artists who refuse to prettify human life. Yet there is a quality of delicacy in your work. Riddle me that.

AS • When you look at Chaucer, you find enormous lyricism, a kind of gauzy lyricism. As well as the bawdiness – tales that are just so crass and funny and silly – there's that beautifully poetic part. In a sense, Chaucer is a little bit like Shakespeare in that he is able to do all those things. Brueghel has it too, this ability to see everything lurid – the brazenness, the crassness of life, its physicality – but there's a delicacy as well.

AC • The delicacy in the visual detail in *Loop* poems such as "Little Stories" (1-5) and "A Name, Many Names" (6) reminds me of Kenneth Rexroth's translations of poems from the Chinese. In this second volume is the Far East an influence on your poetry?

AS • That gesture, the single line you get in Japanese calligraphy, is such an elegant thing. I am drawn to the simplicity that is also elegance.

AC • Even more so than in *Light*, here in *Loop* there is a preoccupation with the way things blur into one another or lose definition – "I see only / edges, one blurred with another" (4) and "Things glazed with heat / waver, diminishing in size" (7). This suggests an Impressionist aesthetic, which was, of course, influenced by Japanese art. Is that a period of painting with which you have some sympathy?

AS • Yes. Only because it is not resolved. It's not determined. I'm not fond of Nicholas Poussin and the Baroque Classicists. I don't really like their work. I was so taken, as so many people are, by the Impressionists because what they are saying is that in paint, one thing becomes another thing. It all depends on, say, light or shadow.

AC • Earlier we were talking about how you contextualize a present-day situation or circumstance through reference to events occurring in myth. Frequently, however, without any reference to myth, you create parallels between similar situations. In "The Lilacs" (*Loop* 10-11), for example, the narrator walks a dog on a leash. Meanwhile, another character is attached, by a cord, to an oxygen supply. Is this perception of difference in similarity the ground of metaphor-making in your poetry?

AS • Yes, and in my fiction too. The things could be quite similar, as is the case in that poem, or they could be a bit further apart. What I like to do is to set one thing up, neck and neck, with something else and see what the buzz is between those two things. That's the structure of metaphor. In the betweenness of things, we find out the surprising thing that poetry gives us.

AC • I am struck by how easily an observed fact becomes metaphor in your poetry. "In the morning / it's cold, but each breath translates / as a plume, a prancing horse" (*Loop* 12). Anyone who has experienced a Canadian winter has seen that, noticed that. A few lines later, however, an entire scene fulfils the metaphor suggested in "plume": "High up, / a peak. A helmet. Breastplates / of gold .... The branches of the Douglas fir, / those sentinels, guard / some bright city of the air" (*Loop* 12-13). The plume of breath has sprung an entire army. Is this glide from fact to metaphor fairly unconscious for you?

AS • Mostly it's unconscious. The conscious part is that I'm aware of, say, the evocative nature of a word like "plume." Even as I write it, the army – if you like – is already taking shape. I suppose it's an example of synecdoche. The other aspect of this is, as a poet-mentor reminded me, that images accrue, or build, in a given poem.

AC • "The New Year" (*Loop* 18), which prefaces the series "Seven Paintings by Brueghel" (19-25), presents revelry with something dark lurking around the edges of the circle created by bonfire and sparklers. Would you say something about that darkness?

AS   • It's the fear of the unknown. The fear of what came before and what will come after. This was a New Year unlike any other because it was the end of one millennium and the beginning of another. I wanted to write something about that, but it was shadowed by all the things that had happened and all the things that inevitably will happen again. In a case like this, I'm reminded of *Beowulf*. In that poem, there is celebration after Grendel has been killed, and then there is another descent into darkness, a world of darkness. Then we come out of it, and there is a golden light of celebration. Maybe I am striving after that same thing.

AC   • The prose poems "Gesture Drawings" (*Loop* 26-36), of which there are 11, follow immediately upon the highly wrought sonnets of "Seven Paintings by Brueghel" (*Loop* 19-25). In this arrangement, are you drawing attention to a formal difference between the two series, parallel, let us say, to the difference in the visual arts between painting and drawing?

AS   • Don McKay said that these are the two wings of my art, and I think what he meant was one is the very rigorous, highly wrought corona and the other is a series of improvisations. That series is made up of gesture drawings and it's quick. Those poems were written very fast, and it took a long time to write and rewrite the sonnets.

AC   • In "Gesture Drawings," I hear a voice I don't often hear in your poetry, sassy, a bit sarcastic: "Give the guy a picnic, a chance to fondle old memories with his sister" ("Wordsworth" 27). What I am interested in here is, does voice find form or the reverse?

AS   • I know that particular voice comes up from time to time. Can we call it sardonic? I don't know about voice finding form. All I know is at that time, I had to write in that particular voice. There was a lot I was critical of in those poems, such as the blunders in the civil war, "Union vs. Confederate" (*Loop* 28), and so a number of those poems are in that voice. Others are sad or wistful, and some are whimsical. There's a whole range, and they were all to do with love. The challenge was how to do gesture drawings of love. Then I removed love from the title, which was probably a good move. It's good not to say it.

AC   • In "Carpets," the speaker says, "I might have been pulled into the blue-black, / too high, too far, but something called me / back" (*Loop* 44). This speaker may or may not be a stand-in for the poet, but let me ask you anyway: Are there risks in poetry?

AS • Oh, yes. There are risks. You might lose the ground you stand on. You risk losing yourself. If you are writing with your whole soul, with everything that you are, you risk everything.

AC • In "Remains," the speaker, looking at animal body parts – "claws, dark fur, cable of spine" – says, "we've felt teeth at our own necks, / been dragged, bitten, / ripped open" (*Loop* 40). Similarly, the owl's presence in the poem "Owl," means "something clutched at the neck" (*Loop* 46). Is this noticing of nature "red in tooth and claw" really about human vulnerability?

AS • Our world isn't so very different from the animal world. So, yes, these poems have to do with *our* vulnerability, but they also have to do with our instincts to hunt, to kill. We're both predator and prey.

AC • In "First of July," we're cautioned, "Latch the heart / when you go out" (*Loop* 45). In another poem, the body is a "locked gate" (*Loop* 50) and back in *Light*, in the title poem, memory has a "latch" (4). Tell me about the recurrence of the latch/lock metaphor.

AS • It appears again in "Seven Paintings by Brueghel" (*Loop* 19-25). Certainly there are metaphors that poets return to again and again: This must be one of mine. It's possible that what I'm getting at with this image is the way we're restrained by convention, among other things, and so can't free ourselves.

AC • Both *Light* and *Loop* give evidence of wide reading in history. When you're not writing, are you more likely to read history than a novel or poetry?

AS • I have a fascination for it, which comes from my father, who is enormously well read in history. It may be that I'm trying to fill gaps in what I've learned. I vividly recall a volunteer teacher in Nigeria, a man from Scotland, who had a list of philosophy books that he was going to read. And he did read them while he was there, and maybe he checked them off as he went along. So, yes, now I read history, a little philosophy, a smattering of science. Lots of poetry. When I'm writing fiction, though, I don't read many novels, except the classics, because I find contemporary novels have too much of an influence on my own work. My reading goes all over the map.

AC • It seems to me "The Body Tattoo of World History" (*Loop* 47-49) is a signature Simpson piece. Like "North, South, East, West" (*Loop* 14-

17), which comprehends the four cardinal points of the world, "Body Tattoo" records not just "History," but "*World* History" (*Loop* 47-49). You seem to want to wrap the world in words. At the same time, the locus of many of the poems in *Loop* is the body. Is it an exaggeration to say that in your work the world and the body are conflated?

AS   • That particular poem, "The Body Tattoo of World History," was written sometime after I'd seen a show of Tim Hawkinson's art at the Power Plant Contemporary Art Gallery in Toronto. I was amazed by the sheer brilliance of his inventiveness, his wit and intelligence, but also his scope, his reach. At the time I saw the show, I'd been thinking a lot about the body, and here was someone who was obsessed with it – to the point of making tiny birds and eggshells out of his own fingernails. He'd also made a *Wall Chart of World History from Earliest Times to the Present* (1997), a large scroll of red-inked patterns, which could depict the rise and fall of nations, but which Hawkinson loosely modelled on the digestive system of the human body. In many ways those wall charts of history are meaningless, which is partly, I think, what Hawkinson is pointing out: No one really cares when Otho the Great ruled Germany, for instance. But it's all part of a script about the world, which could, just as easily, be a script about the body, something that's written in blood. And around the same time, I was reading *An Unfinished History of the World*, but never finished it, which seems somehow fitting. Anyway, these things came together. I thought if you could take history and the body together, you could regard the body as a container, and that's how I thought of it in terms of this poem. I wanted to find a way to say that the body contains time, and also that it is marked, or let's say tattooed, by time. But the poem is also an elegy for a teenager who was killed, a student with whom I'd worked. So there is a fierceness about this poem, a deep anger. The way it shaped itself was different – in terms of form – than other poems I'd written, and maybe that came from wanting to give voice to an intense vision in a way that opens the poem up rather than closes it down.

AC   • This is poetry that frequently remarks the absence of gods and angels. In "Watching the Game," the speaker wonders about the pitchers in the dugout: "Perhaps they waited / for the gods who weren't attending" (*Loop* 66) and in "The Imperial Asylum," what is absent is "the many-feathered angels / who will not descend" (*Loop* 78). Are the gods remarkable now only for their absence?

AS • We can't rely on the divine to save us, if saving is what we want. But it's not just a case of the divine not being available to us, it's that we are no longer available to the divine. I think, for the most part, we've lost that capacity, though I should point out that I'm speaking of 21st-century North American consumer culture when I say this.

AC • "[O]rdinary lives are always / embellished by the papers" (*Loop* 74). What does poetry do with or for ordinary lives?

AS • Poetry can give us whatever limns the ordinary, which can be, occasionally, the extraordinary. I was especially concerned with this when I wrote my first novel, *Canterbury Beach*, because the lives of those characters – ordinary ones – were ones in which I was deeply interested. None of those characters was going to set the world on fire, but I wanted to examine them carefully, with tenderness.

AC • "The Imperial Asylum" (*Loop* 75-79), although it begins in the asylum at Vincennes, as photographed by Charles Nègre, suggests that the whole world is an asylum: "we are, all of us, crowded together, / or wandering in circles" (*Loop* 75). This is a rather Dantean view of the world, isn't it?

AS • I don't always regard the world as an asylum, but an asylum can also mean a place of refuge or sanctuary, and I was thinking along those lines at the end of that poem. Essentially, it's a poem about transcending fear and grief.

AC • "Trailer Park" (*Loop* 80-91) juxtaposes the history of physics – naming major figures such as Kepler, Copernicus, Galileo – and a night scene in a trailer park, including a couple in a tent making love: Gravity's embrace of the world and the couple entering one another are parallels. Is desire expressed in the structure of the world?

AS • Desire could be regarded as gravity, if we want to see it that way. I gave a lot of thought to John Wheeler's fascinating description of gravity: "Mass grips space by telling it how to curve; space grips mass by telling it how to move" (Greene 72). Wheeler could have been talking about making love, it seems to me.

AC • "[T]ime's loop, gravity's // laws" (86): These are huge concepts, yet they find a place in your poetry.

AS • We tend to think of time or gravity in the way we've been taught to think about it. But what if those ideas were exploded? We'd have to think about time and gravity in new and different ways. I experienced a real jolt when I read Brian Greene's *The Elegant Universe* because string theory really does explode the way we think about these things. I've been influenced too, by Andre Linde, a Russian physicist who is now at Stanford. He figures in "The Trailer Park" (*Loop* 80-91). He says things that blow me away, like the fact that the big bang wasn't a one-time phenomenon, but that universes bang into existence all the time. And then he adds, as a kind of afterthought, it's just that these things happen in dimensions we can't see. So it's kind of like magic is happening all around us, except it's happening in other dimensions. As for the scope of the concepts, well, I guess I think what's to stop us from considering these things in poetry? I had an art teacher once who told us to use the whole piece of paper we were working on, and even to draw outside the borders of the paper. It didn't matter if we contained the thing we were drawing or not. And I think this is true in writing. You can't afford to be afraid: You have to be fearless. If you want to do it, you can draw outside the borders of the page.

AC • I can't imagine anything more unlike a novel than your poem "Möbius Strip" (54-63), which is the most minimal of your poems. What do these two forms – the minimalist poem and the novel – answer to?

AS • In the case of "Möbius Strip," I wanted great economy so it would work as a Möbius strip, but also because the poem seemed to expand, paradoxically, the more I contracted it, and I was intrigued by that. Of course, a novel is a different thing altogether, like working on house construction as opposed to making a cat's cradle out of string. You can toss all kinds of things into the novel, and it can be accommodated with room to spare.

AC • What urges you in one direction or the other?

AS • I think that poetry is a way for me to work out big ideas in small containers. It's kind of like finger painting was for me when I was young: You can make a big mess and use all the colours you want and have a lot of fun. So while the subjects I choose are serious, the work itself can be enormously playful. The novel is larger, so the play is different for me, but it's still there. In the novel, I want to tell stories – big stories, small stories. It comes of wanting to understand why people do what they do. For me, this is a very rich and intriguing thing: I like to weave the stories together and make a kind of tapestry of the telling. For instance, in *Canterbury Beach*, I was interested in making a novel that was a memory theatre – that Renaissance concept of retaining ideas by means of an imagined memory theatre – for a family, by examining the individual lives within that family. It's a whole world you can construct, though you have to do it with care and precision, but the thing is that people will *believe* in this world. I love that about the novel.

AC • The short stories seem closer than your novel to your poems. What gear shifts in writing a novel?

AS • The short story can do something that neither poetry nor the novel can do. Perhaps it retains the best of both. It has a jewel-like quality that poetry has, but it also allows for character to unfold within a sharp, glinting world. Raymond Carver once mentioned that [Anton] Chekhov wrote, in a short story, that "suddenly everything became clear to him" (Carver 14) and this notion – of things becoming clear – is fundamental to a good short story. That's the moment I look for in a short story: That one moment when everything changes. The novel has moments like this too, but it works on a larger scale.

AC • It surprises me that your poetry and fiction are not more alike. Of course poetry takes place in time, and fiction, or at least plot-driven fiction, takes place in space. But is their difference more than that?

AS • I couldn't write fiction without poetry, or poetry without fiction. I need them both. But I want to talk further about what you say about time in poetry and fiction. Interestingly, I see poetry as stopping time, rather than "taking place in time," as you put it. I don't think it depends on a narrative line, or linear time, let's say, in the way that fiction does. Poetry can have bits of story in it, and it can even have a narrative line, but in the end, I don't think poetry cares about story in the same way. It is not *required* to tell a tale. So I see poetry as the knife that cleaves through linear time. Fiction depends on time, though. Even unconventional novels – and I'm thinking of *Time's Arrow*, by Martin Amis, as an example – depend on our knowledge of chronological time.

AC • In a conversation with Jan Zwicky, you said, "Poetry remains a touchstone for all other writing that I do" (116). Why is poetry the "touchstone"?

AS • Poetry is at the heart of things for me. It's that simple. It's like air: I need it to breathe. I didn't always know this, but I know it now.

WORKS CITED

— • —

Carver, Raymond. *Fires: Essays, Poems, Stories*. 1968. New York: Random House, 1984.

Gilbert, Jack. *The Great Fires: Poems 1982-1992*. New York: Knopf, 1996.

Greene, Brian. *The Elegant Universe*. New York: W.W. Norton, 1999. Vintage, 2000.

Simpson, Anne. "Bowing Before the Light." Banff Centre for the Arts. Unpublished conference paper.

– – – . *Canterbury Beach*. Toronto: Viking Penguin, 2001.

– – – . *Light Falls Through You*. Toronto: McClelland & Stewart, 2000.

– – – . *Loop*. Toronto: McClelland & Stewart, 2003.

– – – . "There Is No Place That Does Not See You." Anne Simpson Interviews Jan Zwicky. *Where the Words Come From: Canadian Poets in Conversation*. Ed. Tim Bowling. Roberts Creek, BC: Nightwood Editions, 2002. 115-22.

Tegmark, Max. "Parallel Universes." *Scientific American* 288.5 (May 2003): 40-51.

"THE LONG WORK IT'S BEEN JUST TO OPEN":
SUE GOYETTE TALKS ABOUT WRITING

At the time of this interview, May 2003, Sue Goyette was about to publish her second collection of poetry, *Undone,* and she was at work on a new novel "Miracle." Goyette's previous collection, *The True Names of Birds* (1998), was shortlisted for a Governor General's Award, the Gerald Lampert Award, and the Pat Lowther Award. *Lures,* her debut novel, was shortlisted for the Thomas Raddall Award for Fiction. Goyette grew up in St. Bruno, Quebec, and has lived in the Halifax area for 13 years.

The interview took place in St. John's, NL, on an airplane between St. John's and Halifax (very noisy, that), and at Bob & Lori's Food Emporium, Gottingen Street, Halifax. Three days of talk.

AC   • "This road // has filled my shoes with birthstones / and turned my mother into a full / length mirror" (13). I know roads and mirrors, but these lines, and others like them, have the logic of a dream. Would that be an appropriate way to describe the mix of strangeness and familiarity in *The True Names of Birds*?

SG   • Yes, the logic of a dream, a kind of underground knowing – how trees know each other through root systems, the way root systems are connected underground in forests. It's something you don't see, but it's there.

AC   • The personae of these poems seem fairly consistent from first poem to last. Do you think of these personae as one character, a bit like a character in a short story?

SG   • I suppose I might. I'm in the driver's seat, so I'm taking myself down roads I want to go, but I don't really think in character when I am writing a poem. I think I am probably present in a way I am not even able to articulate. I am in the poem – it's me – but it's autobiographical in a lyrical, not in a factual or non-fictional, sense. You know, it's kind of like a pair of pants. The "I" just fits. With my poetry, I attempt to use my experience more as a palette than I do in my fiction. Ultimately, though, I am a writer and every day I get out of bed thinking, *This day will be a fabulous story*. So, I am in my life as a writer. I don't think I could begin to separate the two.

AC • And the consistency of the personae?

SG • There is a consistency in the voice because I wrote the poems very close together. They occupy a certain time in my life, which that voice witnessed.

AC • In *Illuminations*, Walter Benjamin says, "No poem is intended for the reader, no picture for the beholder, no symphony for the listener" ("The Task of the Translator" 69). Do you have some sympathy with Benjamin's statement?

SG • Yes, because if I were to begin to think of readers, I wouldn't be writing. That's like trying a bathing suit on under a group of spotlights. I don't want an audience watching. I need to forget about myself when I write: It becomes just the words on the page, the energy that takes place, that blending between head, heart, and page. I can't afford to think about anything else.

AC • The poems in *True Names* are forthright and honest: I feel rather abashed asking you questions about them. Did you feel revealed, exposed, when the collection was published?

SG • Oh, yes, but I feel that way when anything of mine comes out. Writing for me is an incredibly solitary, intense, and private activity. It is necessarily so, but it doesn't occur to me while I am writing to even think that it will be a book. When I first got *True Names*, it was delivered by the guy who coached my son's baseball team. He used to go around and pretend to check to see if all of the boys were wearing their cups for the baseball diamond, and so when the book came I thought, *Oh my God, protection, protection, we need protection*! A weird metaphor, I know. When I held the book, I thought, *Shit, there's no hiding*. If I'm going to be a writer, eventually things will be public, and I need to face that fear, that challenge. And it has been a challenge, even with *Lures*. People who don't usually read a lot of poetry – friends, neighbours – read my novel because they knew me. They assumed a lot of things because of what they read, and I found myself having to

ANNE COMPTON

defend it and myself. It is not something that I am complaining about. I think it is an aspect of being an artist you have to come to terms with. Each time, it doesn't get better, but it is different, and I have more faith in myself as an artist and I know the process.

AC • Your poetry begins with a house, the people in it. How do you set off from there into a poem?

SG • There are small universes everywhere, and I just happen to use my house as metaphor. Art for me is the transformation of house into universe.

AC • You prefer a long line. In fact, your lines frequently overrun the margin. What does that long line enable you to do?

SG • I do prefer them. I can go all the way to the end and further. I try to write short ones, but it's not natural. I feel more at home in long lines. The more you can figure out who you are, the writing follows. When I teach writing to students, I tell them about how each of my kids takes a bath. One kid locks the door and pulls out the drawer so that there is no way to get in. Then she comes out with three towels on, goes to her room, and eventually comes out dressed. The other one streaks to his room, leaves the door half open. If you can figure out how you take your bath, that's how you write.

AC • Most of these poems take the form of unrhymed tercets or couplets. In one of his essays, Billy Collins says that "the physical shape of the poem" is a "spatial guide for the reader's passage through the poem" (7). How do you go about determining the shape a poem will take?

SG • I generally lean towards couplets. They look good on the page, and I like the idea of long couplets. It is kind of like navigating for me. You navigate to each couplet, like an island, and are able to make a stop and visit. I like ghazals too for that reason. The couplets just stand there, and then you leave just one line at the end. I like that tension. I like the three lines as well, but I have to admit I probably like couplets more. I was talking to another poet about baseball, and it dawned on me that outside the foul lines is the rest of the world. The baseball game is in the diamond, and I realized that outside the poem is the rest of the world too. You have the whole world pressing against the poem. The couplets are important, and so is the space around them.

AC • "Magic" is a word the recurs in this book: "magic symbol ... magic trick" (21); and there are "fairy godmothers" (14), "toothfairies [and] medicine men" (30). Where do these words spring from?

SG • Probably from the way I perceived the world. I think I imposed a system, which I've outgrown since. In growing up, growing older, and having my own children, I had to re-address that system. My particular system – the magic in my world – came because my growing up was hard. I needed to believe in magic, and that changed as I began to address my issues, and my need for that system of magic changed. What replaced it was true magic. The poem is maybe the mass for the moment. The celebration of it. That exchange with the moment is really important.

AC • Are poems "reminders of the unrejoiced" (15), as one poem puts it? Is that why you write?

SG • That's what I hope to be doing with my poetry. Monks sweep every day and make their sweeping a prayer. I think that if we can be convinced again by our everyday, then we would stay in it. We often forget to be in our bodies and worry about what we should be doing. Writing is an act of doing something celebratory. The human condition is fraught with loneliness, and if we learn to live with it, instead of shutting down to it, then we can be alive.

AC • In the first section of *True Names*, in such poems as "I Know Women," adulthood means loss. The speaker in that poem asks, "When did you grow so big? / So heavy?" (12). Similarly, in "Again to Be a Daughter," the speaker says, "I want to turn into a daughter / again" (14). What's been lost, and what in adulthood is unwanted?

SG • "Again to be a Daughter" is more about looking back and realizing there was a point in life when you realized that your mother was a person, a woman who had her own battles. I wasn't really aware of them growing up. I was more aware of who I was. "Again to be a Daughter" pays homage to my mother as a woman. As for the question, "When did you grow so big? / So heavy?" (12), growing up startled me. It still startles me how old I am. I have this essence of myself, and then I catch myself in the mirror and think, *Oh, you look tired*, and the next day the same thing, and then I realize that I am getting old. Aging is a surprising thing for me. I had my children really young, so when I was writing *True Names* there was a part of me which was like when you are camping and sitting in the tent and hearing everyone else laughing and thinking they are all having a better time than you. There was a time in my life when I thought everyone was having a way better time than me, so I wrote *True Names*.

AC • In "I Know Women," the speaker seems to be suspended in a kind of limbo: "This is your punishment; not to have become // the owl, but to no longer be the girl" (12). The full transition would be to arrive at "owl"?

SG • Well, I don't know. I can talk about writing poems and about poems, but there's a space between where the poem starts and how it ends that is, to me, just wilderness. That's the reader's space. I have been there, and I'm done.

AC • The reader walks around in that space, and sometimes comes back – as I'm doing – and asks, "Well, how does that happen?"

SG • Yes, and I find that kind of demystifies it.

AC • I don't. That's the Romantic position. Wordsworth says, "We murder to dissect" (79). My field in literature is 17th-century Metaphysical poetry, where thought and emotion are wedged together from the beginning. As far as I am concerned, analysis – and thinking about poems – strengthens, and certainly doesn't weaken, a poem.

SG • I don't think thinking messes things up. I'm just not used to talking about "How does that happen?" It's very rare that I get to. When I am out for beer with my friends, they don't really care about the wilderness. They're like, "What did you have for supper?" I think it's really important to talk about it and I love reading about it. I think my hang-up is not that I will demystify it, but hose it down.

AC • There's a drive towards inclusiveness in this book. Let me give you some examples: "[T]here's a ceremony for everything" (12); "everything [is] a sign" (20); "every moment is a bargain" (20); "Everywhere you look you see distance" (45); and "I give birth everywhere" (44). Can you say something about this *every moment, everywhere* inclination in your poetry?

SG • I was driven by the need to believe that every moment was important. I don't know if I am as driven now.

AC • The traditional muse for the male poet is female, sometimes maternal. In your poetry, it seems to me, the muse is not behind the poetry, but in it: "I give birth everywhere" (44). Do you feel in reading women's poetry these days that the muse has bypassed the intermediary stage and simply taken up residence in the poetry?

SG • I hope so. It's kind of like the lantern in the park. Instead of conjuring up the muse, or thinking it is around us like the air, it's in the poetry.

AC • Sadness is a cat "wrapped in burlap" for drowning (16). Regret is a houseguest, a "woman who watches her reflection / in soup spoons and still water" (41). Sadness and regret are not abstracts. They have solidity and presence. Can you say something about the quality of emotion in your poetry?

SG • These emotions absolutely have solidity and presence. I think they inform us and the way that we are in the world. Metaphor is just the birdcage, the mayonnaise jar we catch the fireflies and the butterflies of loneliness in. It allows us to go right up to that houseguest and sit beside her and see what she is like. Regret is sleeping in my nightgown. Not everyone is comfortable with that.

AC • In *Undone*, the new manuscript, light is an "ancient relative in the corner" (15). This metaphor is comparable to the visitation of "Regret" (*True Names* 41). There is in your work a tendency to conceptualize emotion and observation as character.

SG • I like the idea of something sitting in the room of the poem. I wave my wand in the poem and, *presto*, there is loneliness, and we can finally talk to it.

AC • Metaphors in *True Names* are strong and startling. I've picked three, more or less at random: "This season is a breech baby ... winter, on its back, lies moaning" (46); "My dreams are shoeboxes // filled with bones from my feet" (50); and "Mornings are double- / jointed, wanting to go either way" (61). All of these are copula metaphors. Why do you think you favour this form?

SG • I guess it takes the abstract by the collar and sits it right on my lap. There is nothing in between. I like that directness. I don't like pussy-footing around: "Let's get to it, let's not bullshit." I think in metaphors. It's just the way I am. Metaphors are the shortcut. They're the better fly nets. They're the way we can get close to wilderness. They're our tool and tour guide. You can use them both ways. They're double-jointed.

AC • The other thing about those metaphors is the fact that they all involve the body. Why do such things as seasons and mornings get referred to the body?

SG • It goes back to the whole cup. I think the body is ultimately our metaphor in that it contains it all. My body is part of my craft, and it contains a wealth of information. I remember something someone said, "Oh, once you have children, you won't be able to travel," and I was really dismayed and didn't write for a whole year. Then I thought that writing, using my body as litmus paper for the world, would be really interesting.

AC • Is there a risk in that?

SG • I think you have to have a distance. There is a very fine line between exploration, navigation, and indulgence. When you start taking yourself a little too seriously, you hold up words implying an importance they haven't earned, and that frightens me. I use my body the way I use my family and house. I don't want to be a person. I don't want to get in the way of the writing when it works so that it can *swoosh* right through me. "Use me," I say every day.

AC • A lot of naming happens in *True Names*. Sadness has "all the names / I can give to it" (16). Elias Canetti says, "The act of naming is the great and splendid consolation of mankind" (Atwood xiii). Are naming and defining consoling acts? Other people might say that naming is a negative thing: "It's about ownership."

SG • It's the opposite of ownership. It's about loving. For me, it is about giving something its space to be what it is. I don't want to keep relying on the mass thing, but it's a way of just holding something up and letting it be what it is.

AC • In "Solstice and Other Long Days," the speaker is a reader of "signs" and "warning[s]" (*True Names* 19), and in another poem "everything [is] a sign" (20). In the final poem, trees are "some kind of forecast" and birds are "signs" (63). Is that because the world is full of danger?

SG • I think because the world is full of danger, we insinuate signs. I don't know which came first, the danger or the signs. I think maybe for me the danger came first.

AC • In "Solstice," birds feed at a feeder above a poised and ready-to-pounce cat; children go to "the edge of all those steep places" (19). Is poetry a precipice-avoidance system?

SG • Not a whit. Not for me. Poetry's a way to investigate my experiences as a human being.

AC • A specific geographical place does not come into view in *True Names*. Is a specific geography or locale not important to you in the creative process?

SG • Oh, it is important to me. It informs me. I live very close to the ocean, and a five minute drive away from a wonderful walk along the salt marsh. I used to go there a lot and still try to every so often. It's very important to me to go to something I can't see the edge of. There are a lot of times in the day when I mentally touch it: "There you are." It keeps me in my place. I am so steeped in it, I don't need to name it in my poems because it just simply is. It is the horizon line. It probably comes up more in *Undone* because I relied on it more. Outside became the inside.

AC • "There are roads // weaving between mountains and the ocean / that can lead you to the very place / you're running from" (13). In *True Names*, topography transmuted into a mythical topography. Is that so?

SG • It did. It is like taking a road and watching it transform into The Road. It is like taking a small thing and watching it enlarge into it all – the way the cup holds the universe; the way the window holds the universe. I think the universe presents itself in those small ways all the time. So the road that was an actual road – I was on a road between mountains and ocean – did lead me back to that road we all travel. I think that's what I hammer. That's what I work on. I use the particular and hammer it until I can see the big picture, the mythology, the truth.

AC • An article in *The Chronicle Herald*, referring to work by you, Lynn Davies, and Anne Simpson, speaks of your "invigorating (and various) approaches to the domestic" (C7). Do you feel sometimes like wringing the neck of the word "domestic"?

SG • Yes. I do worry because I feel I am being confined, as if domestic hangs over me like a bathrobe. If you are coming to me with domestic, then that is what you are going to see. It is like coming into a room and thinking of one colour, you will see it everywhere. Domesticity is there.

ANNE COMPTON

It informs me, and yes, I use the domesticity of my life, but I consider myself more of a naturalist. I am interested in the relationship between inside and outside, and domestic only implies inside. I think that I try to balance inside and outside. If they said, "She is a domestic and wilderness writer," I would wear that. Domestic alone sounds dismissive, putting me back in the kitchen, and that I don't like.

AC • In the world you create in *True Names,* everyday actions and things are raised to the level of ritual: "You need to hear of the prayer / of folding. Of putting away your clothes ..." (20). Household acts are acts of homage, aren't they?

SG • They are. I think that if you can turn acts into that, your days are blessed. It is just a matter of perception. For a long time, I resented the fact that I was doing dishes, and then I thought, *If I am going to be doing dishes every day, I had better be able to make it work for me.* That's the lovely thing: Ecstasy and laundry gallop through our lives.

AC • At the same time, in some of the poems, the speaker suffers a separation from immediate things and is "stranded in this stillness" (21). A divide occurs between the gesture and the voice so that although the speaker pulls "handkerchief after handkerchief from my sleeve /... someone else sings the blues" (21). So there is also a sense of separation from the ordinary from time to time.

SG • That was an investigation of the struggle in being an artist and a mother, the situation in which I found myself. The demands on my time, I found, were hard to reconcile with what I wanted to be doing. I was stuck doing the practical magic tricks while someone else was singing.

AC • The world of *True Names,* for all its familiarity, seems temporary. In the poem "For Robyn," the speaker asks on her behalf, "How many things must you get used to?" and observes, "you're homesick. This house, you think, has too many doors" (24). Is the world at once foreign and familiar?

SG • I think so. I think because it is so foreign and so unpredictable, we make it predictable. We search for things, for patterns, because we don't know anything. We are always at the precipice, and we make assumptions.

AC • Pattern-making is a way to lessen the foreign?

SG · It lessens what is foreign or, perhaps, just puts guardrails on it.

AC · Does the world feel foreign, even while it is familiar, because we really belong in some other world?

SG · I don't think "foreign" is the right word. I know in my experience I make an assumption that my backyard is my backyard. Well, my backyard is quite an independent place. There is a space between out there and me, and I can't do anything about what happens in that space. Though we've fenced our yard and planted our gardens, it's wilderness.

AC · Is there a religious heritage or predisposition behind the pattern in *True Names* that makes even the most ordinary and everyday gestures a penitential ritual?

SG · Probably. I'm not religious, but I think I'm spiritual. I grew up Catholic, but I'm not anymore, and I still feel guilty saying that – that's how Catholic I grew up. I consider writing my ritual. I've heard myself saying that writing for me is prayer.

AC · So your writing calls up a religious heritage?

SG · It calls up awe.

AC · There are poems called "Faith" (32-33) and "Confession" (25-26); the word "penance" appears in the latter. "[B]aptism" is referred to in another (32). These are not poems of religious faith, so why is the vocabulary of the church invoked in this book?

SG · Yes, OK. I definitely used vocabulary that I grew up with and took it for my own. It is like taking a shirt out of your mother's cupboard and tearing out the sleeves. I use the vocabulary.

AC · You move the vocabulary out of the church and into the poem?

SG · I do, and I think when you do something like that, you hold it up at a different angle and it becomes a different thing.

AC · The prose poem "Gardens" retells Genesis, focusing on Eve's internal, physical experience once the curse has fallen upon her: "lobster claws in her stomach ... moles burrowing and scraping tunnels to her heart" (27). The story is shifted away from Adam. Is it your belief that the foundational stories of our culture ought to be reconsidered or recast in those terms?

ANNE COMPTON

SG • I would like to see everyone getting equal time. That would be a fascinating way to revisit it because, obviously, it had to occur that way, although it wasn't always told that way. It would be interesting to go back with flashlights and light it up again. I don't know if it is something I would do. I do it when I come across it, but I don't know if I would specifically pack a bag and go back.

AC • The "Sisters" in childhood "weren't temples or even bungalows. We were apartments. Small / rooms each of us ..." (31). Is that because it is impossible to think of childhood without thinking of the spaces where it was spent?

SG • That's another thing that I explored in *Lures*. When you are living in an unhappy climate, you become very alone and small. We contain ourselves in order to keep ourselves safe. Our bodies are temples. Well, we couldn't be temples. We couldn't be that big. We had to stay very small.

AC • Distance is a painful preoccupation in *True Names*. "The moon on Friday night" reminds "the women of songs / they knew, songs written to gauge distance" (30). In another poem, the speaker says, "in some language / there must be a word for this distance" (39). In a poem called "Distance," the speaker says of a son "Everywhere you look you see distance" (45). What is spoken of here – spatial distance or emotional?

SG • I think emotional, but I don't know if that's the right word. I think the distance is when you are exploring that space between where you are and where you wish you were: It is the distance of the unfinished, the unexplored, the un-begun.

AC • "I'll create the mythology for this house" (47): Is that what you wanted to do in your first collection of poetry?

SG • I think it's an important undertaking. We are responsible for how we remember our stories. When I hear it now, it sounds a little controlling, but it wasn't about controlling. It was about calling up light and calling up stories that would keep us on the right track.

AC • In *Lures*, Eliza draws "to record, to mark down like a kind of charting, a mapping of her children, her home ..." (115). That need is similar to "I'll create the mythology for this house" (*True Names* 47) isn't it?

SG   • It is. I think the day is kind of the tray of things that you can pull out for the collage. It is the choosing and the putting them together, that is art.

AC   • In "Women Drinking Tea or Tequila," the speaker is in a "strange woods" with her friends, "no trousered daddies / pointing out advice with the stems of their pipes" (*True Names* 60). In the first poem in the collection, "The True Names of Birds" (11), an adult speaker is lost in the woods, bereft of "wonder," which is associated with her father. Is "Women Drinking Tea or Tequila" written against that first poem?

SG   • I didn't do that consciously, but when you put the two together, yes. But they didn't bookend each other in my mind.

AC   • Tell me about the shift from poetry to fiction. I understand that *Lures* began as poetry.

SG   • Because I had just finished writing *True Names*, I assumed I was going to continue writing poems so I insinuated the material into poetry form. But the poems struck me as flat. They were just narrative, nothing lyrical to them. There was no leaping around like I always felt when I was writing poems. There wasn't a spark. I thought that if I just kept on writing, I could tap into that vein of poetry, that feeling again. I wrote a lot of poems, and they weren't convincing me. I was thinking that they were failed poems, but I didn't have anything else to write. One day I was writing a series of poems, and I went across the page and wrote a block of prose. Just going across the page unhinged something, and I thought maybe that was the way I should be going. It progressed into a short story, which got longer and longer. For a long time I called it a really long short story. It took me a long time to say it was a novel.

AC   • If I were to identify the bridge poem between your fiction and your poetry, I would name "Women Drinking Tea or Tequila," which introduces women "walk[ing] in storyteller boots" (*True Names* 60). Would I be right?

SG   • I certainly was thinking about the way we tell our stories when I was writing that poem, and how we bring them to the table when we are with our friends, and how people who love us listen to those stories. I was, perhaps subconsciously, mapping something I wouldn't be aware of for a few years. I certainly wasn't thinking of writing fiction then. It never occurred to me that I could.

AC   • Les McIntyre, in *Lures,* is such a sleazy man. Was it difficult to write about him?

SG   • I had to go into the dark, and sometimes I felt like I had to tie a rope around my waist and just sink into it, but other times it felt like I had one of the finest times writing it. It was a tear writing *Lures.* I felt really alive and engaged with my characters. It was remarkable. There is no word that's potent enough to say what that experience was like – a kind of rush. It was a light-bulb turner, and I wouldn't change a minute of it. But it was also difficult.

AC   • Did that feeling of exhilaration stay with you through all of the stages of the novel?

SG   • Writing *Lures* was a totally different experience from the novel I am writing now. The novel I am writing now is difficult, not structurally or narratively, but rhythmically: My life is not set up right now so that I can give it the attention it needs. Once, I was in the position where everything collaborated in my life. I wrote *Lures* hard and fast, and I did have that feeling, that wonderful lunge of feeling you have when you get through a poem, and it is working and everything is falling into place in a way that you couldn't possibly have planned. I had that feeling pretty consistently throughout *Lures.* I was incredibly blessed – I never felt more alive – and I managed to tap into it again when I edited it.

AC   • How long did it take to write *Lures?*

SG   • About eight months. I wrote it, sent it to an agent, and he suggested it be about 60 pages longer. I took a month to do that. So it was fast. And afterwards, when it was finished, I felt like I had been chewed up and spit out. I was exhausted.

AC   • *Lures* is full of watchers. Besides the creepy child molester, there's the gangster Ralph who spies on people; Gary says, "all he had to do was watch" (45); and Curtis wants "just to watch" (47). In these instances, watching is either aggressive or a retreat. Jerry begins to realize, however, that "it was seeing that was important, not what was being looked at" (153). Tell me the difference between watching and seeing.

SG   • Watching is more pedestrian. Seeing is more aggressive. Seeing is being more awake to what's actually happening. Maybe the characters aren't doing anything, but they're partaking in the scene in a way that makes them more involved than if they were just watching. Seeing is making a connection. It's more of a muscular watching.

AC • Obsession is in all of the characters in *Lures*, but they are not – with the exception of Les – unwell people. Through her endless copying from the encyclopedia, Lily develops to the point where she is going to stop being a copier and is going to become a writer. Her obsession delivers her into something.

SG • Which is what happens I think in a lot of human experience, especially if you grow up with some dysfunction. You are born into a family, and you have to learn to adapt a rudder or a sailing system so that you can move through it, and that system is either going to tear you apart – be destructive – or it's going to help you become more who you are.

AC • Can you tell me about the comparable satisfactions of poetry and fiction in terms of writing?

SG • I think a novel costs something you don't realize you are paying. When you write poetry, you pay it out poem by poem. At the end, you have a collection, whereas a novel requires dedication and concentration and a corralling in of the story to keep it herded together. It is very hard to maintain any semblance of life while you are writing a novel. It's easier to live writing poems, but it's harder to make a living.

AC • "[T]he long work it's been just to open" (49): This new collection of poetry, *Undone*, might have been called "Open." Tell me about its title.

SG • I think I had to become undone to become open. Undone was one of those steps before open, and undone was the step I got snagged at while I was writing. I think you have to burn down to start building yourself up again.

AC • But the manuscript is largely about being rebuilt: It's more done than undone.

SG • Yes, but I think the undone is the basis from which I started, and it was imperative that I was undone.

AC • Between *True Names* and *Undone*, there's a move from an interior world to an exterior. Light, in particular, is carefully observed: "The Season of Forgiveness" (15) remarks the difference between fall light and the greedy light of summer. In another poem, light, the "true narrator ... documents // her loss" (62). Is there a sense, then, in which light is the narrator of this book?

SG • There's a sense of light having narrative qualities. It is something that happened organically because the book was written from a very dark place. When I first started writing it, I was really, really hungry for light, and then it started to present itself in its own way.

AC • You wrote it quickly?

SG • Nine or 10 months. I was writing every day, and I write hard and fast. I don't like admitting how fast I write, but I also know that I write a lot, and a lot of the stuff I write is no good. I have friends who write really slowly and everything they do is impeccable.

AC • You wrote your novel – well, a huge chunk of it – in eight months and *Undone* in nine months, and you write, you say, "hard and fast." You're a cowboy.

SG • Yes, it's a rodeo ride, giddy-up, absolutely. But then afterwards, I can't do anything for months. I go comatose – emotionally drained.

AC • What stage are you in at this moment?

SG • Well, I'm writing right now, but I'm not riding hard and fast. I also know from the experience of writing poems that you have to write through every poem, and you have to write through the poem as it presents itself. You have to follow its lead, its trail, whether its uphill or downhill, rocky or smooth. I've learned that, and I know you have to write the poem that is in front of you to get to the poem that comes after that. I believe that. A lot of the voice in *Undone* was a voice that I wasn't even comfortable with, that I didn't recognize at all, and I didn't trust it for a long time because it was so new. But I learned from that. I learned that it's OK not to recognize yourself. That it is, sometimes, actually a good thing. I'm OK with the fact that I'm not galloping with this new novel. I'm completely faithful to it, and I will turn up for it every morning. It's beginning to trust me in that way.

AC • Speakers are out of the house in *Undone*, on the road, or on their way: "Roads stretch all the way to morning / or all the way to night" (70). Are you putting distance between yourself and the house?

SG • In a way, I am obviously out of my house. I'm also in the middle of two things. I was finishing one thing and hadn't started another. I was looking behind and I was looking ahead. I hadn't started walking yet. The writing was the walking.

AC • *Undone* editorializes on the past and on *True Names* in particular: "Anything spoken with the word / distance in it used to interest me greatly" (19) – which relates to our earlier talk about distance – and "I used to think that way. Life was often just verging on, about to, had to // get better" (20). In *Undone*, were you consciously writing against the emotional register of the first collection?

SG • I was writing against the emotional register of that part of my life represented by *True Names*.

AC • There is a relationship between *Undone* and *True Names* that exceeds the usual relationship between a first collection and a second collection.

SG • In between there was a huge moment. My marriage broke up. So I think it's like "[t]he stone of truth" (92) in a poem. The stone is dropped, and it informs the truth backwards and forwards. It informs *True Names*, and it informs *Undone*.

AC • Not only are poems longer in *Undone*, but they are also more layered. "Tattoo" (91-95) is an example: It interweaves Georgia O'Keeffe painting the irises; Robyn riding the Gravitron; and the speaker's experience of love: "I want the man about to tattoo me / to think of light and love with every needle" (94). Would you agree that there is a greater density of texture in the second book?

SG • Oh, yes. It sprawls. I think that was just the next, the inevitable step in my writing. I like *True Names*. I look back on it and think that it's a sturdy little book, but I didn't want to rewrite it. After *True Names*, it was really easy to write the same kind of poems. So easy that I didn't want to. In fact, I think that's one of the reasons I didn't fight the idea of writing fiction. It was like the second-album syndrome. I didn't sit down to write *Undone*. I was just visited again by poetry. I didn't realise I was writing a book, and I didn't realize how connected it all was until it was done. I was reading a lot, and my life was split open in a way that I think *Undone* reflects.

AC • In "Tattoo," the "stone of truth" finally gets dropped into the vase of irises that O'Keeffe is painting.

SG • Which represents the life-to-art transition. That line about "light and love with every needle" (94) is actually true: I was getting tattooed at the time. The Chinese symbol of light. I had to get that done after I wrote *Lures*. It was a bargain I made with myself. I wrote so dark in *Lures* I needed a tattoo.

AC • Where's the tattoo?

SG • It's right at the base of my spine. So it works metaphorically .... I want it down that I showed you my tattoo!

AC • "Tattoo" is not the only poem where O'Keeffe is present. There's also "Inspire" (111-12). What is it about her work that fascinates you?

SG • I was reading a lot about her at the time. I was reading her letters. She was wild. She put herself in a landscape that was, at first glance, so stark. I liked that she stayed. I wasn't interested in her so much as a person. The more I read about her, the more I didn't like her. She didn't really maintain her friendship with that best friend of hers. She didn't honour the friendship in the end. But I like what she did with her art and how she stayed true to her art. In an interview, she talks about those bones and how she liked to paint around things. I thought that was really interesting.

AC • Painting around things might be a way of defining metaphor.

SG • I think so. As I said earlier – in St. John's, in the last province we were in – I see metaphor as a net catching something wild. I do think that's true.

AC • In terms of metaphor, one never gets to the centre?

SG • We can't. Just as we can never get to the centre of anyone else's truth. We can just gesture and hope that readers take the time to travel all of the way there. That's why I think it's difficult for me to talk about the part of a poem I leave with the reader. It's their wilderness. It's their place to go. Yes, you are right: I can come back and shine lights on the hieroglyphics on my walls, but they are my walls, and I am hoping that the readers will find their own. I can hear them through the trees. Metaphor is the Holy Grail. If you got there, you wouldn't have to do it again. You get close though, don't you? You can smell it.

AC • There's exhilaration, though, when you think that you've got it right?

SG • I was walking down a dirt road near St. Peters, in Saskatchewan. I had just gone for my run, and I was cooling down. I didn't have my glasses on, and I was convinced I saw a deer a ways down the road. I was very excited and I had the whole deer experience – the creeping up to it, the stalking: "It's letting me get so close." And then when I got close enough, I realized it was a fencepost. But before that, I was having a deer experience. What's true? Thinking that it was there – whether it was or not – or being face to face with the fencepost? When you are in the emotion and the presence of that instance – when you don't know it is the wrong thing – you are moving towards the deer, and it seems that everything in that moment is in harmony with that movement. Everything just hushes, the road rises, the sun is at the right slant, it is just deer-ready.

AC • Ophelia also appears more than once in *Undone*. O'Keeffe and Ophelia: That's an odd pairing. It's true that Margaret Laurence and Elizabeth Bishop appear, but theirs are cameo appearances. What can you say about this unlikely duo, O'Keeffe, who was so ruthless, and Ophelia?

SG • When I was writing a chunk of this manuscript, my life was a total mess. I was hardly getting out of bed, but I was reading a lot. That middle section of *Undone*, where there are a lot of poems for other people and characters, was my way of thanking my banisters and light bulbs in my dark. I was reading Shakespeare like a fiend. Anyway, I was stuck on *Hamlet* because of the grief and the haunting. Ophelia seemed to me someone that I could relate to – the misunderstanding and all of that. One of the first poems I ever wrote was called "Ophelia" so it was also a way of looking back at that. I think that the sensibility of Georgia O'Keeffe and of Ophelia live in me. In that period of my life, I was like that: I was bone and I was suicidal. I was high drama: "Oh, my life, my life!"

AC • In reading *Undone*, particularly the lines in the first "Mahler" poem (31-34) – "already my day has convinced me / that light can conduct anything" (34) – I am reminded of Wordsworth's title "Surprised by Joy." Was that your experience in composing these poems?

SG • I was surprised. I was surprised because it is a book that sprang from a very dark time, and yet it's kind of like when you walk out of a funeral. Or when you have been dumped by a man, and you walk out and the sun is still shining and the birds are still singing. At first you think, *Bastard!* but then you think, *It goes fine, doesn't it?* And then you let it in, and it saves you. This book saved me. Daily, when I wrote – a poem a day basically – I would phone Helen [Humphreys] and read it to her, and she would say thumbs up or thumbs down. That saved me as well. When I wrote the last poem, I knew it was done. I finished that one and thought, *Phew, I'm done.*

AC • Although the speaker is "convinced" by joy in "Before Mahler's 9th" (31-34), the respondent poem, "And After" (35-38), overturns that conviction: "The sky, I wrote, was exquisitely left behind. / I lied. There is nothing exquisite about this" (38). *Undone,* in its first section at least, is cautious about joy, isn't it?

SG • Yes, it took me a long time to trust joy. It was easy to move through the murk. I can do that anyday. Trusting happiness is a totally new thing for me. I was mapping something in those poems: I was pushing against the side of joy and saying, "Now, how long are you going to stay?" There were days when it just deserted me, and I didn't want to write. I wasn't convinced by Mahler. I wasn't convinced by the day. I wasn't convinced by any of it. That was when it was the darkest. I think I was situationally depressed. It wasn't a clinical depression. It was like when you run just far enough away from a burning building and get to sit down and look back to watch your house burn down.

AC • The first Mahler poem says that the day will conduct the light, and there is joy in that. The second Mahler sabotages it. There is a chug-ahead and pull-back movement in the first section.

SG • I think that's what happens. When you are trying to move away from something, you bravely go off in a new direction for as long as that courage lasts, and then you run back and play all of your Beatles tapes. Then the next day, you go a little further.

AC • "And After" (35-38) is skeptical about poetry as well as joy.

SG • It is. I lost my faith in poetry. That was the lowest rung. I can still taste the day I wrote that poem.

AC • The cautious speaker in that skeptical poem "And After" also says, "let me step from these lines breaks and unbutton / the metaphors" (19). Interestingly, the desire to get out of metaphor is itself metaphorically presented.

SG • There is a lot of unbuttoning in *Undone.*

AC • Would you say that *Undone,* at the same time, reaches for a plainer speech than *True Names?*

SG • A plainer speech, yes, I think so. When I wrote *True Names,* I was more idealistic as an artist, and I thought there was a special language that poets used to talk about love. I have since realised that is the thing which, if I don't quite despise, I find fake. I think we should just cut the bullshit and talk about it. I think a lot of times there is a distance between the poet, the poem, and life. I know that when my friends read poems, they have that feeling of not being touched, moved, or being searched through because there is that distance. I think that if I can bridge that distance and yet still bring someone to their own wilderness, then I have succeeded. It's not that I am using language more plainly. I'm just using language that is sturdy and can get us through all the currents. The everyday talk enacts what I am writing about.

AC • Poems are longer in *Undone,* especially in the third section, and there's a greater tendency toward narrative. Might these formal shifts be connected to the fact that you wrote a novel between the two collections?

SG • Absolutely. It taught me about that longer reach, and it taught me about trusting the impulse of that reach to get me where I wanted to go in a way that poetry hadn't previously taught me. I could get close with the long line, but with the novel, I was writing something on page 48 that reappeared, without my really planning it, on page 104. I began to trust that. It taught me a lot to write a novel: Discipline and trusting the structure of it. It knew more about itself than I did. When it came to *Undone,* I was not concerned about the narrative drive in the last section, but I certainly knew it was there, and I was OK with that.

AC • The conceptualizing of emotions as figures has been there all along in your work. It's part of the way that you give them presence. Regret sits at the morning table just as some visitor might. Maybe that capacity to "think character" was there even in *True Names. Lures* allowed you to let the characters fully live – not calling them regret, or grievance, or folly, but Les McIntyre and Lily.

SG • Right. And in *Undone,* perhaps, I have gone back to regret and loss and let them walk their stories.

AC • In *Undone,* there are multi-sectioned poems, and this is a new move. Not only are you working with longer poems – and in the third section, with narrative-based poems – but also you are working in multi-sectioned poems, the sections separated by asterisks or in some other way.

SG • For me, these sections – it's an impulse more than anything – were kind of like what I did in *Lures* with characters. They allow me to explore the same themes but from different perspectives. I was filled with what knew I wanted to explore, and I gave myself different vantage points on the same things. I think ghazal is my native, my creative DNA. I wrote *Lures* as a ghazal. I know that sounds ridiculous, and I don't even know how to explain it, but I saw each section as a couplet, and what's in the middle, or between, is not spoken yet informs all the other parts.

AC • There are shifts of these sorts in *Undone*, but the fondness for paradox, which appears in *True Names*, continues. In "Neruda's Nets," the speaker says, "the thing that rescues ... is the same thing // that holds you here. Under" (26), which reminds me of the paradox in "You Know This" – "the candle you need for [winter's] darkness may be what burns your house down" (*True Names* 22). Paradoxical statement in your poetry generally functions to undercut security, doesn't it?

SG • In *Undone*, I was dealing with the huge ideas of love and marriage and how you have security, and then all of a sudden, *shazam*, it's gone. I wanted to investigate what was secure. Nothing. Security is an illusion.

AC • A more cryptic paradox appears in the second section of *Undone*: "The nature of loss is everywhere / it isn't" (66).

SG • Isn't that true! I think that's one of the truest things I've said. It's seamless. It is like a reflection, very close to itself. When you have lost something and you are in the world without it, soon it becomes everywhere. Its absence accompanies you.

AC • In order to write this manuscript, you had to exist in *isn't* rather than *is*?

SG • Yes. It's not that I chose to look there. Even when I was editing the manuscript, poems like "And After" (35-38) and "Alone" (27-30) and "Back When We'd Try Anything To Fix It" (19-20) were very, very painful poems for me to read.

AC • In *True Names,* "[g]rief has so many stages" (57). In *Undone,* sadness has "seven levels" (22). Is conceptualizing grief and sadness in these terms connected to the recurrence of the ladder image in *Undone?*

SG • Yes. The ladder image is really important. Absolutely. It will be the cover. A lovely painting by Carol Fraser, a Halifax artist. There are also references to rope. I needed to insinuate a sense of moving out of something. All of those images were really important in order to suggest that, yes, I went down. I went really down. I went flatter than down – the other side of the horizon. But there were ladders.

AC • Do you want to do it again? Pay the ferryman, take the crossing, be in the awful place of darkness? Do you want to climb down?

SG • Of course. I'm not afraid anymore. It's hell. I drank more beer than I should have and listened to the blues way more often than I should have. I ate a lot of chocolate and nothing green for almost six months.

AC • The larger world of *Undone* includes references to many other writers – [Pablo] Neruda (25-26, 36); Dylan Thomas (18, 53-54); Rilke (36, 121-22); John Thompson (55-56). Why these particular poets? What's the connection?

SG • They were the ones I was reading. They were my peep string [my people] in a very lonely time. I really made my life small. I saw very few people. I was really a mess. Those writers populated my life at that point. Dylan Thomas is there, and Caitlin is mentioned. I was interested in their relationship. I was interested in John Thompson's relationships – his marriage breaking up and then falling in love with his editor, and his loss. He was really quite a pioneer in loss. He went in there with his rifle and his hunting jacket and his six-pack and went to the other end of loss. I was interested in that. Neruda, on the other hand, kept seeing light. There's also that book of love sonnets, and there's that picture of Neruda and Mathilde that I look at almost daily because he's open to the world in a way I aspire to. And Rilke. Well, actually, Helen and I were going to translate *The Duino Elegies*, and then we started reading them and thought, *Are we on crack? Let's not do this.* I am very interested in Rilke's marriage and the way he – like Shakespeare – at the age of 38 or 39, had a meltdown. That was the age that I was, and I thought, well, Shakespeare wrote *Hamlet* when he was 38 or 39, and he couldn't write for a year, which, in Shakespearean writing time, is like dog years, a really long time. Rilke left his wife when he was 39, left his family. That whole breaking-up thing interested me. These were people who do what I do – not that I'm comparing myself to them – but I could look to them as guides, and see that they did this, and then kept writing.

AC • Would you say that John Thompson is an important influence on your work?

SG • Thompson's ghazals are stunning. Yes, absolutely. I think he is a fine, fine poet. Definitely, anything I read usually inspires me. I have to be careful. I can't read fiction when I am writing it because I am very magpie. I will steal all of the shiny bits. I find I can read poetry when I'm writing it, and I don't take those shiny bits. Intellectually, poetry's a different terrain for me. When I am writing a story, I have to keep the story corralled so that it doesn't straggle away. It is a huge sprawling beast. I don't go out as often as I do when I am writing poetry. I wear the same clothes. It's pretty pathetic – I have my novel socks. I don't want to think too much. I just want to think about the story. Whereas with poetry, there are more breaks. I can go out and talk to people, and it actually feeds me. When I talk to people when I am writing a story, it irritates me. Writing a novel is a difficult way to be in the world. When I am writing poems, reading other poets is having coffee with an excellent friend.

AC • "A Late Horizon" (55-56), the poem for John Thompson, has a line-repetition pattern.

SG • It's a pantoum. Lines 2 and 4 repeat as lines 1 and 3. The repeating line is an extension of repeating the theme in different sections of the poem. You take the same line and put it in a different climate, and it will change. I'm drawn to form, even to things like couplets, not just for themselves, but also for their anti-selves, working against the form. When you try to fulfil a form, you are led into a direction that you might not necessarily go in if you were writing free verse.

AC • Throughout *Undone* you make use of the exclamatory "O."

SG • Yes, and there's the line, "how we've always ached, // for more O's" (58).

AC • Is intensity of emotion a distinguishing characteristic of poetry for you, both as a reader and practitioner?

SG • Generally, I'm a pretty passionate person, so I try and herd O's into my day. I used to think I should change: I should simmer down. I tried doing that, and I thought, well, you just have to figure out who you are and learn how to be the best way you can. It's probably like embracing an Ophelia ending. But O's can be good. I mean that they aren't always *Ohhh*. They can be rejoicing as well.

AC • In "Here Lies the Water and Here Stands the Man" (59-60), actress Ellen Terry turns into the words, the role, she is memorizing. Does a poet similarly turn into her poetry?

SG • There is that. I think ultimately you have to lie down for your poem. It has to trample over you onto the page. Then you have to remember to get back up.

AC • And do you?

SG • I do. I have kids. I know how to balance it. I know that when I go to Banff, and am a poet for five weeks without being anything else, I have a very difficult time re-entering my real life.

AC • Who are you in Sobey's grocery?

SG • In Sobey's, I am a poet, but also a poet who has to defrost chicken. Whereas in Banff, there is a kind of suspension from that reality, and for someone like me, that is quite dangerous.

AC • *Undone* contains the poem "On Hearing Elizabeth Bishop Read Her 'Crusoe in England'" (87-88); her voice is "gossip," "gospel," and "testimony," but the first line of the poem is "Her voice is a blouse ..." (87-88). Does poetry – poetry by others – move you through its sound or its saying?

SG • Oh, it's a combination. That particular poem was written after Helen and I had spent a night listening to a CD of poets reading. I had read a biography of Edna St. Vincent Millay, and I had fallen in love with her because of the way she read. I was expecting her sultry voice. But then Elizabeth Bishop came on and she has this lovely voice. She completely surprised me, the way she came up with this sultry voice. I've read various things about Bishop and I've read her poems. We went to see her house last year. I really do like her, but in all her pictures she has this conservative look. You think that you have an image of the poet, and then she reads and you think, *This is so intimate*. She lives in her poems.

AC • You're going for a job interview today?

SG • And I'm also going to be talking to my agent today about "Miracle," my next novel. "Miracle," by Sue Goyette. Yes, I have been fortunate.

WORKS CITED

— • —

Atwood, Margaret. *Negotiating with the Dead: A Writer on Writing*. Cambridge: Cambridge UP, 2002.

Benjamin, Walter. "The Task of the Translator." *Illuminations*. Ed. Hannah Arendt. Trans. Harry Zohn. New York: Harcourt, Brace and World, 1968. 69-82.

Collins, Billy. "Poetry, Pleasure, and the Hedonist Reader." *The Eye of the Poet: Six Views of the Art and Craft of Poetry*. Ed. David Citino. New York: Oxford UP, 2002. 1-33.

Goyette, Susan. *Lures*. Toronto: HarperCollins, 2002.

- - -. *The True Names of Birds*. London, ON: Brick Books, 1998.

- - -. *Undone*. London, ON: Brick Books, Forthcoming 2004.

Robinson, Matt. "Golden Age of Poets: Nova Scotian Women Add Their Formidable Voices to Canadian Poetry." *Chronicle Herald* 21 January 2001: C7.

Wordsworth, William. "The Tables Turned," *The Prelude with a Selection from the Shorter Poems, the Sonnets, The Recluse, and The Excursion*. Ed. Carlos Baker. New York: Holt, Rinehart and Winston, 1948: 78-79.

"NOT FROM HERE AND NOT A TOURIST EITHER":
CAPE BRETON IN SUE MACLEOD'S POETRY

Poet Laureate of Halifax, Sue MacLeod is the author of two collections of poetry – *The Language of Rain* (1995) and *That Singing You Hear at the Edges* (2003), a collection described as "art that says what it sees and feels" (Clarke C6). Macleod's poem "The God of Pockets" won the 2000 *Arc* Poem of the Year Award. In 1998, she participated in the Hawthornden International Retreat, Scotland. Born in Ontario, MacLeod has lived for 24 years in Halifax, where she works as a librarian. Three generations of her family have lived in Cape Breton.

This interview took place at the Marshlands Inn, Sackville, NB, in June 2003.

AC • Your first book, *The Language of Rain*, was published in 1995; your second, *That Singing You Hear at the Edges*, in 2003. Did you stop writing for a while or were you renovating your poetry?

SM • I didn't stop writing, but I'm not especially prolific. And I didn't always have time to write. As Alastair MacLeod once said, "I do other things as well." I'm a single parent, and I also work at the Halifax Library, and before that I used to do freelance journalism and other freelance writing of various sorts. During the freelance period, I also finished my BA, which I needed for my library job. The eight-year period between books reflects the pace of my life. The other thing is that two manuscripts – "Mercy Bay" and "Five Readings of All This Snow" – ended up getting collapsed into *That Singing*. A lot of writing done during that period did not end up in the book.

AC • What was the relationship between your journalism and your poetry?

SM • They didn't have a very good relationship. I started doing journalism when I was 18. I supported myself on that till my mid-30s, including, especially as time went on, some corporate and public relations writing, and educational stuff. But periodical-type journalism isn't me. The journalism did teach me to have a thicker skin. I'm less disappointed than some of my friends when things don't get accepted. It's made me tougher.

AC • The first poem in *The Language of Rain* says, "we're what he knows / he dreams us with him. Snout to snout, / our noses wet, paws pounding. / Dreaming us / our fur back on" (12). Does this entry into the book signal some aspect of the human that you are going to explore?

SM • It represents a sense of how we are in process in evolutionary terms – both psychologically and physically – as is the dog. Our perceptions and how we live are in the moment and are not the result of some fixed thing that we are. We are changed by the very fact of how we perceive reality. We are shaped by the larger world around us, just as the dog is by looking at the field from a car going "90 k. per hour": "and the ears will be shaped in such and such a manner / to protect them when the head sticks out the backseat window" (11). That is passed on to future generations of dogs, and that would be true of us as well. For example, in our push-button world, I wonder if we have lost certain rhythms that used to be common to us.

AC • Later in *Language,* the poem "Oxymoron Lumbers Forth" (56-57), probably an allegory, tells the story of a bullied kid "knees trim enough for a pantyhose ad / thick hairy ankles," who grows into a man with "ungainly hooves" and "antlers" (56, 57). Tell me about the devolution of the human hinted at in this poem.

SM • "Oxymoron" is a bleaker poem than the first. The human has almost become unworkable. "Oxymoron" is a character who represents environmentally where we are. There's goodness in that creature, but he has become so awkward that his goodness can't be expressed. Is there somewhere that we can evolve to yet that would take us out of that oxymoronic state? I've always been kind of disappointed at the reaction to those poems. People have reacted to the dog poem as a lighter poem, and no one has ever gone near the "Oxymoron" poem. I think there is a lot in my work that connects to the overall human picture: How are we here? How did we ever get to this? How did we happen to develop from the cave to this point? It's an underlying concern. The domestic is an entryway to that.

ANNE COMPTON

AC • Tell me about the impact of Bronwen Wallace on your work. She seems to be a presence in both books. In *Language* you say, "She cracked me open so I can tell you who I really am" (76).

SM • She was one of the first people that I read when I started reading contemporary poetry. There's something in the quality of her voice that drew me. "She cracked me open" refers particularly to the book that came out after she died, *Keep That Candle Burning Bright*, which had to do with Emmylou Harris's music. There's often a class difference between country music and poetry. Bronwen Wallace brought those things together. She freed me up. Both her short stories and her poetry opened up a sense of possibility. When I started writing poetry, I was doing Women's Studies classes where I saw that the domestic was valid territory. She was part of that. It's OK to express what you really want to express. At the time of *The Language of Rain*, there might have been certain things that I had to be liberated from, which I don't feel as concerned about now. My work now sometimes seems more gendered to me than I feel. I used to be more overtly political. I wrote left-wing articles and worked in a co-op bookstore. I'm still political, but it's more incorporated, fully incorporated, into my life now.

AC • What language does rain speak?

SM • The language of how small we are. Rain is a larger language. It's insistent, unstoppable.

AC • Form is freewheeling in the first book: Lines careen across pages; lower case predominates; punctuation frequently disappears; typescript is various, including handwritten paragraphs. In some poems, white space predominates over print (72-73); the logic of syntax is sometimes abandoned (82-83). You put much of this behind you in your second book, didn't you?

SM • Certainly there's less moving around on the page than there used to be. I think I would disagree with the comment about syntax. Or I would like to disagree with it. It sounds restricting.

AC • In *Language of Rain*, syntactical and typographical conventions are questioned.

SM • In *That Singing*, the ideology no longer needs to be demonstrated as much. I would hope, though, that a freedom from the rules of syntax would still be there.

AC • You seem to think working within the rules of grammar is a bad thing.

SM • That's my gut reaction, I guess. If it's the only thing – if I felt bound by it – that would be a bad thing, a shutting down. The beginner mentality is a very open one, and I don't want to think I've closed down.

AC • One reviewer of *That Singing* remarked that "the poems carry such a weight of feeling with such grace and so little evident strain" (Moore D3). Do ease and the absence of strain characterize the writing experience for you?

SM • Only at the finer moments. I will get a chunk of it that way, but I can't imagine when anything – perhaps with a couple of exceptions – came fully that way. Or if it did, it would be after years of having been tucked away and someday finding a way to be able to say it.

AC • According to "The God of Pockets" (11) – the prefatory poem of your second collection, *That Singing* – pockets hold secrets, identity, love ("the knife that carved / the crooked / heart into the tree trunk"), family connections ("the picture / in the wallet, and the smile / in the picture"), violence (the "unbearable weight of the gun"), innocence, luck, and so forth. This inventory of contents is the book's second table of contents, isn't it, a thematic contents?

SM • Those are things one doesn't want to lose. Most of those things you listed are in their rawer form in childhood, and I have a preoccupation with what we don't want to lose as we grow in our lives. The second to last poem in the book, "At the tide pools" (86-87), comes back to that, to the awareness of what must not be lost. There are very few things in life that I'm sure of – a lot of things that I wonder about – but the "pocket" is what you've picked and *chosen* to keep. It connects to where you have come from, but it also refers to what you have chosen as you go along.

AC • The title of one poem "S.M.E.S" (15-16) is made up of your initials, letters your father painted on your belongings against loss or theft. The speaker finds that identity, reiterated in the father's paint, both assurance and oppression. Identity is much explored in this volume. Is it, as this poem suggests, contradictorily burden and comfort?

SM • Oh, yes, as is the tie to place, which is explored in the second section of *That Singing*. The certainty about place, which is in the mother's generation but not in the daughter's, also brings restrictions with it. I am interested in the ways in which place can be both burden and comfort.

AC • There's an interest in this book in the architectural features of your childhood residences: "the thick glass bricks that framed / the doorway. A delicious coolness" and "the serious / grey mail slots" (15). Is it fair to say that you are interested in the architecture of the past where that word is understood in both its literal and metaphorical senses?

SM • I love it when things are literal and metaphoric at the same time – or at least when there's a kind of hinge between the two. As for architecture, I'm obsessed with old buildings, with the details of houses, with rooms – of the past and the present.

AC • So much contemporary lyric poetry is angst- and grief-ridden. *That Singing* is largely characterized by contentment and sufficiency. What are the grounds of that contentment?

SM • It's hard to write of contentment. A sense of smugness can set in, whereas it is easier relatively to write sad poems or songs. I think that if you write out of the parts of your life and your interests, you are going to connect to others. And I'm pleased that includes the parts of life that are satisfying because that's trickier to do. It's easier to expect people to relate to pain. To me, the contentment indicates that I'm expressing a fullness of experience. I think that there is a sense of longing as well in the book, which is not necessarily contradictory.

AC • Tell me why you chose Chagall's *Three Candles* for the cover of *That Singing You Hear at the Edges*?

SM • *Edges* made me think of things that are on different scales, different things happening at once. Chagall's work is full of that. Chagall expresses joy but not in a naive, folk-art sense.

AC • The locus of poems such as "This is the body, consoling itself" (17-18) and "A woman is making" (58) is the body itself. In the former, the body is observed quite clinically. The phrase used throughout is "the body," rather than "my body"; the details, however, are intimate. Is this combination of intimacy and detached observation something that you strive for?

SM • Without the distance, you can't really get the intimacy. You'd get something claustrophobic instead.

AC • Depersonalizing the body by not using the personal pronoun adjective *my* leads ultimately to what is tended in hospitals, what is claimed in morgues – "the body" (68). Is there a desire in *That Singing* to be ruthless and unromantic about the body?

SM • Yes, in some poems there is, but "This is the body, consoling itself" (17-18) is about the state of being *in* a body. It's about the quirky strangeness of having a body. That choice of pronoun universalizes. Your approach to the subject determines naturally whether it will be a personal pronoun.

AC • In "To a friend with her daughter, washing dishes" (19-20), the speaker, watching her friend, contemplates their aging: "Remember how *big* / we were once? We were / giants of women" (19). Why is that sense of size and power cast in the past tense? Are you suggesting this bigness is a function of mothering, something lost when the children are grown?

SM • It's a sense that you have when you are in a certain stage of your adulthood, and probably having young children makes it particularly visible: You are the capable one. It's a scary thought that you lose it in aging, just as you didn't have it in childhood.

AC • The speaker re-imagines the kitchen as classroom: The children are "writing on the blackboard / with their backs to us ... and the chalk they're using / used to be our bones" (20). This turns domesticity – the kitchen – into a danger zone, doesn't it?

SM • It recognizes a certain reality. The sense of capability is passing to the daughter. Children emphasize our mortality. The use of "bones" also refers, though, to how much of us is taken on psychologically by the children. They move on, taking so much of what we have formed and influenced.

AC • "Love me anyway" is the "reedy song // through time" (25). According to "Repetitions, on a Daisy" (24-25), it was the song of Godiva, Rapunzel, the fisherman's wife who squandered three wishes. It's the song of the child, the adolescent, the speaker, the perfect (Godiva, Rapunzel), and the imperfect (the fisherman's wife). Is this a universal song or the song of women only?

SM • I would think it's universal although in my writing it seems to come out in a gender-specific way. Why is the child in that poem a girl? I don't think of "writing from the body" – that's not a phrase that I emotionally feel – nonetheless, things seem to come out in my writing through a woman's experience. That's the natural way for me to write. There's something there that troubles me. I don't know if it's an overly gender-specific way of perceiving the world or if it's language – a problem with pronouns. The title "Especially for a woman, reading" (88-89) also troubles me: Men read, boys read. But "a person, reading" really wouldn't work. A "person" sounds like a bureaucratic entity.

AC • Shifting between prose and poetry, "Brick Lane" (26-30) experiments with form. Visually, the poem varies from dense blocks of print to single-word lines. And in the poem "When mother & daughter discuss the facts of life" (35-36), short poem lines occur within the blocks of prose. Some poets write prose poems, but you insert poetry in the prose passages, intermixing them. Do you find the distinctions between poetry and prose limiting?

SM • I like pieces that bring those genres together and resist the distinctions. Poetry is rhythm-driven and prose is more linear. In "Brick Lane," the poetry is going on within the narrator's mind, but when you move out into the world, the prose comes in. In the second example, "When mother & daughter discuss the facts of life," the daughter's questions – the prose block – are more literal, whereas the mother's answers are in an internal poetic voice. The prose and poetry just seemed to work together in those two poems. There was nothing ideological in those choices.

AC • The evolution of both these poems depends on dialogue. Does this mean that character is a principal interest for you?

SM • I am extremely interested in things I overhear – the sounds of people's voices and their expressions. But I don't take them to make up a whole character. Hearing is very prominent in my poetry, but visual images play a strong role too.

AC • "Swoop like the gulls" (33-34) begins, "It doesn't matter which roof / you light on. All points / lead back to your home / once removed, / your mother's, not quite yours ..." (33). The poem, however, concludes that this is a "place / you'll never reach" (34). So where is home?

SM • Home is a place that isn't ever reached. Changes have occurred in the way that people live. We think, rightly or wrongly, that there might be something that is more authentic, but we've never quite been there. It might be an illusion.

AC • The question is a simple one. What's home for Sue MacLeod? Where do you come from?

SM • I have a little problem with that. I grew up as an army kid, and army kids don't come from anywhere. My mother came from Ingonish, Cape Breton. It was a very different Ingonish from the one I experienced so it became kind of mythological for me. I've lived my entire adult life in a city that just happened to me, and I don't feel overly connected to. I've never really found a place that feels for me like home. Ingonish is certainly a place I want to go back to, but not to spend the whole rest of my life.

AC • The personae in several of these poems appear to co-opt the origins and home of the mother – "your mother, a girl / when the supply boat came in spring / time" (34). One might get the impression the mother's childhood is more central to this collection than the author's own. Would that be accurate?

SM • In a way, yes, but it's a second-hand sense of the mother's childhood as seen through the author's own childhood vision of it.

AC • In the dialogue poem "When mother & daughter discuss the facts of life" (35-36), the child-speaker is incredulous about the facts of her mother's life and curious about its hardships – the deaths of her mother's sibling and the prison-like winters. To the child's key question, "*why* are the bottom / curtains pinned / shut?" the mother replies, "*there are times to turn away, we knew / when not to let things in*" (36). Is this collection of poetry an unpinning of the curtains, letting things both out and in?

SM • There's meant to be a sense of wisdom to the mother's not letting things in. The collection is a way of letting things in and out, but still there's an acknowledgment that the child's question lacks subtlety. Not everything can be laid open. There have to be shadings.

AC • How crucial to your poetry is your mother's history, which has the feeling of another century, a pioneer landscape?

SM • It's very crucial to my way of imagining. There's a way of speaking, a Cape Breton voice, and a sense of connection to landscape that I don't have in the same way.

AC • How many generations since your family came from Scotland?

SM • My mother's great-grandmother lived in Scotland. That's five generations back. My mother's grandmother was born in Cape Breton. But the way Cape Breton was for a long time, it might as well have been Scotland. When you go around Cape Breton, there are people who sound as if they were born in Scotland.

AC • The second section of *That Singing*, "the gathering up of each wave before its breaking," is focussed exclusively upon the mother-daughter relationship and on the familial past. In poems so rooted in your own past and the family past – such as "Picture ..." (38-39) – why do you use the second-person?

SM • That talking to the self as if you were talking to someone else seems to work in that poem, but it's a good one to be careful with because using "you" instead of "I" can seem a little sneaky. I had a feeling of discomfort about that poem because of the directly autobiographical nature of the material. I certainly would not have put it in the first person. I needed to feel that it was not a whiney, self-absorbed poem. Sometimes, though, the "you" can be phoney-feeling because it's being used as a cover-up.

AC • "[T]he tingle / that fills every pore when you've been / in the sea" (40) – a moment of intense physiological awareness, the after-swim moment – is classic Atlantic Coast, but not one that you often find in Atlantic poetry. Coast poems are more often, in the manner of Alfred Bailey or Milton Acorn, about storms, shipwrecks, and hard work.

SM • And that may have been what my mother would have written about, but my experience was more leisurely, a summertime experience. I didn't grow up there. I'm not a tourist, but neither am I from here.

AC • That's an interesting relationship to place: Not from here, and not a tourist either.

SM • A lot of people must feel that. It's not specific to me. People whose families emigrate from another country – a country they haven't even been to – must feel that too, because of the culture that the families bring with them. They're pulled to that culture, but there's a gap between them and their parents because they haven't known that culture directly.

AC • Most of the poems in the second section of *That Singing* take place at the edge, and although it is often a place of pleasure, it is also perilous – from "the slow- / motion // somersault // that waits beyond the guard rail" (34) to the story of "cousin Julia," the "living miracle," who fell from cliff-top to rocks below and survived (44-45). Does your attraction to edge have something to do with the co-presence of pleasure and peril?

SM • Edge is also the place from which we see things with both intimacy and distance. Pleasure and peril come into every poem that has ever been written because to write a poem you have to be keenly alive to the moment you're in. That's the pleasure. The peril is that the moment is so fleeting.

AC • What is the relationship between the "the edge / of the sea" (54) and "the edge / of your mind" (55)?

SM • The shore is the conscious mind, as opposed to the more stirred up unconscious, the sea. "[T]he edge of the mind" is the place where the two meet.

AC • The woman in "How the world might sound" is "Aunt Grace," who is "raising both arms in a gesture / like worship" as she shakes the sand from a towel after a swim (40). Is this goddess-like figure the opposite of the mother figure, who is usually spoken of in relation to her chores?

SM • It's kind of nice for me, somehow, to remember that they do end up going to the dance together in the next section, in the poem "When Night meets Thread & Needle & lies down among the Bedclothes" (61-62). What a mother becomes, or became, in those days was more chore-oriented, more a "workhorse" in a way, than the childless woman.

AC • The mother figure in this book does a lot of housecleaning – "your mother's scrub-brush moving / through the house" (33); "Something white / in her hand – it must be / the dust cloth" (49); "you could eat off her floors" (52); "dust-mop shuffle" (58). Are these two women conflicting models for you?

SM • My experience includes being a mother. To some degree one has to be the cleaning one. But one wouldn't want to be that with one's life. I love cleanliness and order, but that's different: That's an aesthetic enjoyment. That's not what the mother figure is meant to be doing. So yes, there are definitely conflicting roles there. Also, the mother figure

ANNE COMPTON

is a woman of a certain time. I think those roles are not as conflicted now, in a way, as they were then.

AC • Did poetry descend to you from the goddess "Grace" or from the housewife?

SM • More from Grace.

AC • In *Language*, you introduce yet another aunt, a glamorous woman, "my mother's sister / a place my dreams would lead me to ..." (17). The antithetical pair, plain and glamorous, recurs in your short story, "First Comes Love." Why does this pair, exploited in poem and prose, exercise such a hold on your imagination?

SM • It just seems a very primal, shaping kind of material – these two kinds of women. And these two parts of a woman. These two women were there when I was growing up and they've come to *embody* a lot. Probably a good choice of words. There are images you carry, obsessions you carry, and you write about them and through them. And yet I want to be aware of at which point I am doing that as a useful strategy and where I might be doing that without being consciously aware of it. You've got the seashore thing – coast and edge – and you've got those two figures: There's a lot of power in them.

AC • A generation back, Maritime families were, like your mother's, frequently a dozen strong and preoccupied with the basics of survival. Is one of the obligations of your generation to tell the stories that didn't get told?

SM • Yes, I think so. But I think it always remains important to come at it, in some way, with the awareness that it's a story that is only partly known.

AC • In the poem "They buried the 40s in my grandmother's well" (41-43), are you trying to retrieve through the inventory of objects and Gaelic phrases what has been buried in the well?

SM • Yes, it's a whole way of life, including things like the rhythm of the water pump and the *clop-clop* of horses. The subtleties of rhythms and sounds, and how those have changed, all go along with my obsession with voice and rhythm.

AC • In *That Singing*, there is a feeling of time foreshortened because you seem to be so in tune with that earlier sensibility.

SM • I'm sort of caught between times, like I wasn't from here and I wasn't a tourist, and maybe I feel like that in life. My life is contemporary, but perhaps it isn't totally contemporary in that I spend a lot of time on foot, instead of in cars. And I do spend a lot of time in the quiet, instead of in noise, so maybe I am, in some way, in tune with a slightly different sensibility.

AC • There's a lot of family lore – child deaths, the miracle survivals, the codes for summoning good fortune (46-48), warnings (51) – in this book. Is the family past a storeroom of spells?

SM • That would be a fun way of looking at it. I think, however, that material is more my own way of thinking rather than anything in my particular family past. I'm sure Presbyterians weren't overly into spells.

AC • "To summon the angel of rescue" (46-48) contains two crossings: A geographical one and a cultural one. A grandmother crosses from the Catholic side to the Presbyterian and in so doing, crosses a mountain. So is yours a dual heritage? If the spells do not seem at all Presbyterian, is there another side of your heritage that you might be drawing from?

SM • There's obviously an element of something very magical to the mass ritual. I think that's more in the aunt – her gesture of worship. And it's partly, I think, because the child, with all her questions, really likes to make stories. Knowing when not to let things in fits more with the Presbyterian side.

AC • A lot of travel, literal and metaphorical, occurs in this book – "driving home, I pass through other / years" (16); there's bus travel in "Brick Lane" (26-30); "She gave me" describes a train trip (52-53); and a car trip structures "Dissolution" (82). How can this poetry be so rooted in place, yet so obsessed with movement?

SM • They are two sides of the same thing. One thing that I am really interested in is how you can have freedom of movement without losing place, or how much can you? How and where those things interact, and where they don't, interests me. We can go anywhere, but as we do that, almost anywhere begins to look like the same place anyway. It's that thing of what's lost and what's gained. It seems such a delicate thing, and we don't know until it's happened.

AC • In the prose poem "No one like us," a woman newly settled on a city street is thinking "not without nostalgia of the ache in country music,

ANNE COMPTON

of neighbours on a front porch on a summer night" (67). A reviewer of your first book remarked the "comforting twang of a hurtin' country song" (Vaughan 133). Country music is an influence?

SM • Yes. I say that with hesitation because country music is famous for not having much complexity or subtlety, and I certainly don't think that is true of my poetry. There's something that I really emotionally connect with in the older country music, though not so much with the current stuff. Merle Haggard, for example. A politically atrocious example, but his voice seems to carry a sense of place. It's tone of voice, and I was thinking recently that there is an Appalachian overtone of some kind in quite of bit of country music. There's Scottish background there too.

AC • In "She gave me" (52-53), the mother is characterized by speech patterns: "*Oh go away Jim ... the women will do it ourselves*" (53). Is speech pattern part of your Cape Breton heritage? Do you hear those patterns when you are composing a poem?

SM • Not directly, no. I compose orally, and there's something – a rhythm, not a particular voice – I hear. I will sometimes hear someone from Cape Breton or Newfoundland, and I will feel something that's so familiar.

AC • What is distinguishable about Cape Breton speaking?

SM • There's a bit of a lilt. Not as much as in Scotland, but a rising up at the ends of sentences and words. There's a subtle twang in places.

AC • The mother "proud of things Scottish & Cape Breton," nonetheless, denies her origins: "once when a Yonge-Street receptionist said, *you sound Maritime*, she lied" (52). Are pride and apology co-present in the Maritime character?

SM • Well, I don't know if I can speak for the Maritimes, but in that case, yes. It's like the "come from away" expression. You know, there's a defensiveness, isn't there? And a pride. The apology in that line you quoted – not even wanting to acknowledge her identity – is almost a class thing, like being considered a bit lower.

AC • Do you see that doubleness of pride and apology in Maritime poetry?

SM • When I think of contemporary people who I know, I don't really. I mean I think I can see it in Milton Acorn. You might see it in some

Newfoundland poets, but I think only when the poetry's coming out of something about the Atlantic part of their identity. You take your sense of identity from your place and feel that you're being judged by it or you're being protective of it. But because of the nature of writing and publishing at this point, you don't see yourself as rooted even though you may be. You are seeing yourself as a Canadian poet. *Maritime* seems like a political boundary or something. It just doesn't feel like place. It feels like a border had to be drawn between this and that.

AC   • The phrasing "I am her mother's daughter's daughter," in the poem titled "Self-portrait, as sea-shell" (57), puts the emphasis on successive daughters. Are women first and foremost daughters?

SM   • At first. That's the first shaping. That wouldn't always be the sense of identity, but that is the first.

AC   • "[L]earn to be modest" is one bit of advice given and received in "Self-portrait" (57). How does modesty sit with the revelations that occur in so personal a poetry?

SM   • It causes some tension, and I think that is one place where the daughter is insisting on opening the curtains.

AC   • Do those directives about "modest[y]" (57) and "*shame*" (62) still have force in the Maritimes today, and do you feel them as restraints when you write?

SM   • People aren't that removed from a time when those words were often spoken. They still exist, and I wish rather than have them disappear, they would be replaced by something better. Instead, they are either there or they are gone. I think that when I write, I feel more free. I don't feel constrained. When I send it out, or think of having somebody read it, I'm pretty much able to remove myself. There's probably all kinds of self-editing, though, that I'm not aware of.

AC   • The speaker appears to have been defined by "scold[ing]" and reprimand (57). For all the talk about patriarchy and its repressiveness, doesn't "Self-portrait" introduce the idea that the matriarch is the stronger force?

SM   • Teaching a child how to be is a mother's role. Regardless of society's standards or expectations, there is a large weight for the mother to be the one to pass that on. I mean, it's not foot-binding, but it's the same kind of thing – the mother does the work of binding the foot. That's

ANNE COMPTON

AC • Is "A woman is making" (58) the companion poem to "Self-portrait" (57) since in the former the woman is truly a self-maker, whereas in "Self-portrait" the mother seems to be the arbiter of the speaker's identity, creating a daughter rather than a woman?

SM • "A woman is making" picks up from "Self-portrait." I think that's true. Is the mother's intent to make a daughter rather than a woman? I don't know. But the character moves from being primarily a daughter to being a woman in the movement from one poem to the other.

AC • I want to talk about large and "small" in relation to women. "A woman can make herself / small," we're told in this poem (58), and in "To a friend with her daughter, washing dishes" (19-20), the speaker asks, "Remember how *big* / we were once?" (19) Is "making ... small" good for women?

SM • No, not generally speaking, but it can almost be a protective place at times. Not a good place to be stuck in.

AC • "A woman is making" (58) gathers up key motifs from other poems – the relationship between body and landscape; containers (boxes, pockets); the apartments of childhood (58); a clean-obsessed mother. How do these things add up?

SM • *That Singing* opens with "The God of Pockets," which is childhood. It closes with a poem that has a girl still alive in the woman who is reading. How do you take, and maintain, things from childhood yet create a life? It comes together in the poem "A woman is making," which is really about how you take what you are given and yet have the freedom to make things of yourself as you go along. You pick and choose what's in the pocket.

AC • Sewing is the metaphor of this poem and of "When Night meets Thread and Needle & lies down among the Bedclothes" – "scraps," "knots," "thread," "tassels," "nap," "stitch" (61-62). In the latter, "my needle makes / a path for figures" (61). Is poetry like sewing? Is it a matter of bringing things together, threading them into a story?

SM • Threading them together into something more along the idea of a quilt – different textures and patterns. I think of poetry as being more about patterns and textures than narrative.

AC • Is your frequent use of the ampersand connected to the writing-as-sewing metaphor? The ampersand is a knot.

SM • Well, it is, isn't it? That's a delightful thought. I think my liking of the ampersand connects to my liking longer titles. I like a comma in the title. It gives a sense of the visual to a title. And the ampersand can also be like the asterisk. They are like appliqués – a decorative aspect.

AC • Clotheslines are strung through this book (71, 79) and "dishcloth[s]" appear (71). Do you eschew the grand for the homely? Clotheslines and dishcloths are fairly homely, aren't they?

SM • Clotheslines to me are extremely evocative. You know, I would like to do an anthology of laundry poems. I mean, a clothesline is a very obvious place where you can take the domestic and very readily see all the different elements that can be in it.

AC • "Thirteen ways of looking at a clothesline" repeatedly poses the problem of delivering the truth of visual experience as it exists in the everyday: "How do I show you how it is / to hang this laundry out?" (71) and "How do I show you how it is / this fresh June morning?" (72) Why does such urgency attach to this showing forth?

SM • That's an expression of what we try to do with language, but also there's an awareness of the inadequacy of showing. We're surrounded by visual images, but they don't fully express experience. On one level, it's about that, but it's also about the awareness of the inadequacy of our ability to really understand or experience outside of our own skins. I don't know if that is the inadequacy of language or imagination, or a bit of both.

AC • There may be "thirteen ways of looking," but doesn't the speaker's sensibility ultimately determine her look?

SM • I don't think there's really a way around that except there's something to be said for an acknowledgment of it. I think poetry is a great vehicle for empathy. I think those little bodily or rhythmic things are one of the ways. It's interesting what can link or connect us to others. There's such an impossibility in that, and yet I think that's what we love and hunger for so much in art and literature.

AC • The desire to cross over?

SM • Yes, but we can't. It's dangerous to think we can do it too fully or too readily. It becomes tourism, I guess. I have this tourism fear built in from my early background.

AC • In "Day-nighter" (79-81) the preference for train travel, the dislike of the "air-lift of air- // plane[s]" (79) expresses more than travel preferences. Since going is inevitable, the speaker chooses a transport that takes her via "the backdoor" by "fire escapes," through "service lanes heavy / with clotheslines" (79).

SM • There's the dishcloth instead of the grand again.

AC • "Dissolution" (82-84) is one of those poems that interweaves two situations: A pair of lovers on a car trip and the speaker typing the poem. The latter, the speaker, draws attention to the writer and the process of writing, as do other poems.

SM • I remember thinking that I don't like to do that too much. I don't like to see a lot of reference to the writing process. It's not what most people do with their time, and it seems to separate the poem from others in some way.

AC • "Especially for a woman, reading" (88-89), the final poem in the book, is a homage to readers. At any rate, it inventories women of all ages, reading in all sorts of places, including "a grandmother ... who stirred with a book in one hand" (88). With the next line – "For everyone stirring / with words in their hands" – the reader is turned into a writer. How important was reading in your becoming a writer?

SM • Very important, especially my reading as a child. A lot of who I am comes from that. Not in terms of the specifics of what I read, but in terms of the connection with other human beings. Young girls talk to one another with such intensity in ways they don't talk with teachers and parents and others. When you read a poem, there is a similar kind of intense connection.

AC • "Books / thrown into the fire / because supper wasn't ready" (88): Doesn't this poem reflect upon a Maritime world which, in the past, and perhaps still in the present, maintains that reading happens at the expense of the real work?

SM • That's one aspect of that poem, for sure.

AC • "Reading like a girl": Does reading return a woman to childhood?

SM • There's something about the nature of the absorption in reading that can do that. Reading takes you back to what you felt as a child. But "Reading like a girl" also means that you can keep on reading. You don't have to stop to do 20 million other adult things.

AC • What about writing?

SM • Writing brings together the woman and the girl, whereas reading is more truly a return to girl.

AC • Is writing hard work?

SM • Oh, yes. It's about 30 rewrites hard.

WORKS CITED

— • —

Clarke, George Elliott. "Simpson, MacLeod produce compelling work." *Sunday Herald* 18 May 2003. C6.

MacLeod, Sue. *The Language of Rain.* Lockeport, NS: Roseway. 1995.

– – –. *That Singing You Hear at the Edges.* Winnipeg: Signature Editions, 2003.

– – –. "You Mark My Words." *Antigonish Review.* Forthcoming.

Moore, Robert. Rev. of *That Singing You Hear at the Edges,* by Sue MacLeod. *Winnipeg Free Press* 25 May 2003. D3.

Vaughan, R.M. "Five (not so) Easy Pieces." Rev. of *The Language of Rain,* by Sue MacLeod. *Fiddlehead* 193 (Autumn 1997): 130-34.

ETHICS AND AESTHETICS
IN PETER SANGER'S POETRY AND SCHOLARSHIP

Peter Sanger has published two full-length books of poetry – *The America Reel* (1983) and *Earth Moth* (1986); a collection of 20 poems, *The Third Hand* (1994), in conjunction with an exhibition of Maritime agricultural artifacts; *Ironworks* (1996), a suite of seven poems with accompanying photographs by Thaddeus Holowina; and two chapbooks, *After Monteverdi* (1997) and *Kerf* (2002). In *Sea Run: Notes on John Thompson's Stilt Jack* (1986) and *John Thompson: Collected Poems and Translations* (1995), Sanger has helped to ensure a continuing readership for Thompson's poetry. His other work as a literary critic includes *"Her kindled shadow ..."*: *An Introduction to the Work of Richard Outram* (2001) and *Divisions of the Heart: Elizabeth Bishop* (2001), a collection of essays, which he co-edited. In 2002, he published *Spar: Words in Place*, essays on the layers and laminations of rocks and words which, along with *Earth Moth*, won an Alcuin Society Award for Design. For seven years, Sanger was editor of *The Elizabeth Bishop Society of Nova Scotia Newsletter*, and he has been poetry editor of *The Antigonish Review* since 1985.

At the time of this interview (August 2003), Sanger was at work on a new collection of poems, *Arborealis*, and a collection of essays, *White Salt Mountain*, published, respectively, in 2004 and 2005. *Aiken Drum*, poetry, appeared in 2006.

Born in Worcestershire, England, Sanger emigrated to Canada with his family in 1953. Twenty years later, he settled in Nova Scotia. He is a Professor Emeritus of Nova Scotia Agricultural College, where he was Head of Humanities. Sanger's carefully crafted poems focus upon the objects, dwell on "the groundmass," of his immediate world, rural Nova Scotia, and in their allusive nature, the poems reflect a breadth of reading in theology, philosophy, and science.

AC • In *Earth Moth* (1991), your poems are gnomic, not just small but gnomic in the sense in which that term is used in the Hebrew tradition: Poems of calm and philosophical reflection rather than poems of a moment's sudden and impassioned feelings. Or so they seem to me. Is meditation your poetic mode?

PS • Mainly it is, although there are poems of other kinds, poems at the beginning of *Earth Moth* that are satirical, and many of the poems throughout *Earth Moth* have an ironic edge to them. Satire and parody are directed at other people a lot of the time, but also at myself.

AC • Beginning with "Solipsist" (24), there are four poems of a satirical nature, which we are going to come to, but as to the others, would you describe the ethic of your poetry as reverent observation?

PS • If I dared to, yes! In my first book, *The America Reel*, there is an essay at the end which I was asked to put in. I didn't really want to do it, but the publisher thought that the poems were not really understandable and he asked me to write an explanation which, as I say, I was very reluctant to do. In that explanation, I say that there are certain preoccupations that I have, one of them being the relationship between immanence and transcendence. If the collections have a perceptible pattern, it is a movement from objectivity to transcendence. Hopefully, at the end of each collection, the transcendence has an immanent reality, a grip upon the factual. All of the books are meant to be acts of meditation. I brought to poetry a sympathy for, a training in, patterns of directed meditation as it was practised in the 17th century. Poets like [George] Herbert, [Thomas] Traherne, [Richard] Crashaw, [Andrew] Marvell, all of whom are very important to me, meditated on the natural world because it signified – and I'm using that word carefully – something transcendent to them.

AC • You deal with that pattern in prose, as well, don't you, when you argue for the importance of analogical thinking and when you talk about the worthiness of integrating myth and the daylight world, and – to go back to the poetry – in the John Thompson poem (*Earth Moth* 29-31), where you write about "symbolic / taxonomy" (31)? *Earth Moth* itself is structured so that it moves from the concrete, early in the book, towards a dream state at the end.

PS • That's what I intended in *Earth Moth* and, actually, it's a pattern that I have used before. *The America Reel* is structured in three parts. At one point, I was going to number the parts to make the pattern obvious, but I was reluctant to do that because it suggested sharp definitions where there were slightly more subtle margins. The first group of poems in *The America Reel* is really quite objective, almost scientifically objective. The second part moves into history, and the third part involves dreams, quite literally dreams I'd had. And there are links between the sections.

AC   • Things, natural and manmade, solicit such attention in *Earth Moth*. Are you interested in the "finicky nick" (18), the minute particulars, of things as is suggested by "Snow-Wright" (18)?

PS   • Oh, yes. Ever since I was a child I've been interested in natural things. As a child, I tried to make my own natural history museum, and collected shells, pebbles, and that sort of thing. When I came to Canada in 1953, at the age of 10, I continued that collecting activity. My life is a matter of detail, and I want my poems to reflect that. I'm very much against abstractions. One of my quarrels with a good deal of modern Canadian poetry is that it glosses over actuality and the resistance of it. To me, that's the real fault of "the literary." "The literary" does not mean being involved with Shakespeare or Milton. Their work is not "literary." To me, "the literary" is subtracting literature from the fact and resistance of ordinary life.

AC   • I'm reminded of the first essay in *Spar* (2002) where you speak of the "sanity of small, exact things" (18). Those are the things in life that keep us grounded, are they?

PS   • Yes, they are, and the last essay of *Spar* is called "Groundmass," but then you have to deal with the "mass" part of it. And the "mass" is, of course, something grand. It's one of those words where there is transcendence into immanence, which is another aspect of *Spar*.

AC   • The smallest, least noticeable objects and creatures of nature come in to view in your poems – "Crane Fly" (35), "Earth Moth" (20), "The Web" (44). The "Crane Fly" is a "filament gantry" (35). If I searched for something in nature to match your poems, I might choose the web for its intricate design, its near invisibility, its catch function. Should words in poetry have the near-invisibility of a web?

PS   • When I was in my teens, I heard the music of Prokofiev, Bartok, Shostakovich, and Stravinsky for the first time, and I was overwhelmed by the clarity and freshness of their notes. In Prokofiev's piano music, for example, every note is rinsed clear. I made up my mind that any poetry that I wrote would have that quality too, that it would have that rinsed, clear, shining quality. But in poetry, you're dealing with many levels. One level is the narrative, and that level has to be clear even if the poem is not obviously a story. All poems have a story. You just have to work out what the story is. If you write a poem without a story in mind, you're probably lost, and you'll probably lose control of the poem. It won't have any shape. And the narrative has to have other levels. I'm reluctant to use the terms symbolical, analogical, allegorical, but poems do have those levels. That kind of poetry – symbolical, allegorical – has a poor reputation now. I'm entranced by it. I read Spenser and Milton for pleasure. I enjoy poets who aren't really read in English at all now. There are superb translations of Ariosto and Tasso, to whom there are references in many of my poems. The wonderful baroque modes of elaboration – synthetic, syncretic combinations – in poems by the people I mentioned intrigue and fascinate me. They are the real texture of literature. Literature is not a matter of eccentric posturing. It's in the web. And as you suggested in your question, the web is a very strange artifact. It's killing at the same time. And that too is an aspect of poetry.

AC   • Things held in or with the hands – "Skipstones" (11); "Picture Blocks" (13); "Earthenware Bowl" (15); "Basket" (16) – account for many of the titles in this collection. For all its observational exactitude, isn't touch also a pre-eminent sense in this poetry?

PS   • Poetry to me is a manual act. Letters are tangible. There's a passage in one of the *Spar* essays about my feeling the edges of wooden letters when I was a child. When I write, I sense the shape of the poems in my hands. I don't know whether anybody else does, but that's important to me because the poem becomes something existent in time and space. I use the words "manual act" because, again, that has a religious connotation. In Christianity, the chief manual act is the re-enactment of the mass. Other religions have different manual acts. For example, in Islam, I suppose you could say that the Koran is itself a manual act, and in Islam, the Koran is something very much more than a bound sequence of pages with printing on them. It's something that we, in other cultures, find very difficult to understand – the sacredness of this act made by hands. In a culture shaped by Christianity, we still – even though we may not be Christians – have some reverence for the Bible, but we don't reverence words in the way that I just described. I try to. I'm suggesting that objects in the world have a transcendent place of value.

AC • Given its rational grammar and syntax, *Earth Moth* employs some surprisingly obscure words: "feculent" (25), "wimbelled" (31), "tappeting" (45), "crepitance" (56), and so forth. Why's that?

PS • These words are not always obscure. They belong to other worlds. For example, for 26 years, I worked with scientists. I was teaching in an agricultural college. They frequently used words that are probably not part of the ordinary level of conversation, but any trade does. Spend time with plumbers or electricians and you're going to hear words that you may be unfamiliar with. Why limit our vocabularies to what our immediate lives have brought us? Why limit our vocabularies to what contemporary writers offer us? Why not freshen the language? Just think of the flood of language that Joyce and Pound brought into the 20th century – writers who were very important to me when I was in my 20s. It seems to me people who object to a wide vocabulary are insisting upon constraining writers to a limited vocabulary which is really the specialized dialect of contemporary fashion. The other thing to say is that words like those are exact. They're appropriate. I never try and use words simply to show off the fact that I know them. I use words because I know that they fit. There's a word in "Mare's Skull," for example, in the line "earth / unexanimate" (*Earth Moth* 62), which comes out of my readings of 17th-century theology. And if you look at that word carefully and take it apart, you see what it's saying, see what that criss-cross of negatives is doing there, and hear it as something exultant. A reader who is not familiar with it will stumble over it first of all, but if that reader backs off, takes a run at it, the reader may find earth exultant in the sound, which was the effect that I was trying for. In fact, many of the supposedly more recondite words have that function. They are flourishes of energy; and they also, by the way, fit the system of scansion because in my work I'm always working very consciously with the stresses. I'm working for the speaking voice.

AC • Such words often appear as adjectives, as in "[t]entacular / cities, mighty at heart …" in "Wind Storm" (38); "androgynous calm" (13); "anthracitic glitter" (28); "chitinous / dust" (59): Simple nouns accompanied by complex modifiers. "Tentacular / cities" immediately suggests to me tentacles and thus something dangerous. Do those adjectives bear the metaphorical import of what you are saying?

PS • Very much. And they are often referring what you call the simple nouns to another context. For example, "tentacular cities" does what you say, but there's also a concealed literary reference there to Émile Verhaeren who talked about tentacular cities at the beginning of the 20th century. When I used it there, I was thinking, as you say, of the threat of the modern industrial city – the environmental threat but also the mental one. "[C]hitinous" is meant to refer to a body of scientific knowledge. "Androgynous" refers to baroque art and the androgynes who turn up as cherubs in Renaissance painting, but also there's a reference to Greek art and a reference, in a sense, to the *Mona Lisa*, its asexual atmosphere which, to me, is extremely unsettling. It hints at worlds beyond the immediate world, at something that exists beyond our experience.

AC • In *America Reel*, the poem "Heron" has the lovely sounding line "it shoulders a / collop // of sky" (9), where the sound of the word "collop" is connotatively rich, suggesting, to me at least, a priestly cope or chasuble, no matter which meaning of "collop" you had in mind. When a reader is trying to sort out the meaning of a word, she brings a raft of connotations to it, and often that is the result of a word's sound. I went from "collop" to various churchy garments by virtue of collop's sound.

PS • You bring a whole wealth of associations, but the rest of the poem should help decide. When I used "collop" in that poem, I had a very strong sense of the heron's shoulders, especially as it is flying. And, yes, I was thinking of cope and chasuble. But I was also using the word in the sense of a piece of flesh, and, of course, that poem ends with an evocation of the heron as a predator as well as being this antiquarian and approachable "sackbut" sort of figure (9). The "collop" was meant to signal that particular intrication. Of course, the heron in itself refers to the "heron-priested shore" of Dylan Thomas and also the heron in Gaelic mythology. In Yeats, for example, the herons mythologically have a rather sinister part to play. They're partly human and partly bird. They inhabit two worlds and they ferry across these two worlds. You could say that those two worlds are the world of life and the world of death. By the word "collop," I wanted to signify that too, because you're dealing with flesh, and flesh is mortal.

AC • Are words a lot like "Skipstones": They must be "sorted" to find "one, / alive in its bias" (11)?

PS • The words that I reject are the ones without the kind of bias that I need. That could be a bias of meaning or nuance or layering. It could be a bias of sound or stress. Or it could be a bias that leads me on further into the poem. All of my poems begin with the first line. I don't sit down to write a poem with what becomes line 2, or 3, or 4. I have to get the first line right. That's picking the stone. The first stone, when it's skittered across the page, sets up the movement of sound and syntax that continues throughout the poem. By the end of the poem, the stone has pattered itself out. And sinks back into the water.

AC • There's a Chinese proverb that goes, "Recite poetry only with a poet" (Huntington et al. 45). Is poetry a closed shop?

PS • I think any poet writes for an ideal reader, but I don't want to say that I write only for other poets. The truth is most other poets that I've come across in my life don't really catch onto what I am doing. There are wonderful exceptions, but to be blunt about it, I'm 60 years old and have published quite a few books and most of my publishing life has been lived in absolute obscurity.

AC • As much as you like the surprising, seemingly out-of-the-way, multi-syllabic word – such as "its beak's obstetrical slash" in "Kestrel" (46) – you rely on solid, single-syllable sounds – "stiff," "stoop," "slash" to convey suddenness of perception, in this case of the kestrel. Would you say that such words, monosyllabic words, are the rocks within the "groundmass of [your] syntax" (*Spar* 73)?

PS • Absolutely. From the point of view of stress, those are the anchor points. There have to be strong nouns and words that connote use and activity as well.

AC • In "Crabapple Blossoms," "flaw" is of Old Norse origin, as is "snub"; "haul" is Old French, and "scud," Low German or Dutch (47). In choosing a word, are you interested in the depth of time that a word brings with it?

PS • I've always regretted that I don't have any sophisticated form of linguistics background. In fact, I'm not very good at languages, although I am fascinated by the origins of words. For example, in *The Third Hand* (1994), the book of riddles, I was very conscious of working within Old English and Norse forms. I chose words in that sequence, in particular, that were meant to recall a layer of linguistic history.

AC   • In your work, taken as a whole, one finds these interests: Geology (*Spar*); an archaeology of implements (*Ironworks*, 1996), and throughout an interest in etymology. Is depth of time the constant here?

PS   • Since childhood I've been fascinated by history. When I was a child, along with my natural history collections, I used to try to make historical collections. Because of when and where I was born, much in those collections involved the First and Second World Wars. And then later, I chose to study history. I deliberately chose not to study English because I thought that I needed the discipline of objectivity that history would force me into. In my working life, at the agricultural college, among other things I used to teach history. I have a mind that thinks naturally in historical terms.

AC   • The poem "Fisherman" reflects upon the fisherman's methodical casting, although he is "afloat / adrift" (19). Would this be an apt description of what the poet is called upon to do – cast methodically for words – even while he or she is "afloat" or "adrift" in memory or daydream?

PS   • I think all poets are adrift on the sea of whatever you want to call it, the sea of life, or to be more complicated about it, the sea of indifferentiation, where words become the definition of whatever can be retrieved or caught in the magma of the possible, the unconscious. Casting the fly is art. The line to the fly should be invisible.

AC   • Is there a cohabitation of two things at once in the poet: The sense of being "afloat" but also the need to be methodical?

PS   • Well, you have to know how to handle your boat, and you have to be in a good boat. You have to know how to row or paddle; you have to know how to set your sail and how to fish.

AC   • Training. Yet you say in *Spar* that all good poems are "wildings" (52). Everything else that you've said is contrary to that.

PS   • You have to remember what a wilding is. All apples are basically domestic. They were introduced to North America. They may revert to the wild, and then they may be grafted back into domesticity, so there's an interchange going on there. There's an element of unpredictability. The wilding may still carry a genetic element of its domesticity. It's wild, but it has an aspect of domesticity. My choice of the word

       ANNE COMPTON

"wilding" was deliberate too. It's an unusual word that belongs to the realm of the orchard. Otherwise, I would have said "wild," but I did want the connotation of the wild in there. I doubt whether our usual distinctions between the wild and the domestic would mean anything in Eden.

AC · As one nears the end of *Earth Moth*, dream preponderates (54, 55, 58-59, 61). One poem, "The Sleeper," traces descent as the sleeper "dropped, darkness from // dark, down through the pit of his body ..." (58). Does this collection move from the daylit world to the nightlit world?

PS · Yes, and that's deliberate. "Black Mirror" (61), "Mare's Skull" (62), and "The Wish" (63) are quite deliberate indicators of the book's movement from light to dark, but by the time those poems occur, darkness and light are practically synonymous, which is what those poems demonstrate. Again, we are in the area of the fisherman – adrift and afloat, but casting still. I'm really not interested in poems that don't have that kind of intrication, what some people might call ambiguity. I wouldn't say it's ambiguous. I'd say it's realistic.

AC · The fable-telling "Sampler" is about an object of art that describes or enables a "provisional Eden" (14). Is that where poetry takes us?

PS · A "provisional Eden" is about the best a poet can hope for. Some poets, of course, have gone beyond that, though they might for theological reasons deny it. It is impossible to read the end of *The Divine Comedy*, for example, and not feel that Dante has succeeded. He's beyond the "provisional" part of it. But I'm sure he himself would deny that. So I think that's a registration that the reader really has to make. I talk about Traherne's *Centuries* at the end of the first essay in *Spar*, and I speculate as to why he left his last *Century* incomplete. Had he, at that point, reached recollection of Eden? I do believe that some artists have created Eden, but most of us can only hope to create "provisional" ones.

AC · And "Sampler," the poem we are talking about?

PS · "Sampler" is ironic. Partly it's about the 19th century and a very local culture which seemed to reach a kind of perfection, and yet that perfection was very, very tenuous. Like the cod-based architecture of Lunenburg, it was made possible by an ethic of depletion. The gold in that poem is the gold of industrialism, the gold of massive deforestation and environmental degradation, which accompanied the Western civilization that created that sampler. There are a number of similar poems in *The America Reel* – "The Sisters" (26), for example. In fact, all the historical poems in the second part of *The America Reel* have that twist of irony in them. Those poems have been often read as rural idylls, or pieces of nostalgia, but I wrote them very carefully to be that and something quite different, something symptomatic, within a pathology.

AC • "Picture Blocks (about 1800)" (13), a physical form of puzzle, involves three levels of play: Games are depicted on the blocks; the children who played with them are ghostly presences; and the pattern-making speaker, also a player, concedes the "fragments mismatched, [are] / perfections / who almost existed" (13). Is poetry a form of play that takes us closer to "perfections / who almost existed"?

PS • I take play very seriously. And yes, poetry is play in the most profound sense. Play in the adult form is a kind of ritual, and ritual is a form of understanding the cosmos. We know that our games – soccer and baseball and all the rest of them – derive historically from sacred art. That was in my mind when I wrote "Picture Blocks." Of course, adult games have been secularized and that is also implied by that poem. The modern pattern is imperfected, truncated, in that sense. That poem is partly about modern poetry and the condition in which the poet finds himself or herself. The poem is also about the 19th century and the kind of fragmentation that took place then. Like "Sampler," it's about this "provisional Eden," in this case depicted on the blocks, and how the game of the ghostly players was caught in an historical situation that would destroy them. You think of the panoply of power that the Victorian British Empire presented and how it crumbled during and after the First World War. The poem is also about the present circumstances of power and their tenuous nature. There are a number of poems in *The America Reel* and in *Earth Moth* that pursue such matters.

AC • The "androgynous calm" of the children in "Picture Blocks" (13) makes me wonder if the creative act bestows a moment of androgyny on the maker? Is there a great freedom from egotism?

PS • I keep to the gender I have. I agree, though, with your second question. When a poem is going well, conscious interference with it tends to diminish it. The words, at times, can seem to be given. When that

ANNE COMPTON

happens over an extensive period of time – and it can happen during the composition of a whole sequence or collection – you look back and feel, *Really, I didn't write that.* What we're talking about is inspiration, and I'm uneasy with that word because it's one that has been abused so much. But when you write, you do often seem to be taken out of yourself. "[A]ndrogynous calm" was one attempt to describe that situation. Certain works of art do obsess my imagination. Among them are the statues of the Greek maidens, the Kores, the archaic ones. In *Kerf* (XIII), theirs is the "Eleusinian / smile." One of the starting points for *Kerf* is a marble relief from Eleusis, dating from the fifth century BC, showing Demeter, Triptolemus, and Kore. It's a smile that seems to have been rediscovered by Leonardo da Vinci, not only in the *Mona Lisa*, but also in that painting *St. Anne with Virgin and Christ Child*. The smiles on those faces are removed beyond all contradiction, and yet they somehow have encompassed the contradictions that most of us have to live with. That really was what I was trying to get at when I used that phrase "androgynous calm."

AC • Approaching the centre of *Earth Moth*, one finds four portrait poems. These are portraits of types – "Solipsist" (24), "Plagiarist" (25), "Simoner" (26), "Lapidary" (27). Are sins of language the common denominator in this rogues' gallery?

PS • Sins of language, compact with ethical misjudgments or outright opportunism. I would link the misuse of language with the ethics, or non-ethics, of opportunism. That's one reason why Dante is cited in "The Simoner" (26). I deliberately refer to one of the circles of Hell. Wittgenstein wrote in his *Tractatus*, "Ethics and aesthetics are one and the same" (147). That is one of the most profound things that can be said about poetry.

AC • The "Solipsist" "regrets you're the voice he can't play, // an obstinate *thou* refusing to shift / to demotic" (24). In the Introduction to *Divisions of the Heart*, you are at pains to assure us that Kierkegaard's protagonist, "A," or a poet's "seemingly infinite recessions of meaning" (16), is not solipsistic. Is solipsism something you fear in yourself as a poet?

PS • Modern poetry basically has an egocentric basis. Once you cut away all the levels of cosmos we've been talking about, what's left is ego. Under those circumstances, solipsism is easy to slip into, and it's something that I have to fight against in myself. As I said earlier, those poems are about other poets, but they're also about me. The irony is directed outward and inward at the same time.

AC • The "Lapidary" who "often sells lies considered / quite finished" (27) might be a definition of the poet, mightn't it?

PS • The word "finished" is used in a double way. The lies are finished, done with. They're old lies. They have no real currency. They are also highly finished, polished up, recycled. Was I thinking of Plato's suspicion of the poets? Yes, I was. Very much. Poets are like all other artists. They are equivocal figures. They are always tending to offer substitutes. Often they manage to convince themselves that their lives, their own autobiographical experiences, have a validity that is imaginative. But the experiences have to go through a sea change. The "Lapidary" is a figure who does not accomplish this. As a child he is offered the wonderful gift of a glimmering stone beneath the water; but by the time we reach the end of the poem, and by the time he has matured, that particular gift has been levelled out into quartz, which is nothing more in his mind than mere denotation.

AC • Elsewhere, you say that words are never just "nominal" (*Spar* 69).

PS • I understand that in terms of contemporary philosophical thought, I'm probably absurd, but I have to stand on my experience as a poet. What I know of words, and what I've experienced of words, is that they are not interchangeable counters. They have a facticity that is insistent. They're never neutral or interchangeable.

AC • In the eight-part "Properties of Wood (John Thompson 1938-1976)" (*Earth Moth* 29-31), Thompson's poetry-making is understood as woodworking: "words shaped / clear by commonplace things, helves, / shafts, tines ... all manner of tackle / trimmed to form by his knife ..." (29), which echoes Hopkins' "all trades, their gear and tackle and trim" (30). Do you want the reader to bring something of Hopkins to his or her appreciation of John Thompson?

PS • I wanted the reader to think in terms of Hopkins' sinewy syntax, which I think is characteristic of Thompson's best work. I wanted the reader to think of Hopkins' emphasis upon touch, upon tangibility, and his intuitions about the operation of natural forces, which, again, I think are characteristic of Thompson's best work. I also want the reader to think of Hopkins in terms of being a religious poet, which Thompson also was.

AC   • "Properties of Wood" reviews the virtues of Thompson's poetry: "he named / particular things, *cambium,* / *phloem, xylem* ..." (29) and "By touch and smell in the dark / he could name them ... elm ... oak ... [m]aples ..." (30). Is the impulse to write poetry, at bottom, a naming of the world? A true naming?

PS   • Yes, it is. Adam's task is not a nominal occupation. It is a real occupation. And that's another reason why the occupations are alluded to in that poem. Shaping the wood creates shapes just as Thompson shaped, handled, words.

AC   • Speaking of John Thompson's death in the introduction to *John Thompson: Collected Poems and Translations*, you say of his death: "He chose the undifferentiated 'limitless ocean,' from which everything rises and into which everything falls" (43). In "Properties," Thompson is, poetically speaking, a shipwright as well as woodworker: "Each tree is an ark" (30).

PS   • In "Properties," he's the poet. In the introduction, he's Thompson the poet struggling with the problem of finding a vessel for his imagination. He died very young, which is also in "Properties of Wood." I have very mixed feelings about Thompson, as many people do. I've tried to deal with that in "Properties of Wood." But I wrote that poem before I carried out the biographical work that went into the preface of the book on Thompson.

AC   • Thompson making for that sea seems to be present both in "Properties" and the introduction to the *Collected Poems* as if that was what he had always been doing in his life and work. Is that more than a reference to death?

PS   • Oh, yes. I mention in the introduction to the *Collected* that he was embarked on a night sea journey, an archetype in Jungian psychology, where the hero does make a night sea journey. *The Epic of Gilgamesh* has a similar night sea journey. Jonah makes a night sea journey in the belly of the whale, and, of course, Thompson uses that in one of the ghazals of *Stilt Jack*. Earlier we talked about the sea of undifferentiation and, yes, I do have that in mind in "Properties" and in other places. My reference is to life, or to death seen as part of life.

AC   • So these references to the sea don't just mean that he was a death-destined man. Rather, what's important is that it is a night sea.

PS • I am associating the night with unconsciousness, with the dreams that do tell the truth. Incidentally, there's another meaning to *Sea Run* besides the one we've been talking about. At one point in the ghazals, Thompson compares himself to "a salt-water trout spilling seed" (139). A searun trout is one that leaves its freshwater habitat and goes out to sea to feed and then returns to spawn in freshwater. There's a searun into darkness, but also a searun into fruition – the recreation of another life. I was very conscious of that double meaning when I chose the commentary's title.

AC • Your admiration for Thompson's work is tempered by what you know about the life. Is that right?

PS • My admiration isn't tempered. I can read *Stilt Jack*, which I think is a great book, with admiration. For example, I have my own private canon, the way most poets do. When I get obstreperous, I insist that it is the only possible canon. I admire W.W.E Ross' work, especially the *Laconics*. That is wonderful, wonderful poetry. I reverence Saint-Denys Garneau, and regard *Regards et Jeux dans l'espace* as one of the greatest works of Canadian poetry. I reverence Thompson's *Stilt Jack* on the same level. I think of these poets as being absolutely central to any understanding of the best poetry that has gone on in this country. So Thompson is there among a handful for me. My mixed feelings for Thompson derive, at the deepest level, from a sense that his metaphysics were skewed and that he didn't take as much care to think accurately about his mythology as he should. In a poet who was essentially metaphysical and mythological, these are destructive failures. Recently I tried to sort out my thoughts about Thompson at several points in a collection of essays, *White Salt Mountain*, soon to be published.

AC • Some lines in "Properties of Wood" suppose Thompson speaking: "*Those who maddened me / living now market me dead*" (31). Does justice need to be done for John Thompson?

PS • Yes. I think that's still true. I tried to do justice in the *Collected* and also in *Sea Run*. You see him anthologized, but you don't really see him being discussed. Someone once told me that Thompson will never be a well-known poet because his work is too complex. He told me that modern students simply would not be able to understand the implications of *Stilt Jack*. Thompson's doomed because his poetry won't be taught in university. If that's the case, there's not much hope for poetry in Canada.

AC • You name Thompson and Hector de Saint-Denys Garneau in the same breath in *Spar* (71). Is it because they shared an attitude and practice in regard to words such as the one expressed by Saint-Denys Garneau: "A small number of simple words must be found, rooted words, saturated with the beings of things, first words that have barely emerged from things ..." ("Saint-Denys Garneau on Poetry ..." 82)?

PS • One of the reasons that I coupled them together – and added the other poets in the list from which you've taken those two – is because they are poets of tangibility and of metaphysical and mythic range. By the way, Thompson appears throughout those essays in *Spar*. He is both a seen and unseen presence. He could be said to have turned up in "Biorachan Road" (15-25). He turns up in "Keeping: The Cameron Yard" (37-64). His presence is implied in several places throughout those essays. I never met him. There is an encyclopedia entry out there that states that I was his student. I don't know where that came from.

AC • The *Earth Moth* poems are more likely to name the stuff of the world than to deal in abstracts, but isn't naming itself called into question in the poem "Silver Poplar"? Neither the poplar leaf nor the flock of unnamed birds can be certified as to colour: "black on the back, / white as they veer away" (32). Can naming be a "negative game"?

PS • Yes. And it turns out to be a "negative game" in many of the poems. We were talking earlier about naming being a form of stasis, of fixing in time. A poem itself once it's been published becomes fixed in that way. So naming can be a very dubious proposition. That's one reason why all of my poems do have points of reference outside of themselves. Hopefully they exist as poems with their own integrity, but the poems are always referential as well. They point to a world that surrounds them and not to a world that is inherent within them. In the poem we're talking about, the natural object is intended to elude the poem. It was written after I'd made a trip out to Cape John, which juts out into Northumberland Strait. Like a Hopkins' poem, it's a place that's full of wind and waves, really utterly unencompassable. I suppose you could say that the poem is about attempting to encompass the unencompassable and not really succeeding. I was also thinking of "negative theology" – the defining of metaphysical forces by terms of non-existence.

AC • During the freshet, a "Spring River" (*The America Reel* 8) reclaims its original flow path, as it was "before we gave out / the names." Here naming seems to be a harness on nature. Is it?

PS • That poem comes at the beginning of *The America Reel*, and there's a sense in which those first poems are poems of surface. There's irony at work there. The names have yet to be given at that point in the book. The names become more enduring, more solid, as the book continues. The particular locution in that line is deliberate. You give out names the way prizes used to be given out at school graduation ceremonies. The poem is actually set at North River, which flows down into the head of Cobequid Bay, and the North River overflows its banks almost every spring. The people of the town are invariably astonished that this happens. Those are major floods, and once the floods subsides, the people go back to building along the flood plain. The poem is about how nature eludes our attempts at definitions. The river in question is called the North River, and how many rivers of that name are there in the world? The name is unimaginative. It's also a name given it by the Anglo-American settlers who came here, or possibly by the Scots, so what was the name of it when it was a Mi'kmaq river? I don't know, but I expect that the name would have been more appropriate. The poem is about a name that has failed to indicate the sheer physical existence of this river any more than the culture out of which the name came managed to accommodate itself to the force of the river.

AC • If one takes the right path, at the right pace, to knowledge, "[p]erhaps knowing and naming could even prove to be the same," you say in the "Groundmass" essay in *Spar* (67). Is taking time, then, perhaps the most important, and least frequently practiced, virtue of the poet?

PS • What I had in mind when I wrote that was the timing of a poem. The timing that occurs within every line, every stanza, within the full run of the poem. My sense of time is pedestrian: I think as I walk. My sense of touch – my feet on the ground – is what I bring to the syntax of my poems. A walker's sense of time is not like that of someone driving a car or someone flying. Neither one of those is really a poet's time. You understand complex concepts really quite slowly. You have to give your thoughts and feelings time to work themselves out.

AC • The first-person pronoun "I" rarely puts in an appearance in *Earth Moth*. By my count, the speaker draws attention to self four times only

(32, 54, 57, 60). Does the erasure of the "I" spring from a desire to get the subject out of the way so that the object will be the poem?

PS • Whenever I find myself writing "I" or the possessive pronoun, I stop and ask, "Am I simply writing this autobiographically, assertively? Am I really getting in the way of what I want the poem to be?" If that happens, I act accordingly, make revisions. I was very much influenced by Rilke when I wrote both *The America Reel* and *Earth Moth*. Still am. All of his books have meant a great deal to me, but at the time of *Earth Moth*, it was *The New Poems*, the poems he wrote quite deliberately about objects, just as he conceived [Auguste] Rodin to have made his sculptures. Those two volumes were very much on my mind at the time of *Earth Moth*, and those, I think, are part of Rilke's attempt to remain sane and to continue as a poet. And his attempt to avoid solipsism, which we talked about earlier. I'm in a dialogue with Rilke throughout much of my work. *Kerf* is partly a dialogue with Rilke. *Kerf* and *Ironworks* are imbued with Rilke's ideas. In the poem in *Kerf* that is directed to Rilke, where he's called "Serafico" (V), I'm also in a quarrel with another side of Rilke, that of the romanticizer of infinitely postponed love.

AC • You are one of the few critics who refers to the muse.

PS • I have no choice because that is my experience. That again is where I stand just as I stand on the nominal and real meanings of words, and the difference between them. As a man, my experience of the muse has to be a woman, but she can come in many other forms, and at many different levels. She exists as what many people would call a reality. And if you want to see a picture of her, there's one at the beginning of *Kerf*. The muse might exist for me as a figure in a Vermeer painting. Or she can exist as those Greek statues that I mentioned earlier, or as the da Vinci painting of *Saint Anne with Virgin and Christ Child*. Or she can exist in a Byzantine icon. In my experience, the muse does speak. I know there are various psychological explanations for it. I don't wish to say that I just sit and the words come. It's dreadfully hard to write, but there is something that speaks in my experience. Often I have been more or less told, "This really isn't the way it is," and my reaction has to be, "I don't have any choice. This is what I have experienced."

AC • Writing about the critical reception of [Richard] Outram's poetry, you wonder if the shapers of Canadian public literary opinion have "lost touch with poetry's theatrical origins" ("*Her kindled shadow ...*"

45). Do you refer to the masks, personae, guises, poses that a poet might assume, the "dramatizations of aspects" of the self (66)?

PS • I'm using "theatrical" in the classic sense as distinct from egotism – the theatre of the imagination in contrast to what used to be called, in the 1950s and 1960s, Kitchen Sink Theatre. To me, the most profound theatre is opera. Some of the most realistic works of art I know of are *Don Giovanni* and *The Magic Flute*. The theatre of Commedia dell'arte, which is really crucial to an appreciation of Outram's work, is central to the poetic tradition. The theatrical aspect of poetry is what frees us from egotism. If we think that there is a direct line between the author's life and what the author writes, we would be in trouble. And frankly, sometimes I think such authors are in trouble too. It partly comes down to an understanding of the form. I like stanzaic forms. I like poems that have a theatrical shape. I like the modulations of narration through a poem. To me, part of the delight of poetry is the enactment of a pattern.

AC • What is the geographical or topographical locus of your poetic practice?

PS • Right now the focus is here in this house, on this farm that runs down to the river. This farm is the setting of the last two essays in *Spar*. The setting of the first essay in *Spar* is where I used to live in North Colchester County. And the second essay, "The Crooked Knife" (27-36), was really written up there and relies upon the kind of physical activity that I was doing. There are poems in *The America Reel* that are not set in Nova Scotia. There is one set in Bombay, another in Marrakesh. They derive from my travels. Whenever I set poems distant from Nova Scotia, they are meant to be by way of contrast and definition. Usually, they'll be about a range of experience that has unsettled me, has knocked me off my local bearing. The first part of my life, until I was nearly 30, was very unsettled. I never lived anywhere for more than three years. When I arrived in Nova Scotia – I think it was 1970 – I decided I had to dig in, in the physical sense, the topographical sense, as you suggest, but also imaginatively because I had no grip on very much of anything except abstractions. For the kind of poetry that I write, for the kind of poet that I wish to be, that is what I had to do. You have to understand the weather, the animals, the trees, the way things grow, the procession of the seasons. You have to listen to sounds. To me, that's very important. The sounds of the leaves, the sounds of the birds. They all have to enter into the work in one way or another. You can only do that over time.

AC • In each poem, I've noticed, a certain sound seems to give the melodic line. In "Hatch," for example, "L" seems to be the base sound with variation: "Flight of the swallow sleighting / middle air, festival / tilts ..." (45). To what extent does sound take you where you are going in a poem?

PS • I try for a narrative of sound in every poem. In "Hatch" that narrative is the swallow's flight. In each poem, the narrative of sound is also that of the poem's sequence of cognition.

AC • A poem is made, you say, "in a world of many other poems" (*Spar* 71). In *Earth Moth*, I am aware of Wordsworth – "cities, mighty at heart, lie still" (*Earth Moth* 38) – and Shakespeare and Hopkins. Do you belong to a poetic continuity? Are there antecedents and contemporaries with whom you feel a kinship?

PS • A poem which expresses or implies no loyalty to antecedents is not likely to interest anyone beyond the poet's contemporaries. Starting in the 1970s, I tried to express in prose my sense of various kinships wherever I thought I knew enough to say something worth listening to: So there are essays or pamphlets on [Geoffrey] Hill, David Jones, [Paul-Emile] Borduas, Thompson, Saint-Denys Garneau, [Robert] Bringhurst, Outram, [Elizabeth] Bishop, and others. In many cases, these essays or pamphlets or books are parallel commentary upon poems I've published.

AC • "How / much is enough? All there was: / blossom unfalling, its / whiteness falling, / wherever you break to touch" (47). Is sufficiency, abundance, plentitude of nature and of the world, something that this volume celebrates?

PS • *Earth Moth* is a celebration of what you say, as long as you interpret "world" as including a plenitude which might also be called pleroma. *Earth Moth*, as its epigraph from Virginia Woolf indicates, is also about the strength, courage, and beauty of whatever appears most fragile – including *poetry*.

AC • "Wasp's Nest (Winter)" is the occasion for a meditation on death – the wasp's nest, in its shape and structure, replicates the human skull "emptied" (49). Is death "plundered / sweetness"?

PS • Many of the poems, including "Wasp's Nest (Winter)" – whose pro-
tagonist, by the way, might be Hamlet – are concerned with sacrifice:
What gets sacrificed, why, and by whom. We execute many things,
including poems.

AC • The "White Fawn" is "all things / by its form signified, // man, lion,
ox ..." (53), a biblical language. Was, and is, the Bible a formative influ-
ence on your language?

PS • The King James Bible and the Anglican *Book of Common Prayer*, both
of which I grew up with – including a stint as a church chorister in
Chatham, Ontario, where I sang with Sylvia Tyson and was taught by
the organist, her mother, Mrs. Fricker – influenced my language,
including its syntactical structures, to a degree that sometimes catches
me off-guard. As I grow older, I can trace more and more of what I
thought was mine to other, very much earlier voices. "The White Fawn"
also consciously owes a great deal to Malory and Marvell. But it is not,
it should be said, entirely a poem of borrowings. The events narrated
did happen, including the shooting.

AC • The "White Fawn" stepping out of the darkness "was what never /
would happen believed ..." (53), and is "middle kind / and a maker"
(53), a riddling syntax. I asked you earlier if meditation was your poetic
mode, but paradox and reversal are central to your thinking, aren't
they?

PS • You seem to imply that paradox and reversal differ from meditation
– or is that implication a deliberate provocation? Seventeenth-century
prose, Blake, and the poetry and prose of the American 19th century –
Emerson, Thoreau, Melville, Dickinson – which I continue to read a
great deal, are meditative, paradoxical, and full of reversals, and so also
are works in Eastern and Western mystical traditions, Saint John of the
Cross, Saint Theresa of Avila, or to come closer to home, Dame Julian
of Norwich, Walter Hilton, and so on. Their paradoxes and reversals are
ways of saying what can't be said any other way.

AC • *Earth Moth* is a volume that weighs things, and is particularly inter-
ested in the lightness of things – "The Web" (44), "Wasp's Nest" (49),
"Windlestraw" (54): "Your weight / is a breath on my hand" (54). The
"Woodcock Feather" is "As light as whatever you wish ..." (57). Why are
things of no or little weight of such interest to you?

PS • Synecdoche interests me profoundly. As a literary device it parallels the ancient microcosmic reflection of the macrocosm conception, a metaphysical device for joining mind and matter, body and soul, earth and heaven. It's really part of the pneumatic energy of syntax. The study of grammar, like that of subatomic physics, always leads into metaphysics.

AC • *Earth Moth* is also fascinated with "emptiness" as in the "emptied" "Wasp's Nest" (49), the "Windlestraw," which is a "hollow, an emptiness / centred" (54), and the "Mare's Skull" (62). Is absence a metaphysical interest of yours?

PS • Absence is of profound metaphysical interest to metaphysicians, philosophers, linguists and, therefore, necessarily to poets. If language permits one to assert the presence of absence, it can, at least at one level, suggest the void which preceded the *fiat lux* of Genesis. It's an old story. The poem which ends *Spar* is part of my answer. So are the epigraphs to *Spar*. "The Token," which is the title of the concluding poem of *Spar*, comes from the marriage service in the Anglican *Book of Common Prayer*. There is nothing in the centre of a ring.

AC • The poem "Windlestraw" observes "forms // sliding back into bodies" (54). And the first poem of *Ironworks* (1996, 2001) considers calipers "an aspect / of iron returning to nature / approaching her malleable state" (n.pag.). Are you an idealist?

PS • If you are asking whether I'm an idealist as distinct from being a cynic or a utilitarian or a materialist or what is very loosely now called a "realist," then I am an idealist. But if you're using "idealist" in a philosophical sense, then our conversation becomes more complicated. I'm not an idealist in the Hegelian sense because the Hegelian absolute turns into emptiness or tyranny if it is recreated poetically. And Hegelian dialectic – the triad of thesis, antithesis, synthesis – is death to the minute particulars. Idealism in the Platonic or neo-Platonic sense is another matter. No one can read English poetry carefully and with love without acquiring some belief in, or reverence for, Platonic idealism. I think, for example, of Spenser's *Four Hymns*, or Shakespeare's "Sonnet 14," and what I believe to be a meditation upon it at the end of Keats' "Ode on a Grecian Urn." Truth, beauty, love do exist, in my experience, as Platonic archetypes. But on the other hand, I'm realist enough, in the sense of medieval scholasticism, to believe transcendence may become immanent, that it has indeed done so in a few poems – as well as in certain sacred situations, which I don't think this is the place to consider. I can't really conceive of a real artistic making without a religious making. As for the quarrel between a Jungian and a Platonic doctrine of archetypes, I have to be guided by what's in "Keeping" (*Spar* 37-63). Whatever else they involve, love and beauty can be presently incarnate. That's really how we know them.

AC • Is your attention to the small and your use of the short line connected?

PS • Yes, they are connected. Sometimes when writing such poems, I thought of the lines being little more than vibrating filaments.

AC • There's an even shorter line in *The America Reel*, often only four syllables across.

PS • If it works, a minimalist line might offer an infinitely suggestive truth – as, for example, a fragment of Herakleitos. If it doesn't work, the line is vague and banal. The short lines in *The America Reel* are also an effort to reduce language to the irreducible – as counter to an ethos overloaded with egotistical rhetoric.

AC • This is not free verse, nor is it tethered to fixed forms. Nonetheless, it is formal and shaped, what I'd call designed verse. Do things in nature model design in poetry?

PS • Yes, I believe they do. Many years ago I read *On Growth and Form*, the great book by the structural zoologist, biologist, and mathematician D'Arcy Wentworth Thompson. It forever persuaded me that the theoretical excess of open poetics and the prejudices against "closed form" in poetry do not have much to do with nature. Hurricanes are a shaped form. So are sandbars. Nature is nautilus.

AC • *Earth Moth* favours the quatrain, variably shaped. Is a specific traditional form of quatrain – ballad quatrain, hymnal stanza, *In Memoriam* stanza – informing the shape of your four-line stanzas?

PS • Yes, when I write quatrains, the sources you suggest are in my mind. The ballad quatrain is a particularly important one because I think of it as a central carrying form of what was most important in Maritime poetry of European origin during the 19th century. It gives us still an entry into the economical narrative method and profound psychological world of the Anglo-Scottish ballads.

AC • A regular syntax gives way in some poems, as in "Escalade," to parataxis, where Borduas' paintings are "return of the imprisoned sign, / flight of ephemeral dancing / catacombed rock sunk in wine" (23).

PS • Parataxis justifies itself as a mode of intuitive understanding. Actually, the parataxis you quote from "Escalade" is made up of translations from the extraordinary titles Borduas found for his paintings. The quick flight of his choices was the quick flight of his hand and mind – the essence of his kind of abstract expressionism. I suspect one of the characteristics of Borduas' genius was his ability to think coherently in paratactic terms.

AC • "Spinning and splicing poems is ... a matter of eye and hand, foot and belly, working together in the precise rhythms of creation ..." (*The Third Hand* 23). Is the body the "great poem," as Wallace Stevens puts it (974)?

PS • You touch upon one of the central themes attempted in *The Third Hand*: Space is not an altereity. To return to a trope mentioned earlier in our conversation, it is the centre of the ring. Yes, I agree with Stevens, though with the reservation that we are not quite in the position to know whether the body is *the* great poem or *a* great poem. I'd read Stevens' analogy in a Blakean sense, thinking, for example, of Blake's "Glad Day" engraving, or Leonardo da Vinci's naked microcosmic male sketched in inexorable *X*.

AC • "An extraordinary musician is innately gifted with musical ability just as an extraordinary poet is gifted with poetic ability," you say ("*Her kindled shadow ...*" 18). So what is the innate ability of the poet?

PS • I was thinking of musical precocity. The obvious example is Mozart, who seems to have been born with an innate sense of musical form. In the case of poetry, the "innate ability" must obviously involve words – the intuitive sense of how they fit together by sound, meaning, and syntax, how they may run together in detectable but not ostentatious rhythm. Some of the greatest poets seem also to have been born with a sense of the lexicographical history of words – literally, their rootedness. Shakespeare is the great example. How a person can be born knowing philological nuances I don't know. But I can tell you that only the first two or three lines of a poem can reveal whether its author is a poet or not. If word does not lead to word and line to line, no hope.

AC • "Poetry is closer to prayer than confession" ("*Her kindled shadow ...*" 314): What does that mean?

PS • The comment is a provocation in part. Like most provocations, it assumes an unstated context. It is polemic against the kind of autobiographical confessional poetry directed to the public rather than to a real confessor, which has characterized modern English language poetry – particularly in North America since [Robert] Lowell, [Sylvia] Plath, [Anne] Sexton, [John] Berryman, and others. Richard Outram, the real subject of the remark, writes another kind of poetry – as do the other poets I admire and respect. The central mystery of poetry is analogous to the mystery of the mass. The mass takes place during words and manual acts of consecration. An alternative is to take tea with Rikyu. But I keep thinking of Simone Weil's use of George Herbert's poem "Love": "I used to think I was merely reciting it as a beautiful poem, but without my knowing it the recitation had the virtue of prayer" (*Waiting on God* 21).

AC • The simile is the figure of choice in *The America Reel*. In "Bone Yard," grave stones "tilt every way like wind cocked stooks" (25) and "winter [is] ... like someone / who'd entered with snow on his sleeves / and stood unspeaking" (26). Would you agree that *Earth Moth* makes greater use of metaphor?

PS • Yes, perhaps I began to see that metaphor is an inherent condition of language. Simile has an aspect of externality. In his great essay on Dante, Osip Mandelstam talks about Dante's similitudes launching themselves into flight from one another. That is the way one should try to use them.

AC • For you, can there be poetry at all without metaphorical thinking?

PS • There is a social poetry of declarative utterance, isn't there? I think of Juvenal, for instance. But English language poetry is invariably metaphoric. Look what Dryden, Swift, Pope, and Johnson make of Juvenal. The relish and gusto of their language invariably modulates into metaphor. At another level, of course, language itself is conceivable entirely as metaphor – so is calculus.

AC • In *The America Reel*, the object or creature poem tends to have more narrative context as in "When I touched the green / snake with my foot / two carrion beetles ... ran out of its / belly and showed me / expectant antennae ..."(12). Reference to the perceptor gets dropped pretty much in *Earth Moth*, doesn't it?

PS • Yes, I turn up – or a version of me turns up – more frequently in *The America Reel*. But I worked for narrative lines in all the poems in both books. For me, the narrative of a poem may be auricular, ideational, mimetic as well as a matter of plot or sequential events. The perceptor is more evident in *The America Reel* partly because the book honours the storytelling tradition in Maritime culture – although the stories told often reflect upon that tradition with irony.

AC • The narrative impulse in *The America Reel* is, however, more often at the service of local stories involving characters: "The Sisters" (26), "The White Lady" (29-30), "Jerome" (31-32). Were characters, or at least local characters, of paramount interest to you at the time of *America Reel*?

PS • They were of major interest, but not paramount. Poetry was paramount. Had they been of paramount interest, I think I would have produced a sentimental or nostalgic book. There are already too many of those in Atlantic-Canadian writing. *The America Reel* was meant to be, among other things, an abrupt interruption. At least one of its reviewers – I think it was reviewed twice – had some sense of that and called the writer of it cold.

AC • In *The Third Hand*, the collection of riddle poems that accompanied the exhibition of Maritime handmade tools and implements (Halifax, June-September, 1994), which you put together, we see riddle at the service of "praise" [1]. How does that combination work?

PS • The riddles in *The Third Hand* are meant not only to give their readers an understanding of the mode of operation of the tools and implements, but also to locate that mode cognitively as both physical and metaphysical expression. May I say that knowing is a form of praise? David Jones speaks about "the actually loved and known" (25). I don't think his "and" is the equivalent of an addition sign. It indicates a co-inherency.

AC • Isn't laconicism a feature of all your early poetry, not just the riddle poems of *The Third Hand*?

PS • I've been told my poetry stops too soon or is too thin – along the lines of "Is that all there is?" Perhaps the comments are just. But I've always felt I had only so many few words to say, and I'd better try to choose them carefully and say no more. That feeling was acute at the beginning. For me, a poem remains an intensive, packed, precise statement which must elicit several, perhaps many, levels of hearing and reading although some of my favourite poems are lengthy ones. I think, for example, of [Sir John] Harington's translation of Ariosto's *Orlando Furioso*, which amounts to 46 books, containing on average 100 Spenserian stanzas each. But it's a translation of extraordinary speed and fluency, the work, I think, of someone who knew a great deal about horses and the necessary economies of their management. Perhaps I'm wrong, but I also feel laconicism honours the reader.

AC • This collection gets its title, *The Third Hand,* from the first implement not named, a harness-maker's vice. "Now I'm remembering / how all I once held / gripped everything going" (I), which could be a rather melancholy observation on life, couldn't it?

PS • It could be melancholy – or it is not. The choice is the reader's, and there are ironies involved. We may, for example, speak admiringly of someone who has everything going for him or her. But then the slang of the locution could imply that whatever's on the go is a matter for callow acquisition. Remember, there are horses involved here too. This particular vice may not now be in use, but to quote Marlowe, quoting Faustus, quoting Ovid, "*O lente, lente curite noctis equis.*"

AC • Each riddling voice in *The Third Hand* asks us to consider the object. The voices in *Ironworks* ask us to stop, look, and pass through. Isn't malleability – our own as well as the object's – iron's song?

PS • Yes, and iron's song in *Ironworks* is the song of its transformation into light. Is that a stage beyond or one concomitant with rust? The book is meant to answer.

AC • The second poem of *Ironworks* begins magnificently, "Measure restores the museum," but isn't the opposite true also – "The museum restores the measure"? Museum, a place of muses, its original meaning, reminds us that any so-called permanent exhibit is ultimately about impermanence.

PS • The epigraph to *Ironworks* is taken from an alchemical treatise by Michael Sendivogius, which was collected in a 17th-century compilation published in Germany whose title was Englished by A.E. Waite as *The Hermetic Museum*. Yes, a museum is, as you say, definable etymologically as "a place of the muses." That etymological derivation, once made, I believe, returns any museum back to life. It depends upon whether you think muses are still at work. For me, they are.

AC • *Ironworks* employs terms such as "epochs," "an age," "aeon," and "returning to darkness enclosed," yet it begins and ends with the image of the dance. Do these iron objects incarnate the dance of time?

PS • Time is really a human concept. When I used the words "epochs," "age," "aeon" – particularly with the latter – I was trying to indicate the limitations of our conceptions of time. Industrialized time is the most transitory time humankind has ever created. We know the consequences. Our descendants will curse us. Industrialized time really commenced with the iron age. In the aeonic cycles, Hindu mythology distinguishes the inception of the Kali Yuga, when Shiva will dance the dance of destruction. That dance is a restoration. A dance of an analogous kind, a lesser dance with this cosmic cycle of dance, occurs in the "The America Reel" (19), the poem closing the second third of the book to which it gives title. The breaking of the dancers in that reel led to another civilization, on another continent, to another type of Blake's Albion or Stevens' "body," which you spoke about earlier – to another restoration. The restoration occurs over the run of human time, but transcends it.

AC • Dancing and weaving are motions, and metaphors, of utmost importance in *Earth Moth*. Relate these two motions for me.

PS • Dancing and weaving are both repetitive, rhythmical activities which create patterns. In that sense, they are analogous to the syntax, rhythm, and match of words which create poems. In Nova Scotia, during the 19th century, treadle looms were common in many households. The acts of pressing the loom's foot pedal and the hand casting the shuttle were a form of dance. Many religious traditions, including those, for example, of the Navaho, think of the weaver's completed task as analogous to the warp and weave out of which the demiurge made creation. In reading *Earth Moth*, it might help to remember that warp and weave are a cruciform pattern.

AC • When you write that for Outram poetry "must be a mode of accurate metaphysical discourse, both accommodating and transcending temporality" ("*Her kindled shadow* ..." 20), you might be describing what the images and words of *Ironworks* do: Accommodate and transcend the temporality of the objects presented. Is it axiomatic that any poet deeply observant of the natural world will be, necessarily, also a metaphysical poet?

PS • My instinct is to say yes. An apparent exception might be John Clare, but I would argue that his greatest poems enter the archetypal world of the songs of *Comus*, for example, or of *A Midsummer Night's Dream*. My answer is reacting to your "deeply observant," and I take it that those words answer Blake's comment on the division between the natural and spiritual man in Wordsworth. It is not enough to be only "observant." Simone Weil, working from a Platonic basis, wrote that "We cannot contemplate without a certain love. The contemplation of this image of the order of the world constitutes a certain contact with the beauty of the world. The beauty of the world is the order of the world that is loved" (*Waiting on God* 107). I think that deeply observant poets of nature – even if they are secularized – would agree with Weil. Radical Darwinism has never had much effect upon the tradition of English-language nature poetry. That poetry is still basically Platonic in origin, or draws upon traditions which are similar – given the context of our conversation – Taoism and Zen Buddhism, or what very little we know of the pre-Socratics.

AC • Am I right in thinking that *After Monteverdi: Twelve Poems* (1997) marks a return – to some degree – to the narrative tendency of *The America Reel* since the former contains the ballad "Sealskin" (15), a story of selkies, and a variation on the Orpheus and Eurydice story in the title poem (27)?

PS • *After Monteverdi* was published, as a gift to me really, by Douglas Lochhead. He suggested a chapbook collection. I saw a chance to put together poems about love, poetry, and music, and their intrication with the natural world, a theme I'd been working on for many years. "Elegy for the Great Auks" (31-33) and "Mozart's Starling" (43) were written particularly for the chapbook in 1997. The other poems were written earlier. "Sealskin" (15) was written before the poems in *The America Reel*, for example. Like *The America Reel*, *After Monteverdi* deliberately reworks what I think of as Atlantic-Canadian inherited forms. My intention was to show how the same level of inspiration has inhabited and linked all the forms. We know, for example, that Celtic music, which is commonly thought to be a kind of spontaneous folk generation, is, in fact, a very subtle, complex intersection of both folk

ANNE COMPTON

forms and the baroque. [Turlough] Carolan, the Irish composer, is one of my great heroes because in his work we can see the intersection and reformation so beautifully and intelligently accomplished.

AC • Although "Sealskin" is a variant of the ballad stanza (its lines of five and three syllables are really three tetrameter lines, plus a two-syllable refrain line), isn't *After Monteverdi* more varied in form than your earlier books – "Embouchure" (9) and "*Canti Avium*" (13) in couplets, and "After Monteverdi" (27-28) and "To Clytie" (35) unbroken prose paragraphs?

PS • The formal variations are very deliberate – just as the songs of the birds in "*Canti Avium*" are various. I hope the variations can be read and heard as done with some wit. *After Monteverdi* is a book about love and friendship, as its dedication to my wife, who is a pianist and knows music far better than I, implies. The anagrammatic play of the title "Stone Notes" (37-41) is meant to be one of the small jokes, for example, as are the rhymes in "Embouchure." "Cameo" (19) impersonates and, I hope, deflates a certain kind of connoisseur – it could be read with a transatlantic accent. "After Monteverdi" and "To Clytie" are an attempt at blank verse, and if read aloud, should show structured stress patterns.

AC • The word "Keeping" in the title of the third *Spar* essay, "Keeping: The Cameron Yard" (37-63), could mean rather a number of things – observance, a looking after, preservation, maintaining, as in "keeping" a mistress, or in the particular vocabulary of art, tonal values – but you refer to a particular attitude with that word, don't you?

PS • All the meanings of "keeping" you list were intended in the essay, and I'm grateful for your seeing them and hearing them. The particular attitude is love, a love which is indistinguishable from knowing and understanding within the limits each of us is given.

AC • Is generalization the enemy of poetry?

PS • Imprecise generalization, based upon an ignorance of literature, history, theology, philosophy, nature, or whatever else is being generalized about, which is expressed in language without semantic depth and syntactical range, is the enemy of poetry. I don't subscribe to the Imagist dogma of no ideas but in things. As counter, I would reverse the dogma: No things but in ideas. When Weil writes, "... in all beauty we find contradiction, bitterness, and absence which are irreducible"

(*Gravity and Grace* 206), is that a generalization or a statement of empirical, ethical fact? It is both, and it is no enemy to poetry.

AC • "[T]he question is whether poetry itself is nature" (*Spar* 74). Poetry is nature – is this what you mean – if words are seen to carry "latencies" (17), "laminations" (66), and layerings in their very substance?

PS • Yes, poetry is nature in that sense. Both nature and poetry must elicit from us ecological concerns. Poetry's concern is language. Genesis links language and creation. As a poet, I have to believe that the *fiat lux* is the unspoken first line of every real poem. Poetry is sound, not just words on a page. No one, surely, can listen to certain musical forms – Orthodox Christian church music, Gregorian chant, Tibetan temple music, Inuit throat music, or Monteverdi's *Orfeo* – without hearing the possibility of human sound becoming continuous with creation. If there is hope for us, it may lie in the extension of that realization.

AC • What are the implications for the poet's work if the poet is "perhaps ... always last at the feast" ("Late at the Feast" 89)?

PS • The poet is neither victim nor executioner. He is the secret sharer. She is the secret sharer.

WORKS CITED

— • —

Boisseau, Michelle and Robert Wallace. *Writing Poems*. 6th ed. New York: Pearson Longman, 2003.

Hopkins, Gerard Manley. *Poems and Prose of Gerard Manley Hopkins*. Ed. W.H. Gardner. London: Penguin, 1967.

Huntington, Cynthia et al. "How to Peel a Poem: Five poets dine out on verse." *Harper's Magazine* (September 1999): 45-60.

Sanger, Peter. *After Monteverdi: Twelve Poems*. Sackville, NB: Harrier Editions, 1997.

– – – . *The America Reel*. Porters Lake, NS: Pottersfield P, 1983.

– – – . *Arborealis: Photographs by Thaddeus Holownia & Poetry by Peter Sanger*. Jolicure, NB: Anchorage P, 2004.

– – – ed. et al. *Divisions of the Heart: Elizabeth Bishop and the Art of Memory and Place*. Wolfville, NS: Gaspereau P, 2001.

– – – . *Earth Moth*. Fredericton: Goose Lane Editions, 1991.

– – – . "*Her kindled shadow ...*": *An Introduction to the Work of Richard Outram*. 2nd. ed. Antigonish, NS: *Antigonish Review*, 2002.

– – –. *Ironworks: Photographs by Thaddeus Holowina, Poems by Peter Sanger*. Jolicure, NB: Anchorage P, 1996, 2001.

– – – . *Kerf*. Wolfville, NS: Gaspereau P, 2002.

– – – . "Late at the Feast: An Afterword." *Ursa Major: A Polyphonic Masque for Speakers & Dancers*, by Robert Bringhurst. Wolfville, NS: Gaspereau P, 2003. 77-90.

– – – . *Richard Outram: A Preface and Selection*. Occasional Paper #3. Antigonish, NS: *Antigonish Review*, 2001.

– – – . ed. *John Thompson: Collected Poems and Translations*. Fredericton: Goose Lane Editions, 1995.

– – – . "Saint-Denys Garneau on Poetry, Writing, Painting and Music." *Antigonish Review* 64 (Winter 1986): 79-89.

– – – . *Spar: Words in Place*. Wolfville, NS: Gaspereau P, 2002.

– – – . *The Third Hand*. Jolicure, NB: Anchorage P, 1994.

– – – . *White Salt Mountain*. Wolfville, NS: Gaspereau P, 2005.

Stevens, Wallace. From *Adagia*. *The Norton Anthology of Modern and Contemporary Poetry*. 2 vols. 3rd. ed. Eds. Jahan Ramazani et al. New York: W.W. Norton, 2003. I. 972-75.

Thompson, John. *Collected Poems and Translations*. Ed. Peter Sanger. Fredericton: Goose Lane Editions, 1995.

Weil, Simone. *Gravity and Grace*. Trans. Arthur Wills. New York: G. P. Putnam's, 1952.

– – – . *Waiting on God*. Trans. Emma Cranfurd. London: Routledge and Kegan Paul, 1951.

Wittgenstein, Ludwig, *Tractatus Logico-Philosophicus*. London: Routledge and Kegan Paul, 1974.

AFTER THEATRE AND THEORY:
ROBERT MOORE'S POETRY

Born and raised in Hamilton, Ontario, Robert Moore dropped out of high school, working for several years as a machine-fitter and steelworker before entering university. After completing three degrees, he became a university professor at Augustan University College, Alberta, and later at the University of New Brunswick, Saint John. He has lived in New Brunswick for 15 years. An actor, director, and playwright, Moore has written more than a dozen plays for radio and stage and has earned playwriting and directorial awards. In 2002, he published his first collection of poetry, *So Rarely in Our Skins*, shortlisted for the Atlantic Poetry Prize and for the Margaret and John Savage First Book Award. Well received by reviewers, *So Rarely in Our Skins* was praised for its wit and erudition. At the time of this interview – May 2005 – Moore was preparing his second collection, *Museum Absconditum*, for press and working on a third book of poems, "Figuring Ground." Reviews by Moore have appeared in *Books in Canada*, the *Winnipeg Free Press*, and other journals and newspapers.

AC • What impelled you, and continues to impel you, to write poetry?

RM • I don't know that I'm impelled. I'm obviously *inclined*, but impelled suggests that I'm under some sort of compulsion to write poetry, which is a notion I feel I should resist. I just read somewhere something that Mondrian is reported to have said regarding why he painted. "I have no interest in making paintings," he said, "I just want to see what happens." Assuming that interest – of putting one's self in the way of seeing what might happen – what impels me to write poetry is an interest in language, in the relationship between language and self, between acts of language and acts of self. Writing is an opportunity to enter deliberately into that process, to take hold, and if not to remake, then certainly to readjust and otherwise redirect the self, if only by slight and hard-won increments.

AC   • Poets past 40 publishing a first collection is something of a phenomenon in the Maritimes. Why, in your case, did you start late?

RM   • In a formal or literal sense, I suppose I started quite late. In the writing I did before turning to poetry, mostly as a playwright, I was never especially interested in plot, but very much interested in voice. The plays I wrote were rich in moment – in poetical moment – but weak when it came to holding it all together, which I used to put down to a failure of the imagination, never mind a failure of dramaturgy. I guess what I'm saying is that I don't think of myself as a late starter. I recently came across my old copy of Leonard Cohen's *Selected Poems*, a book I was never without 30-odd years ago. It was full of marginalia, illegitimate little Cohen spawn squeezed into every available expanse of white. The ambition to make a book, however, did arrive quite late.

AC   • Was publishing *So Rarely in Our Skins* anticlimactic in ways it wouldn't have been had you published a collection in your 20s or 30s?

RM   • If I had published in my 20s or 30s, I would have worked within and through an entirely different set of interests. For one thing, I suspect I would have had far more confidence in the relevance of the response my work engendered. I would have been much more interested in that response, would have lived much more inside it, in a way I'm no longer capable of. Now I have a much stronger sense of the limited relevance of the part one's readers play in the process of writing, coming in as late and as obliquely as they must. I'm not sure, either, how developed a purchase I would have had when I was younger on the actual place of poetry in the life of my culture. Anticlimactic? I suppose, too, I'm surprised by how little response, how little residue, is created by a book of poetry. Maybe that's just in the case of my work. It just reminds one again of how important the *writing* is as opposed to the reception.

AC   • In "Resolution and Independence," Wordsworth says, "We Poets in our youth begin in gladness; / But thereof come in the end despondency and madness" (138). So what is the trajectory for those beginning late in life?

RM   • Hopefully, opposite the one you quote. Art is the antidote for, not the cause of, madness. I don't know whether or not this applies to other late starters, but I think I began in despondency and madness and set

               ANNE COMPTON

about writing my way out of it. I'm much more well adjusted to the world now that I've written and am writing. Indeed, I have a certain nostalgia for the old despondency, the madness of youth, probably because I'm fairly certain it's behind me.

AC • In reviewing *So Rarely in Our Skins*, Chris Pannell says that when the mature beginner "releases work that has been stored for years, the poetry is highly polished" (103). Does that accurately describe the advantage for the late beginner?

RM • I wonder if there is any necessary relationship between storage and polish. Polish is an effect of craftsmanship and much practice. The logic of Chris's position is somewhat hydraulic: Following a prolonged period under pressure, there's apt to be a gushing forth of the long-fermented and therefore likely fully formed. To accept the premise is, I think, to accept that there's something magical about writing, that it isn't a craft, isn't something you have to learn step by step and work at every day. Poets, like carpenters, are made not born, however late in life.

AC • Would tragicomedy best describe this collection's veering between jest and gravity?

RM • The definition [Samuel] Beckett offers of the term – laughing wild mid severest woe – has always struck me as an honourable posture to take in this life. Of the writers who've taught me the most about writing, Beckett would rank very high. In terms of a note to hit, I do think of tragicomedy as a natural one. Of late, however, I'm trying to write away from it because it comes a bit too naturally. It's become a habit.

AC • Do Hamm and Hamlet, unnamed, hover around between these covers?

RM • Hamlet is a source of endless fascination. If I had to save one play from the proverbial burning library, it'd be *Hamlet*. That said, it's [Beckett's] Hamm with whom my work more often finds itself in conversation. Hamm is the saddest of the 20th-century's monsters. A great and terrible creation.

AC • When you gave the collection five sections, did you have in mind a five-act play?

RM • Never thought of it in those terms. Frankly, I'm all but useless when it comes to the overall organization of a book of poetry. I write poem to poem, and when the moment comes to organize it into a collection, I rely on the kindness of others to make a meaningful form of it. Maybe that's why I no longer write plays. I couldn't quite manage three acts, never mind five. As a maker of forms, I can really only think in terms of the fragmentary and the singular.

AC • When one thinks about the tradition of the lyric, as represented in the canon, there's not a lot of humour. Has postmodernism made greater room for humour in the lyric?

RM • By its very nature the lyric takes the self – and the self's connection to the world – quite seriously. Humour requires a certain ironic distance. The lyric has far too much confidence in the capacities of language to weld experience to the world, to weld self and the experience of the self in the world together, and into a meaningful whole, which is the very assumption, or interest, humour is determined to undermine. Almost by definition, postmodernism's interest – especially with regard to irony – assaults the lyric's putative sagacity, its mystical competence.

AC • Does that mean that postmodernist humour is of a particular kind – ironic?

RM • I'm trying to think of any exceptions to the rule of irony in the humour of postmodernism, and, offhand, I can't. But then, I can't think, offhand, of any exceptions to the rule of irony in humour generally. Humour, at least as I understand it for the purposes of this question, is always calculated to subvert, invert, and otherwise render dubious some sort of dominant discourse. And that absolutely requires an ironic posture, ironic distance. There are risks in irony – a "hipness unto death," as it were.

AC • Are irony and understatement tactics for "working free of the heart" (11)?

RM • I'm increasingly suspicious of my own ironical bent, probably for the reason you suggest. Irony is a function of ambivalence. [Vladimir] Nabokov – and he's following Kierkegaard here, I suspect – said somewhere that the ironist is the bird which has fallen in love with its cage. In other words, the risk of irony is that it turns into a zero sum game: It's a way to embroider stasis. Irony is probably what I'm using to avoid engagement with the genuinely strange and dislocating. Irony allows for a mild dislocation. However, as the pigs say in "Bovinities," "*There are no ironists in the abattoir*" (34).

ANNE COMPTON

AC • In the title section of *So Rarely*, violence is paired to laughter. In "Axe Handle" (59-60), for example, the speaker reminds the father of a story of breath-stopping violence: "the only story you [the father] had to tell ... of your old man" (59). The "difficult breath he made for you / that night in the orchard" is, however, a "breath which every so often / you asked us to hold" (60).

RM • In recently rereading the book, the wedding of pain and laughter did strike me. Not that violence and humour haven't always been the best of bedfellows. But, yes, it's a much darker book than I remember and much darker than the book all but one or two reviewers appear to have read. Much is made of the book's humour, but little is made of its pain. But as you point out, "Axe Handle" is about terrible violence, a history of family violence, a violence which is – at least as inflected in the retelling – Atrean in scope, the violence of a cursed house. It's set in an orchard, a primal space. The way in which my family handled its pain was through humour – my father always told that story as a kind of rueful joke. Mind you, I don't think my pain, or the biography of my family's pain, is either especially unique or interesting. What is potentially interesting, and what I aimed at reproducing, is how pain is transformed, made meaningful, connected to something larger than itself. The interest is in how you go about making form out of what formed you.

AC • Given all the characters – literary, historical, mythic – that appear, is *So Rarely*, in some way, a reprise of your role as director?

RM • In the collocation of voices? Possibly, but I suspect more actor than director. My training and my practice for the longest time involved formally inhabiting roles, inhabiting other skins, working through personae, speaking from behind and through a mask, discovering how liberating an experience that is. When you're obliged to speak, for weeks and sometimes months at a time, as Agamemnon or John Proctor or Hamm, you're treated to a wonderfully dislocating experience, but – and here's where the art comes in – in a highly structured fashion. At the moment of performance you're inhabiting your self – that great dead weight you're obliged to carry about with you wherever you go – but also this provisional "other" in action, in crisis, and before an audience. So it's not that great a leap to arrange to speak as someone else in a poem.

AC   • A poem such as "This Morning on the Phone" (54) strikes me as a perfectly timed poem. Is timing as important in poetry as it is in theatre?

RM   • More so, I would think. The tolerances are finer. For me, the key to the alchemy of timing is knowing the material, certainly, but also knowing your own position as speaker and, perhaps most important of all, the inferred position of the auditor. All three elements have to arrive at the intersection of surprise – the brief irruptive flourish of the punchline – at precisely the same moment.

AC   • These days a new book means a circuit of readings. Does being an actor make readings easier?

RM   • I suspect it may be a little easier for me, if only because I may know something of what's involved in performing work well. Standing up to read your work before an audience of strangers is a terribly complicated undertaking. Not only are you obliged to honour the work as text – that is, deliver it in good voice – you have to honour the author, the very person who's rarely, if ever, present when you speak as an actor. There is also for the actor in me the temptation to cheat, to come between the poem and the audience, to "come over" the poem and not let the poem speak for itself, whatever that might mean. In the culture I knew as an actor, the model for this tendency was John Gielgud doing Shakespeare – a surfeit of plummy and gummy effects for which the text was too often merely an excuse, an occasion to preen.

AC   • To some extent, have you left the actor behind?

RM   • I'm *leaving* but I'll never *have left*. I'm certainly less interested in the actor, less reliant upon his skills, his tricks. That was where I was most comfortable so my interest was in giving myself interesting things to say in front of an audience. "Watches" (31-32) and "Bovinities" (33-34) are two of the early poems written to be performed. I'm not altogether sure how much life they have on the page. I'm always a little mystified when those two poems in particular are singled out as good poems by readers I'm inclined to trust.

AC   • Does the title, *So Rarely in Our Skins*, refer to the unfixability, the fluidity, of identity?

RM   • The title signifies on a number of levels. The first that springs to mind refers to the notion that we're all just nominally, and I mean that liter-

           ANNE COMPTON

ally, just nominally present to ourselves, to the world. I'm very interested in the ontology of the moment of speech, the moment during which self, identity, and being are all aligned. That moment is rare, the moment when we're delivered into ourselves, when we're "in our skins." The original inspiration for the title comes from what may be an Ontario expression, a compliment you'd offer to someone who's present to himself, present to others, to the moment. Not just present, but honest, a kind of integrity. Those moments – pastless, futureless – of consummation with our skins, though devoutly to be wished, are only rarely achieved. Poetry offers the opportunity for those moments, but in its process. The poem that results – and appears on the page – is, presumably, the residue of that state of being.

AC • This book is a collection of skins?

RM • Yes. And not in a false way, either. That is, not skins in the sense of costumes, of surface, of superficiality. Identity is – and I'm taking my direction here from Emmanuel Levinas and company – identity is performative, a "saying" rather than a said. Poems are acts of identity that manufacture skin, a thing soon in need of a shedding.

AC • One poem says that "[a]ll truth is finally local, rooms of skin" (74). Does that line stand in opposition to the title?

RM • We're never out of one or another of our skins. Where could we go but into nothingness? But we're rarely *in* our skins, in the sense of being fully present to the moment. We're ineluctably locked into ourselves even while we're hoping to see into that which transcends the self. I'm not much of an essentialist so, no, I don't find much contradiction in saying all truth is finally local. You know the commonplace – the way into the universal, the materials of the universal, are exclusively those of the particular. Any interest in making general statements about the nature of truth, capital *T*, can only be undertaken from the local. That's the sense I'm after in that particular line, and, in general, in using the trope of the skin: I'm underscoring not just the local but the evanescence of the local. The skin is everything and it's nothing.

AC • The title section of the book, Section 3, with its focus on death, might lead one to believe that the *Rarely* of the title bears the word's oldest meaning, "briefly." And then there's "The Skin You Wore," a tender elegy about a mother's illness (63). Can poetry, if it's done right, trump mortality?

RM • When a poem works – when it's any good – you've managed to put yourself in touch with the thing that death is not. If death is the great unspeakable, the great unspoken, the realm of "not I," poetry is the most "I" one can manage at any given time. The moment of creation is the moment when I'm most possessed by and in possession of what I am. It's Eros and Thanatos, a simultaneous inscription and erasure of the self, and an act which, interestingly enough, produces an object, an artifact which involves a world of others.

AC • So it's the *making* that may be the potential trump against death?

RM • Yes, in that regard, the poem in the book is all but an irrelevant consideration. It very quickly becomes a stranger, dead to the maker but, hopefully – at least so far as one's readers are concerned – not a "deadly" thing. Writing the poem gave life to me, and I can only hope that reading it, in ways I cannot know or control, offers some measure of life to you.

AC • Icarus is on the cover and six Icarus poems close the book. Is Icarus a talismanic figure for you?

RM • He is for *So Rarely*, yes. I'm not sure he has any particular life for me now. Among the mythological figures to whom I might have clung, Icarus is the one with definite biographical connections. The gesture in the Landon painting of Daedalus and Icarus on the cover is an ambivalent one. It's unclear whether Icarus is about to be held back by the father or has just been released by the father. It reads both ways. Writing *So Rarely*, that ambivalence was very much at issue.

AC • Icarus is autobiographical?

RM • Daedalus stands in for a kind of imagination, for faculties I probably possess, but which don't much interest me, whereas Icarus stands in for a poetic energy in which I'm interested. It's akin to the Apollonian and the Dionysian. Daedalus is the guy you'd go to if you wanted a well-plotted five-act play, good on form and structure. Icarus, on the other hand, stands in for improvisation, for possibility. Mind, he's very much beholden to the craftsman. Indeed, he's a kind of epiphenomenon of the craftsman, the part that is sloughed off to crash and burn. The book's interest in Icarus began with Auden's Icarus in "Musée des Beaux Arts," and if it's talismanic to me at all, it's connected to the irony that art isn't especially important to anyone but the artist.

AC • The horse rubbing its bottom on the tree, to which you make refer-
ence in the poem "The Torturer's Horse" (107), expresses what attitude
toward art?

RM • Almost everyone turns away from art in the way everyone turns from
Icarus in Brueghel's painting. As they should. Art, as Auden knew, isn't
that important. It's not for everyone and doesn't change anything. The
Icarus on the cover of my book, and figuring in the art of the poems,
is thus a cautionary figure, an ironic figure.

AC • And also a boy.

RM • In that, I suppose, he also stands for memory, or the autobiograph-
ical, which I'm less and less interested in, at least as regards to the par-
ticulars of my own biography. In one sense, the Icarus who aspires and
expires in this book is the body of a boy upon which an exorcism has
been performed.

AC • In "A Scorcher by the Pool," Icarus, inviting the listener to take a
plunge, also invites her to recall that "the birth of dawn ... work[s] for-
ward to the fact that any exodus from air / ... involves severest strain"
(104). Doesn't this book suppose that everyone is an Icarus?

RM • We're all going to go through that process, travel that arc of ascent
and descent. Every one of us – multitudes of Icarae. Which implies a
degree of demystification is going on in the book.

AC • Through the course of those many tellings, you make a plain person
of Icarus?

RM • The last poem in the book especially makes that point: "small stone
/ thrown by a boy / gone back to sleep / in the sea" (111). We can't help
but have our own little Icarus in mind when we lift him aloft in our
minds. He can, therefore, despite the gorgeously contrived apparatus
on his back, be none other than plain. He's an ape with angel glands,
as Leonard Cohen, in one of his songs, says of us, echoing Hamlet,
echoing the chorus of *Antigone*.

AC • Does the Beckettian humour of this collection rest upon the notion
that birth and "exodus" are coterminus, or, as one poem puts it: "In
poems / *death* will find a way / to *breath* // or vice versa// ... / as if the
two were the oldest of friends ..." (53)?

RM • There's a line from another poem, "A Disaster is an Unfavourable Star," that applies here: "Imagine if we didn't know death / how hopeless / we'd sound" (74). The suggestion is that death is the gift of life – which is, of course, a commonplace. I'm not sure, though, that the poem you quote, "In poems death" (53), is, in its tone, anywhere near as dark as Beckett. His characters crawl through shit, or awful silence, entirely unable, most of them, to stop talking. That particular poem is celebratory, comic in the technical sense: Comedies tend to end with marriages, with the reconciliation of putative opposites. The reference to Brueghel in that poem is meant to suggest the viability of community, which makes death and breath companionable as elements that belong together in the ceremony of a public event, a well-lit event during which the light pulls at everyone's skin. It's a kind of carnival, or circus, as the presence of balloons – frangible bubbles of breath – suggest.

AC • "[L]ight pulls at everyone's skin" (53) and the "casual spill of their [children's] tracks ... [is] a slow fall through sunlight / softer than ash" (104)? It's as if the children don't know, in their play, that what they're walking through is ash.

RM • There is that moment we have as parents when we have to walk our children through the recognition that they're mortal, that they're doomed. Death, for each of them, then becomes the lifework, living with the prospect of death by being alive in a certain kind of way. The child in the poem, watched by the parent, is imagined as an innocent who's poised on the cusp of that recognition.

AC • One reviewer of *So Rarely* describes the poems as "off-kilter glimpses into truisms of some 'universal' state" and as "wink-eyed looks at the familiar" (*Berger* 134). Do you prefer to look at the world aslant rather than straight on?

RM • I wonder at the person who'd opt for the latter. What would it be to look at the world straight on? The space available to you when you're *not* looking at life askance, alert to the action in the corner of your eye, doesn't seem to me to be a space worth occupying. The position you have to take to survive as an engaged individual will inevitably be one of resistance. Your obligation is to find a place where you can invoke, conjure, and batten upon the oblique and the off-kilter. To be in your skin, in the sense we spoke of it earlier, is to be oblique. The tragic always begins with its hero claiming to look at the world straight on: Oedipus, Hamlet, Lear. Steady gazers all, but deeply blind as bats.

AC • Perhaps the most disturbing poem in this book is "Fox Poem," which describes "a fox left behind / in an upside-down aquarium" when "an uncle drop[s]" (55). In the fox's reflective eye, the observer experiences his own end: "dust starting through buttonholes ... mouth worked open." What's odd and disconcerting – as suggested by the "upside-down aquarium" – is the image of the fox, as dead as dead can be, somehow possessed of information the speaker doesn't yet possess.

RM • The poem started as a response to [Ted] Hughes' "The Thought-Fox." In Hughes' last line, the speaker is looking down at the page and, almost magically, "the page is printed" (3). The fox – animal, hatched from the dark, entirely other – stands in for the poem. My interest was in exploring the ways in which a poem is a fox. In "Fox Poem," when the fox looks back at you, when it draws you through its entirely artificial, strangely immortal glass eyes, the intent is to remind you of your mortality.

AC • The situation with the fox reminds me of those tombs in which the mighty are interred, saints in glass coffins. Those are indescribable in the sense that we get to walk around the dead. This poem has something of that quality.

RM • The thing about a stuffed animal is that the part which seems most alive is the part that doesn't belong, which isn't original to the thing itself. It's a curious inversion. The eyes are where the art is, in the gaze that can't discriminate from looking at, looking through, looking beyond you. It's a form of absolute looking. It's the look of the basilisk, of Medusa: If it sees you, or more to the point, if you really see it, you're translated, quick as a wink, from animate to inanimate. If time has eyes, I'll bet they're made of glass.

AC • Do you know where you are going with a poem when you begin?

RM • I have no experience with knowing where I'm going in a poem. It usually starts with a line or image. Then there's the giddy moment of the second line, which changes the chemistry of the first line or image. And the game's afoot, a game that involves any number of blind alleys, false leads, and endless backtracking. More often than not, the second line, the thing that follows the beginning, does so much damage to the first line that it comes near to killing what might have been a poem. It does happen sometimes that you hit upon a series of happy accidents and are able to ride some wave of energy straight through to the end of the poem, to find your way out of the labyrinth in one desperate, intoxicating, headlong rush. That's happened to me maybe twice. The most one hopes for is to end up with enough to come back to. So no, I never begin knowing where I'm going.

AC • A poem for you evolves through what kind of logic: Formal, narrative, metaphoric, associative?

RM • One of the ways I typically organize the chaos of the moment is through character or voice. If I start with Clytemnestra, say, or with Cassandra, then I'm bound, to some degree, to be carried along by their stories, or hope to be. I think of myself as having danced with figures, like the two I've mentioned, a dance in which I'm obliged to lead, but a dance only they know how to perform.

AC • Poet Donald Hall says that there must be a "distraction of the mind in order for there to be poetry" (27). Given your poetry – intellectually lively and full of wit – I would guess that you would disagree with Hall.

RM • I agree with Hall entirely. The business of poetry is to tease you out of thought, to pull you out of yourself. We live the life of prose, but it's the responsibility of poetry to reverse the polarity.

AC • So in other words, your mind has to be turned down, turned off? Intelligence isn't uppermost to poetry?

RM • Using the famous distinction between the Apollonian and the Dionysian, I don't trust Apollo to write my poetry. I think Apollo *wants* to write my poetry for me. Apollonian intelligence is something you'd want at hand for the process of revision, once you've woken from the Dionysian ecstasies. Actually, I suspect it's more accurate to say that the business of writing is the business of steering the chariot when one of your horses is named Apollo and the other is named Dionysus. The latter is much more easily distracted and wouldn't know a flourish of wit from a gadfly. Here's how I'd like to think the process works: I have to begin not knowing where I'm going. I have to take a risk on every line, trusting to something sub-rational to carry me through. The process of revision is then resisting the tendency to allow the material to collapse into a sort of prose-like transparency, a received but enervating logic.

AC • Aren't you equating intelligence with caution?

RM • There's an image from Schiller I was introduced to early in my training as an actor, when I was learning the art of improvisation – the watcher at the gate. The watcher is the figure who stops all departing impulses with a deadly question: *Is this appropriate?* For a poem to begin, and for a poem to thrive and otherwise survive the process of its making, the watcher at the gates of the mind has to be, if not blinded or asleep, then at least distracted. It's what Frost meant in the line I borrowed from him for the opening poem in *So Rarely*: "a poem is a falling forward into / darkness" (11). As the momentum of the falling forward inevitably begins to wane, the watcher awakens, and the process of refining a form begins.

AC • Yeats said, "It is myself that I remake" in the song (Gibbons 187). Is the poet remade in the making? Is poetry not a revelation of the self but a constituting of a self?

RM • It would have to be both. Poetry would be both a subverting of the self, and a making. There's a curious dialectic between the ineluctability of this burden of the self and these gestures you make as a maker, or creator, when you're attempting to reconfigure the given. You are always speaking from deep within your history, working around inside the limited vocabulary you've managed to put by. But there are, as I say, those moments when you manage to come up with a novel arrangement of the "already received."

AC • In composition, does the body, as the first poem suggests, experience a decomposition: Frost "consider[s] ... the way a body / comes loose in the dark / gradually working free of the heart" (11)?

RM • Yes, but keep in mind that the heart in that poem is "driven" like a nail deep "into the warm pine floor" (11) above Frost's head. Dissolution is the interest of the poet, but you couldn't get more grounded and placed than having your telltale heart nailed to a floor. So in that poem, those coeval impulses we've discussed already, calling them variously Apollonian and Dionysian, or speaking even as you're already spoken, or to escape the self is to make the self, are happening at the same time.

AC • One prose poem asserts that "man is no more than the sum of his remarks, a temporary if surprisingly sticky concatenation of the found and already-fashioned" (46) According to this speaker, persons are the sum of their talk, and talk is just recycled matter. Do you share that notion with your speaker?

RM • No. When Frankenstein's monster – the figure responsible for the remark you quote – offers that bit of wisdom, he manages to both say and unsay the truth of the remark. Frankenstein's monster is compounded out of others. He, more than any, is the sum of his parts, and as such, he's the sum most in search of, most longing for, identity. It's his life's work. My thought was, though, that the moment of his saying this, the moment of recognition that he's doomed to inhabit ground already occupied, is in fact the first original thing he's said.

AC • But in his case, he doesn't say anything remarkable. He says something banal.

RM • But the remark has to be considered in context, which is the lesson Cleanth Brooks teaches us about how to hear Keats' remark about the equivalence of truth and beauty at the end of "Ode on a Grecian Urn" – the meaning lies not simply in the remark but in the context in which the remark is made. In "Frankenstein's Monster," for example, right after parroting that cynical and materialist account of man, the monster speaks of attaching his yellow eye to the children in the playground who think the sun loves them, which is new. The moment we're parsing is very complicated. Even in the act of recognizing how "already said" he is, he opens up the possibility of escaping, however briefly, the jurisdiction of that knowing. It's the usual dividend of the metapoetic. If I could do this book again, Frankenstein's monster might be on the cover. It's the problem: How do we, as poets, move beyond or position ourselves inside the great "already said"? We, whose work is put together out of dead parts. That poem is a sustained attempt to enact a kind of cubist portrait cum monologue – an agglomeration of perspectives on the problem, a welter of voices. Only in toto does the monster utter anything of moment. The patchwork of clichés, item by item, are, as individual pieces, all but unremarkable.

AC • If Icarus frames this collection, Robert Frost is the herald at the door. Frost goes down into the cellar for a poem: "a poem is a falling forward into / darkness said robert frost who late / one evening maybe got up from his chair / made his way to the cellar ..." (11). How does that "falling" relate to Icarus' plunge?

RM • As an invitation to chaos, accident, of pushing beyond. It's the opportunity to make a new darkness.

AC • A poem "fall[s] forward" (11), and Icarus' plunge is recounted numerous times. I would like to know how all the photographs – stopped moments – mentioned in this book (26, 56, 57, 62, 66, 79) relate to "falling."

RM • I suppose I should begin by saying what I think a photograph is. There's something uncanny about a photograph, which arrests time, arranges the living in a dead space. What photographs do – made as they are from activated light – is belie the darkness. They make terrific sense out of life in the sense that they don't seem to be as mediated, as selective, as other modes of description. On this level, they pass themselves off as disinterested, as nearly actual. Unlike the descent into Hell, or the adventure in the wilderness, or the place off the edge of the map where monsters be, the photograph asserts itself as a map of a real and particular place. The authority of the photograph comes from its confidence in its powers of description, in the authority of a common reality, of surface. In this, it's the obverse of a poem. The poem's responsibility, on the other hand, as [Robert] Lowell puts it in "Epilogue," is to give each figure in the photograph his *living* name (838).

AC • Reading a poet's work – poem to poem, book to book – one notices patterns of images, patterns of subject. Are you at ease, or troubled by, such recurrences in your work?

RM • My initial response would be that I'm troubled by the demonstration that my mobile army of metaphors isn't nearly as mobile as I might have imagined. But, frankly, I find I'm awfully interested in the terms of my repetitions, why I return, as Beckett puts it, like a dog chained to its vomit.

AC • Reviewers of the collection made much of its humour, but isn't there also despair at the world's intransigent resistance to the word: "men at war with the speechless / woods dream of sliding their tongues under / axes" (23)?

RM • What's at issue here is an attitude toward nature. I'm not a nature poet. I don't understand, or frankly, have much sympathy for, nature poetry. I don't think a bird is any more appropriate a subject for a poem than a slice of processed cheese. I'd like to think that I'm in agreement here with William Carlos Williams, who said that a poem can be made from anything. The act that my poem describes is the act of someone unable to speak to the woods, who's enacting a radical form of de-personification, if you will, in a desperate attempt to get connected. Rather than sing the woods, the poem sings the dream of songlessness as a means to connect with that which presumably lies outside of speech, of what can be said.

AC   • "[T]he wet root smell" to which Frost descends is "air the house is slow to breathe" (11). Are poetry and domesticity at odds?

RM   • If by domesticity you mean comfort, routine, the warmth of the familiar, I suppose so, though I wonder what Emily Dickinson would say in answer to that question. When Frost goes down into the cellar, he's moving from one realm of the domestic to another. The warmth and light of the rooms above is built upon a wet root smell, as life is built upon death. The imaginative space Frost is after – even as he pulls on the length of butcher string that turns on his basement light – is a chthonic space. The archetype for this little domestic scene is Orpheus' descent, or Dante's, or Christ's, into the underworld. It's the beginning and end.

AC   • And the line "air the house is slow to breathe" (11)?

RM   • Yes. This poem does align poetry and domesticity as being at odds, but they're the elements of a necessary and productive chafing. Each depends on the other, each defines the other.

AC   • The first section of the book, "Dispossessions," is the most domestic. The speakers are variously "In the Garden" (16), "in the backyard snow" (18), remarking "what's left / of last year's / tumid hand" (20), attentive to the effects of winter. And when a better season approaches in these poems, it stops "cold in its tracks" (25). Is nature, which is the prized "possession" of many Canadian poets, what dispossesses these speakers?

RM   • Nature here stands in for what the basement stands for in the poem we were just discussing. It's something final and entirely other. My contact with nature in poems is always a highly mediated contact. It's where I came from and that to which I'll return but, for the present, it provides the outline – describes the edge of, the limits of – me. So yes, nature is a source of dispossession. But so is an open refrigerator door.

AC • If I said that there is nothing particularly Canadian, let alone Maritime, about these poems, would you agree?

RM • I'd be *inclined* to agree. My first impulse is to say that these are poems from nowhere. I mean, I certainly have no sense of writing as a Maritimer, though I've been one for 15 years. But, as Maritimers themselves would be quick to remind me, my 15-year residency constitutes merely the first down payment on a claim that will take several generations to pay off. That is, I'm still "from away" in their view. Come to think, who are these *pur laine* Maritimers to tell me I'm not from here? I'm probably here in a different way than they are, but I'm most decidedly *here*. I only need to start down the 401 and come within a 100 miles of Toronto and Hamilton to be reminded that I'm no longer from there. Wallace Stevens says somewhere in *Adagia* that life is an affair of people, not places, and I absolutely agree. So all that remains to be said in aid of special pleading for my status as Maritimer is, of course, "Some of my best friends are Maritimers." I have little, if any, sense of place. Apart from the homes of my childhood, my sense of place comes from the books I've read and the people I've known.

AC • In *So Rarely*, men alone – or men in pairs – exist on islands of isolation. Besides Frost alone in the cellar, there's Frankenstein's solitary contemplation of his parts (44-46), Rumpelstiltskin's confession that he's "a night feeder, eyes from the bottom of a well" (42), a man drinking alone in a garage (52), van Gogh and Gauguin quarrelling over breakfast (35), and there's Crusoe's letter to Friday (40), the archetypal image of men isolated. Are these figures – literary and historical – versions of the male artist?

RM • To some degree they're all artists, if only because they're engaged in self-fashioning, in representing themselves. The other interest all of these figures have in common has to do with the nature of the masculine, particularly the vicissitudes of how we're asked, as men, to connect with women, with other men. The more I think about your question – about what holds these figures in common – the more I'd say it has to do with the failure to connect, to see the other as anything beyond an extension of the self.

AC • Men appear in groups in "World Series" (51), "Stelco Song in Three Parts" (79-80), and "Siren at the Full-Service Station," where a calendar girl triangulates the attention of three men in a garage (41). Taken collectively, do these poems tell us something about the masculine sensibility in the 20th century?

RM • Those poems are self-consciously masculinist poems, poems which dramatize situations or points of view in which women are fixed in the debilitating gaze. The area of theory which most interests me is gender study, the construction of gender. To study the construction of one gender is to study the construction of the other. So yes, I hope they're saying something about the masculine sensibility, with particular attention paid to the way in which the grand homosocial network that is our culture traffics in women and results in the chronic isolation and sadness of men. To be the man our culture encourages us to be is to be ill-equipped for intimacy with a woman. The speakers in these poems are men who have mistaken themselves and mistaken the world, and that mistake is grounded in how they're reading women.

AC • The speaker in "Siren at the Full-Service Station" is "gobstruck // peering through the porthole of the garage sailing off the / coast of Greece" (41). Is it possible – and is this the point of this and other myth poems in *So Rarely* – to look "through" 20th-century cultural icons, such as the calendar girl, and see the past, attitudes of the past, not as remote but as inherent?

RM • If you mean by "Inherent" that these attitudes, these manners of reading and relegating matters of gender, have come down to us from the ancients, then yes, "inherent" is what I mean. I don't see these attitudes as essential or biological – as written at the level of the cellular – so much as a function of culture, which means that they're textual, subject to change. For the speaker, the moment reproduces, albeit on a terribly banal and workaday level, the scene from *The Odyssey* when Odysseus shepherds his crew past the sirens. The calendar woman, in her "deathless open-toed shoes" (41), is what makes the men's conversation possible, and has always made it possible, at least since Odysseus plied the waters of the world.

AC • As a writer, is your preference for "big time" rather than "my time"?

RM • My interest is in synthesizing the two. The way into the universal, at least as I understand that universal, is through the local, the personal. "My time," if correctly told, if honestly rendered, is a window on "big time." We've known that at least since Wordsworth set out imaginatively for Tintern Abbey. Though you begin in "my time," the interest

ANNE COMPTON

is writing out of that time, of overcoming the self before death does it for you.

AC • One reviewer remarks your "sympathy for women" (Simpson 111), yet we hear one speaker say, "For most men are nothing / without detachment" (86). Supposing that "sympathy" present, how do "sympathy" and "detachment" work together?

RM • I assume what this reviewer is picking up on is my interest in addressing, and thereby rendering less toxic – on behalf of my own two daughters, if for no one else – someone like Rumpelstiltskin. He's a master of detachment, as are Achilles, Frankenstein's monster, Orestes, and so forth. I sympathize not just with the women at the other end of *their* interest, but also with the detached – for those obliged, for whatever reason and to whatever end, to detach.

AC • At some point in the distant future, an anthropologist of 20th-century culture – reading this collection – might remark that such "detachment" coexists with the male gaze: In "One Time" a father directs a "backseat of eyes" – the boys riding in the car – to regard the woman in yellow shorts on a lawn (76).

RM • It would be my hope that the anthropologist of whom you speak would find in my work, and maybe in that poem in particular – which tells a sort of bildungsroman of a gazer – an ironic interest in its machinations. The gaze is everywhere: It's part and parcel of what it means to be gendered. I'd like to think that poems like "One Time" are seen as strategic, as acts of resistance and intervention, as reading against the gaze the father in that poem performs for the boys in the back seat.

AC • Reviewers have rather tiresomely talked about the postmodernism of this collection, the setting, for example, of ancient myth in modern circumstance: Persephone making a phone call to her mother while Hades searches fruitlessly for his briefcase (100-101). Does postmodernist sit well with you as a description of *So Rarely in Our Skins*?

RM • Postmodernism, like deconstruction, is hopelessly fashionable as a term, and regularly misused. It tends to serve as a kind of crude shorthand, especially in reviews, for a very wide range of styles and interests. The hallmark to which these reviewers are referring – the mix of high and low culture – is common in postmodern writing, but it's also common in modernist writing. Try to imagine Joyce or Pound or Eliot without such a mix. Where the book is most consonant with the sort of postmodernism that interests me is the way it seeks to move beyond modernism's confidence in the self, the ways in which it inscribes the self as deeply imbricated in – almost to the point of being a function of – language. The perspective subtending the book is, I think, a decentred one, but it's also marked by a real nostalgia for all of the things God once legitimated in our lives, or at least in my life.

AC • "Watches" (31-32) and "Bovinities" (33-34) are similar in form. Each pithy two-line unit, end-stopped and extractable from the whole, concentrates a quirky truism or maxim. Does Alexander Pope's use of couplets – terse and self-contained – inform these two poems?

RM • If I had to hazard an informing literary source for the two poems you name, it would be Restoration comedy, its wholesale embrace of wit as *the* currency of self-fashioning. "Watches" (31-32) actually began as a ghazal. I remember reading John Thompson and trying to attempt something similar. What failed miserably as a ghazal – probably because I wasn't yet capable of managing that considerable, suggestive, and oblique space you need between images, between couplets – succeeded as the creation of a fairly novel form of utterance, a weird hybrid of Pope and Thompson, seasoned with the stylings of stand-up comic Stephen Wright: Experience is something you don't get until just after you need it.

AC • Isn't metonymy the informing figure here since "Watches" (31-32) is really about time, and the cows (33-34) not only tell but also tell on humans. Does the sideways slide in metonymy make it your preferred figure not only here but throughout?

RM • Both poems are organized along two lines, one metonymic and one metaphoric. As you say, the watches stand in for time, and the cows stand in for humans, which is the metaphoric, but the first half of the metaphor doesn't change from couplet to couplet. Each of the couplets in "Watches" is written over the same space. Each couplet is, in effect, cancelled out by the one that follows. Metonymic logic is the logic of prose, and these couplets are, individually, terribly prosy, as in this couplet from "Watches": "Persons who keep their watches on during sexual intercourse / are bound to arouse suspicion" (31). There's a bit of semantical action around the verb "arouse," but the horses of metaphor are being kept mostly in check throughout. None of that "force that through the green fuse" business here. It's only cumulatively, as a consequence of the accreted substitutions, that these poems aspire to metaphor. I have powerful metonymic inclinations and very high metaphoric aspirations.

AC • Couplets are used in other ways in this collection. They are small steps through story, as in "Lines out of Winter" (27) and "Siren at the Full-Service Station" (41), where the couplets are enjambed, tugging the narrative forward. Do you find couplets to be a particularly flexible form?

RM • It's the smallest unit you can make and still have it function as a stanza. And perhaps more important, it's associated with a particular use in our tradition. The couplet, as in Pope or at the end of a Shakespearean sonnet, seems made for discrete or summary estimation. My use of the couplet is often in conversation with – written over – that traditional function.

AC • So you take the sentence, which your couplets often are, and set it askew?

RM • Yes. The couplet's status as unit – the length of a sentence, a complete thought – allows you to do what Hemingway said Cezanne was doing in his paintings. That is, you set them up, arrange them, as a series of planes, balanced off against each other, occasionally running, through enjambment, into each other. A poem made of couplets has a very particular kind of tectonic, a tension not available in an arrangement of three-or-four line stanzas. Anything longer than two lines, at least on the level of stanza, doesn't lend itself to such dramatic counterpoint. Or counterpoise.

AC • Some of the poems, particularly the prose poems, are out-takes from larger forms – a "Biography" (36-39), a "Confessions" (42-43), Mary Shelley's *Frankenstein* (44-46). Is it your intention to blur the lines between literary forms?

RM • I'm interested in the consequences of writing from within or against a genre. In a way, these are ekphrastic poems, opportunities to see what results, not only when two imaginations enter into relationship – as in Mary Shelley's and mine in the "*Frankenstein*" poem – but two different genres. The "*Frankenstein*" poem – comprised of parts, a collocation of voices, sewn together perspectives – is both homage and a form of assault on the original, a work which, by its very nature, is in constant need of retelling.

AC • Has your engagement with theory determined your approach to poetry?

RM • The influence of theory on my poetry must have been considerable. Theory changed the way I read. I found it very liberating. Very early in my involvement in theory, the distinction between literature and philosophy, and between creative and scholarly writing – indeed, the distinctions we use to construct and maintain any form of discourse – broke down. Not entirely, of course, but in ways which allowed for a wonderful cross-fertilization among categories I'd always assumed needed to be kept discrete. For me, good theory is as exciting, as much a source of estrangement, as the best "creative writing." Which is not to say, by the by, that I'm especially comfortable theorizing what it is I do in poetry. My sense is that in order to write poems, I have to go to the place where theory is not. Theorizing, as we have been here today – about the nature of the poetry I've written – feels awkward, a bit of a violation of the spirit in which the poetry was written. The natural extension of a poem is another poem, not a theory about the poem. Theory allows me to make theory out of poetry, to upgrade my poetics. I can't think it's been of much practical assistance in the actual writing of a single poem. Different, if cognate, skill set.

AC • In "Translation of an Early Draft of a Poem by Basho," the speaker, who is filming a woman in a bath, says to her, "You represent my representation of you / and of course the cruel limits / of representation itself" (86). Does this suggest that the subject of a poem exists only in the poem and does not exist in any real way?

RM • The point the poem is making is a commonplace, at least among idealists: We don't ever have unmediated access to the world. I'm listening to Kenneth Tynan's diaries on an audiotape at the moment, and at one point he makes this discovery about the great characters in Western drama, like Hamlet, Macbeth, Oedipus. What they have in common is that they're pretending to be somebody else. It follows for Tynan, then, that an actor is a person playing a person playing a person. The line you've just cited about representation makes a similar point in metapoetic fashion. The speaker, whose apparent object is the naked woman filmed in her bath, moves to the foreground of his meditation the likelihood that these representations of the naked woman – the dominant locus of secular truth in the West – are like memory itself. We think we have memories, but what we have are memories of memories. What

ANNE COMPTON

this poem is saying about the woman is akin to what Gertrude Stein said of California: *There is no there there* (289). I don't agree with the speaker, but I understand his concern.

AC • In the final section, "Inversions of Other Travels," is subversion, not just inversion, the intent? Penelope – "eyes swimming through seas of their own" – is, for example, the traveller of consequence in "Room with a View" (93), isn't she?

RM • Yes, there are subversions. They're called inversions rather than sub-versions because, as psychology uses the term, "inversion" denotes taking on the role of the opposite gender. Most of the poems in this section are written from the point of view of women, are spoken by the gender opposite my own. In "Room with a View," for example, Penelope's travels, as the artist of the tapestry, are construed as consti-tuting a voyage as meaningful as those of Odysseus.

AC • Her travels end badly. She ends up weeping at having to give up tap-estry now that her husband is home.

RM • When Odysseus arrives, her period of development as an artist is effectively over, the mortgage has come due on the room of her own she's occupied since her husband went off to make himself a name. The subject of the tapestry she made, however, was tapestry. The conceit here is that Penelope as artist – as the maker of a proto-modern mas-terpiece – has actually travelled farther than her husband. Her fate, however, is unwritten. Her rest – the rest of her life – will be silence.

AC • In this section, poems look at myths through the wrong end of a tel-escope. Polyxena seeing Achilles for the first time finds him to be "exactly like in that *Classics Illustrated* comic book" (97); Helen is a "neon-breasted" runway dancer (94-96); and from Hades, Persephone phones home (100-101). Are you insisting upon the situatedness of our understanding of the Greek stories?

RM • Our understanding of the Greeks is always situated. The point at which any age's horizon fuses with the Greek horizon is always changing. So my interest in putting Persephone on a phone shaped like the jawbone of a hero isn't to put my capacity for whimsy on display, as one reviewer seemed to think, but to point out that these myths always and ineluctably have to pass through a glass made dark by the fact that, unlike the Greeks, we know what it is to talk to our mothers on the phone. I wouldn't presume anything like an understanding of how the Greeks understood Persephone. I'm not now, nor have I ever been, an ancient Greek farmer. Practically, I am a bit of an essentialist when it comes to Greek myth: I believe there's some germ of the eternal or the universal housed in those stories, if only because those stories were so instrumental in making us who we are. To get at that germ, the story needs to be retold. Telling a myth is a form of confessionalism. When I tell the story of Persephone, I'm doing what dreamers do when they tell the "facts" of their dreams: Secondary revision. It's in the suppression, invention, and arrangement of the given – in this case, the story of Persephone – that I *re-present* myself. Which is why the term "confessionalism," at least as applied to Lowell and company, is so dubious as a term of reference. *Life Studies* is no more confessional than Eliot's "Love Song of J. Alfred Prufrock."

AC   • You might say that the high is brought low in *So Rarely*. Is irreverence a healthy stance in a poet just as skepticism is a necessary attribute in a critic?

RM   • Yes. But the ghost the skeptic inevitably invokes, and probably is always serving in some respect, is the figure of the true believer, the person capable of making the Kierkegaardian leap of faith. Which, come to think, is another reason why Icarus is the figure around which *So Rarely* is organized. In some sense, the only way I can keep the possibility of belief alive is through the rigorous exercise of skepticism. The skeptical poet is, for me at least, the healthy poet, which may be why political poetry is so often deadly. If you know where you're going at the beginning of the poem, if you're convinced already of the ethical or moral reality of the position you're about to embroider, the poem is effectively over.

AC   • Early on in the new manuscript, *Museum Absconditum*, a speaker at a "New Year's Eve house party," observes: "Dark fields under ice; veneer of nothing / over everything; / breath merely / damaged air" (22). Because of this and other poems, *Museum* seems both more elliptical and more nihilistic than *So Rarely*. Would you agree?

RM   • I'd like to think I'm exploring darker waters in this book, and with greater concentration, greater conviction. Elliptical? I do know that I'm less enamoured with narrative, and the sundry joys of the metonymic we discussed above, which, not surprisingly, has occasioned a greater reliance on metaphor and the magic thinking it allows. I'm also older and that much closer to death than the fellow who might have spoken to you before the publication of *So Rarely*. And not just in terms of the vulgar count of years. What aged me enormously – and in an entirely good way – was publishing a first book of poetry. It put paid to a whole welter of cherished, if woefully unexamined, beliefs of the Parnassian kind, as in: Poetry matters to anyone beyond a crushingly small circle, or good writing changes things. A lot of holdovers from a much more romantic, much younger man. It's a good thing because the gunnels are now clear for a different kind of action.

AC • Given a poem like "The transfiguration of the commonplace" (4-6), which collapses do-it-yourself TV and Christ the carpenter, is it fair to say that in *Museum Absconditum*, the new collection, you are doing with religious material – Christ, the Virgin, Lazarus, Brébeuf – what you did with the Greek tales in *So Rarely*?

RM • I've visited Athens; now it's time for Jerusalem. Given that I was raised much closer to Jerusalem than Athens, the treatment of the Judeo-Christian, which is such an important part of *Museum*, likely constitutes a return to more deeply held, more primitive models of faith. And by faith I simply mean models of connection between the material and the transcendental.

AC • In poems such as "Not for nothing: a triptych" (7-8), which is about the present-day sightseers of manifestations of Christ and the Virgin, you are mocking not the sightseers, but the long history of belief. That poem ends in the garden "the morning Adam spotted God shimmying / into a snakeskin suit which, figuratively speaking, / damn near ruined the surprise" (8). How do you get the tone right in doing that?

RM • I'm not sure that I have the tone right yet. But keep in mind that the second panel of that triptych says, "Be happy for them. Their foolish-ness / isn't yours to mock." That's meant to be taken seriously, as working in tandem with the poem's hoisting of people who would drive a thousand miles to see the image of the Virgin in the rust of a derelict fridge, which, by the way, is a true story. The key to the whole approach and avoidance business this poem depicts with believers is a genuine respect for these and all the other holy fools on what look to me like bootless excursions in the old RV. In drawing them into the poem, I want them to tell me more about what it is that keeps these modern folks a' goin' on pilgrimage, and, just as important, I'd like to put them in conversation with what I think I know about their religion.

AC • I could say of your tone what Seamus Heaney says of a fellow Irish poet, your "gaiety takes the harm out of it" (*Miller* 56). Still, I want to know if a serious inquiry into matters of belief is going on here.

RM • Belief for me these days is what sex used to be: I think about it all the time. And if I can manage a poem with both in it – God knows, I've tried – well, that's like discovering two bloods in one as Donne said of the flea.

AC • This first section of *Museum* relates, overlays, collapses – whatever verb is right – the Christian story and westerns. Explain that juxtaposition.

RM • The western is among the most compelling of the secular, if masculinist, hymns North American culture sings to itself. I respond on a very visceral level to the western. I find them terribly moving. Really, I could go on and on about them, but perhaps it will suffice to say that I take the western seriously, that I find it as complex and beautiful a genre as those at the other end of the cultural spectrum. Westerns are conversations with God.

AC • Can the "Great Lantern of the West" (12) still light up corners of our existence?

RM • Absolutely, pilgrim.

AC • In *So Rarely*, the longer pieces are prose poems. In *Museum*, there are fewer of those, but there are lyrics of considerable length. What explains that shift?

RM • Here's what I'd like to think explains the shift: The sheer scale of the ideas I'm wrestling with demands a larger canvas upon which to work. Now here's what's probably happening: A vestigial sense of prose's scale is still making its influence felt. I don't think of myself as someone who can write a longer poem. My sense is I always write too little.

AC • As well, in this collection, you've really taken possession of the dramatic monologue. Is that a natural medium for someone who's been in the theatre?

RM • Absolutely. My thinking at this point is that the third book, tentatively entitled "Figuring Ground," will be comprised exclusively of dramatic monologues. Voice is everything to me as a poet.

ANNE COMPTON

AC • A half-dozen fairy tales undergo saucy transformations in *Museum*. Jack, who wanders into "The Little Old Lady Who Lived in a Shoe" (31), asks, "Why don't they ever tell it true?" Is that your aim in these retellings?

RM • I wouldn't regard my retelling of these fairy tales as any less or any more true than the originals, which, as you know, are extremely unstable entities in their own right. Every age tells the same tales in subtly different fashion. Recognizing how larded each retelling is with the interests of the culture doing the telling – how any given age effectively wears any text as a mask through which it speaks – is a liberating discovery. So the telling I'm offering of these fairy tales, like the retellings of any of the texts I reinvent, is in no way to insist on having the last word. It's the opposite: I want to underscore how impossible a last word is on these matters.

AC • Whereas research has shown that many of these tales have political underpinnings, your intent seems to be to sexualize the tales. Are you simply having fun? Or are you bringing forward what you believe to be already present?

RM • The research with which I'm familiar is actually more insistent on the issue of sex than on the political. So the sex you see happening in my retellings is simply my attempt to foreground and make manifest what is already latent and active and effective in the original versions. Why does the little old lady have so many children and no husband? Why does she live in a shoe, of all things? Is the shoe, as [Bruno] Bettelheim said of Cinderella's glass slipper, a displacement for the vagina? I doubt it, but that woman does seem to be inordinately and irresponsibly fertile. And why does she whip them all soundly before putting them to bed? By its very nature – open-ended, replete with narrative lesion – fairy tales, like Rorschach ink blots, demand we fill in the blanks.

AC • Is carnivalesque, as understood in Bakhtinian terms, the spirit you are after in the first sections of this new collection?

RM • If by carnival you mean inversion, reversal of roles, invoking the ying to the official discourse's yang, I'm definitely writing in that spirit. But I want to be careful here not to run off to join the circus without leaving a nice note. For carnival is, in some key respects, the *zeitgeist de jour*. What I mean is that, these days everybody wants to be the Wife of Bath. Not on a deep or genuinely subversive level, of course. Given that the road to Canterbury is lined with sisters wearing their honorary scarlet stockings, the carnivalesque just isn't what it used to be. This isn't to say that carnival isn't always available and operative so much as to underscore the fact that it's always being co-opted, all the better to sell us the latest iteration of Coke. All poetry and, indeed, all art is on the side of carnival.

AC • Historically there's a deep connection between the lyric and innerness, but there's also a contemporary aesthetic, as the poet Alan Williamson says, that distrusts innerness (87). Do your retellings and your dramatic monologues represent an aversion to innerness?

RM • How does the maxim go – there's nothing more boring in an artist than sincerity? Claims of innerness should always be distrusted. Feeling something deeply is entirely irrelevant to the business of making deep feeling a felt thing in a poem. That is, making a form sufficient to house deep feeling is a completely different matter. I agree there's a contemporary aesthetic that feels that innerness is too easy to fake.

AC • If men on their own is a common situation in *So Rarely*, *Museum* is interested in women on their own in towers ("Rapunzel" 32) and in suites of rooms ("*Tous les femmes*" 42). These women are more interested in their relationships with one another than with male visitors. Is this about the sadness of men or the independent sexuality of women?

RM • Both. Certainly in the poems you mention, they're one and the same thing. Kenneth Tynan, coincidentally enough, notes at one point in his diaries that all men fear and envy women (audiotape). Men break my heart. We're so sad, so temporary, so needy, so perishable. Consequently, I've always been a woman's man. Not, I hasten to add, a lady's man. Not my end of the field, as my good friend Kenneth Tynan, no doubt, used to say. Probably comes from having a powerful mother. Who knows?

AC • If Icarus is the abiding figure of *So Rarely*, Prufrock dominates in *Museum*. How might I understand this shift from doomed boy to listless, aging man?

RM • It certainly wasn't a conscious shift of persona. Perhaps *So Rarely* drove a stake through the heart of the spinning boy who'd waited so long to unpack his foolish heart. My affinity for the aging Prufrock is a longstanding one. I'm interested in the life lived in the absence of mermaids singing … apart, that is, from each to each.

AC   • Does the Prufrock persona and situation enable you to deal with romantic matters in a covert way?

RM   • Yes, though I hardly think it's covert. Oblique, I'll grant you, but Prufrock's inability to connect to either the talking women or the mermaids – or, more to the point, what they stand for – is written all over him. At my age, I understand better how monumental an undertaking the proper eating of a peach can be.

AC   • Quite apart from Prufrock, *Museum* is a poetry that explores diminishment, as for example "Father, at sea" (61-62), where the Achilles-proportioned father ends up tending a fish pond. Is the exploration of a father's narrative, in this and in other poems, a way for you to explore where you are now?

RM   • The decline and now imminent death of my father is much on my mind in this collection. More and more, I've got into the habit of trying to remember him when he was my present age. I can't, of course. Not really. Maybe it's because when I try to remember such a thing, the two of us – me and the him that was – end up, in effect, occupying the same ground. I do think of him, as you say, as a sort of scout, there on the sad height, as [Dylan] Thomas said, preparing the way, moving beyond my reach.

AC   • In spite of its variety of voices, this manuscript is, finally, in places, intimate, even autobiographical, in reference. Are the many voices, many masks, in fact mirrors?

RM   • I'm glad to hear you characterize the work as "intimate," given what you said earlier about the contemporary animus toward innerness. What's the difference between a mask – a persona – and a mirror? The mask is the healthier mode of narcissism in that it effects a translation of the self, obliges the self to enter into the space of some other. Wearing a mask can be quite liberating. It's one of the first things you're trained to use as an actor. We tend to think of the mask as a form of hypocrisy, which is a holdover from our medieval nervousness about the non-absolute self. Unlike the curious early Christians, for whom actors, as professional liars, were little better than prostitutes with pretensions, the Greeks understood the possibilities for the soul's enlargement when you take on another voice, cover your face with a mask. The Greek word for actor is *hypocrites*, from which we've fashioned an insult, a failure of character. For them, acting was a means of making the gods present: For us, it's a form of duplicity, a falling away from the self. Mirrors, unlike mask, are deadly; dead and deadly. They're traps for the self. I daresay whenever a mirror appears in my poetry, the work it's doing isn't salubrious. Masks open the self. Mirrors close it down.

AC • Because of all the references, later in *Museum*, to "country" – the one from which we depart, the one to which the dead go – I couldn't help but think of Hamlet's "The undiscover'd country from whose bourn / No traveler returns, puzzles the will…." Is this the puzzle that preoccupies you now?

RM • Yes. Death is the master subject, the end and object of my life's work. If I'm not writing about death, I'm not writing.

WORKS CITED
— • —

Berger, Maxianne. Review of *So Rarely in Our Skins*, by Robert Moore. *Arc* 51 (Winter 2003): 134-35.

Cran, E.E. "Two skilled voices, one master poet." *New Brunswick Reader* 4 January, 2003: 15.

Gibbons, Reginald. "Poetry and Self-Making." *Poets Teaching Poets: Self and the World*. Eds. Gregory Orr and Ellen Bryant Voigt. Ann Arbor: U of Michigan P, 1996. 197-206.

Hall, Donald. *Breakfast Served Any Time All Day: Essays on Poetry New and Selected*. Ann Arbor: U of Michigan P, 2003.

Hughes, Ted. "The Thought-Fox." *New Selected Poems 1957-1994*. London: Faber and Faber, 1995. 3.

Lowell, Robert. *Collected Poems*. Eds. Frank Bidart and David Gewanter. New York: Farrar, Straus and Giroux, 2003.

MacLeod, Sue. "Witty, wild, witchy, weighty". *Atlantic Books Today* 38 (Winter 2002): 22.

Miller Karl. *Seamus Heaney in Conversation with Karl Miller*. London: Between the Lines, 2000.

Moore, Robert. "The Land of Lowell." Rev. of *Collected Poems*, by Robert Lowell. *Books in Canada* 33.4 (June-July 2004): 34-35.

– – – . *Museum Absconditum*. Toronto: Wolsak & Wynn. Forthcoming 2006.

– – – . *So Rarely in Our Skins*. Winnipeg: Muses' Company, 2002.

Pannell, Chris. Rev. of *So Rarely in Our Skins*, by Robert Moore. *Antigonish Review* 134 (Fall 2003): 103-07.

Simpson, Anne. "Things That Shine Through." Rev. of *So Rarely in Our Skins,* by Robert Moore. *Fiddlehead* 217 (Autumn 2003): 111-12.

Stein, Gertrude. *Everybody's Autobiography*. New York: Random House, 1937.

Wells, Zach. "Violent Delights and Private Whims." Rev. of *So Rarely* in *Our Skins*, by Robert Moore. *Books in Canada* 33.3 (April-May 2004): 34-35.

Williamson, Alan. "Falling off the World: Poetry and Innerness." *Poets Teaching Poets: Self and the World*. Eds. Gregory Orr and Ellen Bryant Voigt. Ann Arbor: U of Michigan P, 1996. 84-94.

Wordsworth, William. "Resolution and Independence." *William Wordsworth's The Prelude with a selection from the Shorter Poems, the Sonnets, The Recluse, and the Excursion*. Ed. Carlos Baker. New York: Holt, Rinehart and Winston, 1948: 136-41.

AN ADMIRABLE CLARITY:
ROSS LECKIE'S NEW COLLECTION, *GRAVITY'S PLUMB LINE*

Director of the Creative Writing Program at the University of New Brunswick, editor of *The Fiddlehead*, and poetry editor at Goose Lane Editions, Ross Leckie is the author of three collections of poetry – *A Slow Light* (1983), *The Authority of Roses* (1997), and *Gravity's Plumb Line* (2005). His most recent collection was the subject of our conversation on a hot June day in Fredericton, in 2005. In *Gravity's Plumb Line*, Leckie writes about the towns, rivers, and lakes of New Brunswick, where he took up residence in 1997. The quiet objectivity of the poems belies the gusto and concentration that he brings to the scrutiny of objects and places. Clarity, balance, and civility characterize the latest collection, as they do the earlier ones. Leckie is the author, as well, of critical essays on Cultural Studies and on the American sublime, an interest that dates from the period of his doctoral studies at the University of Toronto. Leckie grew up in Montreal and lived in Toronto for 10 years, first as a student and then, some years later – after his post-doctoral work at Princeton – as a lecturer at the University of Toronto. Immediately before moving to New Brunswick, he taught at the University of Northern British Columbia, Prince George, for three years.

AC   • Helen Vendler says, "Even the most intellectual poets begin as children enthralled by the senses through which the world is made known to them" (13). Do you think that it is in childhood one becomes a poet even though the work may not happen until adulthood?

RL   • In my own case, I don't think so. I had no sense of a vocation or calling as a poet or as any other kind of writer until I was in college. I always thought I was going to be a physicist. I do think there were things about childhood that were important to me. I was always interested in philosophical conundra. I've written poems about childhood, and I think of those as a form of research – in a literal way – an attempt to remember the things from childhood that haunt me in a particular way, unconscious things that I'm trying to make articulate. The more sensual poems about childhood are attempts to grasp what must have seemed transient at the time and certainly seems very evanescent now.

AC • The grip of the mind on the perception or thought that will become the poem: Can you describe that state for me?

RL • I guess the state of mind, in my case, is meditative. It's a kind of an attunement, an opening of the mind to the voices that come from wherever they come from. Typically, it starts with images. I begin with place, or with something that has attracted my visual attention, and then I look for an aural quality that will develop that perception. Most of the poems begin with a visual cue. There are exceptions. The poem "One Gives Way" began when I heard a line, the music of a line, "In the deadlocked heat / of summer's breathy mumble / one leaf can bear no more / and tumbles // into shimmered grass" (*Authority of Roses* 24). But that's pretty rare.

AC • What often happens in the plot of a Leckie poem is a juxtaposition of things remote in kind, a plummeting spider and a moon landing, for example: "A slender thread of silk connects these two / events and catches them in the web's // cradle of concentration" (*Gravity* 36). A line later that "cradle of concentration" becomes "this long corridor," actual perhaps, but also metaphoric. Is a poem, temporally speaking, a "long corridor"?

RL • Poetry inhabits time. I'm really resistant to those theories – Pound's being an obvious one – of poetry creating an instant or moment in time that somehow then becomes transcendent to the quotidian flow of space-time. To me, time is built into everything we do. Poetry has to recognize that. It's not transcending time, but working with time's gravity.

AC • An interior world meets an exterior world: The poem is the causeway that the poet crosses, beginning at one end or another. Where do you begin?

RL • Typically, with the exterior world, although – in the received idea of objective correlative – I think that there's something out there that res-onates with some interior, emotional state. Poetry is constructed out of the back and forth between those two things. There's an arc between. Poetry is attempting to find that moving line between inner and outer.

ANNE COMPTON

It's attempting to define where that threshold of meeting is rather than defining what is out there or in here. Obviously, that line can only be identified by the out there and in here. Any metaphor has to know what's out and what's in, although it may purposefully confuse the two.

AC • Charles Simic says that "all lyric poems are narcissistic. They are the earliest form of personal ads" (Huntington et al. 55). Even if a collection is not self-referential – and *Gravity* is not – doesn't it offer a history of what has pressed upon a mind, upon "the impressionable gravel of the mind" (46) as one poem puts it?

RL • One of the peculiarities of my poetry, especially in *Gravity*, is the relative absence of the first-person pronoun, which just doesn't seem very congenial to me. Poetry is obviously registering a particular self because the very language that we use is reflected through our personality, our habits of thought, our experiences to this stage but, in my view, poetry is also self-effacing. There's a quality in writing that says to the reader, "I'm here, but I'm also trying not to be here. I'm trying to draw your attention to the ways in which I am not here at the moment, and the ways you are here, or perhaps not here." There's a lot of interplay in the activity of certain kinds of metaphor to suggest both absence and presence. Poetry can be full of self and yet not be egocentric or narcissistic.

AC • Are you a poet some days? Or are you a poet every day, all the time?

RL • I'm a poet some days. There are way too many other things going on to think about poetry all the time. I've been through those times where I say that I'm going to write so much every day. One of the things that happens to me when I do that is I run dry really fast. Poetry, for me, is not one large aquifer that I can draw on daily. It's little sloughs of water here and there that I stumble across. There are many days when I don't think of poetry in any way, let alone write a poem.

AC • Your academic interest is the sublime, particularly the American sublime. Does the poetry that you find yourself writing inform and direct your academic interests?

RL • What interests me in the sublime are questions of absence and superfluity in poetry, and in our experience of the world. The sublime has been traditionally talked about as an encounter with the infinite or something much larger than the self – the sublime in magnitude – but, for me, the sublime is really more about understanding the difference between a blankness, or absence, and the idea that the world is present to the observer in an overabundance. I remember my brother describing the Hermitage museum in St. Petersburg. They had all this artwork, which they hung over the walls of this gorgeous palace, but since they had lots left over, they filled in all the leftover corners. Similarly, you have the sense that nature is filling in space and over-laying things on top of one another. It's not just something that is: It *is* and then it is more. Ontology is constantly overflowing its boundaries. There's a superfluity of things in the world, and the self has that elasticity to encompass, and understand, both the blank and the overly full.

AC • In your opinion, do linguistic habits more than anything else – subject matter, for instance – distinguish one poet from another?

RL • Yes and no. I do think that one can see in each poet distinct linguistic habits – distinct voices and styles. Those habits are integral to a way of seeing that is somehow uniquely different from everyone else's – challenging and provocative – and, at the same time, a welcoming gesture, an invitation to see in that way. On the other hand, I think you could probably distinguish poets just as easily by subject matter. When it comes to subject matter, for example, you could say, "Well, Canadian poetry is dominated by nature poets." I don't know whether that's true or not, but let's just take that as a presupposition. The moment you begin to break down towards detail, you suddenly discover that what appeared to be the same subject matter is full of difference. Subject matter is far more important to poetry than 20th-century poetics has tended to make it out to be. It is not trivial or secondary to the linguistic body.

AC • Do you think that analysis of a poem's components damages a poem?

RL • The idea that you must resist analysis in order to sustain some sort of magic or some kind of ecstatic or euphoric relationship to what is gorgeous and glorious in the poem is just wrong. You can pick up some poem for the very first time and read it and go, "Wow, that is amazing" and not really be sure why. That sense of "wow" does not last very long if you don't start asking questions as to why that poem is so amazing. And what happens, of course, is that as you take it apart, your intellect engages with various components of that poem and understands why this works this way and why that works that way. These questions can seem quite detached from the emotional experience of the poem but, of course, they aren't. The analytical mind and the emotional brain are interacting constantly, flickering back and forth. An early reading can be very simplistic and miss so many marvellous things, even as you're aware that the poem is marvellous. For me, [John] Ashbery was the great proof of this. I remember the first time I read Ashbery thinking, *I have absolutely no idea what he's talking about, but I know it's there. I can feel it.* I wanted to know how those poems worked so I spent a lot of time analysing Ashbery. It was exciting to try and figure out how those poems work.

AC   • Many poets – in the absence of end rhyme – rely on alliteration, but you make more use than most of assonance. Tell me what this going away and coming back to a vowel sound does for a poem?

RL   • Vowels in a poem have a music that is more subtle than consonant sounds. It's extremely difficult to write alliterative poetry that doesn't sound alliterative, whereas assonance is less obvious. I think it has something to do with the limited number of sounds that the vowels give and so we get so used to hearing them and we don't notice them as clearly as the consonantal sounds. Assonance is that very quiet sound that you are not aware of, and yet it can be very influential to the sound patterns in a poem. The other thing is that assonance allows a more sinuous sense of variation in sound. To be perfectly honest, I find the variation of vowel sounds in their range far more interesting than, say, Christian Bök's *Eunoia,* where he uses one particular vowel for the types of sounds that can emanate from the same letter. One of the things I find disheartening about that book is the foregrounding of assonance. Why would you do that when you can use it much more subtly in a quiet fashion?

AC   • Would you agree that alliteration hastens a poem, assonance slows it down?

RL   • I think more in terms of syntax when I think of the question of pacing. But exactly how that works sometimes perplexes me. For example, you have the feeling that short sentences are fast and long sentences are slow, and yet when you get something that's really rhapsodic, it tends to be in very long sentences. I can think of passages in Milton, for example, that seem very fast because of that rhapsodic quality even though the sentences are very long. So the question of pacing is one that is really complicated and probably has to do with a whole variety of factors: The syntactical structures, the number and kinds of pauses built into the poem, the endstops, the caesurae, as well as the consonance and assonance that's being used. There are, obviously, sounds that require the voice to kind of shape it. With sounds that are harder, you have to shape the mouth in a certain kind of way to get the sound. It makes the sound slower because it takes you more time to shape your mouth, and "U" sounds tend to have that quality. One of the things that gives a poem something of an illusory feel of being closer to the world occurs when the sounds are short and the beats are heavy.

AC   • I turn to a poem like "Easter, Queen's County," the cow poem, and find pairs of assonantal sounds – "shuffle" and "bump," followed in the next verse by "grunt and snuffle as they grind / shoulder to flank" (37), assonance deepened by internal rhyme, with alliteration also present. Does a poem proceed for you through a narrative of sound?

RL   • There is a narrative of sound in the poems that I like best. A narrative, by definition, is something that is moving through time, and sound patterns also move through time. Even if they're repeating, they're, by definition, temporal. Sound pattern is one way of creating the measure of a poem.

AC   • Yet another mode of sound patterning happens in "Easter, Queen's County." "[C]ollegial," "collision," "cold" occur in three successive lines. All of this is linked in the poem to a music befitting Easter Sunday. Is it your contention that a poem should have a kind of "orchestral beauty" (*Miller* 40)?

RL   • That's what I'm most drawn to in other people's writing – poems that have a clear sense of their own music. People say, "You seem to have an aversion to the anecdotal, ironic school of Canadian poetry." Other people call it narrative poetry, but I think what they mean is this sort of storytelling that we've come to associate with [Al] Purdy, [Lorna] Crozier, and others. I think a number of people who are interested in that kind of writing are more interested in the sensational details of the anecdote than they are in the music that's going to put that story together. The simple telling of the story is what they see as primary. I look at it and think, *This is flat.* It sounds flat. And, therefore, the story cannot sustain itself. This is a poem that has lost its sense of orchestral music. And when you use the word "orchestral," you're not just talking about sound that's harmonious. There's contrapuntal sound, dissonant sound, 12-tone scales, and all of that. If you follow through on the metaphor of the orchestra, then the conductor is at the front, calling on different sections of instrumentation to enter at different times.

               ANNE COMPTON

Sometimes you have passages when the strings are playing, sometimes only the clarinets, or woodwinds, and then you have them all coming together in every imaginable combination. Assonance is, obviously, one of those forms of music, and in that orchestra metaphor, I'd say assonance is more like the basses and violas, the quiet under-sounds, as opposed to the consonants, which can sound like the brass section.

AC • Most people would deem simile the simplest of tropes. I'm astonished by what you can do with a simile, as for example: "The pulp of apple differs from chiseled / granite by its glistening" (44). Because an apple differs from granite in its "glistening," the other comparison – the pulp's *likeness* to "chiselled / granite" – is held in place. Is that strategy or accident?

RL • Well, I hope it's strategy, but it was probably accident! Simile can be a way of accentuating the continuity of things that in their relation are far-fetched. In "Footfall" (19), the poem you quoted earlier, putting together the idea of the little spider landing on the desk and a lunar module landing on the moon was whimsical. At the time, I didn't really know how suggestive it was. What's holding something together is "the web's // cradle of concentration" (36). But simile can also be a way of noting that those things are *really* different, and they're coming together for one particular quality. The simile, in some ways, is already deconstructing itself. In the act of simile, you're comparing certain qualities of each thing as being similar to each other even as you know that other qualities of those two things are different from each other. What I want to ask is: At what point do the things cohere? At what point are we holding in our minds the things, and not the qualities? At what point is a quality not a thing in itself? At what point do those invert, and the quality becomes the thing and what we thought was the thing is actually a quality of the new thing?

AC • You like to install a metaphor and then tug it in different directions, as with the quilting metaphor of "Textures" (41), but you also do something more complicated. "Psyche" begins with a simile that likens the tongues of irises to the tongues of "lolling ... dogs" and the "purple splotches" of the irises to "paw prints." And then, in a surprise move, "their crania nodding" are like "human heads" bent over "summer books / whose plots are crisp and narrow as the stem of an / iris might be ..." (42). Comparing "plots" to iris "stem[s]," you have collapsed vehicle and tenor, haven't you?

RL • When I say "iris," we think of a flower, but what are we really thinking about when we think of the flower? We're thinking of the blossom, right? When we say "iris," we think of the blossom because we're distinguishing it from, say, tulip. And also it's the colour we're interested in. So we've already broken this object apart in our minds in order to describe it in this way. If I begin with the flower and compare it to one thing and then another thing and then come back to the stem and suggest that the stem is now the most important thing, which part is the iris? Is it the blossom or the stem? Is it the whole thing? Do we hold the whole thing in our mind at once? The thing is not as integral as we might like to think. Therefore, in the associative patterns of the metaphor, we're constantly moving from possibility to possibility in order to see relations that don't occur if we are held to what I think of as a dichotomous version of metaphor – whether that's vehicle and tenor or some other elaboration of dualism.

AC • In posing that question, I was interested in the way in which you develop a simile.

RL • Certain kinds of metaphors are so apt that there seems to be a kind of inevitability to the metaphor itself, and when one reads a poem with a striking metaphor, one feels compelled by it, feels a certain kind of implosion into the bonding that the metaphor has accomplished. A simile allows us to realize that as cohesive as that metaphor could seem, it's striking because it's so suggestive across a number of associative fields. And so by pulling apart those associative fields with the tool of simile, we can move from field to field to field. A metaphor arrives and you see two things colliding, an impact, a collision of worlds. There's tremendous excitement in seeing how those two things collide together, but the life of the metaphor is, ultimately, in the ways in which the associations you didn't see were always already there. They were inherent in the metaphor, and so the metaphor is always a breaking away from that collision as much as a moving into it. The simile allows us to see some of those steps because a simile is suggesting a greater distance. We don't allow the identity formation in a simile. We don't allow the collision. We're always saying the collision never quite happened.

AC • Later in *Gravity*, the poem "Character" begins "The profile of the face was stamped in bronze / as if on a coin" (87), after which the comparative term, the coin, itself becomes an object in the poem, one that measures character's lack of self-knowledge. This move – let's call it the substantiation of the simile – throws the weight on the comparative term, doesn't it?

RL • To me that's just so interesting. You begin by thinking that this is your topic and that the metaphor is going to support the topic, but it just doesn't seem to work that way for me. The comparative term already has a whole set of associations, some of which, obviously, are going to lead you back to what you thought the topic was, which, in this case, is character. And, of course, there's a certain self-reflexive quality in the poem at that point because the coin gets flipped, and as it's spinning, it's suggestive of possibility – heads, tails, and so on – but in the poem, the person is unaware of those possibilities in the same way that we can become unaware of time, that time is always spinning its way through character. We start off with character stamped as if it were frozen, and the coin seems to be representative of that: Character is as solid as a coin, metallic and solid.

AC • The coin liberates itself, and shows how unfixed character is?

RL • Put simplistically, consciousness always thinks of itself as unified. I'm the same person now as I was 10 minutes ago, or 10 years ago, from the point of view of consciousness. There's this continuous thing that is my perceiving "I," my awareness. To stop and consider how much that's changed through time gives people a sense of the uncanny. I don't mean to play too heavily, though, on that idea of the unstable and unreliable because I do believe in continuity. I don't hold too much with ideas that say that relativity is all, and continuity is nothing. I believe in continuity, and I believe in many respects I am the same person I was when I was five years old. Perhaps in the most important respects, I am the same person, and consciousness is the record of that historical continuity. Although people talk about the fluidity of memory, there is, nonetheless, the historical record. We can sometimes put memory to the test against the historical record. Literary critics who have a biographical bent will discover the poet was at this place and saw these things, and doesn't that inform the poem and help us understand more about the poem? And, yes, I think it does. I enjoy that kind of biographical criticism, the filling in of context. It really helps me enjoy Elizabeth Bishop's poems to know she was in Nova Scotia, and she was related to these people and she lived in this house so long. That helps me understand why somebody who rarely had the opportunity to return to Nova Scotia was, nonetheless, obsessed with the place and kept writing about it through all of her life.

AC • You like to flex a sound through a whole stanza and explore a metaphor through the length of a poem. In writing, do you think in terms of the whole poem rather than the line?

RL • Over the last 15 years or so, I have tended to think far more of sentences instead of lines. Sentences have tended to be more important to me than the line and perhaps that's why blank verse is so appealing. It gave me a sense of measure that I could worry about after the fact. What I really wanted to do was create these marvellous sentences.

AC • When you use a stand-alone metaphor, as different from an extended metaphor, it is frequently a noun-phrase metaphor – "the guitar notes / of the ice" (20); "the impressionable gravel of the mind" (46).

RL • What's going on there is the torque of the sentence. Even little things like the proleptic devices, or the relative pronouns or the conjunctions or what have you, have already indicated a set of relationships within which that metaphor is going to be held or contained. The smaller noun-phrase metaphor is going to be already given shape by what's come before or what's going to come after. Metaphors can be stronger or weaker depending on the syntax that leads in and out of them. Syntax has some kind of strange pull on how the metaphor is going to be understood.

AC • Wit is subtle rather than flashy in your poetry and often involves metaphor, but wit is present in other ways, as for instance in the parodic ornithology of "The Ice Bird" (31-32).

RL • The kind of humour I most admire is sly humour. The humour that sneaks up on you and is quite laconic. One of the things I really admire about people in the Maritimes is that they love wry humour and laconic wit. But in "The Ice Bird" (31-32), I was definitely trying to imitate metaphysical wit. I wanted that poem to be a kind of contemporary equivalent to Donne. "A Valediction: Forbidding Mourning" might be somewhere behind that poem's playfulness. I was definitely thinking this poem will be out there advertising its play and wit.

AC • Many of the poems of Section 2 focusing upon objects – irises, oranges, apples – use words such as "Something" (42) or "Somehow"

(43) as if the object withheld revelation. Is this not-quite-knowing an attitude of awe?

RL • For me, it's more often a question of surprise, that sense of something that you've always known suddenly revealing itself to be there. There is something tentative, obviously, about those words "somehow," "something." I'm trying to get at a feeling of evanescence not just in terms of transitory nature – its mutability – but also the evanescence of perception when you look at something. There's a sense, *Is it there, or not there?* There's an absence of presence working simultaneously through the object that I find fascinating. It's that sense of space between existence and nothingness in which, I think, most things adhere. We tend to think of these solid things – table, book, glass – as stable, and they just aren't that stable. There's a flux and an uncertainty about all things. I'm interested in the movement from the mundane to that sense of presence and absence lurking in the mundane. You can suddenly become aware of it in a small object.

AC • "Apples" are "perfections that paradise couldn't hold" (44). From apples "A firmament / is deduced," complete with "curvature" of sky, "nebulae," and "gravity." Are we to understand that each small thing – ordinary, homely – is a universe?

RL • What I'm interested in is the sense of the scalability of things. Chaos theory suggests that there's a reiterative nature in things that repeats in smaller and larger forms. Well, of course, that mathematical process doesn't really suggest that the universe is like an apple. There isn't anything like an apple out there on the grand scale. But there is something about an apple that suggests its own completion in a way that the universe does, and its own imperfections.

AC • The similarity of hands and leaves occurs more than once in this book (35, 39, 48), but in "Variations After a Summer Storm," a third hand is introduced: "But what hand wrought this landscaping, / this brush of lawn that sweeps across the hill // in its weightless sunlight and says, 'Shadow me. / Lay your small palm of night on my shoulder'" (48). The human hand, hand-shaped leaves, and this third hand – what are the relationships here?

RL • As an adult, I've always been an atheist. But I'm interested in all the forms the mind inhabits in order to think about itself in relation to the world, universe, or whatever. *Authority* was, in some ways, determinedly atheist poetry, whereas *Gravity* is more interested in considering how systematic thought, systematic philosophies, systematic theology relate to those small emotional moments that we feel in passing through daily life. In "Variations After a Summer Storm," I'm looking at a scene and asking, "Well, what kind of hand has made this?" And I'm thinking one answer is as good as another. Perhaps it just is. Or is it because God's hand has wrought all things? I'm leaving that question open, but I'm asking it in a way that I never would have before. Is there a spirituality that can be seen in this experience? Probably in the end, my thinking mind would say no, but there's some emotional part of me that wants to believe.

AC • There is great joy in *Gravity's Plumb Line*: Sky is a "Danceland" (45) and sunshine is "gaiety" (41) and "hilarity" (48), but there's a sense in which this bounty is unearned: "We didn't deserve / the hilarity of sunlight, its banter in the leaves" (48). Why's that?

RL • I think there are two things happening. On the one hand, the ultimate benediction, the ultimate moment when the hand is laid upon your head, is death. And if we have to go through death, we've earned everything we find in this world. On the other hand, there are the ethical and cultural questions, and political questions for that matter, which suggest that we've really made an unholy mess of things and maybe we should think about that and think about what we deserve and what we don't deserve to have in this world. I'm not by nature apocalyptic, and so I tend not to feel that just around the corner is nuclear winter, or some kind of utter devastation but, nonetheless, we're destroying biodiversity and species at an extraordinary rate. There are all kinds of things we can do about it, but we don't bother to do them. We don't seem to have, as a culture, the political will. My poetry is not openly political, but I'd like to think that, on some level, it is.

AC • One might say that honouring the abundance is itself a kind of political stance.

RL • Beginning in ethics and moving to politics – exactly.

AC • The sky is a "Danceland" if rightly approached. There are instructions: "It won't work if you do it that way, / squeezing the rough can-opener / onto the metallic sky, / hoping to spill its mackerel" (45). These could also be instructions for poetry, couldn't they?

ANNE COMPTON

RL • I love those kinds of writing metaphors that are a little deflationary because I think that so often amongst students and amongst people that I talk to at readings, there's the constant discourse of inspiration, of emotion, and even of thought in a grand form. Of course, I love things grand – opera, the sublime, and all of those things – but every poet knows that feeling of trying to get the damn can-opener onto the can and seeing if anything'll come out of it.

AC • In *Gravity*, even the "innocuous" (54) is subjected to scrutiny, and yet such emotion attaches to the ordinary: A glass of water "is the pure / source of the present, its transparent anguish" (54). The exactitude of the observer gives emotion a kind of precision. Is that so?

RL • I like the word "discipline" in that regard. There's a sense in which you're schooling the mind, but you're also schooling the emotions and that's what's meant, in many respects, in a word like "sensibility."

AC • "Love is in the details" (36): Does this declaration reflect upon your poetic practice?

RL • Yes, I think so. You can only love someone or something by under-standing the little things that go into making that thing such as it is, or that person such as they are. Otherwise, what you're doing is projecting a fantasy world, and I think that is ultimately a form of narcissism. That's love as self-expression. Or love as mirror, as echoing pond.

AC • For the protagonist walking the boardwalk of the bridge, the realiza-tion is that "You are alone and then you are not alone ..." (49). This walker may or may not be the poet, but let me ask you anyway – is aloneness, if not loneliness, a necessary condition for poetry?

RL • There's a long tradition of associating thought with walking. Peripatetic, perambulatory – such words speak about walking and philosophising simultaneously. Loneliness is required to write poetry because loneliness is the emotional component of the sense of longing, that sense of *nostos*, the desire to belong, to be at home, to be, somehow, at one with both the natural world and with other people and the recognition that you can never have that, that you will always be that "thinking reed," as [Blaise] Pascal says. So yes, loneliness is required for poetry. Not because poetry has to be about negative experiences or suf-fering. There's that Romantic notion that poetry always has to involve suffering. It's more that in suffering, we're aware of how truly alien everything is around us and how, therefore, alienated we are from our place – alienated in a Marxist sense, in an existential or Heideggerian sense. In some essential way, we always feel we do not belong where we are, and so poetry that finds its beginnings in loneliness is a poetry that is recognizing that gap. And from that gap can come ecstasy, joy, love. There are many things that cross that gap. We don't always exist in that space of separation. Poetry can begin from loneliness and move to joy, or it can remain lonely, but somewhere always lurking in poetry is that sense of aloneness that is next door to loneliness.

AC　• Six people – the acknowledgments tell us – had an editorial hand in *Gravity's Plumb Line*. Are solitude and community successive stages in the writing experience?

RL　• Yes, and for me it's an experience of intimacy. You know that old question "Do you write for an audience or do you write for yourself?" My answer is often enough that I'm writing for particular people. I get down a few lines and think, *So-and-so would really like this*, and it motivates me. It's a way of speaking to other people about things that you mutually understand and are trying to explain so that anyone who is familiar with the language of poetry can pick up the book and read it and hopefully both feel at home in the book and feel surprised by it. Certainly that's the way I am as a reader. When I read a book, I'm constantly excited by the ways in which it's both familiar and strange simultaneously, the way the writer opened up perceptions in ways that I felt I could almost have done but didn't. I suppose that the great poetry that I don't like is probably poetry that sees the world in such a completely different way that I simply don't understand it and, therefore, can't find an entry point.

AC　• There's an admirable clarity – an avoidance of ambiguity – in this poetry. Is that a quality you look for in others' work?

RL　• Ambiguity is a really problematic concept because as paradoxical as this might sound, for ambiguity to really resonate, you have to be precise. You have to choose the ambiguities you want to push and pull against each other, and those ambiguities have to be connected to the entire context of the poem and to what the poem's logic is articulating. Ultimately, ambiguity has to be articulate. There are productive values in the way things are contextualized that returns us to a notion of the beautiful. Perhaps postmodernism has been about the sublime of the unknowing. I like the notion, however, that there might be beauty in the poems – in the way they're shaped, the way they're crafted — that

　　　　　　　　　　　　　　ANNE COMPTON

they might be *objets d'art* in and of themselves. Certain kinds of post-modernist poetry see notions of beauty as bourgeois, very much constrained to certain kinds of privilege. And that is a problem, but the solution isn't to throw it out. For me, politics evolve from aesthetics. A sensibility is what brings somebody to a sense of compassion, a sense of desire for change, an awareness that privilege, either earned or undeserved, exists at the expense of other people.

AC • The Saint John River sequence, which opens *Gravity's Plumb Line*, moves from north to south, from headpond to harbour. Was this – after eight years here in the East – a way of situating yourself in the province?

RL • When I arrived here, I deliberately set out to write poems about New Brunswick as a way of arriving and as a way of beginning to inhabit a place that I, at that point, expected to live in for a very long time, perhaps for the rest of my life. I thought that was important. I thought there was a kind of settling I was doing that required my imagination of the place. I turned to the Saint John River because there's a mythic quality about rivers, obviously, the way they speak to a certain kind of circularity of life. But also because of the way rivers become the conduits of transport. The water is the first mode of transport, and people settle along the river. Other modes of transport follow the river. Highways and roads follow the river and reinforce the towns and settlements that have grown up there. Obviously in this day and age, people have spread out all over New Brunswick and don't necessarily live on the river, or on other rivers, but still in terms of cultural history, the river has that almost primordial feel. And as a child – up until the age of eight – I'd travelled up and down the river on the way back and forth to Shediac for summer holidays so the Saint John River then had a historical significance for me personally as well as for the province.

AC • The vocabulary of light in the river section, and generally throughout the book, is notable: "blistering brightness" (18); "glitter" (19); "luster" (68); "luminiferous" (67), and so forth. Did moving to New Brunswick and getting to know the Saint John River involve a new experience of light?

RL • Well, the light's certainly different from Prince George, which is the place I came from before coming here. It was very clear to me that I'd moved into a different kind of light. The other thing to say, though, about the area of New Brunswick in and around Fredericton, where I live, is that it is like Quebec. The temperatures are similar; the light is similar; contours of landscape and vegetation are similar. All that is very different from Saint John, and from any of the coastal areas of the Maritimes. There's an extensive ecosystem through Quebec, Maine, northern and central New Brunswick, down to and including Fredericton. Many things, including the light, were familiar to me except, perhaps, for the river itself, which was familiar only in distant memory.

AC • Writing a river, like tracking one, is a way of sorting out where you are. Is writing a river also an investigation of time – "a skein of liquid time" (24)?

RL • Absolutely. And I think that those conceptions of time overlay the historical. Somewhere in the process of writing these poems, I came to the clear conviction that space and time, in some senses, are the same thing. Or that they operate in continuum with each other, and I thought that is, in some senses, what we mean by poststructuralist. We mean a way of thinking past this great structuralist discovery that one could take history and lay it out spatially. And a metaphor could do this, could take a fluid passage of time and lay it out in a kind of spatial arrangement for us to understand how it functions. I'm not trying to suggest that my poems are deconstructionist or poststructuralist. What I was interested in was the way in which we think of ourselves as inhabiting space, but we're also inhabiting time, not in the sense of history only, but also at the level of cognition and perception. The fluidity of the river became a powerful metaphor for the idea that we're always looking at time, that time is far more intimate than structuralist ideas of time have suggested or certain kinds of visionary movements that want to somehow transcend time.

AC • How we experience time – Is that a preoccupying subject for you?

RL • Because our binocular vision allows us to establish spatial relations in a way that is very immediate, we have a sense we are seeing space, in and of itself. Time doesn't present itself to us in the same way because most things that we see in the world are at rest. Of course, even as they're at rest, they're moving through time. I wanted to find ways of evoking that sense of how everything is moving through time.

AC • There's a trinity of things – thought, perception, and the physiology of the brain – that appear in these poems in surprising ways.

RL • In "Below Florenceville" (19), I was trying to weave together a sense of historical time and a sense of phenomenological time, and the ways in which those relationships are metaphorical to the relationship between thinking and the brain. It's impossible, in my view, to reduce thinking to the firing of synapses. Most mornings when I get up, I'm a materialist: I don't think that there's anything in consciousness beyond the brain. Nonetheless, the thoughts there are not the brain's: A synapse firing is not the same thing as the thought that it creates. Maybe some smart scientist in the future will figure out how thought is actually physical, but to me it's intangible. Thought has an incorporeal existence. There's a huge portion of us – namely our thinking, our awareness, and our consciousness – that is incorporeal.

AC • "[T]he outer stairs" of a pavilion – though the pavilion is gone – is the "apparition // of some long forgotten thought" (73). This striking image, seen in understated elegiac terms, seems to me a key moment in the collection. Thought – Is that what we grieve, what is ghostly?

RL • Let me say one more thing about thought, before I get to the elegiac sense of it. Maybe it's something endemic to poets, but I suspect everybody has this constant movement of thought going on. There's a constant babble of voices in your head and some of that babble is formed intellectually, and much of it isn't. Built into the process of thinking is a huge amount of superfluity. It's inefficient in some basic way. If thought is strictly for the purposes of finding shelter and propagating the species, it sure is going about it the long way around. That part of thinking that is constantly emptying itself out and going into dead ends and leading nowhere – just musing, just reflecting – is somehow perhaps stored up in recesses in the mind and emerges again in very unusual moments. In fact, I imagine that many of the driving ideas in our poetic thinking are probably ideas that have begun as dead-end thoughts: *But what about this now? Forget it.* We have about a billion of those a day. But some begin to coalesce and they start to shape over time. I have a sense that poems are often a distillation of this murky liquid of thinking that's gone on before. By definition, that process is elegiac – in the Coleridgian sense of the elegiac as simply commemorative of a consciousness as it moves through its mutability toward death. It has often been said that virtually all poems are commemorative in the sense that they are all articulations of a self that is at a particular point in space-time, that is moving through mutability to its inevitable conclusion. Poetry, then, is an articulation of that mutability even as it seeks to commemorate the moment. A poem is both an articulation of a unique way of being in the world and a cultural artifact. In socio-political terms, the poem becomes a document of everything that was informing that moment. So it is historical. When you're sitting and writing the poem in the present, you are giving testament. And in giving testament, you are creating a document that will become a part of history, literary history if one is really good at it, and if one isn't, then it will be hidden somewhere in a library.

AC • And the pavilion?

RL • Yes, the pavilion is ghostly. The actual source of that metaphor is Expo '67. I was probably 14 or 15 when Expo occurred, and I was given the run of the place. My parents, bless their hearts, gave me a season passport, as they were called, and they taped a dime in it so I could phone home if I was ever in an emergency. I went to the place every day. There was this incredible, imaginative world, made literal in all these pavilions, and it was an extraordinary thing, but it was only there for one summer. The pavilion that everybody loved the best, and that seemed to be the most successful, was the Czech one. When they tore it down, they left the staircases, ones that just went up into the air and then stopped. I guess somebody must have said, "Instead of tearing them down, let's hang plants on them." That's where that poem began. Obviously it gets transplanted into another kind of environment, but I was fascinated by the idea that you had this incredible structure of the imagination that then gets removed, but the staircases that led there are still in existence. It suggests that even after the memory is gone, we remember the process of having had the memory. Or even as the memory is vanishing, the scaffolding of that memory is still present. I suppose, in some ways, the Saint John River was like that for me: It had a kind of imminence, on the one hand, but on the other hand, it was a kind of ghost of all kinds of things that, in many respects, I've forgotten, or I'm simply recreating. The whole scene of seeing my parents' initials carved in the wood on the Hartland covered bridge is fabricated ("Hartland" 18). I was reinhabiting these props of memory that were left, these vestiges, and I think we're fascinated by things that suggest presence, suggest we can walk up and find the pavilion, or whatever, that has now gone. An empty staircase, or a staircase leading nowhere, is, in that context, elegiac. Maybe a book is the tangible fragment of both a life and a culture.

AC   • The houses reflected on the water at "Grand Falls" (16-17) are inhabited by ghost figures. The narrator reflecting on himself as an eight-year-old on the Hartland Bridge (18) might also be seen as a ghost, and both poems are especially tender. How does the river evoke such tenderness in the perceptor?

RL   • One of the feelings I had when I moved here was that feeling of being a foreigner and an inhabitant simultaneously. I can lay claim to this place. My ancestors were New Brunswick Loyalists but, on the other hand, I'm not from here. Of course, as you know, these kinds of roots to both the land and the place are extremely deep in the Maritimes, partly because they have a fairly long historical heritage and partly because families have tended to form stronger kinship networks than in other places in Canada, especially, obviously, in the cities. New Brunswick, like Saskatchewan, still has that sense of being quite a rural place. As I follow the river, I'm not that often in cities. It struck me that so much of the river is about ways of life that are dying. So here I am coming to a place for what is, ultimately, a well-paying job, to work and teach people who live here, who have grown up here, but who, by the same token, are often leaving because they can't find a means to survive. The students I'm teaching graduate and head off somewhere else. I'm preparing the exodus, to some extent. I'm part of that process, and so there's perhaps, at times, an element of culpability in the poems, or maybe guilt. And at times, there's a sense of elegy. I refer specifically to that movement away in "Saint John Harbour" (27-28) and "Below Florenceville" (19), where I talk about the communicants to a church, with the suggestion that the church is still there but the people have gone: "children who have moved to the city, / ... who are at home there now" (19). I was very much aware, in that poem, of the way in which these places are inhabited by ghosts. The past itself can be thought of as a kind of ghostly presence along the river. That's a very important aspect of the river: It flows through history as much as it flows through the present.

AC   • *Gravity's Plumb Line* takes its title from a poem that begins with the metaphor "sleep's pillowed conservatory" (59), a place that enables the narrator's memory of his piano-playing father. Do memory and gravity share characteristics?

RL   • I think so. It's something I've been thinking around for the last five to 10 years. There seems to me to be certain kinds of very strong memories that have weight to them. They have a gravity that pulls the mind in and around them as if there were a particularly strong well of gravity there, around which the mind perpetually circles. As I layer different, later experiences, as those get woven into my life, they start interacting with each other around a profound memory and, hence, I start to confuse when different things happened because things from very different times are linked to the same memory, or to the same set of memories. Memory has gravity because it's condensed so many things into it.

AC • Why did "gravity," which appears here and there in this collection (59, 75, 80), come uppermost in the title?

RL • I think it was Andrew Steeves, my editor, who took that phrase, "gravity's plumb line" from the poem about my parents skiing and suggested it as a title ("Sleeping Over" 59). The moment I heard it I thought, *Yes, that really resonates with the book*. Of course the "plumb line" part of it is very important because that suggests to us where the gravity actually lies even as our visual perception is tricking us into thinking differently. Poetry, in some ways, is like a plumb line. It's a way of indicating where the weight really is and how one should experience the light and weight of language and of poetic attention. At the same time, though, a "plumb line" is also something that we work against. I'm thinking, for example, of cantilevered buildings. Or of skiing. When you're skiing, you don't just go straight down the gravity line. You weave back and forth. I really like the idea that we're not just looking to find gravity in order to find orientation, but we're looking to gravity in order to find out how we can push against it, deliberately play with it, how we can confuse ourselves with it, and how interesting and playful and fun that can be, and, in some ways, how it is defining for both memory and experience. I was hoping that when people first saw "plumb line," they would think it's a way of taking a sounding, which is another metaphor that's often been used to describe poetic attention. I was hoping when they came to that poem (59), they'd also see the other side of the idea – the deliberate attempt to confuse gravity and to play against it. Obviously a cantilevered building won't work if it isn't counterweighted against gravity. In some ways, that's the point of it. The play of cantilevering is in the idea that it appears to be counter to gravity.

AC • After the river (Section 1), after the objects of interest (Section 2), a narrating "I" makes its appearance in Section 3. Does this structure reflect your feeling that the "I" is always already situated in the midst of things?

RL • I would have felt very uncomfortable having that "I" in the front of the book before I had established what I wanted to establish about the way consciousness forms and un-forms, or coalesces, around a whole variety of processes of thinking, of understanding the world, culture, and so on. If one gives oneself over to the metaphors as they emerge, one will have a deeper understanding of how that self is constructed than if you just step on the stage with an "I."

AC • Is a variety of moods, rather than a variety of narratives, a better way of thinking about Section 3?

RL • Mood is more of a key to the structure of the book. Mood is like hue, and that brings us back to an earlier question – "Is light different in New Brunswick?" It's the light that gives us a sense of hue, and hue and mood are transformative to a poem. Perceptual interaction is dramatically changed even if the mood itself is not greatly changing. The way things are seen *is* changing. In the process of revision, a primary question had to do with those poems in Section 3 and whether they were, in their variety, breaking the guiding mood of the book.

AC • In this collection one finds majesty in the river, in trees, and as one poem says, in "All Things Great and Small" (60-61), but it also remarks the paint-peeling, "shrivel[led]" houses of the "backwater" (76), the "scrabbling" efforts of "The Clam Diggers" in their "seasonal work" (74). Is the experience of the sublime available if poverty is present and witnessed by the viewer?

RL • Yes. What is not present for the viewer is the picturesque unless the poverty is shoved out of focus, unless it's ignored, which in some ways is what a tourist does. A tourist ignores the poverty in order to see what it is they want to see, the pretty landscape. But the sublime, on the other hand, encompasses that poverty, reconnects us to the ferocity of those questions about class structure, about hardships, about terror. "The Clam Diggers" is wondering what terror those people experienced: "does their world close in on them like a glassy shell?" (75). Do they feel like they're digging their own graves when they're out there? They're digging for their life, in a way, but they're also digging their own graves. Just knowing what I know from various summer jobs I've had, I felt the terror of what that might be like.

AC • Are you suggesting that there is something inherently political about the poetry of the sublime?

RL • When I first started thinking about the sublime in relation to modern and contemporary poetry, I was curious to find out if the sublime was a form that could encompass political action. We often think of the Romantic sublime as that moment when the self is alone in a vast wilderness or on a precipice. In creating that vertigo of perspective, that sudden opening up, everything has lost its order, and so the social order itself is liable to being overturned. The potential upsetting of the self into emptiness and superfluity is an experience of terror, but it can lead to an experience of empathy that urges you to consider different ways in which the world can be configured. Looking out over the precipice – in the Burkean sense of the sublime – you are in a position to imagine possibilities. The best poets enacting the sublime – Ashbery or Jorie Graham, or back further, Stevens and Bishop – have a vision of a more egalitarian society.

AC • A river opens this book; Aristotle closes it. In writing a suite of poems on the elements of tragedy, are you suggesting that lyric poetry is closer to drama than it is to narrative?

RL • Perhaps so. Although the Aristotle sequence was very much conceived of as a lyric sequence. I was very conscious of a form of translation, the attempt to take tragic ideas and to make them suggestive, rather than narrative or dramatic. I wanted to make a singing of a narrative or dramatic space, rather than trying to invoke something of an epic quality.

AC • Aristotle places the elements in hierarchical order, plot first. In arranging your book as you have, did you have a plot structure in mind?

RL • I would say that there is not a plot structure to *Gravity*. If there's any kind of structure – and sometimes I wonder if there is – it's lyric, by which I mean that it's an associative structure. It's one that works through the semiotics of the metaphors, creating parallel meanings and exploratory meanings that nonetheless cohere in the logic of the progression of each poem – its syntax, its rhythmical movement through time. I see the book as trying to experience space-time as a single continuum.

ANNE COMPTON

AC • "Was this, then, to be our first principle, / that suffering makes human the echoing // woods?" (83): Is this a revisioning of nature, which, earlier, had been "gregarious" in its sunshine (41), a vision of "carousing / celebration" in "Late Spring" (39)?

RL • I see in nature a variety of types of existence. We have our empirical sense of the world. We see its phenomenal nature, which is open to scientific investigation, to measurement. We also have a world of plenitude, a world of superfluity – the natural world filling in every possible space. There seems to be a sense of overwhelming presence that's exhausting itself. It seems continually to replace and expand at an extraordinary rate. That's a fulfilment that goes beyond empirical measurement. There's also the sense of absence: Appearance is all there is. There's nothing behind it. In deconstructive terms, the natural world is an endless play of signifiers. We sense presence, absence, superfluity. All of these things. My poems are a movement back and forth between these various ways of perceiving the natural world. I hope people will see that – the carousing and gregariousness of a world fuller than we can comprehend. A world that is replete and then some, which involves this superfluous spending of itself.

AC • When I read this final section, I'm tempted to go back and read the earlier poems in its light. Did you want the last section to cast a retrospective light?

RL • Although the Aristotle poems were written earlier than the others, once I had written them I realized that they had a summational effect. They have a quality whereby they do cast a backward light on the other poems. The other poems are pulled toward the gravity of that final section.

AC • Seeing one thing in terms of another is the ground of metaphor. The final section of the book sees nature as the mimesis of human suffering, or the reverse. Is mimesis metaphor writ large?

RL • That's a hugely complex question. Much of the discussion of metaphor in the Canadian context – [Jan] Zwicky's *Wisdom and Metaphor*, Don McKay's discussions of it, Anne Simpson's talks on it – sees metaphor as a very special form of mimesis. I agree with that, with the proviso, which I take from Stevens, that metaphor can also be a sleight of hand. It can be an empty rhetoric, a machine of human devising that somehow loses its geared connection to the wheels of the world. The cogs don't quite mesh. So metaphor is mimetic in the sense that nature moves in ways that are structured in different forms of thinking. In one way, I do agree with Zwicky: Both metaphorical thinking and propositional logic – two kinds of thinking – are engaged with a real world that we are attempting to know. Metaphorical thinking really does get at something essential in our perceptual acts, and, therefore, is mimetic. In terms of Kantian thinking, space and time are the immediate ordering principles of perception. That, in turn, is followed by the analytical categories. My sense is that Kant gives primacy to the analytical categories. I'm less certain of that neoclassical or rationalist view of the world. If space and time are immediate ordering principles of the mind, metaphor is what fills in and gives us knowledge of that immediate ordering because of its associative structure. It is already determining what the analytical categories are going to be discovering. Furthermore, I often have the feeling that analytical thought is constantly interactive with perceptual thought or with metaphorical thinking. I'm not necessarily equating perception itself with metaphor, although they're highly interactive. We have to realize that there's a constant movement between rationality and metaphor. They are in constant conversation and exchange with one another.

AC   • "Hamartia" is understood, in your poem of that title, as the ambition of the human mind: The "devour[ing]" mind "longs ... to see the distance of the stars // and galaxies flattened like kernels of grain / sprinkled across the shadowed floor of an old // silo" (85). This might describe the poet's ambition. Is the poet a tragic figure?

RL   • I remember Sheldon Zitner saying to me once that the literal translation of hamartia referred to archery, and to a missing of the mark. That's always intrigued me – the idea that one can project oneself on the world and somehow miss. But, in some senses, that's what we do all the time and, therefore, there is this constant enactment of tragedy. We are always missing our lives. We never, or rarely, hit the target. Occasionally we have that glimpse of ecstasy and feel that we have touched something in the world that is truly resonant with ourselves. So often in life, though, we extend that desire only to find that it has fallen short.

AC   • In a poet so interested in thought, perception, and the brain (19, 71), in what sense am I to understand the word "soul" (55, 85)?

RL • One of the things that structures our notion of what it is to be a self, even in a secular age, even in someone like myself who tends towards atheism, is the sense that thought and emotion are non-corporeal. Those may very well be dependent on the firing of neurons in the brain or the electrical-chemical reactions between cells. Nonetheless, we come back to the idea that there is a soul-like quality or characteristic to the way that we experience – a non-corporeality in the way in which consciousness extends from materiality. If I sometimes use the word "soul," I'm obviously using it in a way that is different from traditional religion, especially Christian conceptions of that word. In "Woodstock," in the Saint John River sequence, I imagine the dead constructing their souls in the ground (20). The soul becomes the tombstone upon which their names are engraved, which is almost a satiric conception of soul.

AC • Throughout *Gravity's Plumb Line*, I'm aware of trees, sky, flowers, a river, but in the fourth and final section, fire is present. Is this tragedy's element?

RL • Conflagration has a lot to do with the sense of tragedy as I'm trying to define it or experience it within these poems. The notion that fire consumes what it burns is somehow elemental to tragedy. If we are tragic figures, we are tragic because we must die. If we lived forever, what meaning would tragedy have? We live a tragic existence precisely because consciousness, like the sun, is burning its own hydrogen. Ultimately it will burn itself out.

AC • If "you are not a guest" (86) at the party, you are either at the wrong party or you're the principal figure. Does one discover "after the fact" one's role in "Plot" (86)?

RL • Absolutely. Do I as a participant in my life understand where the story is going? I have no idea. I'm constantly surprised by the narrative twists and turns my life is taking. It's one of the reasons why people are so interested in biographies. Why is the life of Einstein, for example, relative to his discoveries? Only because we get the faintest glimpse into how his mind worked. There's something else going on there, though: There's a fascination with plot. How did the life unfold, allowing it to arrive at the point where it would make extraordinary discoveries? That's what we're interested in, but we can't see our own narrative trajectory. There's a tendency to want to see one's own life as an essential narrative in the plot of oneself. Just as one wants to see humanity as an essential character in the plot of the universe. I somehow doubt that it is.

AC • In "Plot" (86), "Character" (87), "Thought" (88), and "Diction" (89), there's mistake, misunderstanding: The self, in thinking, creates "little comedies" (88), and in speaking, deviates from the truth of "the first word" (89). Is failure the human horizon?

RL • I think it is. Imagine if one could be a perfectly articulate being. I sense that would be the end of poetry. We'd say what we have to say, and it would be full and complete. It is fundamental to human life that we continually mis-prize what we experience, that we project ourselves in foolish ways, in ways that mistake the circumstances and misunderstand the intentions of others. We spin our own ridiculous little comedies, but we also expand to heroic proportions. Does heroism imply tragedy? Ultimately it does. Aristotle had it right when he suggests that there is already inherent in heroism a movement towards hubris and the notion that we can act in a way that will transform our own lives and others'.

AC • The "stark nobility" of the "elm tree" is "the misunderstood branchings of its disease" (88). Does this subtract "nobility" from the inevitable tragedy of human life?

RL • In an ironic age, there's a tendency to see human failure as pathetic, perhaps even as stupid. Ultimately we're all idiots in an idiotic world. But I want to suggest that although misunderstanding can be catastrophic, it can also be noble. It is the mark of the attempt to understand. Perhaps something of understanding is carried forward into the misunderstanding.

AC • "You were crying by the river, watching / the swollen river shadows carry with them // the bodies of the dead" (94). That "you," in the concluding poem, "Catharsis," is every reader, isn't it?

RL • Some of that poem was meant to be literal. It came out of reading accounts of different conflicts – mainly in Africa – where people are butchered and dead bodies are floating down the river. The bodies in the river "say," "This is what you have wrought." And "you" in that poem has to be humanity. In one way or another, we are complicit with the conditions that create these kinds of circumstances. But the river also became a metaphor for the way one sees mutability in one's life and in others'. The realization that as much as you would like to be the grand figure on the stage – the one who makes giant changes – you are not that person. Typically you are the "single / blade of grass washed by the rain's catastrophe" (94), the bystander, who is himself ultimately washed over or carried away.

WORKS CITED

— • —

Huntington, Cynthia et al. "How to Peel a Poem: Five poets dine out on verse." *Harper's Magazine* (September 1999): 45-60.

Leckie, Ross. *The Authority of Roses*. London, ON: Brick Books, 1997.

– – – . *Gravity's Plumb Line*. Kentville, NS: Gaspereau P, 2005.

Miller, Karl. *Seamus Heaney in Conversation with Karl Miller*. London: Between the Lines, 2000.

Vendler, Helen. "Indigo, Cyanine, Beryl." Rev. of *Never*, by Jorie Graham. *London Review of Books* 23 January 2003: 13-16.

MAGIC PROSE:
JOHN SMITH'S *MAPS OF INVARIANCE*

Prince Edward Island's first Poet Laureate, John Smith, was born and raised in Toronto. After an undergraduate degree in physics and mathematics, Smith did postgraduate study in philosophy in London, England. Returning to Toronto, he earned his MA in English and taught high school. In 1967, he moved to Prince Edward Island, teaching at Prince of Wales College, and later at the University of Prince Edward Island, where he served a term as Dean of Arts. He is the author of seven collections of poetry – *Winter in Paradise* (1972), *Of the Swimmer Among the Coral and of the Monk in the Mountains* (1976), *Sucking-Stones* (1982), *Midnight Found You Dancing* (1986), *Strands the Length of the Wind* (1993), *Fireflies in the Magnolia Grove* (2004), and *Maps of Invariance* (2005). *Fireflies in the Magnolia Grove* was shortlisted for the 2005 Atlantic Poetry Prize. His most recent collection, *Maps of Invariance* – a collection of 15 intellectually and formally complex prose poems – was the subject of our conversation in Charlottetown in August 2005. A Professor Emeritus of UPEI, Smith was Poet Laureate from 2002 to 2004.

AC • *Fireflies in the Magnolia Grove*, your 2004 book, is a collection of sonnets; *Maps of Invariance* is prose poems. One might think of the prose poem as the sonnet's opposite, but intuitively I know that's wrong. Does the prose poem relate genealogically to the sonnet?

JS • The sonnet, I thought, was the typical Western lyric form, and I had something of that reference in mind when I started writing all those sonnets. My attitude to the sonnet form has been somewhat irreverent. I rather capriciously add lines on occasion, and I don't rhyme. My lines tend to be longer than 10 or 11 syllables and to substitute prose rhythms for metre. But, then, so do the sonnets of Robert Lowell. The sonnet is well grounded in the Western tradition, but stylistic prose goes back even farther, to Cicero and earlier, and is central to the

Western literary experience. In these two choices that I've made – looking at them in retrospect – the sonnet is true to the tradition, although I'm doing something a little bit quirky with it. In the prose poems, again, I'm leaning on what I take to be a long and distinguished tradition, although the continuity that one normally thinks that one needs in prose I often dispense with. I slide from one topic into another, trying not to bat an eye in the process. I'm adhering to the form – the shape of the sentence – but the content is all over the place. There is that relationship. I'm very much a traditionalist, but I'm playing with the tradition.

AC   • In the prose poem, is the sentence, rather than the line, pre-eminent?

JS   • Yes, the sentence, or perhaps even the phrase, is the basic form, and the sentence expands on the form of the phrase. The paragraph expands on the form of the sentence, the poem expands on the form of the paragraph, and the book on the form of the poem. It's a nest of self-similar structures, each larger structure exhibiting more detail.

AC   • If the undulations of sand in a desert, which result from the "racket and ricochet" of grains, contain the secret of "the escape of formlessness into form" (28), and if, "As time goes on, chaos will be revealed to exhibit definable preferences ..." (38), isn't the prose poem, which is the freest of free-verse modes, by parallel, already on its way back to form?

JS   • If you abandon metre, you put more emphasis on the shape of the sentence. We have analyzed our world, from pre-literate times, in terms of sentence form: Something does something to something else – period. And then something else does something to something yet other. There is a progression from sentence to sentence, but there is also a very definite form in this basic linguistic structure. It may be partly accidental that we, way back in the past, struck upon this sentence form when we might have chosen other forms, but now it's very difficult to analyze the world in any other way. What we call consciousness might be the outcome of that kind of structural analysis. Clearly, sentence form has had a good deal to do with our survival and development. In the second example that you quoted, I was thinking of the research that is being done on chaos theory. Chaos also has a form that can be managed. It's just a case of extending our notion of what form is. There is nothing and nowhere without order. It's a matter of seeing what kind of order it is or trying to mimic or recreate the order that is already there that has gone unnoticed.

AC • How does the shape of the sentence arrive?

JS • First, there's the music of the sentence, a music that hasn't yet been filled in with words. This was something that I was quite conscious of in the writing of the poems. Often the next thing to happen will have a kind of rhythm. I will feel that rhythm before I'm conscious of fitting words into it. It's an intuitive process. It may be that the unconscious has decided what the specific words, or specific figures, are going to be, and that decision first emerges to consciousness as a rhythm rather than in semantic form. My own experience is that I don't always know the rhythmic form of the sentence right to the end, but I know it for the next phrase or two. In fact, it's more exciting not to know the form of the sentence right to the end. I rather like long sentences because there is that element of discovery, of uncertainty.

AC • For the reader, there's chaos in this book, but the two passages about "formlessness" I quoted earlier suggest, "You're not really lost because order inheres in what you think is chaos." Is that order as basic as subject, predicate, object?

JS • The reader may feel a little disoriented in first reading these poems, but very soon should catch on that there is a principle of stability in them. There is the sentence form, which I do not abandon, but in fact accentuate, thinking of different ways in which to cast sentences. At the same time, there's a dependable voice. Whatever the conflictual or multifarious situations the voice is placed in, it is able to maintain a kind of authority and say something relevant, witty perhaps, and unexpected about that situation. We're not lost because we have our consciousness and this dependable prose form with which to deal with anything that comes along.

AC • Is the engine of the prose poem shaped in the warehouse of narrative or the laboratory of lyric?

JS • I'd like to be inclusive. Narrative is an important feature of these poems. Often the narrative doesn't last for any longer than a paragraph. In fact, it may be just a phrase suggesting the fragment of a narrative, and then we go on to something else. Narrative is certainly one of the structural features that I bear in mind in writing these, and there is a certain lyricism to the voice and to the treatment of things. There's the kind of whimsicality and fast footwork that lyric allows. I also have in mind the shape of a normal essay. So I'm thinking of narrative and expository essay, and of a lyric voice that's often playful. It's all of these things together. I'm not just telling a story and not just arguing a point.

AC • Charles Simic has described the prose poem as "quick unpremeditated scribble" where "intuition rules" (46). Does this correspond to your experience?

JS • That says quite a lot about my experience in writing these particular poems. There's a sense in which you have to move quickly in order to pre-empt your own conscious analytic processes. On the other hand, some of these poems did take a long time. I might have taken a month to write some of the longer poems, writing a paragraph or two each day. I did attempt to give intuition fairly full freedom, not inquiring whether what I had to say logically followed from what preceded it, but asking whether it was an interesting evolution.

AC • I've heard you say that these poems, in their generation and procedures, have a dream logic.

JS • I've been in the habit of dozing off and coming back to consciousness a number of times in the course of a day. Generally, I come back refreshed and wishing to prolong that period when I'm somewhere between asleep and awake. Frequently, in the waking-up state, I'm conscious of being, but not being anyone in particular. It's a kind of generic being that one experiences. But, of course, I know that I can't sustain the state. There is, therefore, a certain mannerism in the writing to make these poems seem as if they occurred between dream or dreamlessness and full waking.

AC • Did you have any model in mind – someone else's ventures in the prose poem – as you wrote these?

JS • The influence that I'm most conscious of is John Ashbery, whom I interpret as a neo-surrealist, a mannerist surrealist. I believe he's producing the result of surrealism without being carried away in the way the original surrealists thought they could be or actually were. It's a reflective, reconsidered kind of surrealism. There are also great prose writers that I admire very much, in particular [Marcel] Proust and Joseph Conrad. I admire the elegiac shape of the Proustian sentence, the Proustian paragraph. Woolf and Joyce, too, have something to do with this. I love Henry James also. I think there's something of James in *Maps*. There's an article by Richard Howard in which he illustrates the fact that when a good many American free-verse writers are reaching for something that will substitute for metre in traditional poetry, they reach to Henry James' prose.

AC • As compared to the lyric, is the prose poem closer to, or more distant from, the spoken voice?

JS • It's closer to the spoken voice.

AC • These lines from one of your earlier volumes might be describing the prose poem: "Something that breaks the prose line to let tracing tools reach opened surfaces. / Something that reveals in hiding, like a spreading fan" (*Midnight* 27). Is the poetry in a prose poem – the poetic devices, tropes, and so forth – an archaeological tool that reveals and conceals at the same time?

JS • The second element in the quotation seems better to describe some of the effects achieved in the *Maps* poems. We've refined the art of hard-nosed tracing tools in all the fields in recent years – often to productive effect – but, alas, lost the subtle art of the fan, which hides, yes, but also reveals in spreading – reveals itself and, more importantly, forces us to create, in desire and imagination, what we would otherwise see behind the obscuring fan. I think that's quite like some of the effects in *Maps*.

AC • Is *Maps*, in some ways, your most autobiographical work, an autobiography of a mind?

JS • I grew up on T.S. Eliot. I came of age in the 1940s when the *Four Quartets* were the latest blockbuster poems. I was very much influenced by Eliot's idea that poetry is not an exposé of the self, but an attempt to escape from the personality. I've been governed by that. I haven't been very successful in writing directly about myself and my own experiences. For 55 years, however, I've kept a little book, which has now grown to 20 volumes, in which I jot down ideas, some of them worked out in detail, some just fragments, a phrase or sentence. It's my book of *obiter dicta*. That is a kind of autobiography of the mind. These prose poems that we are talking about read like an astute selection of items from this long-gestating book of *obiter dicta*.

AC • *Maps* is not only travel, but also a "final voyage," on which there is "no reprieve" from "speculation" (21). Is "speculation" burden or liberty?

JS   • I suppose it's both, but I tend to think of it more as liberty. Mine is quite a speculative mind. I like to consider all of the options, but I don't always like choosing one rather than the other. In literature, you can let it all be. There's a concept in quantum theory known as the superposition of states. Until a phenomenon is observed, it exists in a superposition of states. It could be any one of a number of things. Once it's been observed, it becomes definite. There's one tick on the Geiger counter, or there's one track in the detection chamber, and reality is caught in flight. In these poems, I'd like to evince a kind of state in which reality is not caught in flight, a sense of that superposition of states in which anything that could be, is.

AC   • At one point, the "prose voice" tells me that these are "commentaries" that "take you back to point of origin through a set of observations quite familiar, though in unexpected order, and with most of the transitions omitted" (54). Within each of the book's three sections, might I read the poems in any order? Or is there linearity here?

JS   • At the time of writing, the poems weren't thought of in any particular order. Each one set its own regulations as it developed. When I came to look at the poems afterwards, it seemed to me that they fell into a kind of order. It took me several years to figure out what that order was. But I also think of the book as one that the reader can open at random and simply plunge in. There is, however, an added pleasure, I hope, in reading the whole poem from beginning to end. It starts somewhere and it gets somewhere.

AC   • The prose voice is metaphor in *Maps*. This metaphor is "acted out ... as the very body of the poem" (10). Is it voice that holds the thing together?

JS   • The voice is very important in the integrity of the work. The voice is dependent upon a certain tone, and although there are variations, I wanted to maintain a general consistency of tone throughout. *Jubilant perplexity* is a description of the voice that comes to mind. It's a confident voice, which is different from my own. The voice is a kind of superego that one constructs. It's an authoritative voice, although often its authority is only that of posing significant questions, rather than deciding which of a number of answers fits the question. There may be other things that hold the poem together – the constant recasting of the sentence form, which is not exactly voice, for example.

AC • The circuitous wanderer-speaker says, "I write so that I may see to read what I desire to hear" (15). Isn't the further conceit of the book, then, that we're reading what he has written?

JS • If you mean it's a narcissistic process that invites eavesdropping, I'd agree to that.

AC • Although the borders of his identity are fuzzy, the narrating character of *Maps*, whether we call him "voice" or map-maker, has personality. He makes jokes, indulges in irony, relishes understatement, and is charmingly self-deprecating at times. Did you begin with this character?

JS • That's probably a persona that I developed over many years of teaching and trying to make the whole process of lecturing interesting. It wasn't a persona that was specifically developed for the purpose of writing this book. And this persona probably enters into dialogues with friends over lunch and so forth. How that differs from me, I don't know at this stage. Maybe one creates a favourite persona and becomes so identified with that persona, one abandons the project of being anyone else.

AC • The squirrel (10, 67) seems to be a figure for the way the wanderer moves through time or, at least, thinks about movement through time.

JS • I was quite conscious of identifying with the squirrel. I admire the sprightliness of squirrels, their apparent good humour, their playfulness, and their ability to survive and rejoice in a world that is sometimes threatening. And there's a squirrel-like quality to the way in which these poems move. They are like the squirrel finding his way through the infinite, or almost infinite, number of ways available to him through the forest. He chooses one way, and he is quite confident that that way will open up new options for him. He is not frustrated. There will always be a way onwards.

AC • Early on, transcendence is identified with a high ledge in the mountains, home of an "unspecifiable bird" whose solitude is as familiar and comforting to him as "the cytoplasm of the wing muscles" (21). For one who walks the flat to hilly landscape of PEI, as you do, does the otherness of mountains become the fit figure for transcendence?

JS • Probably so. I've done some walking in the Rockies and in the Lake District and Scotland and Maine although I've never climbed a big mountain. Living in PEI, I miss mountains, and I do like occasionally to get to a landscape that has more profile to it. But then there are all sorts of examples of self-similarity in nature. You can walk the dunes of PEI – none of which is more than 80 feet high – and you can see in the structure of the dunes something that is very similar to the structure of mountains. You can experience mountains in little, or in imagination, even when you are living in a relatively flat landscape. The mountain as a figure for transcendence is something of a cliché, and I have availed myself of that cliché. It plays an important part in Wordsworth's *Prelude*. There's the ascent of Snowdon at the climax of *The Prelude*.

AC   • By times, the wanderer has a companion, sometimes male, sometimes female. This companion, "entwined and twinned" (20), may be, in truth, an aspect of the wanderer. If so, doesn't that make these prose poems interior monologues taking place in an internal theatre, "the black box" (52)?

JS   • I suspect that we all have an interlocutor, or a variety of them, partly based upon people that we know. We also have the ability to recreate a version of ourselves inside so that we can have conversations with our twinned selves. I don't know that there's anything unusual about that. As you suggest, these poems are managed and edited interior monologues.

AC   • Did the circuitous wanderer claim your attention – ask you to witness to his adventures and record the "words ... that insist on being said" (62)?

JS   • Probably he did. In the conclusion of *Sohrab and Rustum,* Matthew Arnold speaks of the river as a "circuitous wanderer" (144). But rather than being lost, I wanted my wanderer always to be in a state of finding and being found. My recollection is that from time to time I wanted somehow to dart out a hand or a word to someone, and I very quickly manufactured a person on such occasions to be the object of my attention. I created these people almost on the spur of the moment to be the respondents or the auditors. I didn't give them very much time to be themselves or to establish a specific identity as separate from the questioner or speaker.

AC   • I've referred to a first-person speaker, but in fact pronouns in this book shift among "I," "we," "he," "you," "one." Entire poems – such as

   ANNE COMPTON

"In his later years" (38-40) – are presented in the third person. Were you after a kaleidoscopic perspective on the wanderer, or to put it in terms the book uses – Were you "bend[ing] the maximum number of vectors of attention ... round the centre from which apperception springs" (68)?

JS • Both of those, I think. In the poem "In his later years," the wanderer is addressed as "he" throughout, and yet he consists of a number of discontinuous vignettes. He's a person whose pieces don't really fit together, and yet he's given a kind of coherence by what I would call the authority of the voice that addresses him. He begins the poem as someone like Henry James, and he ends the poem something like Jackson Pollock.

AC • Actually, the pronoun "we" enters that poem (38-40) as well. "We" see him at a café where he's reading, or pretending to read, a newspaper. The question for the reader is: Is the reader with the wanderer? Or is the reader included in the "we" observing the natty dresser reading the newspaper?

JS • I don't think I had asked myself those specific questions. It just seemed to me right at that time that there would be two of us observing this man at the café table, and we would say to each other, "Shall we go over and join him?" And, yes, "Let's. Let's see what outrageous thing he is up to today." It seemed right and interesting that such a thing should happen. I guess maybe there's something a little bit cinematographic about these situations.

AC • I'm trying to sort out the "you" whose attention is often solicited here. Isn't that "you" sometimes outer-directed at the reader: "In your country of origin too, the network of old drovers' tracks ... still scores the landscape" (22)?

JS • Yes, definitely, and the "you" suggests that this is simply a non-specific other.

AC • Finally, it doesn't matter who the auditor is – character or reader – because the ultimate audience for this prose voice is – isn't it – "the encompassing silence" (62)?

JS • That goes back to my confession of perplexity. What does happen to all the things that we say? What has happened to all the things that people have said since the time people began to say things? Are they recorded somewhere? Certainly they very slightly and subtly changed the physical distribution of the universe – these vibrations in the air – but is there some sort of realm where everything that has been, or has been said, is saved? At the point in the poem where I use the phrase "encompassing silence," I'm presumably saying that there is no permanent record. What we say and do are absorbed into an ultimate silence. The "encompassing silence" must be the ultimate auditor, which is a paradox, of course, because it is an auditor that gives no sign of having heard. At this stage, we're reaching the limit of what words can perform. There's a poem by Wallace Stevens that I'm very fond of – "Prologues to What Is Possible." Stevens had a fine sense for the limit that language can reach, and he has a profound sense of something beyond that limit. My "encompassing silence" may derive from Stevens. Finally, I suppose it's almost inevitable that when we think of transcendence, we give it some human presence, the ability to listen even though it doesn't talk back, cannot talk back.

AC • A woman playing a musical instrument is a figure that recurs in your work. In *Maps*, "She plays the lute becomingly ..." (18). In "You Wanted to Hear," she "bends at a lonely instrument ..." (*Strands* 15). In *Midnight Found You Dancing*, she's one of the embroiderers whose "hands are clusters of arpeggios" (31). Could you say something about your interest in this figure.

JS • It seems to me appropriate that what I hear would be generated by a harpist, a pianist, a lutanist-female, an anima figure possibly. She is always speaking a language beyond what I'm speaking, which, perhaps, I'd like to be able to incorporate into my speaking. She's speaking the language of music.

AC • "Left-handed versions" (46-50) is given over to the story of the woman who's an avid reader. She surmises a "metasphere ... more jubilant than anywhere we could pragmatically go" (50). Doesn't this woman – given her ideas – forecast where the wanderer will arrive in the final poems of Section 3?

JS • She forecasts where the wanderer would *like* to arrive.

AC • I could say that *Maps* is Ulysses' journey had he travelled on the surface of the mind rather than the surface of the sea. Or I could say it's Wordsworth's *Prelude or Growth of a Poet's Mind* played backwards from its end point. Would these be good approximations of what's going on in *Maps*?

JS • Ulysses is certainly an archetypal presence in my mind, and he gets some explicit coverage in *Maps*, although his name is never mentioned. Even if readers don't recognize this figure, they'll know this is a man making a journey home. They would also do well to remember Tennyson's Ulysses, tired of home and bent on a final voyage: "To follow knowledge like a sinking star, / Beyond the utmost bound of human thought" (67). The Ulysses parallel, I could certainly agree to, and I certainly have spent a good deal of time reading, thinking about, and admiring Wordsworth's *Prelude*. "[P]layed back from its end point" suggests that any later poet will come to the end of *The Prelude* and will begin his own poetic enterprise from the point that Wordsworth gets us to at the end of that poem. That doesn't mean that I will do as good a job in what I'm trying to do as Wordsworth did in what he was trying to do, but it does mean that the history of poetry is an ongoing affair. It's developmental.

AC • I intended my question more literally: Supposing we read *Growth of a Poet's Mind* beginning with where he arrives in Book 14 and reading back to his origin. I'm floating the notion that where the wanderer arrives at the end is origin.

JS • You may well be right, but not in the Wordsworthian sense of the recovery of his childhood and of its heightened perceptions. My own intellectual life has been guided throughout by a number of ideas, one of which is the *arche*, that Greek term that means the origin or first principle. My inquiry of my own experience, and of history, the world, and philosophy, has had that objective. This is what makes the figure of Ulysses significant. *The Odyssey* is about the *nostos* or return – the voyage home in one man's particular case, a return to the scenes of his childhood or early manhood, somewhat as with Wordsworth. But the object of the earliest Greek philosophers was to get back to the first principle, which would have been first in time, but also first in authority and in logical necessity. It's an objective that has been fol- lowed by 20th-century physics: What are the fundamental particles, the fundamental substances and relationships?

AC • Perhaps "the end is origin" idea applies to the methodology of *Maps* if not to the character's travels?

JS • At the beginning of *The Prelude*, he's wandering "free as a cloud." If he follows any cloud, he will get to his destination because he has that trust in nature: "Nature never did betray / The heart that loved her" ("Tintern Abbey" 100). One of the premises of my poems is that Wordsworthian one that I can follow any cloud. I can pick up the end of any thread, and it will lead me ultimately anywhere. It's an encouraging kind of philosophy because it says that you are at home wherever you are. It's the transformation of a situation that could be interpreted as being lost into its opposite, a benign lostness or a fortunate fall.

AC • "[S]ince we're here, there's everywhere else to go and we're in process of getting there" (13): Does *Maps* enact the inexhaustible hunger of the mind?

JS • Desire occurs frequently in these poems. *Maps* takes the "inexhaustible hunger of the mind" as a kind of premise. It does what it can to enact that human trait.

AC • If I stand transfixed in a doorway, all compass points available to me, plus up, down, and out, doesn't the house, metaphorically speaking, collapse behind me. What happened first here: The collapse of the house or besottedness with all the possibilities that lie beyond the house?

JS • I can see the house as tradition. We've been secure in traditional interpretation, and Christian theology has a lot to do with that interpretation. I grew up in a century that, to a large extent, saw that house collapse. One is left destitute and alienated, but then one finds that destitution and alienation – if one is fortunate – are guarantees of one's freedom. I'm free now to think anything, to consider any possibility. I don't feel that socially or philosophically I have to subscribe to the current dogma. The house has collapsed in the process of time and the modern person is left without a house, but discovers that the whole of reality is a bigger house that is out there to be explored. It doesn't have the comfort of old walls. It's more like Wordsworth's cloudscape than Dante's universe, let us say. It imposes challenges of self-discipline and self-direction, as the old house imposed challenges of conscience and obedience.

AC • Does Wordsworth's assertion "The Soul that rises with us ... / Hath had elsewhere its setting ..." (154) have resonance for you?

JS • I don't believe literally in Neoplatonic pre-existence, but I find the theory of pre-existence poetically attractive and meaningful. I believe that was Wordsworth's position also. We come into being from a deep and abundant background – physical, geological, microbiological, not to speak of a long cultural history – which science is presently exploring. Current understanding of the way nature works seems pretty much to preclude belief in individual souls with persisting integrity through many lives or after this life. The non-deterministic element in natural process would preclude that persisting integrity. But a deep pre-existing background there indubitably is, and as individuals, like new leaves on a tree, from that background we come.

AC • It certainly piques my interest to hear you imply that the wanderer has no belief in an eternal soul. I thought the wanderer had not only a belief, but a delight, in something eternal.

JS • I would agree that the wanderer has a strong sense of eternity, of something that is not bound by time and by sequence. The poetry itself is a kind of illustration of a world that is not bound by normal logical sequence.

AC • The collection's called *Maps of Invariance*, but doesn't the traveller find the world to be capricious and variable and, second, doesn't he find the fact that he's in *this* world and not some other similarly capricious?

JS • There's an element of irony in the title. However, there are invariances in the poems – the voice is a kind of invariance. The presence of the speaker is an invariant in the midst of lots of things.

AC • The title's a misfit for what he's feeling?

JS • But there's also a kind of fit because, as I read it, each of these poems is a map, and it is a map of the invariability of possibility. Possibility is always there, and these poems are maps of that possibility. Here one is trying to create a map of a moving, fluctuous thing.

AC • You like to think about – this is a preoccupation in your other books – "[a]lternative runs of the universe" (*Maps* 13). Does the wanderer have in mind other unfoldings of his life, and do those in fact intersect with the one he's experiencing?

JS • There is one episode, in the poem "Sympathy yes" (58-63), where he talks about intersecting universes – that is, universes that share one moment, or something in common, and yet diverge at other times or in other parameters. I'm thinking of "alternative runs of the universe" in the context of contemporary cosmological speculations. I'm thinking of the larger frame rather than the personal frame of the wanderer's life, although I certainly would not deny that there is some reference to the personal frame: I am what I am, but I might well have been very different.

AC   • Twice the wanderer draws attention to the preponderance of "left-handed" molecules over right-handed in Earth's matter (46, 83). Is the wanderer preoccupied with what seems to be the idiosyncratic nature of what is?

JS   • Yes. A reference here would be Stephen J. Gould. His view of evolution is that there was no inevitability that man as a species would emerge from the organic life on this planet. He thinks that evolution is a series of highly idiosyncratic moments of decision that happens to have led to us.

AC   • Whose decision? And the other thing is that although *this* "run of the universe" gave us opposable thumbs, what is it we didn't get? In another "run," we might not have gotten opposable thumbs, but we might have gotten the most beautiful pair of wings.

JS   • I haven't read any convincing description of what other universes might have arisen. As far as I know, no one has given that question the kind of intense and detailed thought that would be necessary to create a plausible and viable alternative. As to "decision," I'm not implying that someone has to make the decision. I wouldn't want the word "decision" to be taken to imply that there is a great overarching intelligence of some sort that has numbered every hair of our head and every sparrow that falls and every electron that turns up with a left-handed, rather than a right-handed, spin.

AC   • In "Not only the weak," in *Strands the Length of the Wind* (1993), "when the recording engineer sets up equipment at point X, // only one guest stands at the gate, a lone survivor ..." (10). Is the idea in that poem, and here in *Maps*, that although X versions of the universe got ruled out in an originating space-time event, these "runs" (*Maps* 13) "exist" parallel to the present?

JS   • The paradox of quantum measurement, which I am attempting to use for figurative purposes, both in the *Strands* poem and in the *Maps*

           ANNE COMPTON

poem, is still a subject of debate. The standard version, to which I allude in both, contends that once a measurement of a quantum phenomenon is made, or once a detection-event of some sort takes place, one of the quantum options becomes actual – happens in this physical world – and that rules out all the other possible states. Another version of the situation, called the "many-worlds interpretation," leads to parallel universes. The difference between the two poems is that in the *Strands* poem, I imagine the detection-event to take place at any time during the life of the universe, whereas in the *Maps* poem, I imagine the detection-event at the earliest possible moment in the history of the universe, the moment when, it may be, the particular characteristics of this universe would have been determined. The people who professionally speculate about these matters generally work on the hypothesis that the system is self-actuating and self-regulating. They could well be wrong in this premise, but they normally don't assume a divine fiat to get the universe going. That's also the position implied in these poems.

AC   • "By this process, the old work of divine signification, turned outside in, becomes the new work of art ..." (14). Does art locate the sacred grove, the temple, the monastery in the human mind?

JS   • Art is a thing that transfers the locale of divine signification from some sort of sacred precinct to the mind and then we try to externalize that as art galleries or art books. In the case of *Maps*, it is externalized as an art gallery. What I had in mind there was the large room in The British Museum in which they display the Elgin Marbles. They have the remains of the two pediments of the temple of Pallas Athene, which, in the original design on the Acropolis, faced outward from either end of the temple, but in The British Museum they turned the pediments around – one at each end of the gallery – so that the two pediments face each other down the gallery. I'm playing with this idea as a complex metaphor for the historical transition from the dominance of religion to the dominance of art.

AC   • The wanderer remarks a number of devolutions: The "palace" epic, that "embrac[ed] all others," fragments into dissonant rooms (23-24); tribal gestures – "rub[bing] their palms together ... to emphasize points" – devolved to liturgy (28); and "in a pianistic age ... [there's] nostalgia for the lifestyle embodied in the sound of the harpsichord" (38). In these three examples, but especially in the movement from tribal gestures to doctrinally defined liturgy, there's a sense of stepping down. Is that right?

JS • There's the original, spontaneous meaningful act and then this becomes regularized and becomes compulsory. Certainly that would be consistent with my own world view that tends to respect moments of initial revelation or awareness and to be suspicious of the doctrinaire repetition of those moments. So yes, there is some dissatisfaction expressed here with the house of art, the city of art, but that simply means that art and the city of art must change as Wallace Stevens says in "Notes Toward a Supreme Fiction."

AC • The prose voice of *Maps* ranges over time. He expresses elegiac feelings for the past and whimsy in regards the future, but he reserves his most pointed remarks, doesn't he, for the present: "At the end of the cycle, poster art, protest art, the entire rigmarole of the avant-garde, co-opted by the establishment, fit not uncomfortably into the museums .... However hard they try, the regular polyhedra never become true spheres, but they can dream, can't they?" (52).

JS • Yes, and to further the illustration, there's a placc in London called the Institute of Contemporary Arts that houses art that is quite avant-garde, but they've co-opted it. They've created an establishment out of an art that was meant to disassemble the establishment.

AC • Is the elegiac feel for an old order of things – the epic "palace," the tribal gesture – compensated for by a richness of the mind, "a kind of urlinguality" (29) that is found beyond language and reason?

JS • This state of "urlinguality" is another way of talking about the super-position of states. Everything is there, but nothing has yet been decided or chosen. There's a special joy in holding everything in consciousness rather than having chosen. Before a word has been spoken, everything possible that is to be said is somehow there. We can have everything there is, so long as we don't make it explicit – a paradoxical situation. Once we've made it explicit, we have to take one thing rather than another.

AC • Might I take the following for the anti-methodology of the wanderer's thinking: "The marbles tumble around in your head alarmingly, and to let them follow their will taxes whatever negative capability you can muster" (36)?

ANNE COMPTON

JS • He recognizes that we have a constant desire to simplify things or to stop the flux, but if we do that, we're giving up on the creation of that map of invariance. It seems that we're getting a map of invariance because everything is still, but it's a false map. The real map is a map that is alive – just as cosmologists now think of space-time itself as rather like a living thing, an idea that would not have been outrageous to the Greeks, but would have been outrageous for the two centuries following Newton.

AC • The wanderer-speaker begins the first poem of Part 2 with "The legendary entrance is a gate you won't find if you keep circling the walls, as you do, in a factual mode." Comments on the "country round about" the city abruptly shift into: "To be interested in the shapes of sentences is inevitable, nonetheless ..." (33). The wanderer's leaps in thought are actually associative, rather than chaotic, aren't they?

JS • Yes. So talking about the structure of cities is a way metaphorically of talking about the structure of sentences. I suppose I'm being somewhat influenced here by [Jacques] Derrida and Claude Levi-Strauss. What I'm assuming is that the structure of humanity is observable in the structure of language, the structure of cities, and in everything that we design and make. There is a kind of human invariance in all of these things that at first look very dissimilar. The plan of a city doesn't look anything like a dictionary or a rhetoric, and yet it is a kind of speaking. The text precedes everything in that sense. The text, as such, emerges fairly late in the history of man's residence on this earth, but it was implicit from very early on. That, at any rate, is the hypothesis. Texuality takes these other forms – works of art, methods of hunting game, designs woven into fabrics, and so forth.

AC • To put that distinction another way: The thinking here is not so much a "tumbl[ing]" (36) as it is a dancing, an escape dance from one image "into the other. From the second ... into a third. And so on" (54). Would you agree with that distinction?

JS • Yes, I would, as a matter of fact. It reminds me of watching Margot Fonteyn dance. She had a way of looking as if she was going to fall and a terrible mistake was going to be made. She then recovered in such a way that it became a very expressive moment. She put herself at risk, and out of that act of daring, she was able to achieve an artistic expression that couldn't have been achieved otherwise.

AC • Within each of the 15 poems there's discontinuity due to the leaping about, but individual paragraphs, as if they were small, stand-alone poems, cohere, don't they? I'm going to cite an example of how a paragraph end line makes sense of the out-of-nowhere paragraph beginnings: "The legendary entrance is a gate you won't find if you keep circling the walls, as you do, in a factual mode .... And so you persist, out of touch with your preferred self, although others remain real enough – up to a point" (33). A sinuous set of associations connect the image of the city with the concept of the self.

JS • If I can generalize, often an end of a paragraph makes a return to the idea with which the paragraph begins, but in between there may be a lot of material that is not obviously related to the opening or the closing. I'm an Aristotelian at heart, I guess: Things have beginnings, middles, ends, and the whole should make some sort of coherent sense. There's a similar structure in the small scale as well as in the large scale.

AC • Cities are related to sentences (33); maps are linked to textuality (41). Breaching the citywalls results in disappointment (34), and laminated maps peel and scatter. Is there any articulation – verbal or graphic – that is adequate to, capable of embodying change?

JS • If change is such a notable characteristic of the world, then all that poetry can do, all that a writer can do, is to keep recasting what it is, though inevitably there will be something left out, and in the subsequent recasting there will inevitably be something new. So we're in this constant process of casting away, rearranging, and discovering. This is why, perhaps, there has to be a history of literature. And why the supreme fiction is never finished.

AC • The wanderer is lost – happily perhaps – because maps of invariance can't tell him about the world in which he finds himself. Is this because we now know the world in a post-Newtonian way?

JS • The short answer is yes. When Newton published his *Principia* toward the end of the 17th century, it seemed a remarkable revelation about the world. It seemed that the world, perhaps, was governed by a few very simple principles: If you knew the equations, you could calculate exactly what would happen before it happened. Confidence in the exactness of Newtonian predictions was an important element in the movement we call the Enlightenment. But, as it turns out, there are slight variations from this exactness, and when we reach extreme conditions – for example, particles that are moving relative to each other at something close to the speed of light – there are very significant differences. Einstein took the decisive steps in redesigning physical science in his 1905 papers: High-speed mechanics, which he develops into the special theory of relativity, and electron-photon interaction, which others develop into quantam electrodynamics. We now live in a post-Einsteinian world where we know, or we're beginning to suspect, that there are no exact equations that will predict things in a deterministic way. However, there's always an upside to these down things. Anxiety about indeterminism is actually a source of energy, and in the upside there can be a sense of freedom. We are free to construct any patterns that we like and attempt to apply them to reality. Some may work under certain conditions, but under other conditions you may need to apply a different pattern, a different template, a different set of equations. The usable or pragmatic truth depends upon the circumstance.

AC   • Might we understand *Maps* as an anti-literary gesture – poetry that's not verse, prose that is neither fiction or non-fiction – and is this because "change itself is the durable form" (41), and there's no literary form equal to it?

JS   • I didn't know I was beginning a large poetic project when I began to write these poems. Looking back on it now, I can say to this question, yes, *Maps of Invariance* is a kind of anti-literary gesture. It's an attempt to find a different way from the ways that we've used prose essays and fiction and regular verse to express our position in the world, our sense of reality. I think among his other attitudes the wanderer has a sizable dose of skepticism. There is, I think, some discernible skepticism about literature and about literary forms, but that's part of his addiction to freedom. He doesn't want to be bound by things so he's always ready to criticize them. At the same time, it seems to me clear that he loves the literature of the past. There are quite a few allusions to it, even if he doesn't mention Wordsworth and Milton and other people. He loves, but he's skeptical of the things that he loves. He wants to be free of them to do his own thing. Often he talks in a very cavalier manner of a whole variety of things – science, art, poetry, whatever. Byron's narrator in *Don Juan* is one of the literary ancestors. So is Hamlet.

AC   • If the forms we create, graphic and literary, are always late to the state of things, is changeability approachable only by metaphor, metonym, or some other trope?

JS   • I think it's arguable that nothing that we attempt to approach is approachable in any other form than figuratively. I seem to be returning for support more and more often to Stevens, but he does say in the poem "Asides On the Oboe," "final belief / Must be in a fiction" (102). In *Adagia* he adds, "there being nothing else" (973), by which, I take it, that he accepts the idea that all of our so-called knowledge and all of our response to our lives and the world is, in a broad sense, figurative.

AC   • Change coheres, at least metaphorically, in the way "the heterogenous news of the day congregates under a dateline. Or, according to the lyric logic of the lucid dream" (41). Might we, then, understand *Maps of Invariance* as a form of newspaper?

JS   • Yes. I owe the newspaper idea to an essay of Marshall McLuhan's entitled "Joyce, Mallarmé, and the Press." McLuhan argues that the phenomenon of the newspaper page, with its variety of subject matter, tone, and levels of seriousness, has changed our poetic sensibility and hence our relationship with the world. The date line is a great metonymizer: It establishes relationships between widely disparate things solely by their propinquity in time. McLuhan derives his idea from Lamartine, who said, as early as 1831, "The only book possible from today is a newspaper" (McLuhan 5). To pick up the second part of that quotation – The "lyric logic" of the dream, as Freud and others have illustrated, creates not only piquant and meaningful juxtapositions, as does the newspaper page, but deep and dense fusions of many things, as though many lines of music were playing concurrently in various states of concordance and discordance. Counterpoint would be another trope for what goes on in the rhetoric of these poems.

AC   • Isn't the wanderer, though, as skeptical of tropes as he is of literary forms: "*Incomparable* is the epithet that comes to mind in defiance of all similes that stand in the way, jostling for advantage and urging agreement and sympathy" (62)?

JS   • In that, there's a reflection of an experience that most writers of poetry have had. There are all sorts of possibilities at any given point for figures, and the better poem is distinguished from the less good poem because the writer has managed to find a more telling figure. This is not only a feature of writing poetry, but also a feature of our everyday experience. Whether we're aware of it or not, we're always interpreting the world in some way, and we're interpreting, probably subliminally, by searching through an inventory of figures and analogies that come up and offer themselves as suitable interpreters.

AC • The wanderer thinks about change, and he thinks about the adequacy and inadequacy of forms to articulate that change. Then, he thinks about figures of speech and the way in which they are more adaptable to the nature of change, but then, I thought, he comes to a point where even figures are not up to the character of the world in which we live.

JS • You're right. One can grow impatient with the inexactness of tropes, of substitutions and surrogates, with awareness of a thing's being always distanced from what it is in itself, fended off by a metaphor or simile. One may then be driven, as the wanderer is in the passage you quote, to say in effect, "Let the thing be itself and nothing but itself. Let it be declared *incomparable*." There's a strong strand of negative theology in these poems, as there is in my thinking generally. It goes back a long way in my life, but one central document is *The Mystical Theology of Pseudo-Dionysius, the Areopagite*, a Syrian monk of the sixth century. *The Mystical Theology* talks about the seeking of reality by casting aside everything that one feels is not the ultimately real thing. Cast aside physical perceptions, memory, words, metaphoric substitutes, anything else that comes before you as a kind of pretender to be the ultimate object of your search. All of these things are ephemeral; there's a degree of arbitrariness to them all. The objective, achievable or not, is to reach beyond the arbitrary.

AC • We're used to talking about the themes of a poem or of a work of fiction. Does this book have themes?

JS • I didn't think of the book consciously in terms of themes. I very frequently, though, designed a poem around a theme or two. The poem is somewhat like a musical work, maybe like sonata form, a first-movement form, in which the themes are stated at the beginning and then explored, expanded, familiarized, defamiliarized, and finally come together, restated, but in an illuminated way, at the end. I had that pattern in my mind. The title of one of my poems is often like the opening chord of a symphony, a chord that later gets taken apart, examined, exploited, and then put back together in unexpected ways.

AC • "[W]e are awash in them [the body's molecules] as we are awash in the spicular fragments of fossil starlight from without" (40) and "the subsoil continues to reverberate with its prehistory, and wherever we stand we pick up signals" (52). In spite of that biological and molecular determinacy, "participants in the drama" of "the black box" mistakenly believe all happens by "will," that "character creates destiny" (53). Is the idea of tragedy mistaken?

JS   • There is a suggestion here that we are judging things from a limited point of view. We're using a figure – the figure of will – to interpret many of the influences that we feel upon ourselves, but it is only a figure. From that figure, however, we may deduce that character creates destiny, and that's the central theme song of tragedy. Northrop Frye thought that comedy was a more inclusive form than tragedy because normally in a comedy there is a point in the middle somewhere where tragedy threatens but is somehow overcome. Tragedy is a part of the comic cycle. Frye's chief example, the Christian paradigm, is scarred by the tragedy of the crucifixion. But as atonement, crucifixion leads to salvation and regeneration, creating good out of evil. My poem may be less sanguine at this particular point, but it has been written by one who has listened attentively to Frye's argument, and to Milton and Dante on the same theme, not to speak of St. Paul.

AC   • "I incline, myself, to adopt a principle of complementarity: To assume a transcendence and not to assume a transcendence .... I'm not so convinced of the virtue of consistency as to believe only one if I can choose both" (61). Although deep-time environments shape us mole-cularly, doesn't the speaker himself embrace indeterminacy?

JS   • More precisely, he embraces the superposition of states, the condi-tion of things before a decision has been made – whether it's to be tran-scendence or not transcendence, whether it's to be consistently this, rather than consistently that. It's like keeping things in some kind of solution before the key chemical precipitates out of the solution. He likes that state, and I think that's what he tends to embrace.

AC   • I don't recall ever having come across the phrase "superposition of states" in *Maps*. Perhaps he's enacting it?

JS   • Yes, he himself is an embodiment of it. So is the text itself.

AC   • I don't mean to belabour themes, but isn't another one – recurring from section to section – the notion that the "totalitarian human uni-verse" (79) has wreaked havoc on nature, creature, and self?

                                         ANNE COMPTON

JS • Very definitely, unfortunately. A sense of despair – a sense of frustration, and guilt also – has mediated the choice of the word "totalitarian." We've heard the human universe spoken of in glowing terms by various people, by Frye, for example, who thinks that the object of life should be the humanization of the world. Of course, he's thinking of the humanization of the world in a Blakean sense, the restoration of the true universe, which is identical with the resurrected and reintegrated giant mankind. We've heard the human universe extolled glowingly, but then when you look at the human universe that we willy-nilly created, it looks a very arrogant affair, painfully narrow-minded, animated by greed and self-interest and by the attempt to impose one simplistic interpretation on things, or one simplistic way of doing things.

AC • Does *Maps*, in its totality, move from a point of origin – "when expansion began" (13) – to a foreseeable end point, a "Dark Age" (77)?

JS • I hope the "Dark Age" is not the end point, but certainly a dark age has to be considered possible, but I think the celebratory vein of the poems suggests that a dark age is traversable, as the dark ages of the past have been – the so-called Greek Dark Age, the centuries between Minoan and Mycenaean civilization and Classical Greece; the supposed Dark Ages of the period between the fall of the Roman Empire and the beginning of the Middle Ages and the Renaissance. There are examples of dark ages we have gotten through.

AC • It's here, in the third section, it seems to me, that the prose voice is at its most optimistic: "no variables are endemically destined to lie hidden forever, and that ambivalence, nonterminability, undecidability, paradox, complementarity, and broken parities and symmetries ... far from being blemishes on an otherwise perfect body, are real precursors to higher-level celebration" (79). My question would be then: Doesn't the title *Maps of Invariance* only really apply to this larger, longer view?

JS • The "Dark Age," uncertainties, perplexities – these are way stations, not necessarily the end of things. They're incentives to some sort of transcendence. "[R]eal precursors to higher-level celebration" – that's a kind of map, as you're pointing out, a supreme map, not unlike the pattern articulated by Frye, which I sketched a few moments ago.

AC • Moreover, towards the end of the journey, the wanderer we've been listening to hears another: "Over the obliterative glacial advance of flames ... a voice that admits no forgetting ... comes to us apparently out of the future, sings. And sings. And sings" (78). Is there any reason why we can't call that voice *God* under any of his or her various names?

JS • I would not object to that myself, but I would have to point out that the singing is a trope, and the personal deity is also a trope. And there are other tropes that could be chosen. We could have chosen, for example, *saccidanda*, the bliss of perfectly clarified intellective being springing from within. We happened to have moved into a trope of singing, and singing is usually done by a person. The supreme personality singing the supreme song seems a reasonable image. But if the wanderer had chosen a different trope than singing here, we might have ended up with something else. We might have ended up with a community, rather than a single voice, the image of a symphony orchestra, let us say, an 18th-century symphony orchestra without a conductor, the Elohim, perhaps, rather than Jahweh.

AC • "[D]esire" and "detachment" is one dialectic at work in *Maps*. Alternatively, we could call it attachment and transcendence. Is it "detachment" from "desire" (77) that makes such a view of the future possible?

JS • I guess what is at issue in the passage that you've quoted is the appropriate interpretation of the disengagement from desire. It's not rejection. It's more like the elimination of ego-centred interference and self-promotion. The wanderer would be happier, I think, with a condition in which he experienced desire but was not governed by it. He can detect the desire within himself. He can see where it points. He can experience its energy, maybe divert and apply its energy, if he chooses. But in his detachment he asserts his superiority to the desire. He is master of the desire, in that sense.

AC • Does the wanderer have, if not the conviction, the imminence of a conviction that where he, it, we, will arrive is synonymous with a beginning that could be called "an emanative singularity" (78)?

JS • A journey that ends with the discovery of a beginning, whether his own past beginning or a new one, would be consistent with his effort to embrace the coincidence of opposites. He wants a pair of contrary things. He always wants both, or he wants the advantages of both, which will propel him into some sort of Hegelian transcendence that embraces the advantages of the contraries, but, at the same time, transcends them. The "emanative singularity" would be, I suppose, another universe. The end of all our striving will not so much be, as T.S. Eliot says, "to arrive where we started / And know the place for the first time" (*Four Quartets* 59), but to regenerate. Maybe Eliot would not be predisposed against that idea of regeneration either. Where we arrive is the beginning of a new universe, literally, or more probably, metaphorically.

AC   • Is it also the notion that where we will arrive is the beginning of *this* universe? Singularity is often used in physics as synonymous with the starting point.

JS   • A singularity is a geometrical feature that comes up in the mathematical representation of extreme gravitational phenomenon – black holes, of which there are many – and of extreme emanative phenomena, for which role, as far as I am aware, there is only one candidate in the present universe – the big bang, the event that started everything. "Only in intercourse with this self-grounding emanative singularity can what happens to be actually mean what it is" (78). My goodness, that's loaded, isn't it?

AC   • That's why I've been asking if it's the beginning of *this* universe …

JS   • Yes. The big bang is with us now. The rather mixed message it sent out is the universe in which we exist. We're part of the message. That's more or less how today's cosmology sees things. Tomorrow's cosmology may be different. If we could penetrate the barrier or barriers that lie behind the cosmic microwave background radiation (CMBR), we could conceivably detect in some way the naked singularity, the big bang itself. As it is, the CMBR is providing us with much information about the state of the universe about 99.99 per cent of the way back in time to the big bang. It's physically meaningful to say that the so-called "era of recombination" that gave rise to the CMBR is immediately with us – its microwaves are bathing us every moment of our lives. And so, by extension, we could say that the big bang is *almost* immediately with us. We live in the presence of a perpetual beginning, and it is the beginning of the natural process that has led, among other things, to us. It's almost like saying the creator God is with us. From the point of view of poetry, however – I'm not talking theology or physical cosmology now – from the point of view of poetry, big bang and creator God are tropes, among others, with whose help we attempt to habilitate our minds and sensibilities to the blinding mystery of the origin of the world in which we find ourselves.

AC • Although the wanderer implores us or himself to "walk resolutely into the vanishing point," a moment later, this supremely abundant, if not heavenly, future is described as "peachy" (80), which makes me wonder if he hasn't been having us on with all this talk of a recuperative future?

JS • "[P]eachy" seemed to me exactly the right word among all of those pretentious, multi-syllable, Latinate, absolutist terms. It seemed to be the appropriate leavening word.

AC • So the word did not mean to open up the possibility that it was time for the wanderer to burst into one of those chuckles where I, the reader, might be the object of his amusement?

JS • I don't read that passage in that particular way, but I'm not setting limits on how other readers might read it. You may find it a discomforting reading, but that reading is possible. It's a crucial passage, though, isn't it? One of my tentative theories about this book is that it reaches its climax in that very sentence: "the long-desired and -feared, the repeatedly re-hypothesized, the perpetually immanent, imminent, peachy and immitigable fullness" (80). The fullness suggests the pleroma, the everything. The fullness of time is referred to in scripture, so that evokes the notion of the pleroma, but there's more involved than that, I think. It involves everything, everybody, and everything together, the complete society. Frye talks about the society of all things that are in harmony at the end of the dramatic adventure. But then, I suppose too, that the choice of the word "peachy," in part, is governed by the alliteration with "perpetually" and also by the semantic influence of the word "fullness." Peach is a kind of tactile symbol of fullness.

AC • "What has not been sufficiently appreciated in the iconography is that the very turning-away of the goddess both allows and implores the god .... Her own lifted arms ... signify her willingness – indeed, her urgency" (70). If this pair is a trope for origins and end, and the desire one has for the other, doesn't that imply that circularity is the "resolving" (10) diagrammatic figure for the "cosmic geometry" (84)?

JS • What I had in mind was the god and goddess in a sort of tantric image of embrace. The goddess is in the arms of the god. He has a number of pairs of arms, and she's facing him, but her torso is turned through 180 degrees, like an owl's head. The lower part of her body is facing his body, but the upper part of her body is facing away from him

ANNE COMPTON

so that his hands can conveniently cup her two breasts. That's the image from which I started, and it is a kind of circular affair. It is the complete male-female person talked about in various cultural traditions. The Indian version is the image of *maithuna*, which is the copulatory engagement of the god and the goddess, of the male and the female. Copulatory engagement without ejaculation, we are told, and that is somehow an image of the peachy fullness of things, a pleasure that is never disappointed. It is never disappointed because it is always deferred. It is a symbol not only of an eternal relationship, an eternal and immortal pleasure, but also of supreme control of our destiny, both parts of our nature in some kind of harmony. A map of invariance, for sure, that map of *maithuna*. Embodied there is the circularity, the "resolving" diagrammatic figure for the "cosmic geometry," as you point out. There are cosmologists who like the neatness of circularity. The universe will expand; it will then contract. A lot of them would prefer the universe to be that way, even if it isn't. The other major geometrical figure on offer has been the linear form. History has a beginning and an end. If it's Christian history, it begins with the creation of the world, and it ends with the redemptive uptake of everything, with the possible exception of the rebel angels and so forth, into the divine bosom. We're familiar with that linear vision of the universe. But it just could be possible that neither of these geometrical figures is accurate. Each is only one trope among many. Each does seem to tell us something about the way we experience reality. Something about the world does look like a linear operation. The second law of thermodynamics seems, for example, undeniable. Things move toward higher and higher entropy, to greater and greater disorder, which is to say shallower and shallower heat gradients. That seems to be the way the physical universe is developing. On the other hand, we've recently discovered, so it seems, that what we think of as the substance of the universe, matter, is only about four per cent of the mass/energy that is actually out there. So what is the rest doing? There's much speculation about that. So all of these things may influence whether it's the trope of linear evolution or the trope of the eternal return that gets our preferential nod.

AC   • As well as a speculation on the end point, *Maps* is an inquiry into sources. At one point, the wanderer says that "loss" may be more important than a knowledge of sources since "loss is itself a source that rides with us, a perpetual infusion of novelty, a novelty by negation that, yes, in time transforms the past beyond recognition, recovery, and finally nostalgia ..." (81). Is the axiom of that proposition: Foregoing scrutiny of sources is a healthful thing?

JS • Origin is in every moment. Loss is in every moment as well. Well, is this just the wanderer's double talk to reconcile himself to the vicissitudes of time? To what degree is the wanderer practicing a very clever game of disillusions, replaced by new illusions? There may be something of that to it, I suppose. I've thought from time to time that one of the strategies that appears in my work, as in the work of many poets, not to speak of clergy, is a strategy of resolution by euphemism. By finding pleasant ways of saying things we can somehow resolve problems, or reconcile ourselves to things that we've found very difficult to bear. And of course we use this strategy in life constantly. But to answer your question: Deliberate refusal to scrutinize sources, or anything else, would not be a healthful thing provided that the means to effect that scrutiny were available.

AC • I'd say two things happen in the third section: On the final stages of the journey, the wanderer feels more affection towards his home world as it is at the moment, and second, love is more frequently spoken of. In terms of the first, "tussocky grasses grow among stones [where once there'd have been 'a grand processional route'] and each of us finds a solitary way to the ruined tabernacle" (84-85). Beginnings, when we were supposedly closer to the divine, are now not lost. Is that so?

JS • I think that is so. The ruin is still there, and it has a kind of richness that it didn't have when it was a functional temple, text, or whatever. So in spite of the fact that we've just been talking about loss as a necessary concomitant of creation, or novelty, now we're being told, "not everything is lost after all." It may be altered, but it is not lost. We can return to it, and the return is an enriching experience.

AC • Does the wanderer believe that consciousness, in the end, is incorporated elsewhere or otherwise, rather than lost?

JS • I don't think he does have such a belief, though I stand to be corrected. In writing the poems, I was not aware that he differed from me on this point. As I've indicated before, given its intimate association with my physiology and neurology, my present consciousness could hardly be expected to exist after my bodily death, or to have existed before my bodily birth. So my consciousness is likely doomed to be lost, but consciousness remains a continuing possibility. It will be the consciousness of others, however, not mine. The genome persists – and evolves – and in that sense, we're all cut to a similar pattern and can be said to participate in a single consciousness. I'm straying from the question here, but I don't want to leave the impression that a simplistic materialism is enough. Our ignorance is great in these matters – at least mine is. Clearly, reality is not simply what we see and touch. Reality is what we think, what we feel. It's what we love, what we desire, what we aspire to. It's what we question and, in a poetic sense, what we figure. There are many dimensions to reality, and the wanderer is alive, I hope, to all of these. He has, however, as far as I know, only his brief moment in the sun of consciousness, as do I.

AC • In spite of the multi-universes, string theory, p-brane, and so forth that we hear about in his company, doesn't the wanderer emerge from his travels with confidence in an "infinitely nameable absolute" (89)?

JS • He's certainly receptive to the idea. Confidence is a measure of our ability to take charge of the situation. This is the world, we say, and point to it. This is "a moment in time, or the crisis of self-reflection, or first shy swallow at the feast of love, or first intimation of the infinitely nameable absolute" (89). The image of the wanderer in those lines is not unlike the image of Atlas on the cover of the book. This is an Atlas in the true Renaissance spirit, one who is taking charge of the universe. The picture that I'm suggesting here – "This, we say, is the world" and so forth (89) – is a sort of recreation of the scene in the garden when Adam names the animals. Except that here he's naming more than the animals. He's the source of names, in fact, the source of distinctions, the source of distinctions between different realms of reality.

AC • The traveller is, finally, beyond art, beyond science. That leaves religion, doesn't it, and maybe love?

JS • Near the end, there's a paragraph on self-reflexive prayer, the kind of prayer that is not asking someone for something, but a prayer that venerates prayer itself, or the prayerful attitude (93). But then on the next page, we return to the singing, and I suppose that's art. My impression is that these things all get mixed together somehow in the final bit – and not just mixed, but melded. Indeed, all these poems are meant to be interdisciplinary fusion reactors.

AC   • The penultimate piece is set at a ruins. The last piece begins in a desert, "A desert of consolation" (88). A speaker in *Winter in Paradise* (1972) says mantra-like, "There is no consolation" (65). Does it take 33 years to find "consolation"?

JS   • It never occurred to me to link the *Maps* poem to that poem from 1972 – which, I think, by the way, is quite good. I reread it and it stands up alright – but it is strange, isn't it? This may be a kind of revelation of my own journey, this confluence of consolations, starting with no consolation and ending, as of now, with a "desert of consolation." It's as though it's taken 33 years to realize that the absence of consolation is, in fact, a consolation.

AC   • In his introduction to *Winter in Paradise*, Henry Beissel quotes a letter from you in which you say, "unity, if it is not to be spurious, must come, if at all, only at the end; all before the end must be uncertainty" (11). Did you imagine something like *Maps* in your future when you said that?

JS   • I can't recall having anything in mind at that stage that would have looked like *Maps of Invariance*. I did, however, conceive of a grand synoptic vision, if not a theory of everything, as the objective of the human quest. To know has always been important to me. Another strong belief, then as now, was and is that uncertainty is a condition with which we learn to live, that in an age of scientific investigation in particular, yesterday's apparent truth is today's discarded hypothesis, that we should rejoice in new information and sound interpretation whether or not it disrupts our comfortable convictions. I also believed and believe that most of the major questions of philosophy – what is being, where do we come from, why are we here, where do we go, what should we do, and so on – are likely to remain active questions, perhaps indefinitely, that philosophy is a process, a kind of intellective metabolism rather than a table of dogmata. Past dogmatic systems, nevertheless, constitute a cherishable heritage as points of reference. To sum up, I'm still just as resistant to premature declarations of iconic unity as I was when I wrote those words to Henry, and it's even clearer to me that we may never be able to eliminate uncertainty.

AC   • It seems to me the earlier poems that are closest to *Maps* are "Letters from the Remembered World," in the 1976 *Swimmer Among the Coral* (1-15), reissued as "Letters from the Possible," in the 1982 *Sucking-Stones* (25-27). In the 1976 version, a first-person speaker, experiencing

ANNE COMPTON

many incarnations – "I have come back to this place ten thousand years from today" – "decant[s] / the divinity of art, / the divinity of science, / the divinity of contemplation ..." (4). Would you agree that there are some similarities between the early "Letters" and *Maps*?

JS • Yes. One of the invariants that survives from the time of "Letters" to the time of *Maps* is the dedication to "the divinity of art, / the divinity of science, / the divinity of contemplation ...." One difference is that "Letters" is more elegiac than *Maps*. Another is that *Maps* is much more concerned with what goes on in the middle of the action. *Maps* is interested in the enormous intricacies and possibilities in getting from a beginning to an end.

AC • You like propositions. Here are some related ones for you – The sonnet is the "liturgy" of English language poetry. The sonnet, like "liturgy," is characterized by "routine devices" (28). The prose poem is the ritual from which the doctrinal sonnet descended. The moment before ritual is – if I've read *Maps* at all closely – the "emanative singularity" (78). Here's my question: Did the prose poem take you to an earlier, rawer – without pejorative accent – experience of time?

JS • I'm initially wary of the hieratic paradigm that you propose. Nevertheless, I think you may be on to something. The pattern you sketch is that first comes primary creation, whether of a universe or of the next moment in time – creation and revelation. In my secular scheme of things, the corresponding symbol is the "emanative singularity." After creation and revelation comes the reverential behavioural response, ritual – in my scheme, the often dreamlike or magic prose of the *Maps* poems. We speak of "magic fiction," so why not "magic prose"? In the third step, out of ritual behaviour crystallizes the iconic articulation of the liturgy, represented in my world by the relatively formalized, finite and bounded expression of the sonnets. It seems to correspond somehow to what has happened: After the making of those liturgical gestures, the sonnets, you conceive that I move back a step closer to the mystery and surprise of creation and revelation. This suggests that magic prose is a closer re-enactment of primary creation and revelation than is the sonnet. I'm sure that there are linguistic forms yet closer than magic prose to creation and revelation. But yes, I think I could buy your interpretation.

AC   • Given that the "palace" epic housed all kinds in its roominess (23-24), is a collection of prose poems a 21st-century return – or effort to return – to the epic?

JS   • *Maps* has some features that we associate with epic – ample scale, unhurried movement, an encyclopedic spectrum of allusion, an engaged but largely impersonal and non-partisan voice. Other traditional epic features it lacks – a gallery of larger-than-life personalities; long, grand, exemplary speeches; character conflict; divine machinery, unless the scientific allusions are an alternative for the gods and their involvement. I've thought about modern epic equivalents since first reading Pound's *Cantos* nearly 60 years ago. I didn't think *epic* as I was composing the individual *Maps* poems although when they came together at the end I could recognize in retrospect that they present a largish ambition. Curiously enough, *epic* was more on my mind during the dozen or so years I spent writing sonnets. It has been remarked that what is of most enduring interest in works of epic scale is a series of special moments, great speeches, memorable descriptions, wise comments, elaborate similes and so on, separated by longish stretches where the verse rolls majestically on and Homer nods. I thought of removing the nodding from the envisaged structure, and putting on record a series of privileged moments. In the course of a decade or so, I had about a thousand sonnets, a collection of epic length if not quality. I also had vaguely in mind as a model – how grandiose can presumption get? – the Rig Veda, that startling anthology of over a thousand celebratory hymns of ancient Vedic culture. Not unexpectedly, my own collection fell short. I'm moderately well satisfied with the selection of roughly 200 sonnets that have been published, but they're nothing resembling an epic.

AC   • You've spent a lifetime in poetry, John. So what's poetry good for?

JS   • Poetry is good for expanding the mind and the sympathies. When I use the word "sympathies," I'm not confining that to relationships between people, but including, also, relationships between percipient and perceived world, a conceiver and conceived world, the imaginative intelligence and the vast possibility of imagined worlds that are out there. The great encyclopedia of poems that have accumulated since the marvellous inventions of the phonetic alphabet and the printed book came on line, is a wonderful resource for personal expansion and exploration. The accumulation of poetry is some sort of recompense for having to live such a short life. There's not a lot of time to appreciate the wonders of existence, but the record of poetry enables us to extend and speed up that process of acquaintance with this universal house in which we have been born.

WORKS CITED

— • —

Arnold, Matthew. "Sohrab and Rustum." *Poetry and Criticism of Matthew Arnold*. Ed. A. Dwight Culler. Boston: Houghton Mifflin, 1961. 124-44.

Eliot, T. S. *Four Quartets*. London: Faber and Faber, 1965.

McLuhan, Marshall. "Joyce, Mallarmé, and the Press." *The Literary Criticism of Marshall McLuhan*. Ed. Eugene McNamara. New York/Toronto: McGraw-Hill, 1969. 5-21.

Simic, Charles. "The Poetry of Village Idiots." *Orphan Factory: Essays and Memoirs*. Ann Arbor: U of Michigan P, 1997. 46-47.

Smith, John. *Fireflies in the Magnolia Grove*. Charlottetown: Acorn P, 2004.

– – – . *Maps of Invariance*. Toronto: Fitzhenry & Whiteside, 2005.

– – – . *Midnight Found You Dancing*. Charlottetown: Ragweed P, 1986.

– – – . *Of the Swimmer Among the Coral and of the Monk in the Mountains: An Anthology for the Stars*. Charlottetown: Square Deal Publications, 1976.

– – – . *Strands the Length of the Wind*. Charlottetown: Ragweed P, 1993.

– – – . *Sucking-Stones*. Dunvegan, ON: Quadrant Editions, 1982.

– – – . *Winter in Paradise*. Charlottetown: Square Deal Publications, 1972.

Stevens, Wallace. "Asides on the Oboe." *Poems by Wallace Stevens*. Intro. Samuel French Morse. New York: Vintage, 1959. 102-03.

– – – . "From *Adagia*." *The Norton Anthology of Modern and Contemporary Poetry*. 2 vols. 3rd. ed. Eds. Jahan Ramazani et al. New York: W.W. Norton, 2003. I. 972-75.

Tennyson, Alfred, Lord. "Ulysses." *Poems of Tennyson*. Ed. Jerome Buckley. Boston: Houghton Mifflin, 1958. 66-67.

Wordsworth, William. "Lines Composed a few miles above Tintern Abbey, on revisiting the banks of the Wye during a tour July 13, 1798"; "Ode: Intimations of Immortality from Recollections of Early Childhood." *William Wordsworth's The Prelude with a selection from the Shorter Poems, the Sonnets, The Recluse, and The Excursion*. Ed. Carlos Baker. New York: Holt, Rinehart and Winston, 1948, 1954. 96-101.152-58.